DOMESDAY BOOK

Wiltshire

History from the Sources

DOMESDAY BOOK

A Survey of the Counties of England

LIBER DE WINTONIA

Compiled by direction of

KING WILLIAM I

Winchester
1086

DOMESDAY BOOK

general editor

JOHN MORRIS

6

Wiltshire

edited by

Caroline and Frank Thorn

from a draft translation prepared by

Caroline Thorn

PHILLIMORE
Chichester
1979

1979
Published by
PHILLIMORE & CO. LTD.,
London and Chichester
Head Office: Shopwyke Hall,
Chichester, Sussex, England

© Mrs. Susan Morris, 1979

ISBN 0 85033 159 5 (case)
ISBN 0 85033 160 3 (limp)

Printed in Great Britain by
Titus Wilson & Son Ltd.,
Kendal

WILTSHIRE

History from the Sources
General Editor: John Morris

The series aims to publish history
written directly from the sources
for all interested readers, both
specialists and others. The first
priority is to publish important
texts which should be widely
available, but are not.

DOMESDAY BOOK

The contents, with the folio on which each county begins, are:

Domesday Book is termed *Liber de Wintonia* (The Book of Winchester) in column 332c

INTRODUCTION

The Domesday Survey

In 1066 Duke William of Normandy conquered England. He was crowned King, and most of the lands of the English nobility were soon granted to his followers. Domesday Book was compiled 20 years later. The Saxon Chronicle records that in 1085

> at Gloucester at midwinter ... the King had deep speech with his counsellors ... and sent men all over England to each shire ... to find out ... what or how much each landholder held ... in land and livestock, and what it was worth ... The returns were brought to him.[1]

William was thorough. One of his Counsellors reports that he also sent a second set of Commissioners 'to shires they did not know, where they were themselves unknown, to check their predecessors' survey, and report culprits to the King.'[2]

The information was collected at Winchester, corrected, abridged, chiefly by omission of livestock and the 1066 population, and fair-copied by one writer into a single volume. Norfolk, Suffolk and Essex were copied, by several writers, into a second volume, unabridged, which states that 'the Survey was made in 1086'. The surveys of Durham and Northumberland, and of several towns, including London, were not transcribed, and most of Cumberland and Westmorland, not yet in England, was not surveyed. The whole undertaking was completed at speed, in less than 12 months, though the fair-copying of the main volume may have taken a little longer. Both volumes are now preserved at the Public Record Office. Some versions of regional returns also survive. One of them, from Ely Abbey,[3] copies out the Commissioners' brief. They were to ask

> The name of the place. Who held it, before 1066, and now?
> How many *hides*?[4] How many ploughs, both those in lordship and the men's?
> How many villagers, cottagers and slaves, how many free men and Freemen?[5]
> How much woodland, meadow and pasture? How many mills and fishponds?
> How much has been added or taken away? What the total value was and is?
> How much each free man or Freeman had or has? All threefold, before 1066,
>   when King William gave it, and now; and if more can be had than at present?

The Ely volume also describes the procedure. The Commissioners took evidence on oath 'from the Sheriff; from all the barons and their Frenchmen; and from the whole Hundred, the priests, the reeves and six villagers from each village'. It also names four Frenchmen and four Englishmen from each Hundred, who were sworn to verify the detail.

The King wanted to know what he had, and who held it. The Commissioners therefore listed lands in dispute, for Domesday Book was not only a tax-assessment. To the King's grandson, Bishop Henry of Winchester, its purpose was that every 'man should know his right and not usurp another's'; and because it was the final authoritative register of rightful possession 'the natives called it Domesday Book, by analogy

---

[1] Before he left England for the last time, late in 1086.   [2] Robert Losinga, Bishop of Hereford 1079-1095 (see *E.H.R.* 22, 1907, 74).   [3] *Inquisitio Eliensis,* first paragraph.   [4] A land unit, reckoned as 120 acres.   [5] *Quot Sochemani.*

from the Day of Judgement'; that was why it was carefully arranged by Counties, and by landholders within Counties, 'numbered consecutively ... for easy reference'.[6]

Domesday Book describes Old English society under new management, in minute statistical detail. Foreign lords had taken over, but little else had yet changed. The chief landholders and those who held from them are named, and the rest of the population was counted. Most of them lived in villages, whose houses might be clustered together, or dispersed among their fields. Villages were grouped in administrative districts called Hundreds, which formed regions within Shires, or Counties, which survive today with minor boundary changes; the recent deformation of some ancient county identities is here disregarded, as are various short-lived modern changes. The local assemblies, though overshadowed by lords great and small, gave men a voice, which the Commissioners heeded. Very many holdings were described by the Norman term *manerium* (manor), greatly varied in size and structure, from tiny farmsteads to vast holdings; and many lords exercised their own jurisdiction and other rights, termed *soca*, whose meaning still eludes exact definition.

The Survey was unmatched in Europe for many centuries, the product of a sophisticated and experienced English administration, fully exploited by the Conqueror's commanding energy. But its unique assemblage of facts and figures has been hard to study, because the text has not been easily available, and abounds in technicalities. Investigation has therefore been chiefly confined to specialists; many questions cannot be tackled adequately without a cheap text and uniform translation available to a wider range of students, including local historians.

Previous Editions

The text has been printed once, in 1783, in an edition by Abraham Farley, probably of 1250 copies, at Government expense, said to have been £38,000; its preparation took 16 years. It was set in a specially designed type, here reproduced photographically, which was destroyed by fire in 1808. In 1811 and 1816 the Records Commissioners added an introduction, indices, and associated texts, edited by Sir Henry Ellis; and in 1861-1863 the Ordnance Survey issued zincograph facsimiles of the whole. Texts of individual counties have appeared since 1673, separate translations in the Victoria County Histories and elsewhere.

This Edition

Farley's text is used, because of its excellence, and because any worthy alternative would prove astronomically expensive. His text has been checked against the facsimile, and discrepancies observed have been verified against the manuscript, by the kindness of Miss Daphne Gifford of the Public Record Office. Farley's few errors are indicated in the notes.

[6] *Dialogus de Scaccario* 1,16.

The editor is responsible for the translation and lay-out. It aims at what the compiler would have written if his language had been modern English; though no translation can be exact, for even a simple word like 'free' nowadays means freedom from different restrictions. Bishop Henry emphasized that his grandfather preferred 'ordinary words'; the nearest ordinary modern English is therefore chosen whenever possible. Words that are now obsolete, or have changed their meaning, are avoided, but measurements have to be transliterated, since their extent is often unknown or arguable, and varied regionally. The terse inventory form of the original has been retained, as have the ambiguities of the Latin.

Modern English commands two main devices unknown to 11th century Latin, standardised punctuation and paragraphs; in the Latin, *ibi* ('there are') often does duty for a modern full stop, *et* ('and') for a comma or semi-colon. The entries normally answer the Commissioners' questions, arranged in five main groups, (i) the place and its holder, its hides, ploughs and lordship; (ii) people; (iii) resources; (iv) value; and (v) additional notes. The groups are usually given as separate paragraphs.

King William numbered chapters 'for easy reference', and sections within chapters are commonly marked, usually by initial capitals, often edged in red. They are here numbered. Maps, indices and an explanation of technical terms are also given. Later, it is hoped to publish analytical and explanatory volumes, and associated texts.

The editor is deeply indebted to the advice of many scholars, too numerous to name, and especially to the Public Record Office, and to the publisher's patience. The draft translations are the work of a team; they have been co-ordinated and corrected by the editor, and each has been checked by several people. It is therefore hoped that mistakes may be fewer than in versions published by single fallible individuals. But it would be Utopian to hope that the translation is altogether free from error; the editor would like to be informed of mistakes observed.

The maps are the work of Jim Hardy and Frank Thorn.

The preparation of this volume has been greatly assisted by a generous grant from the Leverhulme Trust Fund.

Conventions
*   refers to a note to the Latin text
[ ]   enclose words omitted in the MS.   ( )   enclose editorial explanations.

CORNWALL DB 1,6

R̃EX ten̄ *GLYSTONE* . Ibi st̄ . IIII . hidæ . ſed geld ꝑ , II . hid̄.

Tra.ē.xxx.cař.De ea.ē in dn̄io.I.hida.7 ibi.II.cař.7 XII.

ſerui.7 XL.uiłłi 7 xx.borđ cū.XVII.cař.Ibi.I.ač p̃ti.Paſtura

III.leū lḡ.7 una leū 7 dim̄ lat̄.Silua.I.leū lḡ,7 dim̄ leū lat̄.

Redđ.VI.lib̄ ad pondus.

De hoc m̃ ablata.ē una hida in *PENDAVID* . Tra,ē.VI.cař.

Boie p̄br ten̄ de comite moriton̄ , Oli.xx.ſot.m̃ uat.x.ſot.

BLISLAND. 4 h. but it paid tax for 2 h. Land for 30 ploughs; in lordship 1 h; 2 ploughs; 12 slaves.

40 villagers and 20 smallholders with 17 ploughs.

Meadow, 1 acre; pasture, 3 leagues long and 1½ leagues wide; woodland, 1 league long and ½ league wide.

It pays £6 by weight.

In PENDAVEY 1 h. has been taken away from this manor. Land for 6 ploughs. Boia the priest holds it from the Count of Mortain. Formerly 20s; value now 10s.

Exon 101 b 1 - 2

101.*b.* V̆ Rex ht̄. I. manſione que uocat Gluſtona. q̃ tenuit herald⁹ comes.

ea die q̃ rex E. f u. 7. m.   In ea st̄. IIII. hide. 7 reddidert̄ Gildu p II. hid̄.

has IIII. poſst̄ arare xxx. carř.   De his ht̄ Rex. I. hida 7 II. carř indn̄io. 7 uilla

ni hn̄t III. hid̄. 7 x. 7 VII. carř.   Ibi ht̄ R. uillanos. 7 xx. borđ. 7 XII. ſeruos.
_{xl.}

7 III. uaccas. 7. lxx. oues. 7. I. leuga nemoris in long̃. 7 dim̄ ĩ lat̄. 7. I. agru pti.

7. III. leugas paſcue ĩ long̃. 7. I. leuga 7 dim̄ ĩ latitud̄. 7 reddit p annu VI. lib̄ ad

pondus. V̆ manſione ea die q̃ rex. E. f. u. 7. m.   In ea eſt. I. hid̄ tr̃e q̃ poſst̄ arare VI. carř.
de hac manſione ablata eſt. I. manſio q̃ uocat pendauid. q̃ ꝑtinebat ad p̃ſcript̄a
de comite.
m̃ ten& ea̅ boia ſacerdos de bomine. 7 ual& x. ſot 7 q̃do comes acceꝑ ualebat. xx. ſot.

The King has a manor called BLISLAND, which Earl Harold held in 1066*. 4 hides there; they paid tax for 2 hides. 30 ploughs can plough these 4. Of them the King has 1 hide and 2 ploughs in lordship, and the villagers have 3 hides and 17 ploughs. The King has 40 villagers, 20 smallholders, 12 slaves, 3 cows, 70 sheep, 1 league of woodland in length and ½ in width, 1 acre of meadow, 3 leagues of pasture in length and 1½ leagues in width. It pays £6 a year by weight. From this manor has been taken away a manor called PENDAVEY, which belonged to the above manor in 1066*. 1 hide of land there, which 6 ploughs can plough. Boia the priest of Bodmin holds it now from the Count. Value 10s; when the Count received it**, value 20s.

* *ea die qua rex Edward fuit vivus et mortuus* ('on the day on which King Edward was alive and dead'); it is always translated in this edition as 'in 1066' and is equivalent to DB *TRE*, 'before 1066'.

** *quando Comes accepit* is equivalent to DB *olim*, 'formerly'.

For the South Western counties there exists another set of returns, the Exeter Book (*Liber Exoniensis*). This contains the returns, differently arranged and worded, for Somerset, Devon and Cornwall, with part of Dorset and one Wiltshire holding. Comparison with the Exchequer version shows that some information is clearly missing in Exon, such as the rest of Wiltshire, a great part of Dorset and some entries for Devon. Arrangement is by fiefs, and within these by counties, though the counties do not always follow each other in the same order each time. Within each county places are often grouped in Hundreds, although without the Hundred name given, and frequently the Hundreds occur in the same order under different holders. This provides primary evidence for the identification of places and in part supplies the lack of Hundred headings in the text of Exchequer DB here. Information is often duplicated, as for example in Cornwall where the same 11 hides are listed under the holdings of both the King and the Count of Mortain. After the fiefs in Exon there are details for Devon, Cornwall and Somerset of 'Appropriated Lands' (*Terrae Occupatae*), folios 495-525, which usually repeat information given in the main entries. Exon also includes the returns of the tax levied in 1084 for all five counties, which it is hoped will be published in a separate volume. Wiltshire is unusual in having three versions of these tax returns, MSS A, B, C (folios 1a-3b; 7a-12b; 13a-16a). The Exon folio dealing with the one fief in Wiltshire, that of William of Mohun (DB ch. 34), is 47a. Totals of the holdings in Wiltshire of Glastonbury Abbey, Ralph of Mortimer, Miles Crispin, Durand of Gloucester and Gilbert are to be found in the imperfect folios 527b; 530b-531a. A convenient contents table of the whole of Exon is printed in V. H. Galbraith, *Domesday Book*, Oxford 1974, pp. 184-88.

The MS is preserved in the library of Exeter Cathedral and was printed in 1816 by Sir Henry Ellis in the third volume of the Record Commission's edition of DB, from a transcript made by Ralph Barnes, Chapter Clerk. No facsimile, such as the Ordnance Survey made for Exchequer DB, exists for Exon. The MS consists of 532 folios of parchment, measuring about 6½ by 9¾ inches (16½ by 25 cms). Each folio contains a single column on each side of about 20 lines. These folios fall into a series of quires, or gatherings, varying in number between one and twenty folios. Generally a new quire was started for each major landholder, and a new side for most tenants. This led to many blanks, which were increased by spaces sometimes left for information not to hand. There is no indication of the original sequence of quires, and the present order and system of reference dates from the last rebinding in 1816. The MS is the work of about a dozen scribes and the hand changes often between entries and even within them.

The text cannot here be economically reproduced; nine tenths of it repeats the DB survey, with discrepancies of a fraction of one per cent in many tens of thousands of figures. Ellis' edition has here been used in the main, though the MS has been checked where Exon and DB differ and in a number of other places. The principal corresponding Exon reference is given beside each entry in the translation, with other references in the Exon notes; the last number refers to the order of the entry on each side, as indicated in the MS generally by gallows marks. All discrepancies and all additional information are given, either in small type in the translation, or in the Exon notes, signalled in the translation by E, or by L (for details of lordship omitted in DB). A specimen entry, with the DB equivalent, showing the differences in formulae, is given opposite. The substance, though not the wording, of the whole of the Exeter Domesday returns is therefore here reproduced.

For a detailed description and evaluation of Exon, see R. Welldon Finn, *The Liber Exoniensis*, London 1964; N. R. Ker, *Medieval Manuscripts in British Libraries*, vol. ii, pp. 800-807; Sir Henry Ellis, *DB3*, Introduction, pp. ix ff.

The county editors would like to thank Mrs. A. M. Erskine of Exeter Cathedral Library for her help in making available the Exon MS.

In Burgo *MALMESBERIE* habet rex .xxvi . mafuras
hofpitatas.7 xxv . mafuras in qb⁊ ſt dom̄ quæ n̄ reddŭ geld̄
plufquā uaſtā tꝵa . Vna quaq̕ harū mafurarū redd .x. den̄
de gablo . hoc . ē ſimul . xl.iii . ſol 7 vi . den̄ ⸗ ſeruitiŭ reddit.
⸗ De feudo eṗi baioēſis . ē ibi dimidia mafura uaſta . quæ nullŭ
⸗ Abb̄ malmeſbie h̄t .iiii. Mas 7 dimiđ .7 foris burḡ .ix . cofcez
q̇ geldaꝶ cū burgſib ⸗ Abb̄ Glaſtingbienſ h̄t . ii . mafur.
⸗ Eduuard .iii. mafur ⸗ Radulf de mortem . i .7 dimiđ ⸗ Durand
de Glouuec . i .7 dim ⸗ Wilts de ow . i ⸗ Hunfrid de infula . i ⸗ Oſbn
Gifard . i ⸗ Alured de Merleɓge . dimiđ mas uaſtā ⸗ Goiſfrid ſimilit.
⸗ Toui . i .7 q̇rtā parte uni mas ⸗ Drogo . F . ponz . dimiđ ⸗ Vxor Edric . i.
⸗ Rog de berchelai . i . mas de firma regis .7 Ernulf . i . ſimilit de firma
regis . quā incaute accep̄ . Hæ duæ nullŭ ſeruitiŭ reddŭꝶ.
Rex h̄t unā uaſtā mafuram de tꝵa quā Azor tenuit.

WILTSHIRE

M	In the Borough of MALMESBURY	64 c

1   the King has 26 occupied dwellings, and 25 dwellings in which are houses which do not pay tax any more than waste land; each of these dwellings pays 10d in tribute, that is 43s 6d altogether.

2   Of the Bishop of Bayeux's Holding, half a derelict dwelling which pays no service.

3   The Abbot of Malmesbury has 4½ dwellings, and outside the Borough 9 Cottagers who pay tax with the burgesses.

4   The Abbot of Glastonbury has 2 dwellings.

5   Edward the Sheriff, 3 dwellings.

6   Ralph of Mortimer, 1½.

7   Durand of Gloucester, 1½.

8   William of Eu, 1.

9   Humphrey de L'Isle, 1.

10   Osbern Giffard, 1.

11   Alfred of Marlborough, half a derelict dwelling.

12   Geoffrey Marshall, the same.

13   Tovi, 1, and the fourth part of 1 dwelling.

14   Drogo son of Poyntz, ½.

15   Edric's wife, 1.

16   Roger of Berkeley, 1 dwelling, of the King's revenue; Arnulf of Hesdin 1, likewise of the King's revenue, which he received injudiciously. These two pay no service.

17   The King has 1 derelict dwelling, of the land which Azor held.

.I.Rex Willelmvs.

.II.Eps Wintoniensis.

.III.Eps Sarisberiensis.

.IIII.Eps Baiocensis.

V.Eps Constantiensis.

.VI.Eps Lisiacensis.

.VII.Abbatia Glastingberiens.

.VIII Abbatia Malmesberiens.

.IX.Abbatia Westmonasterij.

.X.Abbatia Wintoniensis.

.XI.Abbatia Creneburnens.

.XII.Abbatissa Sceftesberiens.

.XIII Abbatissa Wiltuniensis.

.XIIII Abbatissa Wintoniensis.

.XV.Abbatissa Romesiensis.

.XVI.Abbatissa Ambresberiens.

.XVII.Æccla Beccensis.

.XVIIIGiraldus pbr de Wiltune.

.XIX.Canonici Lisiacenses.

.XX.Comes Moritoniensis.

.XXI.Comes Rogerius.

XXII.Comes Hugo.

.XXIII.Comes Albericus.

.XXIIII.Eduuard de Sarisberie.

.XXV.Ernulf de Hesding.

.XXVI Aluredus de Merlebergh.

.XXVII.Hunfridus de Insula.

.XXVIII.Milo Crispin.

.XXIX Gislebertus de Breteuile.

.XXX.Durand de Glouueceftre.

.XXXI.Walterius Gifard.

.XXXII.Wilts de ow.

.XXXIII.Wilts de Braiose.

.XXXIIII.Wilts de Moiun.

.XXXV.Wilts de Faleise.

.XXXVI.Walscinus de Dowai.

.XXXVII.Waleran uenator.

.XXXVIII.Willelm filius Widonis.

.XXXIX.Henricus de Ferieres.

.XL.Ricard filius Gislebti.

.XLI.Radulf de Mortemer.

.XLII.Robertus fili Girold.

.XLIII Robertus fili Rolf.

.XLIIII Rogerius de Curcelle.

.XLV.Rogerius de Berchelai.

.XLVI Bernard Panceuolt.

.XLVII Berenger Gifard.

.XLVIII.Osbernus Gifard.

.XLIX.Drogo filius ponz.

.L.Hugo Lasne.

.LI.Hugo filius baldrici.

.LII.Hunfrid camerarius.

.LIII Gunfrid malduith.

.LIIII.Alured de Ispania.

.LV.Aiulfus uicecomes.

.LVI.Nigellus medicus.

.LVII Osbernus pbr.

.LVIII.Ricard Puingiant.

.LIX.Robtus marescal.

.LX.Robertus flauus.

.LXI.Ricardus Sturmid.

.LXII.Rainald canud.

.LXIII Maci de Moretania.

.LXIIII Gozelin Riuere.

.LXV.Godescal.

.LXVI.Herman ⁊ alij seruientes regis.

.LXVII Odo ⁊ alij taini regis.

.LXVIII.Herueus ⁊ alij ministri regis.

64 c

LIST OF LANDHOLDERS IN WILTSHIRE

1 King William
2 The Bishop of Winchester
3 The Bishop of Salisbury
4 The Bishop of Bayeux
5 The Bishop of Coutances
6 The Bishop of Lisieux
7 Glastonbury Abbey
8 Malmesbury Abbey
9 Westminster Abbey
10 Winchester Abbey
11 Cranborne Abbey
12 The Abbess of Shaftesbury
13 The Abbess of Wilton
14 The Abbess of Winchester
15 The Abbess of Romsey
16 The Abbess of Amesbury
17 The Church of Bec
18 Gerald, priest of Wilton
19 The Canons of Lisieux
20 The Count of Mortain
21 Earl Roger
22 Earl Hugh
23 Earl Aubrey
24 Edward of Salisbury
25 Arnulf of Hesdin
26 Alfred of Marlborough
27 Humphrey de L'Isle
28 Miles Crispin
29 Gilbert of Breteuil
30 Durand of Gloucester
31 Walter Giffard
32 William of Eu
33 William of Braose
34 William of Mohun
35 William of Falaise

36 Walscin of Douai
37 Waleran Hunter
38 William son of Guy
39 Henry of Ferrers
40 Richard son of Count Gilbert
41 Ralph of Mortimer
42 Robert son of Gerald
43 Robert son of Rolf
44 Roger of Courseulles
45 Roger of Berkeley
46 Bernard Pancevolt
47 Berengar Giffard
48 Osbern Giffard
49 Drogo son of Poyntz
50 Hugh Donkey
51 Hugh son of Baldric
52 Humphrey the Chamberlain
53 Gunfrid Mawditt
54 Alfred of Spain
55 Aiulf the Sheriff
56 Nigel the Doctor
57 Osbern the priest
58 Richard Poynant
59 Robert Marshall
60 Robert Blunt
61 Richard Sturmy
62 Reginald Canute
63 Matthew of Mortagne
64 Jocelyn Rivers
65 Godescal
66 Herman and other King's Servants
67 Odo and other King's thanes
68 Hervey and other King's officers.

Rex habet de Burgo *WILTVNIE* . L . lib . Qdo Herueus recepit
ad cuſtodiend . reddeƀ . xxii . libras.

De *WILTESCIRE* . ht rex . x . lib ꝓ accipitre . 7 xx . ſolid ꝓ ſumario.
7 ꝓ feno . c . ſolid 7 v . oras.

De dimid molino a ꝑ *SARISBERIE* . ht rex . xx . ſolid ad penſum.

De tcio denario *SARISBERIE* . ht rex . vi . lib . De tcio denario *MERLE*
BERGE . iiii . lib . De tcio denar *CRICHELADE* . v . lib . De tcio denario
BADE . xi . lib . De tcio denario *MALMESBERIE* . vi . lib.

De Cremto . lx . lib ad pondus . Ħ reddit Edwardvs. _{uicecomes}

Walterivs de . ii . partiƀ burgi Malmeſberie . redd . viii . lib regi.
tantund reddeƀ ipſu burgu T . R . E . 7 in hac firma erant placita Hundret de
Cicemtone 7 Suteleſberg q̄ regi ꝑtineƀ . ꝆDe moneta redd ipſu burg . c . ſolid.
In eod burgo habuit Heraldus un̄ agr̄ træ . in q̄ ſunt . iiii . maſuræ . 7 vi . aliæ
uaſtæ . 7 un̄ molin̄ redd . x . ſolid . Hoc tot reddeƀ . c . ſol . T . R . E.
Qdo rex ibat in expedition l̄ tra l̄ mari . habeƀ de hoc burgo aut . xx . ſolid
ad paſcendos ſuos buzecarl . Aut un̄u homin̄ duceƀ ſecu ꝓ honore . v . hidaru.

64 d

Terra Regis.

Rex tenet *CAVNA* . Rex . E . tenuit 7 nunq̄ geldauit .
ido neſcit quot hidæ ſint ibi . Tra . e . xxix . car.

In dn̄io ſunt . viii . car . 7 viii . ſerui . Ibi . xxxvii . uilti 7 lxxviii.
bord . 7 x . colibti . hn̄tes . xxi . car . Ibi . xlv . burgenſes . 7 vii.
molini reddtes . iiii . lib 7 xii . ſot 7 vi . den̄ . 7 l . ac p̄ti . 7 paſtura
ii . leu lḡ . 7 una leu lat . Ħ uilla redd firma uni noctis cu om̄iƀ
Ꝇ Huj̄ ম̄ æcclam ten̄ Nigell de rege . cu . vi . hid træ . Ꝇ c̄ſuetud̄.
Tra . e . v . car . In dn̄io ſt . ii . 7 vi . ſerui . Ibi . vii . uilti . 7 ii . bord.
^{cu̅ . iii . car̄}
7 xi . cozets . Ibi . ii . molini de . xx . ſot . 7 xxv . burḡſes redd . xx.
ſolid . Silua . ii . q̄ƺ lḡ . 7 una q̄ƺ 7 xxiiii . ac̄s lat . Paſtura . iiii.
q̄rent lḡ . 7 ii . q̄ƺ lat . Tot uat . viii . lib.
Ꝇ Alured de hiſpania ten̄ . v . hid træ . q̄s Nigell calūniat̄.
Ħ tra teſtimonio ſciræ ꝑtinuit ad æcclam . T . R . E.

(WILTSHIRE CUSTOMS)

B 1 The King has £50 from the Borough of WILTON; it paid £22 when Hervey acquired it in charge.

2 From WILTSHIRE the King has £10 for a hawk; 20s for a pack-horse; for hay 100s and 5 *ora*.

3 From ½ mill at SALISBURY the King has 20s by weight.

4 From the third penny of SALISBURY the King has £6; from the third penny of MARLBOROUGH, £4; from the third penny of CRICKLADE, £5; from the third penny of BATH, £11; from the third penny of MALMESBURY, £6. From the increase, £60 by weight. Edward the Sheriff pays this.

5 Walter Hussey pays £8 to the King from the two parts of the Borough of MALMESBURY . The Borough itself paid as much before 1066. In this revenue were the pleas of Chedglow and Startley Hundreds, which belonged to the King. From its Mint the Borough itself pays 100s. Also in this Borough Earl Harold had an acre of land, on which are 4 dwellings and 6 others derelict, and a mill which pays 10s. The whole paid 100s before 1066.
When the King went on an expedition by land or sea, he had from this Borough either 20s to feed his boatmen, or he took with him one man for (each) Honour of five hides.

[1]   **LAND OF THE KING**   64 d

The King holds

1 CALNE. King Edward held it. It never paid tax, so it is not known how many hides are there. Land for 29 ploughs. In lordship 8 ploughs; 8 slaves.

37 villagers, 78 smallholders and 10 freedmen who have 21 ploughs. 45 burgesses.

7 mills which pay £4 12s 6d; meadow, 50 acres; pasture 2 leagues long and 1 league wide.

This village pays one night's revenue, with all customary dues. Nigel holds the church of this manor from the King, with 6 hides of land. Land for 5 ploughs. In lordship 2; 6 slaves.

7 villagers, 2 smallholders and 11 Cottagers with 3 ploughs.

2 mills at 20s; 25 burgesses who pay 20s. Woodland 2 furlongs long and 1 furlong and 24 acres wide; pasture 4 furlongs long and 2 furlongs wide.

Total value £8.

Alfred of 'Spain' holds 5 hides of land which Nigel claims. This land belonged to the Church before 1066, by the witness of the Shire.

Rex ten̄ *BEDVINDE* . Rex . E . tenuit . Nunq̇ geldauit.

nec hidata fuit . Tra . ē q̇t . xx . car una min . In dn̄io suy̌

xii . car . 7 xviii . ſerui . Ibi q̇t . xx . uilli . 7 lx . cozets . 7 xiiii.

cū Lx.
vii . car.
coliḃti . Ibi . viii . molini redd̄ . c . ſol . Duæ ſiluæ hn̄tes . ii . leu

lḡ . 7 una leu lat . Ibi . cc . ãc p̃ti . 7 xii . q̇ꝛ paſturæ lḡ . 7 vi.

q̇ꝛ lat . Huic m̄ p̃tin . xxv . burgenſes.

H̄ uilla redd̄ firmā uni noctis cū om̄ibꝛ c̃ſuetudinibꝛ.

In hoc m̄ fuit T . R . E . lucus hn̄s dimid̄ leu lḡ . 7 iii . q̇ꝛ lat.

7 erat in dn̄io regis . Modo tenet eū Henric̄ de ferreres.

Rex ten̄ *AMBLESBERIE* . Rex . E . tenuit . Nunq̇ geldau.

nec hidata fuit . Tra . ē . xl . car . In dn̄io ſunt . xvi . car.

7 lv . ſerui . 7 ii . coliḃti . Ibi q̇t . xx 7 v . uilli . 7 lvi . bord̄

hn̄tes . xxiii . car . Ibi . viii . molini . redd̄ . iiii . liḃ 7 x . ſol.

7 L . ãc p̃ti . Paſtura . iiii . leu lḡ . 7 iii . leu lat . Silua

vi . leu lḡ . 7 iiii . leu lat.   c̃ſuetudiniḃ.

Hoc m̄ . . . cū appendic̃ ſuis redd̄ firmā uni noctis . cū oīḃ

In hoc m̄ numerant tre . iii . tainoꝛ quas ipſi teneḃ . T . R . E.

Has ded̄ Wills com̄ in Ambleſḃie p mutuatione *BOVECOME* . ☞

De huj̇ m̄ tra . ii . hid̄ ded̄ rex . E . in ſua infirmitate

abbatiſſæ Wiltunienſi . q̇s nunq̇ antea habuerat . poſtea

ū eas tenuit . ☞ Wills com̄ ded̄ Quintone 7 Suindone

7 cheurel quæ erant tainlandæ . p tra de inſula de With.

quæ p̃tineḃ ad firmā de Ambleſberie.

Rex ten̄ *GVERMINSTRE* . Rex . E . tenuit . Non geldau.

nec hidata fuit . Tra . ē . xl . car . In dn̄io ſt . vi . car.

7 xxiiii . ſerui . 7 xiii . porcarij . Ibi . xv . uilli 7 viii . cozets.

7 xiiii . coliḃti . cū . xxx.vi . car . Ibi . vii . molini de . iiii . liḃ.

7 q̇t xx . ãc p̃ti . Paſtura . i . leu lḡ . 7 dim̄ leu lat . Silua.

ii . leu lḡ . 7 ii . lat . Ibi . xxx . burgſes.

Hoc m̄ redd̄ firmā uni noctis cū om̄ibꝛ c̃ſuetudiniḃ ſuis.

2 **BEDWYN.** King Edward held it. It never paid tax and was not
assessed in hides. Land for 80 ploughs less one.
In lordship 12 ploughs; 18 slaves.
  80 villagers, 60 Cottagers and 14 freedmen with 67 ploughs.
  8 mills which pay 100s; two woodlands which have 2 leagues
    length and 1 league width. Meadow, 200 acres; pasture, 12
    furlongs long and 6 furlongs wide.
  To this manor belong 25 burgesses.
This village pays one night's revenue, with all customary dues.
  In this manor before 1066 there was a wood which had
½ league length and 3 furlongs width and was in the King's
lordship; now Henry of Ferrers holds it.

3 **AMESBURY.** King Edward held it. It never paid tax and was not
assessed in hides. Land for 40 ploughs. In lordship 16 ploughs; 55
slaves; 2 freedmen.
  85 villagers and 56 smallholders who have 23 ploughs.
  8 mills which pay £4 10s; meadow, 70 acres; pasture 4 leagues
    long and 3 leagues wide; woodland 6 leagues long and
    4 leagues wide.
This manor ... with its dependencies pays one night's revenue,
with all customary dues.
  In this manor are enumerated the lands of 3 thanes, which
they held themselves before 1066.
† Earl William gave those to Amesbury in exchange for Bowcombe.
  King Edward when he was ill gave 2 hides of this manor's land
to the Abbess of Wilton, which she had never had before, but she
held them afterwards.
† Earl William gave *QUINTONE* and Swindon and Cheverell, which
were thanelands, for the Isle of Wight land which belonged to the
Amesbury revenue.

4 **WARMINSTER.** King Edward held it. It did not pay tax and was not
assessed in hides. Land for 40 ploughs. In lordship 6 ploughs;
24 slaves; 13 pigmen.
  15 villagers, 8 Cottagers and 14 freedmen with 36 ploughs.
  7 mills at £4; meadow, 80 acres; pasture 1 league long and ½
    league wide; woodland 2 leagues long and 2 wide.
  30 burgesses.
This manor pays one night's revenue, with all its customary dues.

Rex ten̄ *CHEPEHÁ*. Rex. E. tenuit. Non geldauit. nec
hidata fuit. Tra. ē. c. car̄. In dn̄io funt. xvi. car̄. 7 xxviii.
ferui. Ibi. xlviii. uilti 7 xlv. borđ 7 xx. cot. 7 xxiii. porcarij
Int om̄s hn̄t. lxvi. car̄. Ibi. xii. molini de. vi. lib̄. 7 c. ac̄
p̄ti. Silua. iiii. leu In lḡ 7 lat. Paftura. ii. leu lḡ. 7 una leu
lat. Hoc M̄ cū appenđ fuis redđ firmā uni̅ noctis cū om̄ibʒ
c̄fuetudinibʒ 7 uat. cx. lib̄ ad numerū.
Huj̄ M̄ ecclam cū. ii. hiđ ten̄ Ofb̄n ep̄s ex T.R.E. Vna ex his
hiđ ē tainlande. altera p̄tin̄ æcclæ. Tot uat. lv. foliđ.
Huic M̄ p̄tin̄ una tra quā rex. E. dederat Vluiet uenatori
fuo. 7 erat de dn̄io fuo. H̄ in firma regis. ē m̄. 7 p una hida habet̄
Tra. ē. ii. car̄. 7 ipfæ ibi ſt. 7 iii. ferui. 7 iiii. uilti 7 iiii. cozets
cū. i. car̄. Paftura. iiii. qʒ lḡ. 7 una qʒ lat. Vat. iii. lib̄.
In firma huj̄ M̄. ē dimiđ v træ quæ fuit tainlande. ˌ
Edricus tenuit T.R.E

65 a
Rex ten̄ *BRETFORD*. Rex. E. tenuit. 7 p una hida
geldauit. Tra. ē. xx. car̄. In dn̄io ſt. ii. car̄. 7 vi. ferui.
7 x. colib̄ti. Ibi xii. uilti 7 vi. borđ 7 xiiii. cozets.
cū. xvii. car̄. Ibi ii. molini de. xx. fot. 7 c. ac̄ p̄ti.
Paftura. i. leu lḡ. 7 dim̄ leu lat.
Hoc M̄ redđ. xxx. lib̄ ad penfū. Silua. ē in manu regis
7 inde ht̄. xl. fot in firma fua.   ⌠Vat. xl. fot.
Huj̄ M̄ æcclam ten̄ Ofb̄n p̄br cū. i. hida træ p̄tin̄ æcclæ
Rex ten̄ *THEODVLVESIDE*. Rex. E. tenuit. Non gel
dauit nec hidata fuit. Tra. ē. xl. car̄. In dn̄io ſt. ix. car̄.
7 xxii. ferui. 7 x. colib̄ti. Ibi. xxxiiii. uilti 7 xxxii. cozets.
cū. xviii. car̄. Ibi. ix. molini de. c. fot 7 xxx. den̄. 7 lxvi.
burgenfes. redđtes. l. fot. Ibi. i. leu p̄ti jn lḡ. 7 dim̄ lat.
Paftura. i. leu 7 dim̄ lḡ. 7 una leu lat̄. Silua. ii. leu lḡ.
7 una leu lat̄.   ⌠c. lib̄ ad numerū.
Hoc M̄ redđ firmā uni̅ noctis. cū c̄fuetudinib̄ fuis. 7 Vat

5 CHIPPENHAM. King Edward held it. It did not pay tax, and was
not assessed in hides. Land for 100 ploughs.
In lordship 16 ploughs; 28 slaves.
   48 villagers, 45 smallholders, 20 cottagers and 23 pigmen;
     between them they have 66 ploughs.
   12 mills at £6; meadow, 100 acres; woodland 4 leagues in
     length and width; pasture 2 leagues long and 1 league wide.
This manor with its dependencies pays one night's revenue,
with all customary dues.
Value £110 at face value.
   Bishop Osbern holds the church of this manor, with 2 hides,
since before 1066. One of these hides is thaneland; the other
belongs to the church. Total value 55s.
   To this manor belongs one land which King Edward gave
to Wulfgeat his Huntsman; and it was of his lordship; now
it is in the King's revenue and is recorded as 1 hide.
Land for 2 ploughs; they are there; 3 slaves;
   4 villagers and 4 Cottagers with 1 plough.
   Pasture 4 furlongs long and 1 furlong wide. Value £3.
In this manor's revenue is ½ virgate of land which was thaneland.
Edric held it before 1066.

6 BRITFORD. King Edward held it . It paid tax for 1 hide. Land   65 a
for 20 ploughs. In lordship 2 ploughs; 6 slaves; 10 freedmen.
   12 villagers, 6 smallholders, and 14 Cottagers with 17 ploughs.
   2 mills at 20s; meadow, 100 acres; pasture 1 league long
     and ½ league wide.
This manor pays £30 by weight.
   The woodland is in the King's hands, and from it he has 40s
in his revenue. Osbern the priest holds the church of this manor,
with 1 hide of land which belongs to the church. Value 40s.

7 TILSHEAD. King Edward held it. It did not pay tax, and was not
assessed in hides. Land for 40 ploughs. In lordship 9 ploughs;
22 slaves; 10 freedmen.
   34 villagers and 32 Cottagers with 18 ploughs.
   9 mills at 100s and 30d; 66 burgesses who pay 50s.
     Meadow, 1 league in length and ½ wide; pasture 1½ leagues
     long and 1 league wide; woodland 2 leagues long and
     1 league wide.
This manor pays one night's revenue, with its customary dues.
Value £100 at face value.

Rex ten̄ *Contone*. Herald tenuit. 7 p̄. x. hid̄ geld̄.

Tra̅.e̅.x.car̄. In dn̄io st.ii.car̄.7 ii.serui.7 xxviii.

uilli 7 ii.bord̄ cū.viii.car̄.Ibi molin̄ de.xii.solid̄ 7 vi.

den̄.7 xx.ac̄ p̄ti.7 viii.ac̄ pasturæ.7 xv.ac̄ siluæ.

Hoc M̄ redd̄.xii.lib ad pensū.

Rex ten̄ *Rvsteselve*.Ghida tenuit T.R.E.7 gel

dabat p̄.xxxvii.hid̄ cū appendic̄ suis.

Tra̅.e̅.xxvii.car̄ 7 dimid̄.In dn̄io st.xix.hidæ.

7 ibi.xii.car̄.7 xxxvii.serui.Ibi xxviii.uilli 7 xl.

bord̄ cū.xiiii.car̄.Ibi.v.molini de.lxxii.solid̄.

7 cxii.ac̄ p̄ti.Pastura.iii.leu lḡ.7 una leu 7 dim

in lat.Silua.i.leu lḡ.7 dim leu lat.

Valuit 7 ual.xxxii.lib 7 x.solid̄.

Huj M̄ æcclam hē S̄ Wandregisilus.cū.ii.hid̄ træ

7 ibi.e̅ una car̄ 7 dimid̄.Val.xl.solid̄.

Rex ten̄ *Aldeborne*.Ghida tenuit T.R.E.7 gel

dab̄ p̄.xl.hid̄.Tra̅.e̅.xlv.car̄.In dn̄io st.xviii.hidæ.

7 ibi.x.car̄.7 xxv.serui.7 xiiii.colibti.Ibi.lxxiii.uilli

7 xxxviii.cozets.cū.xxvi.car̄.Ibi.iiii.molini de.xvi.

sol 7 viii.den̄.Pratū.i.leu lḡ.7 v.q̄ʒ lat̄.Pastura

una leu lḡ.7 dim leu lat.Silua.ii.leu lḡ.7 dim leu

lat.Huic M̄ p̄tin̄.vi.burḡses in Crichelade.redd̄tes

lxiiii.den̄.   nisi.lx.lib ad numerū.

Hoc M̄ redd̄.lxx.lib ad pensū.sed ab anglis n̄ ap̄pciat̄

Ad æcclam huj M̄ p̄tin̄.ii.hidæ.Tra.ii.car̄.Has

hē p̄br ejd̄ æcclæ.7 ual.xl.solid̄.

Rex ten̄ *Cosseha̅*.Tosti tenuit T.R.E.Ibi st.xxxiiii.

hidæ.sed p̄.xviii.hid̄ redd̄ geld̄.Tra̅.e̅.l.car̄.

In dn̄io st.xi.hidæ.7 ibi.vii.car̄.7 x.serui.Ibi.lxv.

uilli.7 xlviii.cozets.7 ix.cot cū xxxviii.car̄.

8   COMPTON (Chamberlayne). Earl Harold held it. It paid tax
for 10 hides. Land for 10 ploughs. In lordship 2 ploughs; 2 slaves;
>28 villagers and 2 smallholders with 8 ploughs.
>A mill at 12s 6d; meadow, 20 acres; pasture, 8 acres;
>>woodland, 15 acres.
This manor pays £12 by weight.

9   RUSHALL. Gytha held it before 1066. It paid tax for 37 hides,
with its dependencies. Land for 27½ ploughs. In lordship 19
hides; 12 ploughs; 37 slaves.
>28 villagers and 40 smallholders with 14 ploughs.
>5 mills at 72s; meadow, 112 acres; pasture 3½ leagues long
>>and 1½ leagues in width; woodland 1 league long and ½
>>league wide.
The value was and is £32 10s.
>St. Wandrille's has the church of this manor, with 2 hides
of land. 1½ ploughs there. Value 40s.

10   ALDBOURNE. Gytha held it before 1066. It paid tax for 40 hides.
Land for 45 ploughs. In lordship 18 hides; 10 ploughs;
25 slaves; 14 freedmen.
>73 villagers and 38 Cottagers with 26 ploughs.
>4 mills at 16s 8d; meadow 1 league long and 5 furlongs wide;
>>pasture 1 league long and ½ league wide; woodland 2 leagues
>>long and ½ league wide.
To this manor belong 6 burgesses in Cricklade who pay 64d.
This manor pays £70 by weight, but it is assessed by the English at
only £60 at face value.
>To the Church of this manor belong 2 hides. Land for 2
ploughs. The priest of this church has them. Value 40s.

11   CORSHAM. Earl Tosti held it before 1066. There are 34 hides,
but it pays tax for 18 hides. Land for 50 ploughs.
In lordship 11 hides; 7 ploughs; 10 slaves.
>65 villagers, 48 Cottagers and 9 cottagers with 38 ploughs.

Ibi . ii . molini de . viii . fol 7 vi . den . 7 xxxii . ac p̃ti .

7 una hida paſturæ . 7 ii . leu ſiluæ in lg̃ 7 lat .

Hoc M̃ cũ append: redd . xxx . lib ad penſũ . Angli ũ

app̃ciant ad xxxi . lib ad numerũ .

Huj M̃ æcclam h̃t S Stefan cadomi . cũ . iii . hid træ

Tra . ē . v . car . Has h̃nt ibi . iii . uilli cũ vi cozets

Æcclã de Paueſhou q̃ adjacet huic M̃ ⌐ Val . vii . lib .

ten Edgar . 7 pat ej tenuit . Val v ſolid

Rex ten MELCHESHĀ . Herald tenuit . 7 p̃ qt xx 7 iiii .

hid geldauit cũ appendic ſuis . Tra . ē . lx . car .

In dñio ſt . xxxiiii . hidæ . 7 ibi . xix . car . 7 xxxv . ſerui .

7 xxxi . colib̃t . Ibi . c . uilli . viii . min . 7 lxvi . bord h̃ntes

xxxix . car . Ibi . viii . molini reddtcs . vii . lib 7 vi . ſol .

7 cxxx ac p̃ti . 7 viii . leu paſturæ in lg̃ 7 lat . Silua

iiii . leu int lg̃ 7 lat .   ⌐ ad totid lib ad numer̃ .

Hoc M̃ redd . c 7 . xi . lib 7 xi . ſol ad penſũ . Angli ũ app̃cia͡

65 b

Huj M̃ æcclam cũ . i . hida træ h̃t Rumold . 7 ual . xl . ſol .

Rex ten CVMBE . Ghida tenuit T . R . E . 7 geldb̃ p̃ xxiii . hid

7 dimid . Tra . ē . xx . car . In dñio ſt xi . hidæ . 7 ibi . iii . car .

7 vii . ſerui . Ibi . xxviii . uilli 7 vii . bord . 7 xliii . cozets . h̃ntes

★ xvii . car . Ibi . ii . molini redd . xxv . ſol . 7 xl . ac p̃ti . 7 paſtura

una leu lg̃ . 7 alia lat . 7 x . ac paruæ ſiluæ .

Hoc M̃ redd . xxiiii . lib ad penſũ . T . R . E . tantd ad numerũ .

Æcclam huj M̃ cũ dimid hida træ ten Leuric . 7 ual . xx . ſolid .

Rex ten BROMHAM . Herald tenuit . 7 p̃ . xx . hid geldauit .

Tra . ē . x . car . In dñio ſt . x . hidæ . 7 ibi . ii . car . 7 iiii . ſerui .

Ibi . xiiii . uilli 7 vi . bord 7 xxx . cozets . cũ . viii . car . Ibi . ii . molini

de . v . ſolid . 7 xl . ac p̃ti . 7 xii . ac paſturæ . Silua . v . q̃z lg̃ .

7 iii . q̃z lat .   Valuit . xx . lib . modo . xxiiii . lib .

De tra uilloz ten pb̃r unã hid 7 unã v træ . de rege . Val . xv . ſol .

2 mills at 8s 6d; meadow, 32 acres; pasture, 1 hide;
   woodland, 2 leagues in length and width.
This manor with its dependencies pays £30 by weight; but the
English assess it at £31 at face value.

St. Stephen's of Caen has the church of this manor with 3
hides of land. Land for 5 ploughs. 3 villagers with 6 Cottagers
have them there. Value £7.

Edgar holds the church of Poulshot which is attached
to this manor. His father held it. Value 5s.

12 MELKSHAM. Earl Harold held it. It paid tax for 84 hides
with its dependencies. Land for 60 ploughs. In lordship 34
hides; 19 ploughs; 35 slaves; 31 freedmen.
   100 villagers less 8 and 66 smallholders who have 39 ploughs.
   8 mills which pay £7 6s; meadow, 130 acres; pasture, 8
      leagues in length and width; woodland, 4 leagues in both
      length and width.
This manor pays £111 11s by weight; but the English assess
it at as many £s at face value.

Rumold the priest has the church of this manor with 1   65 b
hide of land. Value 40s.

13 COOMBE (Bissett). Gytha held it before 1066. It paid tax
for 23½ hides. Land for 20 ploughs. In lordship 11 hides; 3
ploughs; 7 slaves.
   28 villagers, 7 smallholders and 43 Cottagers who
      have 17 ploughs.
   2 mills which pay 25s; meadow, 60 acres; pasture 1
      league long and another wide; a small wood, 10 acres.
This manor pays £24 by weight; before 1066 as much at face value.

Leofric the priest holds the church of this manor with ½
hide of land. Value 20s.

14 BROMHAM. Earl Harold held it. It paid tax for 20 hides.
Land for 10 ploughs. In lordship 10 hides; 2 ploughs; 4 slaves.
   14 villagers, 6 smallholders and 30 Cottagers
      with 8 ploughs.
   2 mills at 5s; meadow, 40 acres; pasture, 12 acres;
      woodland 5 furlongs long and 3 furlongs wide.
The value was £20; now £24.

Of the villagers' land a priest holds 1 hide and 1 virgate of land
from the King. Value 15s.

Rex ten Otone. Eddid tenuit. 7 geldb̄ p̄. xxx. hid una v̄ min.

Tra . ē. xxx . car̄. In dn̄io ſt . xiii . hidæ 7 una v̄ træ. 7 ibi . ii . car̄.

7 xii . ſerui . Ibi . xl . uitti 7 xvii . coſcez . cū xiiii . car̄.

Ibi . vi . ãc p̄ti . 7 paſtura . vi . q̃ʒ lḡ . 7 iii . q̃ʒ lat̄ . Silua . vi . q̃ʒ

lḡ . 7 tntd lat̄.   Valuit . xxvi . lib̄ . m̃ . xxx . lib̄.

Huj M̃ æcctas duas cū . i . hida træ ten S̃ Michael de monte.

Rex ten Westberie. Eddid tenuit. 7 geldauit ſ Val̄. xx . ſolid̄.

p̄. xl . hid . Tra . ē . xlvii . car̄. In dn̄io ſt . xvii . hidæ 7 ibi

vii . car̄. 7 xxviii . ſerui . 7 xvi . colibti . Ibi . xxxviii . uitti 7 xxiii.

bord 7 ix . mellitarij . Int om̃s hn̄t . xl . car̄. Ibi potarij reddt̄

xx . ſot p annū. 7 vi . molini reddt̄ . lxx . ſot 7 vi . denar̄. 7 q̃t xx.

ãc p̄ti . Paſtura . iii . leu lḡ . 7 iii . leu lat̄ . Silua . iii . leu lḡ.

7 dim leu lat̄ . Ibi . xxix . porcarij .   ſ 7 ibi ht̄ . vii . car̄.

Hoc M̃ reddt̄ . c . lib̄ ad numerū.

De ead̄ tra huj M̃ ht̄ æccta hida 7 dimid̄ . Witts . iiii . hid 7 dimid̄ . Æccta ualet

Rex ten Wintreburne. Eddid tenuit. 7 geldb̄ p̄. ii . hid   ſ . l . ſolid̄.

7 una v̄ træ. Tra . ē. xii . car̄. In dn̄io . ē dimid̄ v̄ træ. 7 ibi . iii . car̄.

7 xi . ſerui 7 v . colibti . Ibi . xv . uitti 7 xv . bord cū . viii . car̄.

Ibi molin̄ de . x . ſot. 7 viii . ãc p̄ti . Paſtura . ii . leu lḡ . 7 tntd lat̄.

Valuit 7 ual̄ . xxxiii . lib̄ . Æccta ejd M̃ ht̄ . i . hid de ipſa tra

Abb̄ gēmeticenſis ten hanc æcctam cū tra. 7 ual̄ . lx . ſolid̄.

Rex ten Nigravre. Herald tenuit. 7 geldb̄ p̄ . xx . hid.

Tra . ē . xxii . car̄. In dn̄io ſt . ii . hidæ . 7 ibi . vi . car̄. 7 xlvi . ſerui.

7 viii . colibti . Ibi . xxx . uitti 7 xl . bord . cū xvi . car̄.

Ad hoc M̃ ptin̄ . v . burḡſes in Wiltune . reddt̄ . vi . ſot . Ibi . iii . mo

lini redd̄ . xxx . ſolid̄. 7 lxx . ãc p̄ti . Paſtura . iii . leu lḡ . 7 dimid̄

leu lat̄.   Valuit . xl . lib̄ . Modo . lvii . lib̄.

De hac tra huj M̃ ten Herueus hida 7 dimid̄. 7 ibi ht̄ . i . car̄.

Vn̄ tain ht̄ . ii . hid 7 dim. 7 ibi ht̄ . i . car̄.

15 WOOTTON (Rivers). Queen Edith held it. It paid tax for 30 hides less 1 virgate. Land for 30 ploughs. In lordship 13 hides and 1 virgate of land; 2 ploughs; 12 slaves.

　　40 villagers and 17 Cottagers with 14 ploughs.
　　Meadow, 6 acres; pasture 6 furlongs long and 3 furlongs wide; woodland 6 furlongs long and as wide.
The value was £26; now £30.
　　Mont St. Michel's holds the two churches of this manor with 1 hide of land. Value 20s.

16 WESTBURY. Queen Edith held it. It paid tax for 40 hides. Land for 47 ploughs. In lordship 17 hides; 7 ploughs; 28 slaves; 16 freedmen.

　　38 villagers, 23 smallholders and 9 beekeepers. Between them they have 40 ploughs. Potters there pay 20s a year.
　　6 mills which pay 70s 6d; meadow, 80 acres; pasture 3 leagues long and 3 leagues wide; woodland 3 leagues long and ½ league wide.
　　29 pigmen.
This manor pays £100 at face value.
　　The church has 1½ hides of the land of this manor; a minor clerk holds it. William Shield (has) 4½ hides and has 7 ploughs there. Value of the church, 50s.

17 WINTERBOURNE (Stoke). Queen Edith held it. It paid tax for 2 hides and 1 virgate of land. Land for 12 ploughs. In lordship ½ virgate of land; 3 ploughs; 11 slaves; 5 freedmen.

　　15 villagers and 15 smallholders with 8 ploughs.
　　A mill at 10s; meadow, 8 acres; pasture 2 leagues long and as wide.
The value was and is £33.
　　The church of this manor has 1 hide of that land. The Abbot of Jumièges holds this church with the land. Value 60s.

18 NETHERAVON. Earl Harold held it. It paid tax for 20 hides. Land for 22 ploughs. In lordship 2 hides; 6 ploughs; 46 slaves; 8 freedmen.

　　30 villagers and 40 smallholders with 16 ploughs.
　　5 burgesses in Wilton belong to this manor and pay 6s.
　　3 mills which pay 30s; meadow, 70 acres; pasture 3 leagues long and ½ league wide.
The value was £40; now £57.
　　Hervey holds 1½ hides of the land of this manor and has 1 plough there. A thane has 2½ hides and has 1 plough there.

Ǽcclam huȝ ꝳ cū una hida teñ Nigell medicus . Ħ cū oīibȝ
appendic ſuis ual . xxxii . liƀ . Ipſa ū uaſta eſt ⁊ ita diſcoopta
ut pene corruat.

Rex teñ *COLINGEBVRNE* . Herald coīñ tenuit . ⁊ geldƀ ꝑ . xx . hiđ.
Tra . ē . xlv . caŕ . In dīnio ſt . v . hidæ . ⁊ ibi . v . caŕ . ⁊ xii . ſerui.
Ibi . xlix . caŕ . ⁊ xxvi . borđ . cū . xv . caŕ ⁊ xx ti . aͨ ꝑti . Paſtura
ii . leu lḡ . ⁊ una leu lat . Silua . i . leu lḡ . ⁊ tntđ lat . ⁊ tcia pars
ſiluæ quæ uocať cetum.   Val . xl . liƀ . Modo . lx . liƀ.

Ad æcclam ꝑtiñ dimiđ hidā Huȝ æcclæ decimā teñ Girald
pƀr de Wiltone . ⁊ ual . x . ſoliđ . Eccla uaſta . ē ⁊ diſſipata.

Rex teñ *CHENVEL* . Eileua tenuit T . R . E . ⁊ geld ꝑ . xxx . hiđ.
Tra . xv . caŕ . In dīnio ſt . xvii . hidæ ⁊ dimiđ . ⁊ ibi . v . caŕ . ⁊ x . ſerui.
Ibi . xvi . uilli ⁊ x . borđ . ⁊ xviii . coſcez . cū . x . caŕ.
Ibi . xv . aͨ ꝑti . ⁊ paſtura . i . leu lḡ . ⁊ dimiđ leu lat . Silua dimiđ
leu lḡ . ⁊ tntđ lat.   Valuit . xxviii . liƀ . Ṁ . xxx . liƀ.
De hac tra hŕ Giſleƀt . i . hiđ . Ibi ſt . iii . borđ . Val . vii . ſol ⁊ vi . deñ.

Rex teñ *LIDIARDE* . Godric tenuit T . R . E . ⁊ geldƀ ꝑ x . hiđ.
Tra . ē . viii . caŕ . In dīnio . vi . hidæ una v̄ miñ ⁊ ibi . iiii . caŕ . ⁊ ix . ſerui.
Ibi . x . uilli . ⁊ vi . borđ hn̄t . vi . caŕ . Ibi moliñ de . xxxii . deñ . ⁊ xx.
aͨ ꝑti . Silua . i . leu lḡ . ⁊ dimiđ leu lat . Valuit . x . liƀ . Ṁ . xii . liƀ.
Hǽ DVǼ Villæ fueŕ Willi comitis.

65 c

Rex teñ *OCHEBORNE* .   T . R . E . geldƀ ꝑ . xxx . hiđ.
Tra . ē . xxv . caŕ . In dīnio ſunt . xviii . hide . ⁊ ibi . iiii . caŕ.
⁊ vi . ſerui . Ibi . xxiiii . uilli ⁊ xiiii . borđ hn̄t . x . caŕ.
Ibi . vi . aͨ ꝑti . ⁊ paſtura dimiđ leu lḡ . ⁊ iiii . ꝗrent lat.
⁊ tantunđ ſiluæ.   Valet . xxv . liƀ.

ᚵ Radulf pƀr teñ æcclam de *WRDE* . ⁊ ad eā ꝑtiñ . iii . hidæ ꝗ ñ geldƀ
T . R . E . Tra . ē . ii . caŕ . Has hŕ ibi pƀr cū . vi . borđ . ⁊ x . aͨs ꝑti . Val . c . ſol.

Nigel the doctor holds the church of this manor with 1 hide.
Value, with all its dependencies, £32; but (the church) itself
is derelict and the roof so damaged that it is almost a ruin.

19 COLLINGBOURNE (Ducis). Earl Harold held it. It paid tax
for 20 hides. Land for 45 ploughs. In lordship 5 hides; 5
ploughs; 12 slaves.
  49 [villagers] and 26 smallholders with 15 ploughs.
  Meadow, 20 acres; pasture 2 leagues long and 1 league wide;
    woodland 1 league long and as wide, and the third part
    of the wood called Chute.
The value was £40; now £60.
  ½ hide belongs to the church. Gerald the priest of Wilton
holds the tithe of this church. Value 10s. The church is
derelict and dismantled.

20 (East) KNOYLE. Aeleva held it before 1066. It paid tax
for 30 hides. Land for 15 ploughs. In lordship 17½
hides; 5 ploughs; 10 slaves.
  16 villagers, 10 smallholders and 18 Cottagers with 10 ploughs.
  Meadow, 15 acres; pasture 1 league long and ½ league wide;
    woodland ½ league long and as wide.
The value was £28; now £30.
  Gilbert has 1 hide of this land. 3 smallholders are there.
Value 7s 6d.

21 LYDIARD (Millicent). Godric held it before 1066. It paid tax
for 10 hides. Land for 8 ploughs. In lordship 6 hides
less 1 virgate; 4 ploughs; 9 slaves.
  10 villagers and 6 smallholders have 6 ploughs.
  A mill at 32d; meadow, 20 acres; woodland 1 league long
    and ½ league wide.
The value was £10; now £12.

These 2 villages were Earl William's.

22 OGBOURNE...Before 1066 it paid tax for 30 hides. Land for 25   65 c
ploughs. In lordship 18 hides; 4 ploughs; 6 slaves.
  24 villagers and 14 smallholders have 10 ploughs.
  Meadow, 6 acres; pasture ½ league long and 4 furlongs
    wide; woodland, as much.
Value £25.

23a Ralph the priest holds HIGHWORTH church. 3 hides which did
not pay tax before 1066 belong to it. Land for 2 ploughs.
A priest has them, with
  6 smallholders; meadow, 10 acres.
Value 100s.

⁊ Vitalis p̄br ten̄ æcctam de *BVRBETCE* . cū una v̄ træ . Val . xx . sol.

⁊ Rainbold p̄br ten̄ æcctam de *PEVESIE* . cū una car̄ træ . Val . xx . sol.

⁊ Rainbold p̄br ten̄ æcctam de *AVREBERIE* . ad quā p̄tin̄ . II . hidæ . Val . xl . sol.

⁊ Aluuard p̄br ten̄ æcctam de *HESTREBE* . ad quā p̄tin̄ . III . hidæ.
Tra . ē . II . car̄ . Ipſæ ſt ibi cū . II . uittis ⁊ vI . cot . ⁊ vI . ac̄ p̄ti . Val . lx . sol.

⁊ Oſbn̄ eps hī æcctam de *HASEBERIE* . cū dimid v̄ træ . Val . x . sol.

⁊ Scs Wandregiſilus ten̄ æcctam de *SORSTAIN* . ad quā p̄tin̄ . III . virg
træ . Val . xxvIII . solid . Similit ten̄ æcctam de *OPPAVRENE* .
ad quā p̄tin̄ . II . hidæ ⁊ dim . Tra . ē . II . car̄ . Val . x . lib ⁊ xv . solid.

⁊ Oſmund eps ten̄ de rege dimid æcctam in elemoſina . ad quā
p̄tin̄ dimid hida . Ibi . ē . I . car̄ . cū . v . bord . ⁊ molin̄ de . vI . sol.
ualet . xxv . solid.   ⁊ xxx . solid.

⁊ Witts de Belfou hī . I . hid cū una æccta in *MERLEBERGE* . Valet

⁊ Briſtoard p̄br ten̄ æcctam de *BEDVINDE* . Pat ej tenuit T.R.E. Ibi p̄tin̄
una hida ⁊ dimid . Tra . ē . I . car̄ . q̄ ibi . ē .   Valuit ⁊ ual . lx . solid.

TERRA EP̄I WINTONIENSIS.

.II. Eps Wintoniensis tenet *DVNTONE* .

T.R.E. geldau̯ p.c. hid trib̄ min̄ . Duæ ex his n̄ ſt epi . q̄a
ablatæ fuer̄ cū alijs tribꝛ de æccta ⁊ de manu ep̄i t̄pr Cnut regis.
Tra . ē . xlvI . car̄ ⁊ dimid . De hac tra ſt in dn̄io . xxx . hidæ.
⁊ ibi . xIII . car̄ . ⁊ xl . ſerui . Ibi . lxIIII . uitti ⁊ xxvII . bord
hn̄tes . xvII . car̄ . Ibi . vII . molini redd . lx . solid . ⁊ lx . ac̄ p̄ti.
Paſtura . II . leu̯ lḡ . ⁊ una leu̯ lat . Silua . una leu̯ ⁊ dimid lḡ.
⁊ dimid leu̯ lat.

b Vitalis the priest holds BURBAGE church with 1 virgate of land.
Value 20s.

c Reinbald the priest holds PEWSEY church with 1 carucate of land.
Value 20s.

d Reinbald the priest holds AVEBURY church to which 2 hides belong.
Value 40s.

e Alfward the priest holds HEYTESBURY church to which 3 hides belong.
Land for 2 ploughs. They are there, with
    2 villagers; 6 cottagers.
    Meadow, 6 acres.
Value 60s.

f Bishop Osbern has HAZELBURY church with ½ virgate of land.
Value 10s.

g St. Wandrille's holds SHERSTON church to which 3 virgates
of land belong.
Value 28s.
    Likewise it holds the church of UPAVON to which 2½ hides belong.
Land for 2 ploughs.
Value £10 15s.

h Bishop Osmund holds ½ church from the King in alms to which ½
hide belongs. 1 plough there, with
    5 smallholders.
    A mill at 6s.
Value 25s.

i William of Beaufour has 1 hide with a church in MARLBOROUGH.
Value 30s.

j Brictward the priest holds the church of BEDWYN. His father
held it before 1066. 1½ hides belong there. Land for 1 plough,
which is there.
The value was and is 60s.

2   LAND OF THE BISHOP OF WINCHESTER

1 The Bishop of Winchester holds DOWNTON. Before 1066 it
paid tax for 100 hides less 3. 2 of these are not the Bishop's,
because they were taken away with the other 3 from the
church and from the Bishop's hand in King Canute's time.
Land for 46½ ploughs. Of this land 30 hides in lordship; 13
ploughs there; 40 slaves.
    64 villagers and 27 smallholders who have 17 ploughs.
    7 mills which pay 60s; meadow, 60 acres; pasture 2 leagues
        long and 1 league wide; woodland 1½ leagues long
        and ½ league wide.

De eaḋ ̄tra hůj ᴥ̄ ten Wilts de braiofe . xiiii . hiḋ . Waleran̄

v . hiḋ . Radulf . v . hiḋ . Anſgot . iii . hiḋ 7 dim . 7 rex ħ̄ in ſua

foreſta . iiii . hiḋ . Æccla ejḋ ᴥ̄ ħ̄ . iiii . hiḋ . 7 om̄s hi de epo ten̄ .

Qui has ̄tras teneb̄ T . R . E . n̄ ſe poterant ab æccla ſeparare .

Q̇do Walchelin ep̄s hoc ᴥ̄ recepit: ualb̄ lx . lib̄ .

Modo qḋ ħ̄ in dn̄io . ual . lxxx . lib̄ . Qḋ milites: xxiii . lib̄ .

Qḋ æccla: iii . lib̄ .

Idem ep̄s ten̄ *FONTEL* . T . R . E . geldb̄ ꝓ . x . hiḋ . ̄Tra . ē . vii . caṙ .

In dn̄io de hac ̄tra ſt . v . hidæ . 7 ibi . ii . caṙ . 7 v . ſerui .

Ibi . viii . uilti 7 v . borḋ . cū . iii . caṙ . Ibi molin̄ de . v . foliḋ .

7 viii . ac̄ p̄ti . Paſtura . dim leů l̄g . 7 iii . q̄ꝗ lat 7 tntḋ filuæ .

Valuit . x . lib̄ . Modo . xiiii . lib̄ .

7 de ep̄o .
ħ̄ ̄tra fuit Capicerij æcclē . Alſi monac̄ tenuit

Idem ep̄s ten̄ *FIFHIDE* . 7 Eduuard de eo . 7 geldb̄ ꝓ . v . hiḋ T . R . E .

̄Tra . ē . iii . caṙ . De hac ̄tra . iii . hidæ ſt in dn̄io . 7 ibi . ii . caṙ . cū . i .

ſeruo . Ibi . iii . uilti 7 ix . borḋ cū . ii . caṙ . Ibi . iii . ac̄ p̄ti . 7 xxx . ac̄

paſturæ . Silua . iii . q̄ꝗ l̄g . 7 una q̄ꝗ lat . Valuit 7 ual . c . fol .

Hᴀ́c Svnt De Victv monachoꝛ

Idc̄ ep̄s ten̄ *AWLTONE* . 7 geldb̄ ꝓ . xx . hiḋ T . R . E . ̄Tra . ē . xiiii .

caṙ . De hac ̄tra ſt . vi . hidæ 7 una v̄ ̄træ in dn̄io . 7 ibi . iiii . caṙ .

7 viii . ſerui . Ibi . xxvii . uilti 7 xv . coſcez . cū . viii . caṙ .

Ibi . ii . molini de . xii . fol 7 dim̄ . 7 c . ac̄ p̄ti . Paſtura . vi . q̄rent

l̄g . 7 iiii . q̄ꝗ lat . Silua . vii . q̄ꝗ l̄g . 7 ii . q̄ꝗ lat .

Scudet .
De eaḋ ̄tra ten̄ Wilts . iii . hiḋ de ep̄o . 7 ibi ħ̄ . ii . caṙ .

Qḋ monachi hn̄t: ual . xxiiii . lib̄ . Qḋ Wilts: c . foliḋ

65 d

Idem ep̄s ten̄ *HAME* . T . R . E . geldb̄ ꝓ . x . hiḋ 7 dim̄ . 7 dimiḋ

virg ̄træ . ̄Tra . ē . vii . caṙ . De hac ̄tra . v . hidæ 7 dimiḋ

ſt in dn̄io . 7 ibi . iii . caṙ . cū . i . ſeruo . Ibi . ix . uilti 7 x .

coſcez . cū . iii . caṙ . Ibi . viii . ac̄ p̄ti . Paſtura . iii . q̄ꝗ

l̄g . 7 una q̄ꝗ lat . Silua . vi . q̄ꝗ l̄g . 7 iii . q̄ꝗ lat .

Of the land of this manor William of Braose holds 14 hides, Waleran 5 hides, Ralph 5 hides, Ansgot 3½ hides. The King has 4 hides in his Forest. The church of this manor has 4 hides. They all hold from the Bishop.

The holders of these lands before 1066 could not withdraw from the church.

Value when Bishop Walkelin acquired this manor, £60; value now of what he has in lordship, £80; of what the men-at-arms have, £23; of what the church has, £3.

The Bishop also holds

2 FONTHILL (Bishop). Before 1066 it paid tax for 10 hides. Land for 7 ploughs. In lordship 5 hides of this land; 2 ploughs there; 5 slaves.
   8 villagers and 5 smallholders with 3 ploughs.
   A mill at 5s; meadow, 8 acres; pasture ½ league long
      and 3 furlongs wide; woodland, as much.
The value was £10; now £14.

3 FYFIELD. Edward holds from him. It paid tax for 5 hides before 1066. This land was the sacristan of the church's. Alfsi the monk held it from the Bishop. Land for 3 ploughs. Of this land 3 hides in lordship; 2 ploughs there, with 1 slave.
   3 villagers and 9 smallholders with 2 ploughs.
   Meadow, 3 acres; pasture, 30 acres; woodland 3 furlongs
      long and 1 furlong wide.
The value was and is 100s.
These are for the monks' supplies.

4 ALTON (Priors). It paid tax for 20 hides before 1066. Land for 14 ploughs. Of this land 6 hides and 1 virgate of land in lordship; 4 ploughs there; 8 slaves.
   27 villagers and 15 Cottagers with 8 ploughs.
   2 mills at 12½s; meadow, 100 acres; pasture 6 furlongs
      long and 4 furlongs wide; woodland 7 furlongs long
      and 2 furlongs wide.
   William Shield holds 3 hides of this land from the Bishop;
   he has 2 ploughs.
Value of what the monks have, £24; of what William has, 100s.

5 HAM. Before 1066 it paid tax for 10½ hides and ½ virgate of land.   65 d
Land for 7 ploughs. Of this land 5½ hides in lordship; 3 ploughs there, with 1 slave.
   9 villagers and 10 Cottagers with 3 ploughs.
   Meadow, 8 acres; pasture 3 furlongs long and 1 furlong
      wide; woodland 6 furlongs long and 3 furlongs wide.

De ead̄ t̄ra ten̄ Wilt̄s . II . hid̄ de ep̄o . Qui ante eū
tenuit . n̄ poterat ab æccl̄a recedere.

Valuit hoc Ꝏ . VI . lib̄ qdo ep̄s recep̄ . Modo dn̄ium
ual . IX . lib̄ . Qd̄ Wilt̄s ten̄ . III . lib̄.

Idem ep̄s ten̄ *WESTWODE* . T . R . E . geld̄b ꝑ . III . hid̄.
T̄ra . V . car̄ . De hac t̄ra . II . hidæ in dn̄io . 7 ibi . III . car̄.
7 III . ſerui . Ibi . VI . uilt̄i 7 IIII . bord̄ cū . I . car̄ . Ibi molin̄
redd̄ . X . ſol . 7 VI . ac̄ p̄ti . Silua . II . q̄z̄ lḡ . 7 una q̄z̄ lat̄.
Q̄do recep̄ ep̄s ual̄b . VI . lib̄ . Modo . IIII . lib̄.

Idem ep̄s ten̄ *ELENDVNE* . T . R . E . geld̄b ꝑ . XXX . hid̄.
T̄ra . ē . XII . car̄ . De hac t̄ra ſt in dn̄io . XV . hidæ . 7 ibi
. IIII . car̄ . 7 III . ſerui . Ibi . XXV . uilt̄i . 7 XIIII . bord̄ h̄nt
VII . car̄ . Ibi . VI . molini redd̄ . XLII . ſol . 7 VI . denar̄.
7 LX . ac̄ p̄ti . Paſtura dimid̄ leū lḡ . 7 III . q̄rent lat̄.
7 XX . ac̄ ſiluæ.
De hac t̄ra h̄t un̄ miles . I . hid̄ 7 dimid̄ . 7 h̄t ibi . I . car̄.
Godric qui tenuit T . R . E . n̄ potuit ab æccl̄a ſeparari.
Q̄do ep̄s recep̄ ꞉ ual̄b . XIIII . lib̄ . Val modo . XVIII . lib̄.

Ipſe ep̄s ten̄ *CLIVE* . T . R . E . geld̄b ꝑ . X . hid̄ . T̄ra . ē . V . car̄.
de ead̄ t̄ra ſt in dn̄io . VI . hidæ 7 dimid̄ . 7 ibi . II . car̄.
7 III . ſerui . Ibi . VII . uilt̄i . 7 III . coſcez . cū . II . car̄.
Ibi . XXX . ac̄ p̄ti . Silua . II . q̄z̄ lḡ . 7 una q̄z̄ lat̄.
Q̄do ep̄s recep̄ ꞉ ual̄b . III . lib̄ . Modo . VI . lib̄.

Idem ep̄s ten̄ *WEMBERGE* . T . R . E . geld̄ ꝑ . XIX . hid̄.
T̄ra . ē . X . car̄ . De ead̄ t̄ra . IX . hidæ ſt in dn̄io . 7 ibi
III . car̄ . 7 VI . ſerui . Ibi . XIX . uilt̄i 7 XIII . bord̄ cū . V . car̄.
Ibi molin̄ redd̄ . V . ſolid̄ . 7 XL . ac̄ p̄ti . Paſtura dimid̄
leū lḡ . 7 XV . q̄rent lat̄ . De hac t̄ra ten̄ Richer . I . hid̄.
Q̄do recep̄ ep̄s ꞉ ual̄b . XV . lib̄ . Modo ꞉ XVIII . lib̄.

William holds 2 hides of this land from the Bishop;
the previous holder could not withdraw from the church.
Value of this manor when the Bishop acquired it, £6;
value now of the lordship, £9; of what William holds, £3.

6   WESTWOOD. Before 1066 it paid tax for 3 hides. Land for 5
ploughs. Of this land 2 hides in lordship; 3 ploughs there;
3 slaves.
> 6 villagers and 4 smallholders with 1 plough.
> A mill which pays 10s; meadow, 6 acres; woodland
>> 2 furlongs long and 1 furlong wide.

Value when the Bishop acquired it, £6; now £4.

7   WROUGHTON. Before 1066 it paid tax for 30 hides. Land for 12
ploughs. Of this land 15 hides in lordship; 4 ploughs there;
3 slaves.
> 25 villagers and 14 smallholders have 7 ploughs.
> 6 mills which pay 42s 6d; meadow, 60 acres; pasture
>> ½ league long and 3 furlongs wide; woodland, 20 acres.
> A man-at-arms has 1½ hides of this land; he has 1 plough.
> Godric, who held it before 1066, could not be separated
> from the church.

Value when the Bishop acquired it, £14; value now, £18.

8   The Bishop holds BUSHTON himself. Before 1066 it paid
tax for 10 hides. Land for 5 ploughs. Of this land 6½ hides in
lordship; 2 ploughs there; 3 slaves.
> 7 villagers and 3 Cottagers with 2 ploughs.
> Meadow, 30 acres; woodland 2 furlongs long
>> and 1 furlong wide.

Value when the Bishop acquired it, £3; now £6.

9   The Bishop also holds
WANBOROUGH. Before 1066 it paid tax for 19 hides.
Land for 10 ploughs. Of this land 9 hides in lordship; 3 ploughs
there; 6 slaves.
> 19 villagers and 13 smallholders with 5 ploughs.
> A mill which pays 5s; meadow, 40 acres;
>> pasture ½ league long and 15 furlongs wide.
> Richere holds 1 hide of this land.

Value when the Bishop acquired it, £15; now £18.

Idem eps ten̄ *ENEDFORDE* . T.R.E. geldb̄ ꝓ . xxx . hid̄.

Tra . ē . xxiiii . car̄ . De ead̄ tra . x . hidæ ſunt in dn̄io.

⁊ ibi . iii . car̄ . ⁊ vi . ſerui . Ibi . xii . uiłłi ⁊ xv . bord̄

cū . x . car̄ . Ibi . ii . molini redd̄ . xxv . ſolid̄ . ⁊ xvii . āc

p̄ti . Paſtura . ii . leū ⁊ dim̄ lḡ . ⁊ unā leū ⁊ dimid̄ lat̄.

De ead̄ tra ten̄ Wiłłs . v . hid̄ . ⁊ Herald . ii . hid̄.

Vnus anglic̄ . iii . hid̄ . Ibi hn̄t . x . car̄ . Pb̄r ht̄ . i . hid̄

Qui tenuer̄ T.R.E: n̄ poterant ab æccła ſeparari.

Q̇do eps recep̄: ualb̄ . xxx.iiii . lib̄ . Modo dn̄ium

ual . xx . lib̄ . Q̇d pb̄r ⁊ milites ten̄: xix . lib̄.

Idem eps ten̄ *OVRETONE* . T.R.E. geldb̄ ꝓ . xv . hid̄.

Tra . ē . vii . car̄ . De ipſa tra ſt in dn̄io . viii . hidæ ⁊ dim̄.

⁊ ibi . ii . car̄ . Ibi   uiłłi hn̄t . v . car̄ . Ibi . xv . āc p̄ti.

Paſtura . viii . q̇ꝫ lḡ . ⁊ iiii . q̇ꝫ lat̄ . Silua . v . q̇ꝫ lḡ.

⁊ ii . q̇ꝫ lat̄.

De ead̄ tra ten̄ Durand . ii . hid̄ . dimid̄ v̄ min̄ . Qui tenuit

T.R.E. n̄ poterat ab æccła ſeparari . Valuit ⁊ ual . xx . ſoł.

Dn̄ium ual . viii . lib̄ . Q̇do eps recep̄: ualb̄ . vi . lib̄.

Idem eps ten̄ *STOTTVNE* . T.R.E. geldb̄ ꝓ . x . hid̄.

Tra . ē . vi . car̄ . De ipſa tra ſt in dn̄io . iii . hidæ ⁊ dimid̄.

⁊ ibi . ii . car̄ . ⁊ iii . ſerui . Ibi . iiii . uiłłi . ⁊ vi . bord̄ cū . ii . car̄.

Ibi molin̄ de . x . ſolid̄ . ⁊ x . āc p̄ti . Paſtura . v . q̇ꝫ lḡ.

⁊ ii . q̇ꝫ lat̄ . ⁊ xl . āc ſiluæ.   ⌐Ibi hn̄t . ii . car̄.

De ead̄ tra ten̄ Richeri . ii . hid̄ . ⁊ Anſchitil . ii . hid̄ ⁊ dim̄.

Hoc m̄ qdo eps recep̄: ualb̄ . viii . lib̄ . Modo dn̄ium.

ual . c . ſolid̄ . ⁊ x . ſoł Q̇d hōes ten̄ . ual . iiii . lib̄.

Terra q̇ ten̄: n̄ poterat ab æccła . T.R.E. ſeparari.

10   ENFORD. Before 1066 it paid tax for 30 hides.
      Land for 24 ploughs. Of this land 10 hides in lordship; 3
      ploughs there; 6 slaves.
          12 villagers and 15 smallholders with 10 ploughs.
          2 mills which pay 25s; meadow, 17 acres; pasture
              2½ leagues long and 1½ leagues wide.
          Of this land William holds 5 hides, Harold 2 hides, an
          Englishman 3 hides; they have 10 ploughs. A priest
          has 1 hide. The holders before 1066 could not be
          separated from the church.
      Value when the Bishop acquired it, £34; value now of the
      lordship, £20; of what the priest and the men-at-arms
      hold, £19.

11   (East) OVERTON. Before 1066 it paid tax for 15 hides.
      Land for 7 ploughs. Of this land 8½ hides in lordship;
      2 ploughs there.
rq   ....villagers have 5 ploughs.
          Meadow, 15 acres; pasture 8 furlongs long and 4 furlongs
              wide; woodland 5 furlongs long and 2 furlongs wide.
          Durand holds 2 hides, less ½ virgate, of this land.
          The holder before 1066 could not be separated from the
          church. The value was and is 20s.
      Value of the lordship £8; value when the Bishop acquired it, £6.

12   STOCKTON. Before 1066 it paid tax for 10 hides.
      Land for 6 ploughs. Of this land 3½ hides in lordship;
      2 ploughs there; 3 slaves.
          4 villagers and 6 smallholders with 2 ploughs.
          A mill at 10s; meadow, 10 acres; pasture 5 furlongs
              long and 2 furlongs wide; woodland, 40 acres.
          Of this land Richere holds 2 hides, Ansketel 2½ hides;
          they have 2 ploughs.
      Value of this manor when the Bishop acquired it, £8;
      value now of the lordship, 100s and 10s; value of what
      the men hold, £4.
          The land which they hold could not be separated from the
      church before 1066.

TERRA EPI SARISBERIENSIS.

.III. Eps Sarisberiensis ten *POTERNE.*

T.R.E. geldau p. LII. hid. Tra. ē. XL. car.

De hac tra. x. hidæ ſt in dnio. 7 ibi. VI. car. 7 IIII.

ſerui. 7 v. colibti. Ibi. XXIX. uilli 7 XL. bord cū. XXX.

car. Ibi. VI. molini reddt. XLIII. ſol. 7 IIII. denar.

7 XL. ac pti. Paſtura. II. leu 7 dim lg. 7 una leu 7 III.

qrent lat. Silua. I. leu lg. 7 x. qrent lat.

Dniū epi ual 7 ualuit. LX. lib.

De ead tra huj M ten. II. angli. VI. hid. 7 unā v træ.

Vn ex eis. ē miles juſſu regis. 7 nepos fuit Hermanni epi.

7 Aluuard ten. III. hid. qs Wluuard. T.R.E. ab epo. H.

emit in uita ſua tant. ut poſtea redireɴ ad firmā epi.

qa de dnio epi eraɴ. Hi taini hnt. IIII. car ibi.

cū. II. ſeruis 7 IX. bord.   Val. VII. lib.

Qd pbr huj M ten. ual. XL. ſolid.

De tra ejd M ten Arnulf de Heſding. III. hid 7 unā v.

de rege. Eps ū caluniat eas. qm qui tenuit T.R.E.

ñ poterat ab epo ſeparari.

Idem eps ten *CAININGHA.* T.R.E. geldb p. LXX. hid.

Tra. ē. XLV. car. De hac. x. hidæ ſt in dnio. 7 ibi

. v. car. 7 VI. ſerui. Ibi. XLVIII. uilli. 7 XL. bord.

cū. XXVIII. car. Ibi. VI. molini redd. VII. ſot 7 VI. den.

7 XXX. ac pti. Paſtura. I. leu lg. 7 VIII. qrent lat.

Silua. I. leu lg. 7 x. qrent lat. In burgo *CAVNE*

una dom ptin huic M. redd. XX. den p annū.

De ead tra huj M ten pbr. II. hid. Ebrard. x. hid.

Herman. IIII. hid. Quintin. III. hid. Walter. II. hid.

Brictuuard. v. hid. Aluuard. I. hid. Vxor ppoſiti. I. hid.

Hi hnt. VIII. car. cū. III. uiltis 7 XXX. bord hntib. II. car.

Dnium epi. ual. LX. lib. Qd alij ten. ual XXXV. lib.

1   The Bishop of Salisbury holds POTTERNE. Before 1066 it
paid tax for 52 hides. Land for 40 ploughs. Of this land 10
hides in lordship; 6 ploughs there; 4 slaves; 5 freedmen.
    29 villagers and 40 smallholders with 30 ploughs.
    6 mills which pay 43s 4d; meadow, 40 acres; pasture
       2½ leagues long and 1 league and 3 furlongs wide;
       woodland 1 league long and 10 furlongs wide.
The value of the Bishop's lordship is and was £60.
    Of this manor's land 2 Englishmen hold 6 hides and 1
virgate of land. One of them is a man-at-arms by the King's
command; he was the nephew of Bishop Herman. Alfward
holds 3 hides which Wulfward White bought from Bishop Herman
before 1066 for his lifetime only, so that afterwards they should
return to the Bishop's revenue because they were part of the
Bishop's lordship. These thanes have 4 ploughs with 2 slaves and
    9 smallholders.
Value £7; value of what the priest of this manor holds, 40s.
    Of this manor's land Arnulf of Hesdin holds 3 hides and 1
virgate from the King. But the Bishop claims them, since
the holder before 1066 could not be separated from the Bishop.

2   The Bishop also holds (Bishops) CANNINGS. Before 1066 it
paid tax for 70 hides. Land for 45 ploughs. 10 hides of it
in lordship; 5 ploughs there; 6 slaves.
    48 villagers and 40 smallholders with 28 ploughs.
    6 mills which pay 7s 6d; meadow, 30 acres; pasture 1
       league long and 8 furlongs wide; woodland 1 league
       long and 10 furlongs wide; in the Borough of Calne 1
       house which belongs to this manor and pays 20d a year.
Of this manor's land a priest holds 2 hides, Ebrard 10
hides, Herman 4 hides, Quintin 3 hides, Walter 2 hides,
Brictward 5 hides, Alfward 1 hide, the reeve's wife 1 hide;
they have 8 ploughs, with
    3 villagers and 30 smallholders who have 4 ploughs.
Value of the Bishop's lordship, £60; value of what the
others hold, £35.

Idem eps teñ *RAMESBERIE* . T . R . E . geldƀ p qᵗ xx . 7 x .

hiđ . Tra . ē . LIIII . caȓ . De hac tra xxx . hidæ ſt in

dñio . 7 ibi . VIII . caȓ . 7 IX . ſerui . Ibi . LX . VIII . uitti . 7 XL

7 III . borđ hñtes . xxIX . caȓ . Ibi qᵗ xx . ac p̃ti . 7 x . mo

lini redđt . VI . liƀ 7 xxx . deñ . Paſtura . XIIII . q̃rent

lḡ . 7 v . q̃ɜ laȓ . Silua . xvI . q̃ɜ lḡ . 7 IIII . q̃ɜ laȓ .

De eađ tra huj ᙏ teñ pƀri . IIII . hiđ . Otbold . XII .

hiđ . Herƀt . v . hiđ . Quintiñ . v . hiđ . Vxor p̃poſiti . I . hiđ .

Hi hñt in dñio . XI . caȓ . 7 xxxI . borđ cū . vI . caȓ .

In crichelade . v . burḡſes p̃tiñ huic ᙏ redđ . v . ſot .

Dñiũ epi . uat . LII . liƀ . 7 xv . ſot . Qđ alij teñ.̃ xvII . liƀ .

Idē eps teñ *SARISBERIE* . T . R . E . geldƀ . p . L . Ƒ 7 v . ſoliđ .

hiđ . Tra . ē . xxxII . caȓ . De hac tra . x . hidæ ſt in dñio .

7 ibi . VIII . caȓ . Ibi . xxv . uitti 7 L . borđ . cū . xvII . caȓ .

In Wiltune . vII . burḡſes p̃tiñ huic ᙏ redđ . LXV . deñ .

In ᙏ . IIII . molini de . XLVII . ſot 7 vII . deñ . 7 dimiđ

moliñ de . xxx . ſoliđ . 7 cXL . II . ac p̃ti . Paſtura . xx .

q̃rent lḡ . 7 x . q̃ɜ laȓ . 7 alibi . v . q̃rent paſturæ lḡ .

7 una q̃ɜ laȓ . Silua . IIII . q̃ɜ lḡ . 7 II . q̃ɜ laȓ .

De eađ tra huj ᙏ teñ Eduuard . v . hiđ . Odo . v . hiđ .

Hugo . III . hiđ una v miñ . Qui has tenueȓ T . R . E .̃

ñ poterant ab epo ſeparari . Ibi ſunt in dñio . v . caȓ .

7 III . uitti 7 xvII . borđ cū . II . caȓ .　　　Ƒ 7 x . ſoliđ .

Dñium cpi uat . XLVII . liƀ . Qđ hōes teñ.̃ uat . xvII . liƀ

Idem eps teñ *CHEDELWICH* . Algar tenuit T . R . E . 7 gldƀ

p . v . hiđ . Tra . ē . III . caȓ . De hac tra . IIII . hidæ ſt in dñio .

7 ibi . II . caȓ . 7 III . uitti 7 vI . borđ 7 II . coſcez . cū . I . caȓ

7 dim . Ibi . x . ac p̃ti 7 dimiđ . Paſtura . III . q̃ɜ lḡ . 7 II . q̃ɜ laȓ .

Silua . II . q̃rent lḡ . 7 una q̃ɜ laȓ . Valuit . XL . ſot . Ṁ . II . liƀ .

Ħ ē de Excābio *SCEPELEIA* . Hugo teñ de epo .

3 The Bishop also holds RAMSBURY. Before 1066 it paid
tax for 90 hides. Land for 54 ploughs. Of this land 30 hides
in lordship; 8 ploughs there; 9 slaves.
> 68 villagers and 43 smallholders who have 29 ploughs.
> Meadow, 80 acres; 10 mills which pay £6 30d; pasture
>> 14 furlongs long and 5 furlongs wide; woodland 16 furlongs
>> long and 4 furlongs wide.
> Of this manor's land the priests hold 4 hides, Odbold 12 hides,
> Herbert 5 hides, Quintin 5 hides, the reeve's wife 1 hide;
> they have in lordship 11 ploughs; 31 smallholders with
> 6 ploughs.
> In Cricklade 5 burgesses who belong to this manor pay 5s.

Value of the Bishop's lordship, £52 15s; of what the others
hold, £17 5s.

4 The Bishop also holds SALISBURY. Before 1066 it paid tax
for 50 hides. Land for 32 ploughs. Of this land 10 hides
in lordship; 8 ploughs there.
> 25 villagers and 50 smallholders with 17 ploughs.
> In Wilton 7 burgesses who belong to this manor pay 65d.
> In the manor 4 mills at 47s 7d; ½ mill at 30s; meadow,
>> 142 acres; pasture 20 furlongs long and 10 furlongs
>> wide; elsewhere pasture, 5 furlongs long and 1 furlong
>> wide; woodland 4 furlongs long and 2 furlongs wide.
> Of this manor's land Edward holds 5 hides, Odo 5 hides,
> Hugh 3 hides, less 1 virgate. The holders of these (lands)
> before 1066 could not be separated from the Bishop.
> In lordship 5 ploughs;
>> 3 villagers and 17 smallholders with 2 ploughs.

Value of the Bishop's lordship, £47; value of what the men
hold, £17 10s.

5 The Bishop also holds CHARNAGE. Algar held it before 1066;
it paid tax for 5 hides. Land for 3 ploughs.
Of this land 4 hides in lordship; 2 ploughs there;
> 3 villagers, 6 smallholders and 2 Cottagers with 1½ ploughs.
> Meadow, 10½ acres; pasture 3 furlongs long and 2 furlongs
>> wide; woodland 2 furlongs long and 1 furlong wide.

The value was 40s; now £4.
> This is in exchange for Shipley. Hugh holds from the Bishop.

TERRA EP̄I BAIOCENSIS.

.IIII. Ep̄s Baiocensis ten̄ *Todeworde* 7 Odo de eo . Eddulf⁹
tenuit T.R.E. 7 geld p̄ . v . hid̄ . Tra . ē . iii . car̄ . De hac tra ſt
in dn̄io . iiii . hidæ una v̄ min̄ . 7 ibi . ii . car̄ . 7 . ii . ſerui . Ibi
un̄ uilt̄s 7 vi . bord̄ . cū . i . car̄ . Ibi paſtura . iii . q̄ lḡ . 7 ii . q̄
lat̄ . Val . iiii . lib̄ 7 x . ſolid̄ .

Idē ep̄s ten̄ *Wadhvlle* . 7 Odo de eo . Eddulf⁹ tenuit T.R.E.
7 geld p̄ . vi . hid̄ . Tra . ē . iii . car̄ . De hac tra ſt in dn̄io . v . hidæ
7 ibi . ii . car̄ . 7 vi . ſerui . Ibi un̄ uilt̄s 7 iiii . bord̄ cū . i . car̄ .
Ibi . xii . ac̄ p̄ti . 7 paſtura . i . q̄ lḡ . 7 tn̄td̄ lat̄ . Silua
una q̄ lḡ . 7 iii . ac̄s lat̄ . Val . iiii . lib̄ .

Idem ep̄s ten̄ *Svindvne* . 7 Wadard de eo . Leuiet
tenuit T.R.E. 7 geld p̄ . v . hid̄ . Ex his una . ē in dn̄io
7 ibi . i . car̄ . 7 iiii . ſerui . Ibi . v . uilt̄i 7 ii . bord̄ cū . ii . car̄ .
Ibi molin̄ de . iiii . ſol̄ . 7 xxx . ac̄ p̄ti . 7 tn̄td̄ paſturæ . Valuit xl . ſol̄. ꝼ modo . iiii . lib̄.

Idē ep̄s ten̄ *Dechementvne* . 7 Rob̄t de eo . Azor tenuit T.R.E. 7 geld̄
p̄ . ii . hid̄ . Tra . ē . ii . car̄ . Has hn̄t ibi . xviii . cotar̄ . 7 iiii . molini ſt ibi
redd̄ . xxvii . ſol̄ . 7 iiii . ac̄ p̄ti . 7 x . ac̄ paſturæ . Valuit . c . ſol̄ . M̄ . viii . lib̄ .

TERRA EP̄I CONSTANTIENSIS.

.V. Ep̄s Constantiensis ten̄ *Draicote* . 7 Rogeri⁹ de eo .
Aluuard⁹ 7 Elnod tenuer̄ p̄ . ii . Maner̄ T.R.E. 7 geld p̄ . v . hid̄ .
Tra . ē . ii . car̄ 7 dimid̄ . De hac tra ſt in dn̄io . iiii . hidæ una v̄ min̄ .
⁷ ibi .ii . car̄ . 7 iii . ſerui . Ibi . iiii . bord̄ 7 vii . coſcez hn̄t dimid̄ car̄ .
Ibi . lx . ac̄ paſturæ . Valuit . xxx . ſol̄ . Modo . lx . ſolid̄ .

Idē ep̄s ten̄ *Withenha* . 7 Rogeri⁹ de eo . Aluet tenuit
T.R.E. 7 geld p̄ . v . hid̄ . Tra . ē v . car̄ . De hac tra . iii . hide
ſt in dn̄io . 7 ibi . i . car̄ . 7 iii . ſerui . Ibi . v . uilt̄i 7 v . bord̄

4   LAND OF THE BISHOP OF BAYEUX

1   The Bishop of Bayeux holds (North) TIDWORTH and Odo from
him. Edwulf held it before 1066; it paid tax for 5 hides.
Land for 3 ploughs. Of this land 4 hides, less 1 virgate,
in lordship; 2 ploughs there; 2 slaves.
> 1 villager and 6 smallholders with 1 plough.
> Pasture 3 furlongs long and 2 furlongs wide.

Value £4 10s.

2   The Bishop also holds WOODHILL and Odo from him.
Edwulf held it before 1066; it paid tax for 6 hides.
Land for 3 ploughs. Of this land 5 hides in lordship;
2 ploughs there; 6 slaves.
> 1 villager and 4 smallholders with 1 plough.
> Meadow, 12 acres; pasture 1 furlong long and as wide;
>> woodland 1 furlong long and 3 acres wide.

Value £4.

3   The Bishop also holds SWINDON and Wadard from him.
Leofgeat held it before 1066; it paid tax for 5 hides.
Of these 1 is in lordship; 1 plough there; 4 slaves.
> 5 villagers and 2 smallholders with 2 ploughs.
> A mill at 4s; meadow, 30 acres; pasture, as much.

The value was 40s; now £4.

4   The Bishop also holds DITCHAMPTON and Robert from him.
Azor held it before 1066; it paid tax for 2 hides.
Land for 2 ploughs;
> 18 cottagers have them.
> 4 mills which pay 27s; meadow, 4 acres; pasture, 10 acres.

The value was 100s; now £8.

5   LAND OF THE BISHOP OF COUTANCES

1   The Bishop of Coutances holds DRAYCOT (Fitzpayne) and
Roger from him. Alfward and Alnoth held it as two manors
before 1066; it paid tax for 5 hides. Land for 2½ ploughs.
Of this land 4 hides, less 1 virgate, in lordship; 2 ploughs
there; 3 slaves.
> 4 smallholders and 7 Cottagers have ½ plough.
> Pasture, 60 acres.

The value was 30s; now 60s.

The Bishop also holds

2   'WITTENHAM' and Roger from him. Alfgeat held it
before 1066; it paid tax for 5 hides. Land for 5 ploughs.
Of this land 3 hides in lordship; 1 plough there; 3 slaves.
> 5 villagers and 5 smallholders with 4 ploughs.

cū.iiii.car̄.Ibi moliñ red̄.xii.ſol 7 vi.deñ.7 x..ac̄ p̄ti.

7 xvi.ac̄ ſiluæ.Paſtura.ii.q̃ʒ lḡ.7 una q̃ʒ lat̄.

Valuit 7 ual̄.iiii.lib̄ 7 x.ſol.

Idem eṗs teñ *Winefel*.7 Roger de eo.Azor tenuit T.R.E.

7 geld̄ ꝓ.iii.hid 7 dim̄.Tra.ē.iii.car̄.De hac tra.ii.hidæ

ſt in dñio.7 ibi.i.car̄.Ibi.iii.uilti 7 ix.bord̄ cū.i.car̄.

Ibi moliñ red̄.xx.ſol.7 vii.ac̄ p̄ti.7 xx.ac̄ ſiluæ.Paſtura

iii.q̃ʒ lḡ.7 ii.q̃ʒ lat̄ Valuit 7 ual̄.lxx.ſol.

Idē eṗs teñ *Mamesberie*.Giſlebert tenuit T.R.E.7 geld̄

ꝓ una hida.Tra.ē dimid̄ car̄.De hac tra.ſt.iii.Virḡ træ

in dñio.7 ibi dimid̄ car̄.cū.iii.bord̄.Ibi.iiii.ac̄ p̄ti.

7 Paſtura.ii.q̃ʒ lḡ.7 una q̃ʒ lat̄.Val̄.xiii.ſolid̄.

Idē eṗs teñ *Perteworde*.7 Osb̄tus de eo.Wluuard

tenuit T.R.E.7 geld̄ ꝓ.ii.hid̄.Tra.ē.ii.car̄.De hac tra

in dñio.ē hida 7 dimid̄.7 ibi.i.car̄.Ibi.ii.uilti 7 iii.bord̄

cū.i.car̄.Ibi.xx.ac̄ paſturæ.7 iiii.ac̄ ſiluæ.Valuit 7 ual̄

Idem eṗs teñ *Liteltone*.7 Rob̄t de eo. ꝔXL.ſol.

Aluuard tenuit T.R.E.de abb̄e Glaſtingberie.7 ñ poterat

ab ꟾpſa æccła ſeparari.7 geldb̄ ꝓ.v.hid̄.Tra.ē.viii.car̄.

De hac tra in dñio ſt.ii.hidæ.7 ibi.ii.car̄.7 iiii.ſerui.

Ibi.vi.uilti 7 vi.bord̄ cū.v.car̄.Ibi moliñ red̄.vii.ſol

7 vi.deñ.– xv.ac̄ p̄ti.Valuit 7 ual̄.vii.lib̄.

Idē eṗs teñ *Wintreburne*.Leſſida tenuit T.R.E.

7 geld̄ ꝓ.ii.hid̄ 7 dim̄.Tra.ē.ii.car̄.De hac tꝛa in dñio

eſt hida 7 dimid̄.7 ibi.i.car̄.7 ii.ſerui.Ibi.v.uilti 7 iiii. ⁷ᵘⁿ'ᶜᵒᵗᵃʳ'

bord̄ cū.i.car̄.Ibi moliñ red̄.xii.ſol 7 vi.deñ.7 xx.ac̄

paſturæ.Valuit.xxx.ſol q̄do recep̄ eṗs.Modo.iiii.lib̄.

A mill which pays 12s 6d; meadow, 10 acres; woodland,
   16 acres; pasture 2 furlongs long and 1 furlong wide.
The value was and is £4 10s.

3 WINGFIELD. Roger holds from him. Azor held it before 1066.
it paid tax for 3½ hides. Land for 3 ploughs.
Of this land 2 hides in lordship; 1 plough there.
   3 villagers and 9 smallholders with 1 plough.
   A mill which pays 20s; meadow, 7 acres; woodland,
      20 acres; pasture 3 furlongs long and 2 furlongs wide.
The value was and is 70s.

4 MALMESBURY. Gilbert held it before 1066; it paid tax
for 1 hide. Land for ½ plough. Of this land 3 virgates
of land in lordship; ½ plough there, with
   3 smallholders.
   Meadow, 4 acres; pasture 2 furlongs long
      and 1 furlong wide.
Value 13s.

5 PERTWOOD. Osbert holds from him. Wulfward held it
before 1066; it paid tax for 2 hides. Land for 2 ploughs.
Of this land 1½ hides in lordship; 1 plough there.
   2 villagers and 3 smallholders with 1 plough.
   Pasture, 20 acres; woodland, 4 acres.
The value was and is 40s.

6 LITTLETON (Drew). Robert holds from him. Alfward held
it before 1066 from the Abbot of Glastonbury; he could
not be separated from that church. It paid tax for 5 hides.
Land for 8 ploughs. Of this land 2 hides in lordship;
2 ploughs there; 4 slaves.
   6 villagers and 6 smallholders with 5 ploughs.
   A mill which pays 7s 6d; meadow, 15 acres.
The value was and is £7.

7 WINTERBOURNE. Leofsida held it before 1066;
it paid tax for 2½ hides. Land for 2 ploughs. Of this
land 1½ hides in lordship; 1 plough there; 2 slaves.
   5 villagers, 1 cottager and 4 smallholders with 1 plough.
   A mill which pays 12s 6d; pasture, 20 acres.
The value was 30s when the Bishop acquired it; now £4.

EPS LISIACENS ten *ETVNE*. Leuenot tenuit T.R.E.7 geldb ꝑ.II.hid
7 III.virg.Tra.e.III.car.De ea st in dnio.II.hidæ.7 ibi.I.car.7 II.bord
7 VI.cofcez cu.I.car.Ibi molin redd.x.fot.7 III.ac pti.Silua.II.q̃ ℥ lg.
7 tntd lat.Valuit 7 uat.xL.fot.Turstin ten de epo.

Ide eps ten *SVMREFORD* Aluuard tenuit T.R.E.7 geldb ꝑ.x.hid.Tra.e.VII.car.
De ea st in dnio.v.hidæ.7 ibi.III.car.7 v.ferui.7 XIIII.uitti.7 VIII.bord.cu.IIII.car.
Ibi molin redd.x.fot.7 c.ac pti.Silua.III.q̃ ℥ lg.7 II.q̃ ℥ lat.Valet.VII.lib.

66 c

.VII. TERRA ÆCCLÆ GLASTINGBERIENSIS.

ECCLA S MARIÆ GLASTINGEBERIENSIS ten *DOBREHAM*.
7 geldau T.R.E.ꝑ.LII.hid.Tra.e.xxx.car.De hac tra.xvI.
hidæ st in dnio.7 ibi.IIII.car.7 vI.ferui.7 xxxvIII.colibti.
Ibi.xIIII.uitti.7 xvII.bord cu.xIx.car.Ibi.IIII.molini.reddt
xx.folid.7 xxvI.ac pti.Paftura.III.leu lg.7 una leu lat.Silua
.v.q̃ ℥ lg.7 IIII.q̃ ℥ lat.

De ead tra ten Serlo.v.hid.Vxor hugonis.III.hid.Rogeri
una hid 7 vIII.acs.Qui tenuer.T.R.E.n poterant ab æccla feparari.
Ibi st.III.car 7 dimid.

Totu M T.R.E.uatb.xxxvI.lib.Modo redd.LxI.lib.fed ab hoibȝ
n appciant plufq.xLv.lib.ꝓpt cfufione træ 7 ꝓpt firmã q̃ nimis
Terra tainoȝ uat.vII.lib.7 xv.folid.   f e alta.

Ead æccla ten *HANINDONE*.7 Robt de abbe.Ibi st.xv.hidæ.
Tra.e.x.car.In dnio st.III.car.7 vII.ferui.7 xvIII.uitti 7 x.cofcez.
cu.vI.car.Ibi.II.molini redd.vIII.fot.7 una dom red.v.den.
ptu.III.q̃ ℥ lg.7 III.q̃ ℥ lat.paftura.IIII.q̃ ℥ lg.7 III.q̃ ℥ lat

6 LAND OF THE BISHOP OF LISIEUX

1   The Bishop of Lisieux holds YATTON (Keynell). Leofnoth held it
before 1066; it paid tax for 2 hides and 3 virgates. Land for 3
ploughs, of which 2 hides in lordship; 1 plough there;
2 smallholders and 6 Cottagers with 1 plough.
A mill which pays 10s; meadow, 3 acres; woodland
2 furlongs long and as wide.
The value was and is 40s.
Thurstan holds from the Bishop.

2   The Bishop also holds SOMERFORD (Keynes). Alfward held it
before 1066; it paid tax for 10 hides. Land for 7 ploughs,
of which 5 hides in lordship; 3 ploughs there; 5 slaves;
14 villagers and 8 smallholders with 4 ploughs.
A mill which pays 10s; meadow, 100 acres; woodland
3 furlongs long and 2 furlongs wide.
Value £7.

7 LAND OF THE CHURCH OF GLASTONBURY   66 c

1   The Church of St. Mary of Glastonbury holds DAMERHAM.
It paid tax for 52 hides before 1066. Land for 30 ploughs.
Of this land 16 hides in lordship; 4 ploughs there; 6
slaves; 38 freedmen.
14 villagers and 17 smallholders with 19 ploughs.
4 mills which pay 20s; meadow, 26 acres;
pasture 3 leagues long and 1 league wide; woodland 5
furlongs long and 4 furlongs wide.
Of this land Serlo holds 5 hides, Hugh's wife 3 hides,
Roger 1 hide and 8 acres. The holders before 1066 could
not be separated from the church. 3½ ploughs there.
Value of the whole manor before 1066, £36; now it pays £61,
but (the lands) are not assessed by the men at more than £45
because of the confusion of the land and because of the
revenue which is too high. Value of the thanes' land, £7 15s.

2   The Church also holds HANNINGTON and Robert from the Abbot
15 hides. Land for 10 ploughs. In lordship 3 ploughs; 7 slaves;
18 villagers and 10 Cottagers with 6 ploughs.
2 mills which pay 8s; 1 house which pays 5d; meadow
3 furlongs long and 3 furlongs wide; pasture 4
furlongs long and 3 furlongs wide.

In omĩ ualentia ual . xv . lib . De hac ead ͨtra . iii . hiđ uendiderat
abb cuidã taino T.R.E. ad ætatẽ triũ hõum. 7 ipfe abb habeƀ inde
feruitiũ. 7 poftea debeƀ redire ad dñium. 7 modo cũ alijs . xii . hiđ ſt.

Ead æccla ten DEVREL . T.R.E. geldau ᵱ . x . hiđ . Tra . ē . viii . car.
De hac tra ſt in dñio . v . hidæ. 7 ibi . ii . car. 7 ii . ferui . Ibi . x . uilli
7 viii . cofcez . cũ . v . car . Ibi moliñ redđ . v . fol. 7 una ac ᵱti.
Paftura dim leu lg. 7 tntđ lat.   ℏ tra feparari.

De ead tra ten un tain hidã 7 dimiđ . nec potuit neᵹ poteft ab æccla
Valuit ᷄ qdo Turſtin abb receᵽ . viii . lib . Modo . x . lib.

Ead æccla ten CRISTEMELEFORDE . T.R.E. geldb ᵱ . xx . hiđ.
Tra . ē . x . car . De hac tra . xiiii . hidæ ſt in dñio. 7 ibi . iii . car.
7 ii . ferui . Ibi . xi . uilli 7 xii . borđ. 7 xii . cofcez . cũ . vi . car. Ibi . ii .
molini redđt . xl . fol. 7 xxxvi . ac ᵱti . Silua . i . leu lg. 7 dimiđ
leu lat . De ead tra ten Robt dimiđ hiđ. 7 Eduuard unã v.
Ħ tra teinlande ñ potuit ab æccla feparari . T.R.E.
Toĩ ᷄ ualet . x . lib. 7 x . foliđ.

Abb Glaſtingeb præſtitit . vi . ac͞s ᵱti Brictric T.R.E. in Stantone
Osbn gifart ten modo. ⌐ Similit preſtitit . iiii . ac͞s ᵱti in Liteltone
Aluuardo. Goiffrid eᵽs ten modo. Hæ . x . ac ᵱti deƀ jacere in Criſtemford.
Ipfa æccla ten BADEBERIE . T.R.E. geldb ᵱ . xx . hiđ . Tra . ē . x .
car . De hac tra . xiii . hidæ 7 dim ſt in dñio. 7 ibi . iii . car. 7 iiii . ferui.
Ibi . xi . uilli. 7 x . borđ cũ . iii . car . Ibi moliñ redđ . xl . den. 7 c . ac
ᵱti. Paftura . i . leu lg. 7 iii . qᵹ lat . In Crichelade . i . burgſis red . v . den
Valuit . viii . lib . Modo . x . lib.

Ipfa æccla ten MILDENHALLE . 7 Eduuard de ea . Hugolin ante
tenuerat . In manu abbis erat T.R.E. 7 geldb ᵱ . x . hiđ. Tra . ē . x . car
De hac tra ſt in dñio . iiii . hidæ. 7 ibi . ii . car. Ibi . xv . uilli 7 v . borđ
cũ . iiii . car . Ibi moliñ redđ . xxx . fol. 7 x . ac ᵱti. 7 Paftura dim
leu lg. 7 iii . qᵹ lat. 7 tntđ filuæ.
Valuit . xii . lib . Modo . xviii . lib.

Total value £15.

The Abbot had sold 3 hides of this land to a thane before 1066 for the life-times of three men. The Abbot himself had the service from them; afterwards they had to return to the lordship, so now they are with the other 12 hides.

3 The Church also holds DEVERILL. Before 1066 it paid tax for 10 hides. Land for 8 ploughs. Of this land 5 hides in lordship; 2 ploughs there; 2 slaves.

10 villagers and 8 Cottagers with 5 ploughs.

A mill which pays 5s; meadow, 1 acre; pasture ½ league long and as wide.

Of this land a thane holds 1½ hides; this land neither could nor can be separated from the church.

Value of the manor when Abbot Thurstan acquired it, £8; now £10.

4 The Church also holds CHRISTIAN MALFORD. Before 1066 it paid tax for 20 hides. Land for 10 ploughs. Of this land 14 hides in lordship; 3 ploughs there; 2 slaves.

11 villagers, 12 smallholders and 12 Cottagers with 6 ploughs.

2 mills which pay 40s; meadow, 36 acres; woodland 1 league long and ½ league wide.

Of this land Robert holds ½ hide and Edward 1 virgate.

This land, thaneland, could not be separated from the church before 1066.

Value of the whole manor £10 10s.

5 In STANTON (St. Quintin) the Abbot of Glastonbury leased 6 acres of meadow to Brictric before 1066. Osbern Giffard holds them now.

Likewise in LITTLETON (Drew) he leased 4 acres of meadow to Alfward. Bishop Geoffrey holds them now.

These 10 acres of meadow ought to lie in Christian Malford.

The Church itself holds

6 BADBURY. Before 1066 it paid tax for 20 hides. Land for 10 ploughs. Of this land 13½ hides in lordship; 3 ploughs there; 4 slaves.

11 villagers and 10 smallholders with 3 ploughs.

A mill which pays 40d; meadow, 100 acres; pasture 1 league long and 3 furlongs wide.

In Cricklade 1 burgess who pays 5d.

The value was £8; now £10.

7 MILDENHALL. Edward holds from it. Hugolin held it before. It was in the Abbot's hand before 1066; it paid tax for 10 hides. Land for 10 ploughs. Of this land 4 hides in lordship; 2 ploughs there.

15 villagers and 5 smallholders with 4 ploughs.

A mill which pays 30s; meadow, 10 acres; pasture ½ league long and 3 furlongs wide; woodland, as much.

The value was £12; now £18.

Ipſa æccła teñ *WINTREBORNE* . T . R . E . geldb ꝑ . xx . v . hiđ . Tra

ē . xv . car . De hac tra ſt in dñio . x . hidæ . 7 ibi . iiii . car . 7 vii . ſerui .

Ibi . xvii . uiłłi 7 viii . borđ cū . vii . car . Ibi . vi . ac ꝑti . 7 c . ac

paſturæ . De eađ tra teñ Gislebt . iii . hiđ 7 dim . Orgar tenuit

T . R . E . nec potuit ab æccła ſeparari .

Toƚ ꝳ̄ ualuit . xii . lib . Modo . xx . lib .

Ipſa æccła teñ *NITELETONE* . T . R . E . geldb ꝑ . xx . hiđ . Tra . ē

xii . car . De hac tra ſt in dñio . x . hidæ . 7 ibi . iiii . car . 7 ii . ſerui .

Ibi . x . uiłłi 7 xii . borđ cū . vi . car . Ibi . iii . molini redđ . xxii . soł

7 vi . deñ . 7 iiii . ac ꝑti . Silua dimid leū łg . 7 ii . q̇ƶ lat .

Valuit . viii . lib . Modo . xiii . lib .

Ipſa æccła teñ *GRETELINTONE* . T . R . E . geldb ꝑ . xxx . hiđ . Tra .

ē . xx . car . De hac tra ſt in dñio . x . hidæ . ⁊ ibi . xiii . car . 7 ii . ſerui .

66 d

Ibi . x . uiłłi 7 xi . borđ cū . vii . car . Ibi . x . ac ꝑti .

7 viii . ac paſturæ .

De eađ tra teñ eꝑs conſtant . v . hiđ . 7 Vrſo . iiii . hiđ

7 dimiđ . Qui teneb T . R . E . ñ poteraꝵ ab eccła ſepa

rari . Ibi ſt . x . car .   Ꝑ xl . soł .

Dñiū abbis ualet . xii . lib . Epi . vii . lib . Vrſonis .

Ipſa æccła teñ *LANGHELEI* . T . R . E . geldb ꝑ . xxix .

hiđ . Tra . ē . xvi . car . De hac tra ſt in dñio . xi .

hidæ . 7 ibi . iiii . car . 7 iiii . ſerui . Ibi . xv . uiłłi 7 v .

borđ cū . viii . car . Ibi . xv . ac ꝑti . 7 x . ac paſturæ .

Silua . i . leū 7 dimiđ łg . 7 dimiđ leū laƚ .

In Malmesbie uñ burgſis redđ . xv . deñ . ꝑtiñ huic ꝳ̄ .

De eađ tra teñ Vrſo . ii . hiđ 7 dim . Roger . ii . hiđ una v

miñ . Radulf hidā 7 dimiđ . Ibi hñt . iii . car .

Qui has ƚras teneb T . R . E . ñ poterant ab æccła ſeparari .

Dñiū abbis . uaƚ xiiii . lib 7 x . soł . Hōum ū̄ . c . soliđ .

Q̇do receꝑ abb . ualb . viii . lib .

8   WINTERBOURNE (Monkton). Before 1066 it paid tax for 25 hides.
Land for 15 ploughs. Of this land 10 hides in lordship;
4 ploughs there; 7 slaves.
    17 villagers and 8 smallholders with 7 ploughs.
    Meadow, 6 acres; pasture, 100 acres.
    Of this land Gilbert holds 3½ hides; Ordgar held them
    before 1066 and could not be separated from the church.
The value of the whole manor was £12; now £20.

9   NETTLETON. Before 1066 it paid tax for 20 hides.
Land for 12 ploughs. Of this land 10 hides in lordship; 4
ploughs there; 2 slaves.
    10 villagers and 12 smallholders with 6 ploughs.
    3 mills which pay 22s 6d; meadow, 4 acres; woodland
       ½ league long and 2 furlongs wide.
The value was £8; now £13.

10   GRITTLETON. Before 1066 it paid tax for 30 hides.
Land for 20 ploughs. Of this land 10 hides in lordship; 13
ploughs there; 2 slaves.
    10 villagers and 11 smallholders with 7 ploughs.   66 d
    Meadow, 10 acres; pasture, 8 acres.
    Of this land the Bishop of Coutances holds 5 hides, Urso
    4½ hides. The holders before 1066 could not be separated
    from the church. 10 ploughs there.
Value of the Abbot's lordship, £12; of the Bishop's, £7;
of Urso's, 40s.

11   (Kington) LANGLEY. Before 1066 it paid tax for 29 hides.
Land for 16 ploughs. Of this land 11 hides in lordship;
4 ploughs there; 4 slaves.
    15 villagers and 5 smallholders with 8 ploughs.
    Meadow, 15 acres; pasture, 10 acres; woodland 1½
       leagues long and ½ league wide.
    In Malmesbury a burgess who pays 15d and belongs to this
    manor. Of this land Urso holds 2½ hides, Roger 2 hides,
    less 1 virgate, Ralph 1½ hides; they have 3 ploughs.
    The holders of these lands before 1066 could not be
    separated from the church.
Value of the Abbot's lordship, £14 10s; of the men's, 100s;
value when the Abbot acquired it, £8.

In *LANGEFORD* ten abͫ eͥjd eccͫe . ii . hiͩ . 7 Eduuard
de eo . Duo taini tenueͬ de abͫe T . R . E . 7 gldͫ ᵱ . ii . hiͩ .
Tra . ē . i . caͬ 7 dimiͩ . In dͫio . ē hida una . 7 . iii . v̇ de hac
tra . 7 ibi . i . caͬ . 7 ii . ſerui . 7 vii . borͩ . 7 xvii . aͨc ᵽti . 7 xx .
aͨc paſturæ . Valuit 7 uaͫ . lx . ſoliͩ .
In eaͩ uilla ten Eduuard de rege . i . hiͩ . quæ jure
ᵽtiͫn abbatiæ ad tainlande.
Iᵱſa æcclͫa ten *EVNESTETONE* . T . R . E . geldͫ ᵱ . x . hiͩ .
vna ex his jaͨc in Hanteſcire . Tra . ē . vii . caͬ . De hac
tra . ſͭ in dͫio . iii . hidæ . 7 ibi . i . caͬ . 7 ii . ſerui . Ibi . viii .
uiͭli 7 v . borͩ cū . ii . caͬ . Ibi . vi . aͨc ᵽti . 7 x . aͨc ſiluæ .
Paſtura . i . leu lͬg . 7 iii . qᶻ lat .
De eaͩ tra ten Hunfrid . ii . hiͩ 7 dim . 7 ibi hͭ . i . caͬ .
7 iiii . aͨcs ᵽti . 7 xx . aͨcs paſturæ . Qui teneͫb T . R . E . n̄ pote
rat ab æcclͫa diuerti . Valet xl . ſoliͩ .
Dͫium abͫbis . uaͫ . vi . liͫb . Qͩdo receᵽ . uaͫlb . c . ſoliͩ .
Iᵱſa æcclͫa ten *WINTREBVRNE* . T . R . E . gelͩ ᵱ . v . hiͩ .
Tra . ē . iii . caͬ . De hac tra . ſͭ in dͫio . ii . hidæ 7 dimiͩ .
7 ibi . i . caͬ . 7 ii . ſerui . Ibi . vi . uiͭli 7 iii . borͩ cū . i . caͬ
7 dimiͩ . Ibi moliͫn redͩ . xv . ſoͫl . 7 vi . aͨc ᵽti . 7 lx . aͨc
paſturæ . Valuit 7 uaͫ . iiii . liͫb .
De his . v . hiͩ ten Waleraͫn . unā v̇ træ . quā teſti
ficanͪt taini ad æcclͫam debe ᵽtinere . 7 abͫb caͫluniaͭt eā .
Iᵱſa æcclͫa ten *DEVREL* . T . R . E . geldͫ ᵱ . x . hiͩ . Tra . ē . ix .
caͬ . De hac tra ſͭ in dͫio . v . hidæ . 7 ibi . iii . caͬ . 7 ii . ſerui .
Ibi . xiiii . uiͭli 7 xxiiii . borͩ 7 xii . cotaͬr cū . vi . caͬ .
Ibi . iii . molini redͩ . xiiii . ſoliͩ 7 x . denaͬ . 7 vi . aͨc ᵽti .
Paſtura dim leu lͬg . 7 ii . qᶻ laͭt . Silua . ii . leu lͬg . 7 dim leu lat .
De eaͩ tra ten un miles unā hiͩ 7 unā v̇ træ de abͫb
Eiſi qͩ tenuit . T . R . E . n̄ poterat ab æcclͫa ſeparari .
Toͭt ꟁ ualet . xii . liͫb .

12   In LANGFORD the Abbot of this church holds 2 hides
and Edward from him. Two thanes held it from the Abbot
before 1066; it paid tax for 2 hides. Land for 1½ ploughs.
In lordship 1 hide and 3 virgates of this land; 1 plough
there; 2 slaves;
> 7 smallholders.
> Meadow, 17 acres; pasture, 20 acres.

The value was and is 60s.

13   In the same village Edward holds 1 hide from the King which
rightly belongs to the Abbey as thaneland.

14   The Church holds IDMISTON itself. Before 1066 it paid
tax for 10 hides. One of these lies in Hampshire.
Land for 7 ploughs. Of this land 3 hides in lordship;
1 plough there; 2 slaves.
> 8 villagers and 5 smallholders with 2 ploughs.
> Meadow, 6 acres; woodland, 10 acres; pasture 1 league
>   long and 3 furlongs wide.
> Of this land Humphrey holds 2½ hides; he has 1 plough,
> 4 acres of meadow and 20 acres of pasture. The holder
> before 1066 could not be removed from the church. Value 40s.

Value of the Abbot's lordship, £6; value when acquired, 100s.

15   The Church holds WINTERBOURNE itself. Before 1066 it paid
tax for 5 hides. Land for 3 ploughs. Of this land 2½ hides
in lordship; 1 plough there; 2 slaves.
> 6 villagers and 3 smallholders with 1½ ploughs.
> A mill which pays 15s; meadow, 6 acres; pasture, 60 acres.

The value was and is £4.
> Of these 5 hides Waleran holds 1 virgate of land which the
> thanes testify ought to belong to the church; the Abbot claims it.

16   The Church holds DEVERILL itself. Before 1066 it paid tax
for 10 hides. Land for 9 ploughs. Of this land 5 hides in
lordship; 3 ploughs there; 2 slaves.
> 14 villagers, 24 smallholders and 12 cottagers with 6 ploughs.
> 3 mills which pay 14s 10d; meadow, 6 acres; pasture ½
>   league long and 2 furlongs wide; woodland 2 leagues
>   long and ½ league wide.
> Of this land a man-at-arms holds 1 hide and 1 virgate of
> land from the Abbot. Eisi who held it before 1066 could
> not be separated from the church.

Value of the whole manor, £12.

.VIII. TERRA ÆCCLÆ MALMESBERIENSIS.

Eccla S Marie Malmesberiens tenet *Hiwei*.

T.R.E.geldb .p. xi . hid . Tra . e . vi . car . In dnio st . iii .

car . Ibi . iii . uilti .7 vi . bord 7 iiii . cot . cu . i . seruo hnt . iii . car.

Ibi . xv . ac pti .7 totid ac pasturæ . Valuit . c . sol . Modo . viii . lib.

Ipsa æccta ten *Dantesie* . T.R.E.geld .p. x . hid . Tra . e . vi .

car.Robt ten de abbe . Aluuard q̃ tenuit de abbe T.R.E.

n̄ poterat ab æccta separari . In dnio st . ii . car .7 ii . serui.

7 x . uilti .7 xi . coscez .7 iii . cot . cu . iiii . car . Ibi molin

redd . xx . solid .7 xii . ac pti . Silua dim leu lg .7 tntd lat.

67 a   Valuit 7 ual . vi . lib.

Ipsa æccta ten *Svmreford* .7 Gunfrid de abbe . T.R.E

geldb .p. v . hid . Aluuard qui tenuit T.R.E.n̄ poterat ab

æccta separari . Tra . e . vi . car . De hac tra st . ii . hidæ

in dnio .7 ibi . iii . car . Ibi . vii . uilti 7 v . bord .7 xii . coscez.

7 iii . serui . hntes . iiii . car . Ibi molin redd . xx . solid.

7 xl . ac pti .7 viii . ac siluæ . Ad Malmesberie un̄ bur

gensis redd . xii . denar . Valuit . lx . sol . Modo . c . solid.

Ipsa æccta ten *Brecheorde* . T.R.E.geldb .p. v . hid.

Tra . e . viii . car . De hac tra in dnio est una hida.

7 ibi . ii . car .7 iii . serui . Ibi . ix . uilti .7 xiii . coscez.

7 xviii . cotar . cu . vi . car . Ibi . xii . ac pti . Silua

. ii . q̃z lg .7 una q̃z lat . De ead tra ten un̄ miles . i . hid.

Valuit 7 ual . iiii . lib . Tra militis . xv . solid.

Ipsa æccta ten *Nortone* . T.R.E.geldb .p. v . hid.

Tra . e . viii . car . De hac tra st in dnio . ii . hidæ 7 dim.

7 ibi . ii . car .7 v . serui . Ibi . vii . uilti 7 iii . coscez.

cu . iii . car . Ibi molin redd . xv . solid .7 vi . ac pti.

Pastura . ii . q̃z lg .7 una q̃z lat . Valuit . vi . lib . m̄ . iiii . lib.

Ipsa æccta ten *Brocheneberge* . T.R.E.geldauit

.p. l . hid . Tra . e . lx . car . De hac tra st in dnio . viii.

8 LAND OF THE CHURCH OF MALMESBURY

1 The Church of St. Mary of Malmesbury holds HIGHWAY.
Before 1066 it paid tax for 11 hides. Land for 6 ploughs.
In lordship 3 ploughs.
  3 villagers, 6 smallholders and 4 cottagers with 1 slave
    have 3 ploughs.
  Meadow, 15 acres; pasture, as many acres.
The value was 100s; now £8.

The Church itself holds

2 DAUNTSEY. Before 1066 it paid tax for 10 hides. Land for 6
ploughs. Robert holds from the Abbot. Alfward who held
from the Abbot before 1066 could not be separated from the
church. In lordship 2 ploughs; 2 slaves;
  10 villagers, 11 Cottagers and 3 cottagers with 4 ploughs.
  A mill which pays 20s; meadow, 12 acres; woodland
    ½ league long and as wide.
The value was and is £6.

3 SOMERFORD. Gunfrid holds from the Abbot. Before 1066   67 a
it paid tax for 5 hides. Alfward who held it before 1066
could not be separated from the church. Land for 6 ploughs.
Of this land 2 hides in lordship; 3 ploughs there.
  7 villagers, 5 smallholders, 12 Cottagers and 3 slaves
    who have 4 ploughs.
  A mill which pays 20s; meadow, 40 acres; woodland, 8 acres.
  In Malmesbury a burgess who pays 12d.
The value was 60s; now 100s.

4 BRINKWORTH. Before 1066 it paid tax for 5 hides.
Land for 8 ploughs. Of this land 1 hide in lordship; 2
ploughs there; 3 slaves.
  9 villagers, 13 Cottagers and 18 cottagers with 6 ploughs.
  Meadow, 12 acres; woodland 2 furlongs long and 1 furlong wide.
  Of this land a man-at-arms holds 1 hide.
The value was and is £4; [value of] the man-at-arms' land; 15s.

5 NORTON. Before 1066 it paid tax for 5 hides. Land for 8 ploughs.
Of this land 2½ hides in lordship; 2 ploughs there; 5 slaves.
  7 villagers and 3 Cottagers with 3 ploughs.
  A mill which pays 15s; meadow, 6 acres; pasture 2 furlongs
    long and 1 furlong wide.
The value was £6; now £4.

6 BROKENBOROUGH . Before 1066 it paid tax for 50 hides.
Land for 60 ploughs. Of this land 8 hides in lordship;

hidæ.7 ibi.v.caȓ.7 xvi.ſerui.Ibi.lxiiii.uiłłi.7 vii.

cotaȓ.7 xv.coſcez.hñtes.lix.caȓ.Ibi.viii.molini

redđ.vi.liƀ 7 xii.ſoł.7 vi.denaȓ.7 l.ãc p̃ti.7 xxx.

ãc paſturæ.Silua.iii.ỉeu lḡ.7 ii.leu laȓ.

De ead tra teñ Rã Flãbard in CORSTONE.vi.hiđ.

Tȓa.v.caȓ.Ibi hȓ.ii.caȓ.7 ii.uiłłos 7 ii.coſcez.7 ii.ſeru̇

cũ.i.caȓ.7 moliñ de.xii.ſoł 7.vi.den.7 x.ãcs p̃ti.

7 xv.ãcs paſturæ.7 Siluã.iii.q̃ƺ lḡ.7 una q̃ƺ laȓ.

De ead etiã tra teñ Roƀt.iii.hiđ 7 dim.Wiłłs.ii.hiđ.

Vna anglica mulier.i.hidã.Qui has tras tenueȓ.T.R.E.

ñ poterãſ ab æccła ſeparari.   ſhidas 7 dimiđ.

De dñio monachoƺ tra uillanoƺ.teñ.ii.milites.iii.

Dñium abƀis qdo recep ualƀ.xxvi.liƀ.M̊.xxx.liƀ.

Qđ Rãñ   7 alij teñ.ualet.xi.liƀ 7 iiii.soliđ.

Ipſa æccła teñ CHEMELE.T.R.E.geldƀ p.xxx.hiđ.

Tȓa.ē.xxx.caȓ.De hac tȓa ſt in dñio.xii.hidæ

7 ibi.ii.caȓ.7 vi.ſerui.Ibi.xxx.uiłłi 7 xv.coſcez.

cũ.xviii.caȓ.Ibi.ii.molini.redđ.xv.ſoł.7 xl.ãc

p̃ti.Silua una leu lḡ.7 iii.q̃ƺ laȓ.

De ead tȓa teñ Toui.ii.hiđ 7 unã v̋ træ.7 Wiłłs

iiii.hiđ in CELEORDE.Qui teneƀ T.R.E.ñ poterãſ aƀ

æccła ſeparari.Ibi ſt.ii.caȓ.7 vi.ſerui.7 vi.borđ.

7 moliñ de.x.ſoliđ.7 viii.ãc p̃ti.

De tra uillanoƺ teñ Anſchitil.i.hidã.

Dñium abƀis ualet.xiii.liƀ.Qdo recep.ualƀ.x.liƀ.

Qđ hões teñ.ual.viii.liƀ.

Ipſa æccła teñ NEWENTONE.T.R.E.geldƀ p.xxx.hiđ.

Tȓa.ē.xxiii.caȓ.De hac tȓa ſt in dñio.xv.hidæ.

7 ibi.iiii.caȓ.7 iiii.ſeruȋ.Ibi.xix.uiłłi 7 v.cotarij.

7 ii.coſcez.cũ.ix.caȓ.Ibi.ii.molini redđ.xxx.ſoł.

7 xviii.ãc p̃ti.7 q̃t xx.ãc paſturæ.

5 ploughs there; 16 slaves.

64 villagers, 7 cottagers and 15 Cottagers who have
59 ploughs.

8 mills which pay £6 12s 6d; meadow, 50 acres; pasture,
30 acres; woodland 3 leagues long and 2 leagues wide.

Of this land Ranulf Flambard holds 6 hides in CORSTON.
Land for 5 ploughs. He has 2 ploughs,

2 villagers, 2 Cottagers and 2 slaves with 1 plough;
a mill at 12s 6d, 10 acres of meadow, 15 acres of pasture
and woodland 3 furlongs long and 1 furlong wide.

Also of this land Robert holds 3½ hides, William 2 hides,
an Englishwoman 1 hide. The holders of these lands before
1066 could not be separated from the church.

Of the monks' lordship (and) the villagers' land, 2 men-at-arms
hold 3½ hides.

Value of the Abbot's lordship when acquired, £26;
now £30; value of what Ranulf and the others hold, £11 4s.

7   KEMBLE. Before 1066 it paid tax for 30 hides. Land for 30
ploughs. Of this land 12 hides in lordship; 2 ploughs
there; 6 slaves.

30 villagers and 15 Cottagers with 18 ploughs.

2 mills which pay 15s; meadow, 40 acres; woodland 1
league long and 3 furlongs wide.

Of this land Tovi holds 2 hides and 1 virgate of land,
William 4 hides, in CHELWORTH. The holders before 1066
could not be separated from the church. 2 ploughs
there; 6 slaves,

6 smallholders.

A mill at 10s; meadow, 8 acres.

Of the villagers' land Ansketel holds 1 hide.

Value of the Abbot's lordship, £13; value when acquired, £10;
value of what the men hold, £8.

8   (Long) NEWNTON. Before 1066 it paid tax for 30 hides.
Land for 23 ploughs. Of this land 15 hides in lordship; 4 ploughs
there; 4 slaves.

19 villagers, 5 cottagers and 2 Cottagers with 9 ploughs.

2 mills which pay 30s; meadow, 18 acres; pasture, 80 acres.

De ead̃ t̃ra ten̄ Osb̃n . III . hid̃ . 7 Wilts . II . hid̃ . Ibi hn̄t

VI . car̃ . De t̃ra uitto₂ ded̃ abb̃ cuidã militi suo . I . hid̃ .

Q̃do abb̃ recep̃: ualb̃ . x . lib̃ . Dn̄iũ ej . m̃ ual . XII . lib̃ .

Q̃d̃ hões ten̄ . ualet: VI . lib̃ .

Ipsa æccta ten̄ CERLETONE . T.R.E. geldb̃ ꝑ . xx . hid̃ .

T̃ra . ē . XIII . car̃ . De hac t̃ra . XII . hidæ st̃ in dñio .

7 ibi . II . car̃ . 7 VII . serui . Ibi . XXIII . uitti 7 XIII . cotar̃ .

7 II . coscez cũ . v . car̃ . Ibi molin̄ redd̃ . XV . solid̃ .

67 b
7 XII . ãc ꝑti . 7 xv . ãc pasturæ . Silua . II . q̃₂ lg̃ . 7 una q̃₂ lat̃ .

De ead̃ t̃ra ten̄ . R . Flãbard unã hid̃ 7 dim̃ . 7 ibi hr̃ . I . car̃ 7 dim̃ .

De t̃ra uitto₂ ten̄ Radulf hid̃ 7 dimid̃ . 7 ibi hr̃ . I . car̃ .

Q̃do abb̃ M̃ recep̃: ualb̃ . VIII . lib̃ . Modo dñiũ ej tñtd̃ ualet .

Q̃d̃ hões ten̄ . ual . XL . solid̃ .

Ipsa æccta ten̄ GARDONE . Vlueua tenuit T.R.E. 7 geld̃ ꝑ . III . hid̃ .

T̃ra . ē . VI . car̃ . De hac t̃ra in dñio . ē una hida 7 dimid̃ . 7 ibi . II .

car̃ . 7 VI . serui . Ibi . V . uitti 7 v . coscez . cũ . III . car̃ . Ibi . II . molini

redd̃ . xxv . solid̃ . 7 x . ãc ꝑti . 7 x . ãc pasturæ . Silua . dimid̃

leu lg̃ . 7 II . q̃₂ lat̃ . 7 un burg̃sis redd̃ . III . solid̃ .

Valuit . LX . solid̃ . Modo . c . solid̃ .

Ipsa æccta ten̄ CREDVELLE . T.R.E. geldb̃ ꝑ . XL . hid̃ . T̃ra . ē . XXV .

car̃ . De hac t̃ra st̃ in dñio . XVIII . hidæ . 7 ibi . IIII . car̃ . 7 v . serui .

Ibi . XLVIII . uitti 7 XXIIII . bord̃ . 7 x . cotar̃ . 7 VII . colib̃ti . cũ : XVIII .

car̃ . Ibi . XXIIII . ãc ꝑti . Silua . II . leu lg̃ . 7 tñtd̃ lat̃ .

Valuit 7 ual . XVI . lib̃ . De ead̃ t̃ra ten̄ Ebrard̃ . III . hid̃ . 7 ibi

hr̃ . III . car̃ . 7 VII . uittos cũ . I . bord̃ 7 v . seruis . 7 I . car̃ . Guerlin

qui tenuit T.R.E̅ | n̄ poterat separari . Val . IIII . lib̃ . Ibi . IX . ãc ꝑti .

Ipsa æccta ten̄ BREME . T.R.E. geld̃ ꝑ XXXVIII . hid̃ . T̃ra

ē . xxx . car̃ . De hac t̃ra st̃ in dñio . XVII . hidæ . 7 ibi . VII . car̃ .

7 XII . serui . Ibi . XXXII . uitti 7 XIII . bord̃ cũ . xx . car̃ . Ibi . II . mo

lini redd̃ . xxx . solid̃ . 7 XII . ãc ꝑti . Silua . II . leu lg̃ . 7 II . q̃₂ lat̃ .

Valuit . XIIII . lib̃ q̃do abb̃ recep̃ . Modo . XVI . lib̃ .

Of this land Osbern holds 3 hides, William 2 hides;
they have 6 ploughs.
Of the villagers' land the Abbot gave 1 hide to a
man-at-arms of his.
Value when the Abbot acquired it, £10; value now of his
lordship, £12; value of what the men hold, £6.

9   CHARLTON. Before 1066 it paid tax for 20 hides. Land for 13
ploughs. Of this land 12 hides in lordship; 2 ploughs
there; 7 slaves.
    23 villagers, 13 cottagers and 2 Cottagers with 5 ploughs.
    A mill which pays 15s; meadow, 12 acres; pasture, 15 acres;   67 b
      woodland 2 furlongs long and 1 furlong wide.
Of this land Ranulf Flambard holds 1½ hides; he has 1½ ploughs.
Of the villagers' land Ralph holds 1½ hides; he has 1 plough.
Value when the Abbot acquired the manor, £8; value now of his
lordship, the same; value of what the men hold, 40s.

10   GARSDON. Wulfeva held it before 1066; it paid tax for 3 hides.
Land for 6 ploughs. Of this land 1½ hides in lordship; 2
ploughs there; 6 slaves.
    5 villagers and 5 Cottagers with 3 ploughs.
    2 mills which pay 25s; meadow, 10 acres; pasture, 10
      acres; woodland ½ league long and 2 furlongs wide.
    A burgess who pays 3s.
The value was 60s; now 100s.

11   CRUDWELL. Before 1066 it paid tax for 40 hides. Land for 25
ploughs. Of this land 18 hides in lordship; 4 ploughs there;
5 slaves.
    48 villagers, 24 smallholders, 10 cottagers and 7 freedmen
      with 18 ploughs.
Meadow, 24 acres; woodland 2 leagues long and as wide.
The value was and is £16.
Of this land Ebrard holds 3 hides; he has 3 ploughs and
      7 villagers with 1 smallholder, 5 slaves and 1 plough.
Guerlin who held them before 1066 could not be separated
from the church.
Value £4.
Meadow, 9 acres.

12   BREMHILL. Before 1066 it paid tax for 38 hides.
Land for 30 ploughs. Of this land 17 hides in lordship;
7 ploughs there; 12 slaves.
    32 villagers and 13 smallholders with 20 ploughs.
    2 mills which pay 30s; meadow, 12 acres; woodland 2 leagues
      long and 2 furlongs wide.
The value was £14 when the Abbot acquired it; now £16.

De ead tra ten Eduuard . IIII . hiđ.7 Teodric . IIII . hiđ.

Tra . ē . VII . cař.7 totiđ cař ibi ſt.7 II . uitti 7 IX . borđ 7 VII . cotar.

7 IIII . ſerui . Ibi moliñ int eos de . XVI . ſot.7 X . ac pti.7 IIII . ac

ſpineti.7 ſiluæ una q̃ᴣ lḡ.7 tntđ lat . Valet . c . ſoliđ utrunqᴣ.

Qui teneꝥ has VIII . hiđ T.R.E . ab æccta ñ poterant ſeparari.

De tra uillanoᴣ ten idē Teodric . I . hiđ . quā deđ ei abꝥ.

De ead etiā   ten Eduuard . II . hiđ de rege.7 Giſleꝥ

de eo . Has abſtulit de dñio æcctæ q̃dā abꝥ Anglicus.7 dedit

cuidā ꝑpoſito.7 poſtea uni taino . qui nullo m̃ ſeparari poterat

ab æccta . Vat . XL . ſoliđ ꝑ annū.

Witts q̃qᴣ de Ow . ten de ead tra unā hiđ . quā preſtitit abꝥ

Aleſtano . T.R.E . Valet . VI . ſoliđ.

Ipſa æccta ten *PIRITONE* . T.R.E . geldꝥ ꝑ . XXXV . hiđ . Tra . ē

XXIIII . cař . De hac tra ſt in dñio . XXI . hida 7 dim.7 ibi . II . cař.

7 V . ſerui . Ibi . XX . uitti 7 XII . borđ.7 XIII . cotar . cū . XIX . cař.

Ibi moliñ de . V . ſot.7 LX . ac pti . Silua . II . leū lḡ.7 tntđ lat.

In Crichelade un burḡſis redđ . VI . den . ptiñ huic M̃.

Valuit 7 uat . XVI . liꝥ.

.IX.   QĐ HABEŦ SC̃S PETRVS WESTMONASŦ.

Eccta S̃ PETRI WESTMONASŦ ten æcctam de *CRICHELADE*.7 h̃t ibi plu

res burḡſes.7 tciū denariū ejđe uillæ . Tot ſimut redđ . IX . liꝥ.

.X.   TERRA ABBATIÆ SC̃I PETRI WINTONIENŜ.

Eccta S̃ PETRI WINTONIENŜ ten *MANEFORDE* . T.R.E.

geldauit ꝑ X . hiđ . Tra . ē . X . cař . De hac tra ſt in dñio . V . hidæ

7 dimiđ v træ.7 ibi . II . cař.7 V . ſerui . Ibi . VIII . uitti 7 VII . coſcez.

cū . II . cař 7 dimiđ . Ibi moliñ de . XII . ſoliđ.7 VI . denar.7 X . ac

pti . Paſtura . IIII . q̃ᴣ lḡ.7 una q̃ᴣ lat . Valuit . VI . liꝥ . m̃ . VIII . liꝥ.

Of this land Edward holds 4 hides and Theodric 4 hides.
Land for 7 ploughs; as many ploughs there.
   2 villagers, 9 smallholders, 7 cottagers, 4 slaves.
   A mill between them at 16s; meadow, 10 acres; spinney,
     4 acres; woodlands 1 furlong long and as wide.
Value of both, 100s.
   The holders of these 8 hides before 1066 could not be
separated from the church.
   Of the villagers' land the same Theodric holds 1 hide
which the Abbot gave him.
   Of this [land] also Edward holds 2 hides from the King and
Gilbert from him. An English Abbot took these away from
the lordship of the church and gave them to a reeve and
later on to a thane who could in no way be separated from
the church.
Value 40s a year.
   Also William of Eu holds 1 hide of this land which the Abbot
leased to Alstan before 1066.
Value 6s.

13   PURTON. Before 1066 it paid tax for 35 hides.
Land for 24 ploughs. Of this land 21½ hides in lordship;
2 ploughs there; 5 slaves.
   20 villagers, 12 smallholders and 13 cottagers with 19 ploughs.
   A mill at 5s; meadow, 60 acres; woodland 2 leagues long
     and as wide.
   In Cricklade a burgess who pays 6d belongs to this manor.
The value was and is £16.

9   **WHAT ST. PETER'S OF WESTMINSTER HAS**

1   The Church of St. Peter of Westminster holds the church of
CRICKLADE. It has there many burgesses and the third penny
of the same town.
The whole together pays £9.

10   **LAND OF THE ABBEY OF ST. PETER OF WINCHESTER**

1   The Church of St. Peter of Winchester holds MANNINGFORD.
Before 1066 it paid tax for 10 hides. Land for 10 ploughs.
Of this land 5 hides and ½ virgate of land in lordship; 2 ploughs
there; 5 slaves.
   8 villagers and 7 Cottagers with 2½ ploughs.
   A mill at 12s 6d; meadow, 10 acres; pasture 4 furlongs
     long and 1 furlong wide.
The value was £6; now £8.

Ipſa æccła ten COLEBVRNE . T.R.E. geldb ꝑ.L.hiđ.Tra.e.xxxii.
car.De hac tra ſt in dnĩo.x.hidæ.7 ibi.iiii.car.7 xiii.ſerui.
Ibi .xL. uilłi 7 xiii.coſcez.cũ.xv.car.Ibi.ii.ac ꝑti.Silua
una leũ łg.7 dimiđ leu lat.7 tntđ paſturæ.
De eađ tra ten Croc de abbe.x.hiđ 7 dim v træ|7 Fulcred dimiđ hidã.
ii.hiđ.Qui teneb T.R.E. ab æccła n̄ poterant ſeparari.
Ibi ſunt.viii.car.De tainlande h̃ abb in ſuo dnĩo.i.hiđ.
Dñium abbis tot ual m̂.xxviii.lib.Qd hões ten.ual.xii.lib.
Qdo recep.min ualb.c.ſol.

Ipſa æccła ten PEVESEI . T.R.E. geldb ꝑ.xxx.hiđ.Tra.e.xxiiii.car.
De hac tra ſt in dnĩo.vi.hidæ.7 una v træ.7 ibi.iii.car.7 vi.ſerui.
Ibi.xLvi.uilłi 7 xxiiii.coſcez.7 un borđ.cũ.xviii.car.
Ibi .vii.molini redđ.iiii.lib 7 v.ſolid.7 xv.ac ꝑti.Paſtura
una leũ łg.7 tntđ lat.Silua.iii.q̃ʒ łg.7 dimiđ q̃ʒ lat.
De eađ tra ten un tain.ii.hiđ una v min.7 n̄ potuit ab æccła ſepari.
7 Ernulf de Heſding.ii.hiđ ten de rege.quas abb deđ uni taino
T.R.E.qui tam̃ non poterat ab æccła ſeparari.Valet.xxx.ſolid.
Dñium abbis ualuit.xxvi.lib.Modo ual.xxviii.lib.
Ipſa æccła ten in WINTREBVRNE.ii.hiđ.Tra.e.ii.car.De hac tra
in dnĩo.e una hida 7 i.car.7 iii.ſerui.Ibi un uilłs 7 iiii.borđ cũ.i.
car.7 iiii.ac ꝑti.7 Lx.ac paſturæ.Valuit.x.ſolid.Modo.xL.ſol.
Ipſa æccła ten CHISELDENE.T.R.E. geldb ꝑ.xL.hiđ.Tra.e.xxii.car.
De hac tra ſt in dnĩo.xvii.hidæ.7 v.car.7 vi.ſerui.Ibi.xLv.uilłi
7 xiii.borđ cũ.x.car.Ibi molin̄ redđ.xL.denar.7 xL.ac ꝑti.
Paſtura dim̃ leu łg.7 iiii.q̃ʒ lat.Silua.iii.q̃ʒ łg.7 ii.q̃ʒ lat.
Valuit.xviii.lib.Modo.xxiiii.lib.Huic m̃ ꝑtin.vi.burgenſes
in Crichelade . redđt.iiii.ſol 7 un̄ denar.

The Church itself holds

2   COLLINGBOURNE (Kingston). Before 1066 it paid tax for 50 hides. Land for 32 ploughs. Of this land 10 hides in lordship; 4 ploughs there; 13 slaves.

> 40 villagers and 13 Cottagers with 15 ploughs.
> Meadow, 2 acres; woodland 1 league long and ½ league wide; pasture, as much.
> Of this land Croc holds 10 hides and ½ virgate of land and ½ hide from the Abbot, Fulcred 2 hides. The holders before 1066 could not be separated from the church. 8 ploughs there. The Abbot has 1 hide of thaneland in his lordship.

Total value of the Abbot's lordship now, £28; value of what the men hold, £12; value when acquired, 100s less.

3   PEWSEY. Before 1066 it paid tax for 30 hides.   67 c
Land for 24 ploughs. Of this land 6 hides and 1 virgate of land in lordship; 3 ploughs there; 6 slaves.

> 46 villagers, 24 Cottagers and 1 smallholder with 18 ploughs.
> 7 mills which pay £4 5s; meadow, 15 acres; pasture 1 league long and as wide; woodland 3 furlongs long and ½ furlong wide.
> Of this land a thane holds 2 hides, less 1 virgate; he could not be separated from the church. Arnulf of Hesdin holds 2 hides from the King which the Abbot gave to a thane before 1066, who, however, could not be separated from the church. Value 30s.

The value of the Abbot's lordship was £26; value now £28.

4   in ADDESTONE 2 hides. Land for 2 ploughs. Of this land 1 hide in lordship; 1 plough; 3 slaves.

> 1 villager and 4 smallholders with 1 plough.
> Meadow, 4 acres; pasture, 60 acres.

The value was 10s; now 40s.

5   CHISELDON. Before 1066 it paid tax for 40 hides. Land for 22 ploughs. Of this land 17 hides in lordship; 5 ploughs; 6 slaves.

> 45 villagers and 13 smallholders with 10 ploughs.
> A mill which pays 40d; meadow, 40 acres; pasture ½ league long and 4 furlongs wide; woodland 3 furlongs long and 2 furlongs wide.

The value was £18; now £24.

> To this manor belong 6 burgesses in Cricklade who pay 4s 1d.

ECCLA S MARIÆ CRENEBVRNENSIS ten ESSITONE .7 tenuit T.R.E.
7 p.xx.hid geldau. Tra.ē.xvi.car. De hác tra ſt in dnio.x.hidæ.
7 ibi.ii.car.7 v.ſerui.Ibi.xx.uilti 7 xii.bord 7 iiii.coſcez.cū.xiii.
car.Ibi moliñ redd.v.ſolid.7 cc.ac pti.Paſtura una leu lg.7 dim
leu lat.Silua ht tantd.   Valuit 7 ual.xv.lib.

Ipſa æccta ten in DOBREHA unā hid.Tra.ē.i.car 7 dimid.
Ibi ht abb.i.car.7 v.bord cū dimid car. Val.xx.ſolid.

ECCLA S MARIÆ SCEPTESBER.ten BICHENESTOCH.7 Turſtin
ten de abbiſſa. Harding tenuit de æccta T.R.E.7 geldb p.v.hid.
Tra.ē.v.car.De hac tra ſt in dnio.iii.hidæ.7 ibi.ii.car.7 ii.
ſerui.Ibi.vi.uilti 7 vi.coſcez.cū.iii.car.Ibi moliñ redd.xii.ſot.
7 xxviii.ac pti.7 xl.ac paſturæ.Valuit.lx.ſot.Modo.c.ſot.
Hanc trā reddid ſponte ſua æcclæ Harding.q̇ in uita ſua p cuent

Ipſa æccta ten TISSEBERIE.T.R.E.geldb p.xx.hid.f debeb tenere.
Tra.ē.xl.car.De hac tra ſt in dnio.v.hidæ.7 ibi.iii.car.
Ibi.xl.uilti 7 l.bord.cū.xxv.car.Ibi.iiii.molini redd.xxxv.
ſolid.7 xl.ac pti.Paſtura.i.leu lg.7 dim leu lat.Silua.
una leu lg.7 tntd lat.
De ead tra ten de abba Turſtin.iii.hid.Gunfrid.iii.hid.Albic.ii.hd.
Ibi hnt.ix.car.Eduuard uicecom ht.iii.car in tra uillanoʒ.
Dnium abbatiſſæ ualet.xxx.lib.Militū u.xiii.lib.

Ipſa æccta ten DVNEHEVE.T.R.E.geldb p.xl.hid.Tra.ē.xxxii.
car.De hac tra ſt in dnio.xii.hidæ.7 ibi.ii.car.Ibi.xxxv.uilti
7 xxv.bord.cū.xxv.car.Ibi.viii.molini redd.lxvi.ſot 7 viii.
denar.7 xv.ac pti.Paſtura.i.leu lg.7 tntd lat.Silua.vi.qʒ
lg.7 ii.qʒ lat.De ead tra ten Turſtin.vi.hid.7 qdā tain.i.hid.

11   **LAND OF THE CHURCH OF CRANBORNE**

1   The Church of St. Mary of Cranborne holds ASHTON (Keynes).
It held it before 1066; it paid tax for 20 hides.
Land for 16 ploughs. Of this land 10 hides in lordship;
2 ploughs there; 5 slaves.
  20 villagers, 12 smallholders and 4 Cottagers with 13 ploughs.
  A mill which pays 5s; meadow, 200 acres; pasture 1 league
    long and ½ league wide; the woodland has as much.
The value was and is £15.

2   The Church itself holds 1 hide in DAMERHAM. Land for 1½
ploughs. The Abbot has 1 plough there;
  5 smallholders with ½ plough.
Value 20s.

12   **LAND OF THE CHURCH OF SHAFTESBURY**

1   The Church of St. Mary of Shaftesbury holds BEECHINGSTOKE.
Thurstan holds from the Abbess. Harding held it from the
church before 1066; it paid tax for 5 hides. Land for 5 ploughs.
Of this land 3 hides in lordship; 2 ploughs there; 2 slaves.
  6 villagers and 6 Cottagers with 3 ploughs.
  A mill which pays 12s; meadow, 28 acres; pasture, 40 acres.
The value was 60s; now 100s.
  Harding who by agreement should have held this land for his
lifetime returned it of his own accord to the church.

The Church itself holds
2   TISBURY. Before 1066 it paid tax for 20 hides. Land for 40
ploughs. Of this land 5 hides in lordship; 3 ploughs there.
  40 villagers and 50 smallholders with 25 ploughs.
  4 mills which pay 35s; meadow, 40 acres; pasture 1 league
    long and ½ league wide; woodland 1 league long and as wide.
  Of this land Thurstan holds 3 hides from the Abbey, Gunfrid 3
  hides, Aubrey 2 hides; they have 9 ploughs.
  Edward the Sheriff has 3 ploughs on the villagers' land.
Value of the Abbess' lordship, £30; of the men-at-arms', £13.

3   DONHEAD. Before 1066 it paid tax for 40 hides. Land for 32
ploughs. Of this land 12 hides in lordship; 2 ploughs there.
  35 villagers and 25 smallholders with 25 ploughs.
  8 mills which pay 66s 8d; meadow, 15 acres; pasture 1
    league long and as wide; woodland 6 furlongs long
    and 2 furlongs wide.
  Of this land Thurstan holds 6 hides, a thane 1 hide;

7 ibi ſt . vi . car . Qui teneƀ T.R.E . n̄ poteraꝗ ab æccła ſeparari.

Dn̄ium abƀiſſæ ualet . xxii . liƀ . Hōum ů.ˊx . liƀ . 7 ᵖʳⁱᵘˢtantd̄ ualuit.

Ipſa æccła ten̄ BRADEFORD . T.R.E . geldƀ ꝑ . xl.ii . hid̄ . Tra . e͂

xl . car̄ . De hac tra ſt in dn̄io . xiii . hidæ . 7 ibi . viii . car̄ . 7 ix . ſerui.

7 xviii . coliƀti . Ibi . xxxvi . uiłłi 7 xl . bord̄ . cū . xxxii . car̄ . 7 Ibi

xxii . porcarij . 7 xxxiii . burḡſes redd̄ . xxxv . ſoł 7 ix . den̄ . 7 uꝰ

ſeruienꝭ redd̄ . vii . ſextar̄ mellis . Ibi . ii . molini redd̄ . iii . liƀ.

Mercatū redd̄ . xlv . ſolid̄ . Ibi un̄ arpen uineæ . 7 l . ãc ᵽti.

Paſtura . xi . q̃rent łḡ . 7 iii . q̃ʒ lat̄ . Silua dimid̄ leū łḡ.

7 ii . q̃rent lat̄.

67 d

Ad eund ꟲ Bradeford ptin̄ ALVESTONE . T.R.E . geldƀ

ꝑ . vii . hid̄ . exceptis . xlii . ſupioriƀ hid̄ . Tra . e͂ . vi . car̄.

De hac tra ſt in dn̄io . iiii . hidæ . 7 ibi . iii . car̄.

Toƀ Bradeford cū append̄ . ualuit 7 uał . lx . liƀ.

Ipſa æccła ten̄ LEDENTONE . T.R.E . geldƀ ꝑ . xxxviii.

hid̄ . Tra . e͂ . xvi . car̄ . De hac tra ſt in dn̄io . xxiiii.

hidæ . 7 ibi . iiii . car̄ . 7 vi . ſerui . Ibi xxiii . uiłłi

7 xvii . bord̄ cū . vii . car̄ . Ibi . ii . molini redd̄ . v . ſoł.

Pratū . iiii . q̃ʒ łḡ . 7 iii . q̃ʒ lat̄ . Paſtura dim̄ leū łḡ.

7 iiii . q̃ʒ lat̄ . In Crichelade un̄ burḡſis redd̄ . vi . den̄.

Valuit . xviii . liƀ . Modo . xxii . liƀ.

Ipſa æccła ten̄ DOMNITONE . T.R.E . geldƀ ꝑ . xx . hid̄.

Tra . e͂ . xv . car̄ . De hac tra ſt . vii . hid̄ 7 iii . virg̃ tre̅.

in dn̄io . 7 ibi . ii . car̄ . 7 iiii . ſerui . Ibi . xxi . uiłłs 7 x . bord̄

cū . xi . car̄ . Ibi . ii . molini redd̄ . xii . ſoł 7 vi . denar̄.

7 xx . ãc ᵽti . 7 totid̄ ãc ſiluæ . Paſtura . i . leū łḡ . 7 dim̄

leū lat̄ . Duo burḡſes redd̄ . x . den̄.

De ead̄ tra ten̄ Gunfrid̄ . ii . hid̄ . 7 ibi hƀ . ii . car̄ . Qui

tenuit T.R.E . n̄ poterat ab æccła ſeparari.

Dn̄ium abƀiſſe . ualuit 7 uał xviii . liƀ . Gunfridi . xl . ſoł.

67 c, d

6 ploughs there. The holders before 1066 could not be
separated from the church.
Value of the Abbess' lordship, £22; of the men's, £10;
value the same before.

4   BRADFORD (on Avon). Before 1066 it paid tax for 42 hides.
Land for 40 ploughs. Of this land 13 hides in lordship; 8
ploughs there; 9 slaves; 18 freedmen.
    36 villagers and 40 smallholders with 32 ploughs. 22 pigmen
       and 33 burgesses who pay 35s 9d; 1 servant who pays
       7 sesters of honey.
    2 mills which pay £3; a market which pays 45s; 1 *arpent*
       of vineyard; meadow, 50 acres; pasture 11 furlongs
       long and 3 furlongs wide; woodland ½ league long
       and 2 furlongs wide.
    To this manor of Bradford belongs *ALVESTONE*. Before   67 d
    1066 it paid tax for 7 hides, apart from the above 42
    hides. Land for 6 ploughs. Of this land 4 hides in lordship.
    3 ploughs there.
The value of the whole of Bradford (on Avon) with its
dependencies was and is £60.

5   LIDDINGTON. Before 1066 it paid tax for 38 hides. Land for 16
ploughs. Of this land 24 hides in lordship; 4 ploughs
there; 6 slaves.
    23 villagers and 17 smallholders with 7 ploughs.
    2 mills which pay 5s; meadow 4 furlongs long and 3 furlongs
       wide; pasture ½ league long and 4 furlongs wide.
    In Cricklade a burgess who pays 6d.
The value was £18; now £22.

6   DINTON. Before 1066 it paid tax for 20 hides. Land for 15
ploughs. Of this land 7 hides and 3 virgates of land in
lordship; 2 ploughs there; 4 slaves.
    21 villagers and 10 smallholders with 11 ploughs.
    2 mills which pay 12s 6d; meadow, 20 acres; woodland, as
       many acres; pasture 1 league long and ½ league wide.
    2 burgesses who pay 10d.
    Of this land Gunfrid holds 2 hides; he has 2 ploughs.
    The holder before 1066 could not be separated from the church.
The value of the Abbess' lordship was and is £18; of Gunfrid's, 40s.

.XIII. ECCLA S MARIE WILTVNIENSIS teń *STANTONE*.

T.R.E.geldb́ p̄.xx.hid́.Tra.ḗ.xii.car̄.De hac t́ra
ſt in dńio.x.hidǽ.7 ibi.iiii.car̄.7 ibi.viii.ſerui.Ibi
xvi.uitti 7 uń bord́.7 xxi.coſcez.cū.viii.car̄.
Ibi.ii.molini redd́.xii.ſot 7 vi.deń.7 lx.ac̄ p̄ti.7 iii.ac̄
alneti.Paſtura.i.leu lḡ.7 dimid́ leu lat̄.
Valuit.xvi.lib́.Modo.xxiiii.lib.

Ipſa æccla teń *NEWETONE*.T.R.E.geldb́ p̄ xiii.hid́
7 dimid́.7 dimid́ v́ t́ræ.De hac t́ra ſt iṙ dńio.iiii.hidǽ.
7 ibi.ii.car̄ 7 iiii.ſerui.Ibi.xiii.uitti 7 xvi.coſcez.cū.v. n
car̄.Tot ĉ poſſunt arare.x.car̄.Ibi moliñ redd́.xii.
ſolid́ 7 vi.deń.7 xxx.ac̄ p̄ti.Paſtura..iiii.q̃ lḡ.7 ii.
q̃ lat̄.Silua.i.leu lḡ.7 tñtd́ lat̄.
De t́ra uillanoz̧ ded́ abbatiſſa uni militi.iii.hid́ 7 diḿ.
7 diḿ v́ t́ræ.Ibi ht̄.ii.car̄.7 uitti ej̄.i.car̄.
De ead́ t́ra tenuit Aluric uenator de abbiſſa uñā hid́
7 uñā v́ t́ræ 7 dimid́.ea c̄ditione ut poſt mort̄ ej̄ rediret
ad æcclam q́a de dńica firma erat.Modo teń Ricard́. ^Sturmid
Tot ĉ ualuit.xiiii.lib́.q̄do recep̄.Modo.xviii.lib.

Ipſa æccla teń *DARNEFORD*.T.R.E.geldb́ p̄.iiii.hid́.
Tra.ḗ.iii.car̄.Eduuard́ teń de abbiſſa .Tres angli
tenueṙ T.R.E.7 ñ poterant ab æccla ſeparari .Duo
ex eis reddeb̄.v.ſot.7 tcius ſeruieb̄ ſic taiṅ.Ibi ſt.vi.bou
in car̄ dńica.cū.iiii.bord́.Ibi .ii.angli hñt.ii.car̄.
Ibi moliñ redd́.vii.ſot 7 diḿ.7 xii.ac̄ ibi p̄ti.Pa
ſtura.iiii.q̃ lḡ.7 una q̃ lat̄.Valuit.c.ſot.ḿ.ix.lib.

Ipſa æccla teń *SVALOCLIVE*.T.R.E.geldb́ p̄.iiii.hid́
7 una v́.Tra.ḗ.ii.car̄.Ibi.ḗ un uitts 7 ii.bord́.7 ii.
ac̄ p̄ti.Valuit 7 uat.xl.ſolid́.

1   The Church of St. Mary of Wilton holds STANTON (St. Bernard).
Before 1066 it paid tax for 20 hides. Land for 12 ploughs.
Of this land 10 hides in lordship; 4 ploughs there; 8 slaves there.
   16 villagers, 1 smallholder and 21 Cottagers with 8 ploughs.
   2 mills which pay 12s 6d; meadow, 60 acres; alder-grove,
      3 acres; pasture 1 league long and ½ league wide.
The value was £16; now £24.

   The Church itself holds
2   (North) NEWNTON. Before 1066 it paid tax for 13½ hides and ½ virgate
of land. Of this land 3 hides in lordship; 2 ploughs there; 4 slaves.
   13 villagers and 16 Cottagers with 5 ploughs.
   10 ploughs can plough the whole manor.
   A mill which pays 12s 6d; meadow, 30 acres; pasture 4
      furlongs long and 2 furlongs wide; woodland 1 league
      long and as wide.
Of the villagers' land the Abbess gave 3½ hides and ½
virgate of land to a man-at-arms; he has 2 ploughs;
his villagers 1 plough.
Of this land Aelfric Hunter held 1 hide and 1½ virgates of
land from the Abbess on the condition that after his death it
should return to the church, because it was part of the
lordship revenue. Richard Sturmy holds it now.
The value of the whole manor was £14 when acquired; now £18.

3   DURNFORD. Before 1066 it paid tax for 4 hides. Land for 3
ploughs. Edward holds from the Abbess. Three Englishmen
held it before 1066; they could not be separated from the
church. Two of them paid 5s, and the third served as a thane.
6 oxen in the lord's plough there, with
   4 smallholders.
   2 Englishmen have 2 ploughs.
   A mill which pays 7½s; meadow, 12 acres; pasture 4 furlongs
      long and 1 furlong wide.
The value was 100s; now £9.

4   SWALLOWCLIFFE. Before 1066 it paid tax for 4 hides and 1
virgate. Land for 2 ploughs.
   1 villager and 2 smallholders.
   Meadow, 2 acres.
The value was and is 40s.

Ipſa æccła ten̅ CHILMERC .T.R.E. geldb̅ ꝑ.xx. hiđ.

Tra.e̅.xiiii.caɍ.De hac tra ſꞇ in dn̅io.viii.hidæ.

7 ibi.ii.caɍ.Ibi.xv.uilłi 7 xii.borđ.7 xii.colibti

cū.xii.caɍ.Ibi moliň redđ.x.ſoliđ.7 v.ac̅ ꝓti.

7 x.ac̅ runceti.paſtura.i.leū lg̅.7 dim̅ leū lat̅.

Valuit.xiiii.lib̅.Modo.xv.lib̅.

Ipſa æccła ten̅ unā hiđ træ.in WERDORE.7 Britmar̅

de abb̅iſſa ten̅.Tra.e̅.i.caɍ.Ipſa.e̅ ibi cū.iiii.borđ.

7 iii.ac̅ ꝓti.Paſtura.i.leū lg̅.7 dimiđ leū lat̅.Silua

.ii.q̅rent lg̅.7 una q̑ꝫ lat̅.Valet.xx.ſoliđ.

Ipſa æccła ten̅ CHENVEL.T.R.E.ꝑ.x.hiđ.Tra.e̅.vii.

caɍ.De hac tra ſꞇ in dn̅io.iiii.hidæ 7 dimiđ.7 iii.ſerui.

Ibi.xi.uilłi 7 ix.coſcez.cū.v.caɍ.Ibi.v.ac̅ ꝓti.7 paſtura

dimiđ leū lg̅.7 iii.q̑ꝫ lat̅.Silua dimiđ leū lg̅.7 tntđ lat̅.

Valuit.vi.lib̅.Modo.viii.lib̅.

Ipſa æccła ten̅ OVRETONE.T.R.E. geldb̅ ꝑ.x.hiđ.Tra.e̅

iiii.caɍ.De hac tra ſꞇ in dn̅io.vii.hidæ 7 dim̅ v træ.

7 ibi.ii.caɍ.7 ii.ſerui.Ibi.iii.uilłi 7 viii.borđ cū.ii.caɍ.

Ibi moliň redđ.x.ſoliđ.7 v.ac̅ ꝓti.7 xx.ac̅ paſturæ.

7 xx.ac̅ ſiluæ.Valet.c.ſoliđ.

Ipſa æccła ten̅ CHELCHE.T.R.E.geldb̅ ꝑ.lxxvii.hiđ.

Tra.e̅.lx.vi.caɍ.De hac tra ſꞇ in dn̅io.x.hidæ.7 ibi.x.

caɍ.7 xx.ſerui.Ibi qt̅ xx.7 vi.uilłi 7 l.borđ 7 x ⚬colibti.

hn̅tes.l.caɍ.Ibi.v.molini redđ.lxv.ſoł.7 xii.ac̅

ꝓti.Paſtura.iii.leū lg̅.7 una leū lat̅.7 tantđ ſiluæ.

De eađ tra ten̅ Girarđ.iii.hiđ.Qui teneb̅ T.R.E. non

poterat ab æccła ſeparari.Ibi ſꞇ.ii.caɍ.Vał.iii.lib̅.

Dn̅iū abb̅iſſæ ualet.lxvii.lib̅.

5 CHILMARK. Before 1066 it paid tax for 20 hides. Land for 14
ploughs. Of this land 8 hides in lordship; 2 ploughs there.
   15 villagers, 12 smallholders and 12 freedmen with 12 ploughs.
   A mill which pays 10s; meadow, 5 acres; bramble-thicket,
      10 acres; pasture 1 league long and ½ league wide.
The value was £14; now £15.

6 in WARDOUR 1 hide of land. Brictmer holds from the Abbess.   68 a
   Land for 1 plough. It is there, with
   4 smallholders.
   Meadow, 3 acres; pasture 1 league long and ½ league wide;
      woodland 2 furlongs long and 1 furlong wide.
   Value 20s.

7 (West) KNOYLE. Before 1066 (it paid tax) for 10 hides.
   Land for 7 ploughs. Of this land 4½ hides in lordship; 3 slaves.
   11 villagers and 9 Cottagers with 5 ploughs.
   Meadow, 5 acres; pasture ½ league long and 3 furlongs
      wide; woodland ½ league long and as wide.
The value was £6; now £8.

8 (West) OVERTON. Before 1066 it paid tax for 10 hides
   Land for 4 ploughs. Of this land 7 hides and ½ virgate
   of land in lordship; 2 ploughs there; 2 slaves.
   3 villagers and 8 smallholders with 2 ploughs.
   A mill which pays 10s; meadow, 5 acres;
      pasture, 20 acres; woodland, 20 acres.
   Value 100s.

9 CHALKE. Before 1066 it paid tax for 77 hides. Land for 66
ploughs. Of this land 10 hides in lordship; 10 ploughs
there; 20 slaves.
   86 villagers, 50 smallholders and 10 freedmen who have
      50 ploughs.
   5 mills which pay 65s; meadow, 12 acres; pasture 3 leagues
      long and 1 league wide; woodland, as much.
   Of this land Gerard holds 3 hides. The holder before 1066
   could not be separated from the church. 2 ploughs there.
   Value £3.
Value of the Abbess' lordship, £67.

De ead̄ tra ten̄ Ricard̄ poingiant . VII . hid̄ 7 dim de rege.

Ex his . II . hidas teneb̄ Aileua T . R . E . 7 alias teneb̄ hōes

æcclæ feruientes fic uilti . Abbiffa calūniat.

Ibi hr̄ Ricard̄ . v . car̄ . 7 ual . VII . lib̄.

Ipfa æccla ten̄ NEWENTONE . T . R . E . geldb̄ p . XIX .

hid̄ 7 III . virg træ . Tra . ē . XIIII . car̄ . De hac tra ft in

dn̄io . II . hidæ . 7 ibi . II . car̄ . 7 VI . colibti . Ibi . XX . uilti 7 XVI .

bord̄ cū . XII . car̄ . Ibi . II . molini redd̄ . XL . folid̄ . 7 XX . ac̄ p̄ti .

7 CL . ac̄ pafturæ . 7 CC . ac̄ filuæ . Ad iftū m̄ p̄tin habe

p c̄fuetudin̄ in Silua MILCHETI . qt XX . caretedes ligno₂ porco₂

7 ad domos 7 fepes reem̄dandas qd opus fuerit . †

Ipfa æccla ten̄ WILGI . T . R . E . geldb̄ p . X . hid̄ . Tra . ē . V .

car̄ . De hac tra ft in dn̄io . V . hidæ . 7 ibi . II . car̄ . 7 II . ferui .

Ibi . IX . uilti 7 X . bord̄ cū . III . car̄ . Ibi molin̄ redd̄ . X . fot .

7 XII . ac̄ p̄ti . 7 C . ac̄ pafturæ . 7 X . ac̄ filuæ paruæ .

Valuit . VI . lib̄ . Modo . VIII . lib̄ . f̄ NEWENTON . Val . XVI . lib̄

Ipfa æccla ten̄ WICHEFORD . T . R . E . geldb̄ p . IIII . hid̄ .

Tra . ē . III . car̄ . De hac tra ft in dn̄io . II . hidæ . 7 ibi . II .

car̄ . Ibi . I . uilts 7 XVI . bord̄ cū . I . car̄ . Ibi . II . molini

redd̄ . XXIIII . fot . 7 VIII . ac̄ p̄ti . 7 IX . ac̄ pafturæ

Valuit . III . lib̄ . Modo . IIII . lib̄ .

Ipfa æccla ten̄ LANGEFORD . T . R . E . geldb̄ p . III . hid̄ . Tra

ē . II . car̄ . Has hn̄t ibi . II . angli cū . II . bord̄ . 7 II . feruis .

Ibi molin̄ redd̄ . V . fot . 7 XXV . ac̄ p̄ti . 7 XX . ac̄ pafturæ .

Valuit . XL . fot . Modo . L . folid̄ . Pat eo₂ q̄ nc̄ ten̄ tenuit

T . R . E . nec potuit ab æccla feparari .

Ipfa æccla ten̄ OCHEFORDE . T . R . E . geldb̄ p . IIII . hid̄ . Tra

ē . III . car̄ . De hac tra ft in dn̄io . III . hidæ . 7 ibi . I . car̄ .

Ibi . II . uilti 7 IIII . bord̄ cū . I . car̄ . Ibi molin̄ redd̄ . V . folid̄ .

7 VI . ac̄ p̄ti . Valuit . XL . folid̄ . Modo . LX . folid̄ .

Ipfa æccla hr̄ dimid̄ hid̄ træ in DICEHANTONE . Val . XXX . den̄ .

Of this land Richard Poynant holds 7½ hides from the King. Of these Aeleva held 2 hides before 1066 and men of the church serving as villagers held the others. The Abbess claims them. Richard has 5 ploughs.
Value £7.

10 (South) NEWTON. Before 1066 it paid tax for 19 hides and 3 virgates of land. Land for 14 ploughs. Of this land 2 hides in lordship; 2 ploughs there; 6 freedmen.
   20 villagers and 16 smallholders with 12 ploughs.
   2 mills which pay 40s; meadow, 20 acres; pasture,
      150 acres; woodland, 200 acres.
   To this manor belong by customary due in Melchet Forest
      80 cart-loads of timber and fodder for 80 pigs and what may
† be needed for repairing houses and fences.

11 WYLYE. Before 1066 it paid tax for 10 hides. Land for 5 ploughs. Of this land 5 hides in lordship; 2 ploughs there; 2 slaves.
   9 villagers and 10 smallholders with 3 ploughs.
   A mill which pays 10s; meadow, 12 acres; pasture, 100
      acres; a small wood, 10 acres.
The value was £6; now £8.
† (South) NEWTON. Value £16.

12 WISHFORD. Before 1066 it paid tax for 4 hides.
Land for 3 ploughs. Of this land 2 hides in lordship; 2 ploughs there.
   1 villager and 16 smallholders with 1 plough.
   2 mills which pay 24s; meadow, 8 acres; pasture, 9 acres.
The value was £3; now £4.

13 LANGFORD. Before 1066 it paid tax for 3 hides.
Land for 2 ploughs; two Englishmen have them there, with
   2 smallholders and 2 slaves.
   A mill which pays 5s; meadow, 25 acres; pasture, 20 acres.
The value was 40s; now 50s.
   The father of the present holders held it before 1066;
he could not be separated from the church.

14 UGFORD. Before 1066 it paid tax for 4 hides. Land for 3 ploughs. Of this land 3 hides in lordship; 1 plough there.
   2 villagers and 4 smallholders with 1 plough.
   A mill which pays 5s; meadow, 6 acres.
The value was 40s; now 60s.

15 The Church itself has ½ hide of land in DITCHAMPTON.
Value 30d.

Ipſa æccła teñ *BREDECVBE* . T.R.E. geldb ꝑ . vi . hiđ . Tra
eſt . iiii . car . De hac tra ſt in dñio . ii . hidæ . 7 ibi . ii . car .
Ibi . xiii . borđ 7 moliñ redđ . xv . ſoł . 7 xviii . ac̄ ꝓti . Paſtura
viii . q̓ɫ lg̃ . 7 una q̓ɫ lat . Valet . c . ſoliđ .
De eađ tra teñ Eduuarđ . i . hiđ . quæ ñ poteſt ab æccła tolli.

Vał . xv . ſoliđ .

Ipſa æccła teñ *BABESTOCHE* . T.R̄.E. ꝑ . iii . hiđ geld . Tra . ē . iii . car .
De his ſt in dñio . ii . hidæ . 7 ibi . i . car . cū . i . ſeruo . 7 iiii . borđ cū . ii .
car . 7 vi . ac̄ ꝓti . 7 iiii . ac̄ paſturæ . Vałet . lx . ſoliđ .

Ipſa æccła teñ *WAISEL* . T.R.E. geldb ꝑ . viii . hiđ 7 dimiđ .
Tra . ē . vii . car . De hac tra ſt in dñio . ii . hidæ . 7 ibi . i . car .
Ibi . ix . uiłłi 7 x . colibti cū . vi . car . Ibi . xii . ac̄ ꝓti . Paſtura
viii . q̓ɫ lg̃ . 7 vi . q̓ɫ lat . In Silua *MILCHETE* paſt q̓t xx .
porcis . 7 q̓t xx , caretedes ligno̗ɼ . 7 ad domos 7 ad ſepes qđ oꝑ eſt .
Valet . vii . lib 7 x . ſoliđ .

Ipſa æccła teñ *FEBEFONTE* . T.R.E. geldb ꝑ . x . hiđ . Tra . ē
vii . car . De hac tra ſt in dñio . v . hidæ . 7 ibi . ii . car . 7 vii .
colibti . Ibi . viii . uiłłi 7 vii . borđ cū . v . car . Ibi . ii . molini
redđ . xvii . ſoł . 7 vi . deñ . 7 viii . ac̄ ꝓti . Paſtura . iiii . q̓ɫ lg̃ .
7 una q̓ɫ lat . Silua . ii . q̓ɫ lg̃ . 7 una q̓ɫ lat . Vał . vii . lib 7 x . ſoł .

Ipſa æccła teñ *LAVVRECESTOHES* . T.R.E. geldb ꝑ . ii . hiđ .
Tra . ē . iii . car . De hac tra . ē in dñio . i . hida . 7 ibi . i . car .
Ibi . vi . uiłłi 7 viii . borđ cū . ii . car . Ibi moliñ redđ . vii . ſoliđ
7 vi . deñ . 7 xviii . ac̄ paſturæ . Valuit . c . ſoliđ . Modo . vi . lib .
Huj træ quarta pars in foreſta regis . ē poſita .

Ipſa æccła tenebat . ii . hiđ T.R.E. quas Toret dederat ibi cū
duab̄ filiab̓ ſuis . 7 ex eis ſeꝑ fuer̄ ueſtitæ donec eꝑs baioc̄ſis
injuſte abſtulit æcclæ .

Oꝰs redditꝰ quas h̄t æccła de ipſo burgo Wiltuñ . apꝑciant̄
x . lib . 7 xvii . ſoliđ . 7 vi . denar .

The Church itself holds

16   BURCOMBE. Before 1066 it paid tax for 6 hides. Land for 4
ploughs. Of this land 2 hides in lordship; 2 ploughs there.
    13 smallholders.
    A mill which pays 15s; meadow, 18 acres; pasture 8 furlongs
        long and 1 furlong wide.
Value 100s.
    Of this land Edward holds 1 hide which cannot be taken
away from the church.
Value 15s.

17   BAVERSTOCK. Before 1066 it paid tax for 3 hides. Land for 3   68 b
ploughs. In lordship 2 hides of these; 1 plough there,
with 1 slave;
    4 smallholders with 2 ploughs.
    Meadow, 6 acres; pasture, 4 acres.
Value 60s.

18   WASHERN. Before 1066 it paid tax for 8½ hides. Land for 7
ploughs. Of this land 2 hides in lordship; 1 plough there.
    9 villagers and 10 freedmen with 6 ploughs.
    Meadow, 12 acres; pasture 8 furlongs long and 6 furlongs
        wide; in Melchet Forest pasture for 80 pigs, and 80
        cartloads of timber and whatever is needed for
        (repairing) houses and fences.
Value £7 10s.

19   FOVANT. Before 1066 it paid tax for 10 hides. Land for 7 ploughs.
Of this land 5 hides in lordship; 2 ploughs there; 7 freedmen.
    8 villagers and 7 smallholders with 5 ploughs.
    2 mills which pay 17s 6d; meadow, 8 acres; pasture 4 furlongs
        long and 1 furlong wide; woodland 2 furlongs long and
        1 furlong wide.
Value £7 10s.

20   LAVERSTOCK. Before 1066 it paid tax for 2 hides. Land for 3
ploughs. Of this land 1 hide in lordship; 1 plough there.
    6 villagers and 8 smallholders with 2 ploughs.
    A mill which pays 7s 6d; pasture, 18 acres.
The value was 100s; now £6.
    A quarter of this land is situated in the King's Forest.

1   Before 1066 the church held 2 hides itself which Thored had
given to it with his two daughters; from them they were always
clothed until the Bishop of Bayeux wrongfully took them away
from the church.

2   All the payments which the church has from the Borough of Wilton
are assessed at £10 17s 6d.

Eccl̃a S̃ Mariæ Wintoniens ten *Ierchesfonte*.
T.R.E. geldb̃ p̄ . xxx . hid̃ . T̃ra . ē . xx . car̃ . De hac t̃ra ſt in dñio
vi . hidæ . 7 ibi . vii . car̃ . 7 xvii . ſerui . Ibi . xxxiii . uiłłi 7 xxvi .
bord̃ 7 vi . cotar̃ cũ . ix . car̃ . Ibi . iii . molini redd̃ xxi . ſolid̃ 7 iii .
den̄ . 7 lx . ac̃ p̃ti . Paſtura . i . leu lg̃ . 7 dim leu lat̃ . 7 t̃nt̃d ſiluæ .
De ead̃ t̃ra ten̄ Eduuard̃ hid̃ 7 dimid̃ . 7 tciã parte dim̃ hidæ .
Walter . i . hid̃ . Angli ten̄ . ii . hid̃ . 7 ii . partes dimid̃ hidæ
De . vi . hid̃ quæ ſt in dñio tenuit p̃poſit abbiſſæ . ii . hid̃ . T.R.E.
Poſtea ũ reddid̃ eas æcclæ cũ omĩ pecunia ſua . 7 nc̃ ſt in dñio .
Q̃do abbiſſa recep m̃ : ualb̃ . xv . lib̃ . Modo . xxvii . lib̃ qd̃ h̃t
in dñio . Qd̃ milites : iii . lib̃ .
Ipſa æccl̃a ten̄ *Caninge* . T.R.E. geld̃ p̄ . xviii . hid̃ . 7 una v̄ t̃ræ
7 dimid̃ . T̃ra . ē . xv . car̃ . De hac t̃ra ſt in dñio . iiii . hidæ . 7 ibi . v .
car̃ . 7 viii . ſerui . Ibi . xxvii . uiłłi 7 xvii . bord̃ . 7 vi . cotar̃ .
cũ . x . car̃ . Ibi moliñ redd̃ . xiii . ſolid̃ . 7 cviii . ac̃ p̃ti . Paſtura
una leu lg̃ . 7 iiii . q̃z lat̃ . Silua . iiii . q̃rent lg̃ . 7 ii . q̃rent lat̃ .
Valuit . xx . lib̃ . Modo . xxx . lib̃ .

.XV. TERRA ÆCCLE ROMESIENSIS.

Eccl̃a S̃ Mariæ Romeſiens ten̄ *Edendone* . T.R.E. geld̃b̃ p̄ . xxx .
hid̃ . T̃ra . ē . xxxv . car̃ 7 dimid̃ . De hac t̃ra ſt in dñio . ii . hidæ
7 dimid̃ . 7 ibi . vii . car̃ . 7 x . ſerui . Ibi . xx . i . uiłłs 7 xxiii . bord̃ .
7 x . colib̃ti . cũ . xv . car̃ . Ibi . ii . molini redd̃ . xix . ſot̃ . 7 c . ac̃ p̃ti .
Paſtura una leu lg̃ . 7 dim̃ leu lat̃ . Silua . x . q̃rent lg̃ . 7 v . lat̃ .
De ead̃ t̃ra ten̄ Wiłłs . iiii . hid̃ 7 dim̃ . Oſmund̃ . iiii . hid̃ . Herueus
. ii . hid̃ . Angli . v . hid̃ . 7 unã v̄ t̃ræ . Qui tenet̃ T.R.E. Has . xv . hid̃
7 iii . v̄ : ñ poterant ſeparari ab æccl̃a . Ibi ſt . xii . car̃ 7 dimid̃ .
Dñium æcclæ ualet . xxx . lib̃ . Qd̃ hões ten̄ : xviii . lib̃ .
Ipſa æccl̃a ten̄ *Aistone* . T.R.E. geld̃b̃ p̄ . xl . hid̃ . T̃ra . ē . xxx . vii .
car̃ . De hac t̃ra ſt in dñio . x . hidæ . 7 ibi . ix . car̃ . 7 viii . ſerui .

14   LAND OF THE CHURCH OF ST. MARY OF WINCHESTER

1   The Church of St. Mary of Winchester holds URCHFONT.
Before 1066 it paid tax for 30 hides. Land for 20 ploughs.
Of this land 6 hides in lordship; 7 ploughs there; 17 slaves.
    33 villagers, 26 smallholders and 6 cottagers with 9 ploughs.
    3 mills which pay 21s 3d; meadow, 64 acres; pasture 1 league
      long and ½ league wide; woodland, as much.
    Of this land Edward holds 1½ hides and the third part of
    ½ hide, Walter 1 hide, Englishmen hold 2 hides and 2 parts
    of ½ hide.
    Of the 6 hides which are in lordship the Abbess' reeve held
    2 hides before 1066; later he returned them to the church
    with all his goods; from now on they are in lordship.
Value when the Abbess acquired the manor, £15; of what she
has in lordship now, £27; of what the men-at-arms have, £3.

2   The Church holds (All) CANNINGS itself. Before 1066 it paid
tax for 18 hides and 1½ virgates of land. Land for 15 ploughs.
Of this land 4 hides in lordship; 5 ploughs there; 8 slaves.
    27 villagers, 17 smallholders and 6 cottagers with 10 ploughs.
    A mill which pays 13s; meadow, 108 acres; pasture 1 league
      long and 4 furlongs wide; woodland 4 furlongs long
      and 2 furlongs wide.
The value was £20; now £30.

15   LAND OF THE CHURCH OF ROMSEY

1   The Church of St. Mary of Romsey holds EDINGTON. Before 1066
it paid tax for 30 hides. Land for 35½ ploughs. Of this land 2½
hides in lordship; 7 ploughs there; 10 slaves.
    21 villagers, 23 smallholders and 10 freedmen
      with 15 ploughs.
    2 mills which pay 19s; meadow, 100 acres; pasture
      1 league long and ½ league wide; woodland 10 furlongs
      long and 5 wide.
    Of this land William holds 4½ hides, Osmund 4 hides, Hervey
    2 hides, Englishmen 5 hides and 1 virgate of land. The holders
    of these 15 hides and 3 virgates before 1066 could not be
    separated from the church. 12½ ploughs there.
Value of the church's lordship, £30; of what the men hold, £18.

2   The Church holds ASHTON itself. Before 1066 it paid tax
for 40 hides. Land for 37 ploughs. Of this land 10 hides
in lordship; 9 ploughs there; 8 slaves.

Ibi.xl.uilli 7 xxx.borđ cū.xx.cař.Ibi.iii.molini redđ.xxxii.

ſol.7 vi.deñ.7 c.ac̄ p̄ti.Paſtura.xix.q̃ᵹ lḡ.7 una q̃ᵹ lat.Silua

ii.leu lḡ.7 dimiđ leū lat.De eađ tra teñ Eduuard.iii.hiđ.

Wilts.i.hiđ.Angli.iiii.hiđ.Qui teneƀ T.R.E.ñ poteraꝭ ab æccła

Dñiū æcclæ.ualet.xxx.liƀ.Hōum û.vi.liƀ 7 xiii.ſol.⌠ ſeparari.

.XVI. Terra Æcclæ Ambresberiensis.

Eccła Ambresꝑeriens teñ *Boltintone*.T.R.E.geldƀ

p̄.xii.hiđ.Tra.ē.ix.cař.De hac tra ſt in dñio.vi.hidæ.

7 ibi.iii.cař.7 xiii.ſerui.Ibi.iii.uilli 7 xx.coſcez.7 iii.cotarij

cū.v.cař.Ibi.ii.molini redđ.lxv.ſoliđ.7 xxxv.ac̄ p̄ti.

Paſtura.i.leu lḡ.7 dim leū lat.   ⌠ ab æccła ſeparari.

De eađ tra teñ Aluuard.iii.hiđ.Qui teneƀ T.R.E.ñ poterat

Dñium abƀiſſæ.ualet.xiii.liƀ.Qđ tain teñ.ual.xv.ſoliđ.

Ipſa æccła teñ *Boscvbe*.T.R.E.geldƀ p̄.iiii.hiđ.Tra.ē.ii.

cař.De hac tra ſt in dñio.ii.hidæ 7 dimiđ.7 ibi.i.cař.cū.i.

ſeruo.Ibi.ii.uilli 7 v.coſcez.7 ii.cotar.cū.i.cař.⌠ 7 ual.iii.liƀ.

Ibi.iiii.ac̄ p̄ti.Paſtura.una q̃ᵹ lḡ.7 dimiđ q̃ᵹ lat.Valuit

Ipſa æccła teñ *Allentone*.T.R.E.geldƀ p̄.iiii.hiđ.Tra.ē

ii.cař.De hac tra ſt in dñio.iii.hidæ.una v min.7 ibi.i.cař.

7 iii.ſerui.Ibi.iii.uilli 7 v.coſcez.7 un cotar cū.i.cař.

Ibi.viii.ac̄ p̄ti.Paſtura.i.leu lḡ.7 una q̃ᵹ lat.Valuit.iii.liƀ.

Ipſa æccła teñ *Chelestanestone*.7 Aluuard⌠Modo.iiii.liƀ.

teñ de abƀiſſa.T.R.E.geldƀ p̄.ii.hiđ 7 dimiđ.Tra.ē.i.cař 7 dim.

7 tant̄ eſt ibi cū.ii.ſeruis.7 iii.coſcez.Ibi.viii.ac̄ p̄ti.

Paſtura.v.q̃ᵹ lḡ.7 una q̃ᵹ lat.Valuit.xxx.ſol.Modo.xl.ſol.

Ipſa æccła teneƀ.ii.hiđ T.R.E.7 poſt tenuit T.R.Wilti.7 ſunt

de uictu monialiū.Has teñ cōm moriton injuſte.

40 villagers and 30 smallholders with 20 ploughs.
3 mills which pay 32s 6d; meadow, 100 acres; pasture
    19 furlongs long and 1 furlong wide; woodland
    2 leagues long and ½ league wide.
Of this land Edward holds 3 hides, William 1 hide,
Englishmen 4 hides. The holders before 1066 could not
be separated from the church.
Value of the church's lordship, £30; of the men's, £6 13s.

16   LAND OF THE CHURCH OF AMESBURY   68 c

1 The Church of Amesbury holds BULFORD. Before 1066 it paid
tax for 12 hides. Land for 9 ploughs. Of this land 6 hides in
lordship; 3 ploughs there; 13 slaves.
    3 villagers, 20 Cottagers and 3 cottagers with 5 ploughs.
    2 mills which pay 65s; meadow, 35 acres; pasture 1 league
        long and ½ league wide.
Of this land Alfward holds 3 hides. The holder before 1066
    could not be separated from the church.
Value of the Abbess' lordship, £13; value of what the thane
holds, 15s.

2 The Church holds BOSCOMBE itself. Before 1066 it paid tax
for 4 hides. Land for 2 ploughs. Of this land 2½ hides in
lordship; 1 plough there, with 1 slave.
    2 villagers, 5 Cottagers and 2 cottagers with 1 plough.
    Meadow, 4 acres; pasture 1 furlong long and ½ furlong wide.
The value was and is £3.

3 The Church holds ALLINGTON itself. Before 1066 it paid tax
for 4 hides. Land for 2 ploughs. Of this land 3 hides, less 1
virgate, in lordship; 1 plough there; 3 slaves.
    3 villagers, 5 Cottagers and 1 cottager with 1 plough.
    Meadow, 8 acres; pasture 1 league long and 1 furlong wide.
The value was £3; now £4.

4 The Church holds CHOULSTON itself. Alfward holds from the
Abbess. Before 1066 it paid tax for 2½ hides. Land for 1½
ploughs; as many are there, with 2 slaves and
    3 Cottagers.
    Meadow, 8 acres; pasture 5 furlongs long and 1 furlong
        wide.
The value was 30s; now 40s.

5 ⊕ The Church held 2 hides itself before 1066, and it held them
after 1066. They are for the supplies of the nuns.
The Count of Mortain holds them wrongfully.

Ipſa æccła ten in *WINTREBVRNE* . vɪ . hiđ . Tra . ē . ɪɪɪɪ . car.

De hac tra ſt in dnĩo . ɪɪɪ . hidæ . 7 ibi . ɪɪɪ . car . 7 ɪɪ . ſerui . Ibi . v . uilłi

7 x . borđ cũ . ɪ . car . Ibi . ɪɪɪɪ . ãc pti . Paſtura dim leũ lg̃ . 7 tntđ lat.

Valuit . ɪɪɪɪ . liɓ . Modo . c . ſoliđ.

Ipſa æccła ten *WINTREBVRNE* . T . R . E . gelđɓ p . ɪɪɪɪ . hiđ 7 dim.

Tra . ē . ɪɪ . car . De hac tra ſt in dnĩo . ɪɪ . hidæ 7 dim . 7 ibi . ɪ . car.

Ibi . ɪɪɪɪ . uilłi . 7 ɪɪɪɪ . borđ 7 ɪɪ . cotar . cũ . ɪ . car . Ibi . vɪɪɪ . ãc pti.

7 x . ãc paſturæ . Valuit 7 ual . ɪɪɪɪ . liɓ.

.XVII. TERRA SC̃Æ MARIÆ DE BECH.

Eccła S̃ Mariæ de Bech ten de rege *DEVREL* . Brictric tenuit

T . R . E . 7 gelđɓ p . x . hiđ . Tra . ē . vɪɪ . car . De hac tra ſt in dnĩo

vɪ . hide 7 dimiđ . 7 ibi . ɪɪɪ . car . 7 vɪɪɪ . ſerui . Ibi . vɪɪɪ . uilłi 7 vɪɪ.

coſcez . 7 ɪɪ . borđ cũ . ɪɪɪɪ . car . Ibi molĩn de . xxx . den . 7 ɪɪɪɪ . ãc pti.

Paſtura . ɪ . leu lg̃ . 7 v . q̃z lat . Siluæ . ɪɪɪ . q̃z lg̃ . 7 ɪɪ . q̃z lat.

Æccła ejđ M̃ hɓ . ɪ . hiđ de eađ tra . Tot M̃ ualet . xɪɪ . liɓ.

Valɓ . xv . liɓ uiuente Mathilde . quæ deđ eiđ æccłæ.

.XVIII. TERRA GIRALDI DE WILTVNE.

Girald de Wiltune ten de rege *VPTONE* . in elemoſina.

Idẽ tenɓ T . R . E . 7 gelđɓ p . x . hiđ . Tra . ē . vɪ . car . De hac tra

ſt in dnĩo . vɪ . hiđ . 7 una virg 7 dĩm . 7 ibi . ɪɪɪ . car . 7 ɪɪɪɪ . ſerui.

Ibi . ɪx . uilłi 7 vɪ . borđ 7 ɪɪɪɪ . coſcez . cũ . ɪɪɪ . car . Ibi molĩn

rēdđ . xx . ſoliđ . 7 xv . ãc pti . Paſtura dimiđ leu lg̃ . 7 ɪɪ . q̃z

lat . Valet . x . liɓ.   REINBALDI.

Rᵖᵇʳainbald ten *LATONE* 7 *AISI* . Duo taini tenueʳ p . ɪɪ . M̃

T . R . E . Heralđ junxit in unũ . 7 gelđɓ p . ɪx . hiđ . Tra . ē . vɪɪɪ.

car . De hac tra ſt in dnĩo . ɪɪɪ . hidæ . . 7 vɪɪɪ . ſerui . Ibi . xv . uilłi

6   The Church holds 6 hides itself in WINTERBOURNE (Bassett).
Land for 4 ploughs. Of this land 3 hides in lordship; 3
ploughs there; 2 slaves.
>   5 villagers and 10 smallholders with 1 plough.
>   Meadow, 3 acres; pasture ½ league long and as wide.
The value was £4; now 100s.

7   The Church holds MADDINGTON itself. Before 1066 it paid
tax for 4½ hides. Land for 2 ploughs. Of this land 2½ hides
in lordship; 1 plough there.
>   4 villagers, 4 smallholders and 2 cottagers with 1 plough.
>   Meadow, 8 acres; pasture, 10 acres.
The value was and is £4.

17   LAND OF ST. MARY OF BEC

1   The Church of St. Mary of Bec holds (Brixton) DEVERILL from
the King. Brictric held it before 1066; it paid tax for 10 hides.
Land for 7 ploughs. Of this land 6½ hides in lordship; 3 ploughs
there; 8 slaves.
>   8 villagers, 7 Cottagers and 2 smallholders with 4 ploughs.
>   A mill at 30d; meadow, 4 acres; pasture 1 league long
>   and 5 furlongs wide; woodlands 3 furlongs long and
>   2 furlongs wide.
The church of this manor has 1 hide of this land.
Value of the whole manor, £12; value during the lifetime of
Queen Matilda, £15; she gave it to this church.

18   LAND OF GERALD OF WILTON

1   Gerald of Wilton holds UPTON (Lovell) in alms from the King;
he also held it before 1066. It paid tax for 10 hides.
Land for 6 ploughs. Of this land 6 hides and 1½ virgates
in lordship; 3 ploughs there; 4 slaves.
>   9 villagers, 6 smallholders and 4 Cottagers with 3 ploughs.
>   A mill which pays 20s; meadow, 15 acres; pasture ½ league
>   long and 2 furlongs wide.
Value £10.

[LAND] OF REINBALD

2   Reinbald the priest holds LATTON and EYSEY. Two thanes held
them as two manors before 1066. Earl Harold joined them into
one. It paid tax for 9 hides. Land for 8 ploughs. Of this land 3
hides in lordship; 8 slaves.

7 vi . borđ 7 iiii . cotar . cū . v . car̃ . 7 in dñio . iii . car̃ . Ibi . ii . molini

7 cc . ãc p̃ti . Paſtura . i . leu lḡ . 7 dim leu lat̃ . Valuit 7 ual . x .

.XIX.   CANONICI LISIACENSES.   ꟊ lib̃ .

CANONICI LISIACENS ten DEVREL . Eddeua tenuit T . R . E . 7 geldb̃

p̃ . iiii . hiđ . Tra . e̅ . iii . car̃ . De ea ſt in dñio . iii . hidæ 7 dim̃ . iii . aćs min

7 ibi . i . car̃ . 7 ii . ſerui . 7 vi . coſcez cū . i . uitło hñt . i . car̃ . Ibi . iii . ãc p̃ti .

Paſtura . iiii . q̃ɺ lḡ . 7 iii . q̃ɺ lat̃ . Valuit . xl . ſoł . Modo . lxx . ſoliđ .

ALWARD p̃br hł . v . hiđ q̃ ptiñ ad æcełam ALWARBERIE .

de elemoſina regis . Tra . e̅ . iii . car̃ . In dñio . e̅ . i . car̃ . 7 iiii . uiłti

7 viii . borđ cū . ii . car̃ . Ibi . x . ãc p̃ti . 7 iiii . q̃ɺ filuæ in lḡ . 7 iiii .

in lat̃ . Huic eiđ æcełæ adjacet . i . hida . q̃ nunq geldauit .

Tot̃ ualet . lxx . ſoliđ .   ꟊ Valet . xx . ſoliđ .

OSBERN p̃br hł . ii . hiđ de rege in æccła ALWARESBERIE .

AGENVLF ten HORNINGESHÃ . Pat̃ ej tenuit de rege . E . in elemoſina .

ibi . e̅ dimiđ hida . Tra . i . car̃ . Ibi . e̅ un coſcet 7 ii . ãc p̃ti . 7 ii . ãc filuæ .

    ꟊ Valet . v . ſoliđ .

68 d

.XX.   TERRA COMITIS MORITONIENSIS.

COMES MORITON ten ÇOWIC . 7 S̃ MARIA de Greſtain

de eo . T . R . E . geldb̃ p̃ x . hiđ . Tra . e̅ . iiii . car̃ . De hac

tra ſt in dñio . vi . hidæ 7 dimiđ . 7 ibi . ii . car̃ . 7 iii . ſerui .

Ibi . vi . uiłti 7 ix . borđ . cū . ii . car̃ . Ibi . xx . ãc p̃ti .

Paſtura . dimiđ leu lḡ . 7 iii . q̃ɺ lat̃ .

Valuit . viii . lib̃ . Modo . ix . lib̃ .

Idē cõm ten NECHENDVNE . 7 Giſlebt̃ de eo . Goduin̄

tenuit T . R . E . 7 geldb̃ p̃ . iii . hiđ . Tra . e̅ . ii . car̃ . De hac

tra ſt in dñio . ii . hiđ 7 ibi . i . car̃ . 7 ii . ſerui . Ibi . i . uiłts

7 viii . borđ . cū . i . car̃ . Ibi . xx . ãc p̃ti . 7 xv . ãc paſturæ .

Valuit . xxx . ualet m̃ . xl . ſot̃ .

15 villagers, 6 smallholders and 4 cottagers
with 5 ploughs; in lordship 3 ploughs.
2 mills; meadow, 200 acres; pasture 1 league long
and ½ league wide.
The value was and is £10.

19   THE CANONS OF LISIEUX

1   The Canons of Lisieux hold (Kingston) DEVERILL. Edith held it
before 1066; it paid tax for 4 hides. Land for 3 ploughs, of which
3½ hides, less 3 acres, in lordship; 1 plough there; 2 slaves.
6 Cottagers with 1 villager have 1 plough.
Meadow, 3 acres; pasture 4 furlongs long and 3 furlongs wide.
The value was 40s; now 70s.

2   Alfward the priest has 5 hides, which belong to the Church of
ALDERBURY, from the King's alms. Land for 3 ploughs.
In lordship 1 plough;
4 villagers and 8 smallholders with 2 ploughs.
Meadow, 10 acres; woodland, 4 furlongs in length and 4 in width.
To this church is attached 1 hide which has never paid tax.
Value of the whole, 70s.

3   Osbern the priest has 2 hides from the King in (the lands of) the
Church of ALDERBURY.
Value 20s.

4   Agenwulf holds HORNINGSHAM. His father held it from King
Edward in alms. ½ hide there. Land for 1 plough.
1 Cottager.
Meadow, 2 acres; woodland, 2 acres.
Value 5s.

20   LAND OF THE COUNT OF MORTAIN   68 d

1   The Count of Mortain holds CONOCK, and St. Mary's of Grestain
from him. Before 1066 it paid tax for 10 hides. Land for 4
ploughs. Of this land 6½ hides in lordship; 2 ploughs there; 3 slaves.
6 villagers and 9 smallholders with 2 ploughs.
Meadow, 20 acres; pasture ½ league long and 3 furlongs wide.
The value was £8; now £9.

2   The Count also holds NECHENDUNE and Gilbert from him. Godwin
held it before 1066; it paid tax for 3 hides. Land for 2 ploughs.
Of this land 2 hides in lordship; 1 plough there; 2 slaves.
1 villager and 8 smallholders with 1 plough.
Meadow, 20 acres; pasture, 15 acres.
The value was 30[s] ; now 40s.

Idē cōm ten *CLIVE*.7 Gisleƀt de eo. Goduin tenuit
T.R.E.7 geldƀ ꝑ. III. hid. Tra.ē.I.car 7 dim. In dīnio
eſt.I.car 7 II. ſerui.7 x. ac̄ pti. Valuit. xx. ſot. M. xl. ſot.
Idē cōm ten *CLIVE*.7 Gisleƀt de eo. Goduin tenuit T.R.E.
7 geldƀ ꝑ. IIII. hid una v̄ min. Tra.ē.I. car 7 dim. Ibi.ē un̄
uiƚƚs 7 III. borđ.7 xvi. ac̄ pti.7 xIIII. ac̄ paſture. Vaƚ. xl. ſot.
Ipſe cōm ten *LANGEFORD*. Chetel tenuit T.R.E.7 geldƀ
ꝑ. v. hid. Tra.ē. II. car 7 dim. De hac tra ſt in dīnio. IIII. hidæ
7 una v̄ træ.7 ibi. II. car. Ibi. II. uiƚƚi 7 IIII. borđ cū dim car.
Ibi dimid molīn redđ. xxx. den.7 xx. ac̄ pti.7 xxx. ac̄ paſturæ.
Valuit 7 uaƚ. c. ſolid.
Ipſe cōm ten *WINTRESLEV*. Harding tenuit T.R.E.7 geldƀ
ꝑ. vi. hid 7 dim. Tra.ē. vii. car. De hac tra ſt in dīnio. III.
hidæ 7 ibi. III. car.7 vi. ſerui. Ibi. vi. uiƚƚi 7 xii. coſcez.
cū. III. car. Ibi molīn de. v. ſot.7 III. ac̄ pti. Paſtura una
leu lḡ.7 tntđ lat. Silua. I. leu lḡ.7 dimiđ leu lat.
Valet. x. liƀ. ꝑ De hoc cō tenebat abƀiſſa ābreſberie   ☉
II. hid T.R.E.

.XXI.   TERRA ROGERIJ COMITIS.

COMES ROGERIVS ten *ETTGNE*. T.R.E. geldƀ ꝑ. xv. hid.
Tra.ē. xii. car. De hac tra medietas.ē in dīnio.7 ibi. III. car
7 dimiđ.7 vi. ſerui. Ibi. viii. uiƚƚi 7 viii. coſcez. cū. v. car.
Ibi molīn redđ. xv. ſot 7 vi. den.7 c. ac̄ pti. Paſtura
vi. q̇ lḡ.7 III. q̇ lat. Valuit. xv. liƀ. T.R.E. Modo. xii. liƀ.
Ipſe cōm ten *MILDESTONE*. T.R.E. geldƀ ꝑ. III. hid 7 dim.
Tra.ē. II. car. De hac tra ſt in dīnio. II. hidæ.7 ibi. I. car.
7 III. uiƚƚi 7 v. coſcez cū. I. car.7 dim. Ibi. viii. ac̄ pti. Paſ
tura. I. leu lḡ.7 III. q̇ lat. Valuit 7 uaƚ. lxx. ſolid.
H̄. II. cō ten Turold de comite. Oſmund^{tainus} tenuit T.R.E.

3   The Count also holds CLYFFE (Pypard) and Gilbert from him.
    Godwin held it before 1066; it paid tax for 3 hides.
    Land for 1½ ploughs. In lordship 1 plough; 2 slaves.
        Meadow, 10 acres.
    The value was 20s; now 40s.

4   The Count also holds CLYFFE (Pypard) and Gilbert from him.
    Godwin held it before 1066; it paid tax for 4 hides,
    less 1 virgate. Land for 1½ ploughs.
        1 villager and 3 smallholders.
        Meadow, 16 acres; pasture, 14 acres.
    Value 40s.

5   The Count holds LANGFORD himself. Ketel held it before 1066;
    it paid tax for 5 hides. Land for 2½ ploughs. Of this land 4
    hides and 1 virgate of land in lordship; 2 ploughs there.
        2 villagers and 4 smallholders with ½ plough.
        ½ mill which pays 30d; meadow, 20 acres; pasture, 30 acres.
    The value was and is 100s.

6   The Count holds WINTERSLOW himself. Harding held it before
    1066; it paid tax for 6½ hides. Land for 7 ploughs.
    Of this land 3 hides in lordship; 3 ploughs there; 6 slaves.
        6 villagers and 12 Cottagers with 3 ploughs.
        A mill at 5s; meadow, 3 acres; pasture 1 league long and
            as wide; woodland 1 league long and ½ league wide.
    Value £10.   ⊕
    The Abbess of Amesbury held 2 hides of this manor before 1066.

21   **LAND OF EARL ROGER**

1   Earl Roger holds (Castle) EATON. Before 1066 it paid tax
    for 15 hides. Land for 12 ploughs. Of this land half is
    in lordship; 3½ ploughs there; 6 slaves.
        8 villagers and 8 Cottagers with 5 ploughs.
        A mill which pays 15s 6d; meadow, 100 acres; pasture
            6 furlongs long and 3 furlongs wide.
    Value before 1066, £15; now £12.

2   The Earl holds MILSTON himself. Before 1066 it paid tax
    for 3½ hides. Land for 2 ploughs. Of this land 2 hides in
    lordship; 1 plough there;
        3 villagers and 5 Cottagers with 1½ ploughs.
        Meadow, 8 acres; pasture 1 league long and 3 furlongs wide.
    The value was and is 70s.
        Thorold holds these two manors from the Earl. Osmund,
    a thane, held them before 1066.

Idē cõm ten *POLTONE* . Siuuard̃ tenuit T.R.E.7 geldb̃ ꝑ.v.
hid̃ . Tra̅.e̅.viii.car̃. De hac tra̅.ſt in dñio.iii.hidæ 7 dimid̃.
7 ibi .iiii.car̃.7 viii.ſerui.7 viii.uilli 7 vii.coſcez.cũ.iiii.
car̃.Ibi.xv.a̅c ꝑti.Paſtura.iii.q̊ʒ lg̅.7 una q̊ʒ lat̃.
Valuit.xii.lib̃.Modo.xvi.lib̃.

.XXII. TERRA HVGONIS COMITIS.

COMES HVGO ten̄ *RETMORE*.7 Willſ de eo.T.R.E.geldb̃
ꝑ dimid̃ hida.Tra̅.e̅.iii.car̃.In dñio ſt.ii.car̃.cũ.i.ſeruo.
Ibi.i.uilłſ 7 iii.bord̃ 7 xi.coſcez cũ.i.car̃.Ibi moliñ redd̃
xiiii.ſoł.7 v.a̅c ꝑti.Paſtura.iii.q̊ʒ lg̅.7 una q̊ʒ lat̃.
Silua.iii.q̊ʒ lg̅.7 ii.q̊ʒ lat̃.Valuit.l.ſoł.Modo.lx.ſolid̃.
Idem cõm ten *WIFLESFORDE*.7 Haimo de eo.T.R.E.geldb̃
ꝑ.i.hida.Tra̅.e̅.i.car̃.7 ipſa.e̅ in dñio.7 ii.ſerui.7 iii.coſcez.
Ibi.vi.a̅c ꝑti.Paſtura.viii.q̊ʒ lg̅.7 una q̊ʒ lat̃.Vał.xl.ſoł.
Idē cõm ten̄ *HEORTHA̅*.7 Eduuard̃ de eo.T.R.E.geldb̃
ꝑ.ii.hid̃.Tra̅.e̅.iii.car̃.De hac tra una hida.e̅ in dñio.
7 ibi.ii.car̃.7 ii.ſerui.Ibi.i.miles.7 iii.coſcez.7 v.a̅c ꝑti.
7 iii.a̅c ſiluæ.7 xii.a̅c paſturæ.Vał.xl.ſoł.
Idē cõm ten̄ *BREDECVBE*.7 Haimo de eo.T.R.E.geldb̃
ꝑ.iiii.hid̃.Tra̅.e̅.ii.car̃.De hac tra ſt in dñio.iii.hidæ.
69 a
7 ibi.i.car̃.cũ.i.ſeruo.Ibi.i.uilłſ 7 iiii.bord̃ 7 moliñ de.x.ſoł.
7 vi.a̅c ꝑti.7 x.a̅c ſiluæ.7 xx.a̅c paſturæ.
Valuit.iii.lib̃.Modo.iiii.lib̃.
Idē cõm ten̄ *CADEHA̅*.7 Willſ de eo.T.R.E.geldb̃ ꝑ.ii.hid̃.
Tra̅.e̅.ii.car̃.De his.i.hida in dñio.7 i.car̃.7 ii.ſerui.7 viii.
bord̃ cũ.i.car̃.Ibi.v.a̅c ꝑti.Silua.ii.q̊ʒ lg̅.7 una q̊ʒ lat̃.
Valuit.xxx.ſoł.Modo.xl.ſoł.
H̅.v.Man̄ tenuit Ednod dapifer T.R.E.

3   The Earl also holds POULTON. Siward held it before 1066;
it paid tax for 5 hides. Land for 8 ploughs. Of this land 3½ hides
in lordship; 4 ploughs there; 8 slaves;
>8 villagers and 7 Cottagers with 4 ploughs.
>Meadow, 15 acres; pasture 3 furlongs long and 1 furlong wide.
The value was £12; now £16.

22   LAND OF EARL HUGH

1   Earl Hugh holds RETMORE and William from him. Before 1066
it paid tax for ½ hide. Land for 3 ploughs. In lordship 2
ploughs with 1 slave.
>1 villager, 3 smallholders and 11 Cottagers with 1 plough.
>A mill which pays 14s; meadow, 5 acres; pasture 3
>furlongs long and 1 furlong wide; woodland 3 furlongs
>long and 2 furlongs wide.
The value was 50s; now 60s.

The Earl also holds

2   WILSFORD. Haimo holds from him. Before 1066 it paid tax
for 1 hide. Land for 1 plough; it is in lordship; 2 slaves;
>3 Cottagers.
>Meadow, 6 acres; pasture 8 furlongs long and 1 furlong wide.
Value 40s.

3   HARTHAM. Edward holds from him. Before 1066 it paid tax
for 2 hides. Land for 3 ploughs. Of this land 1 hide in
lordship; 2 ploughs there; 2 slaves.
>1 man-at-arms and 3 Cottagers.
>Meadow, 5 acres; woodland, 3 acres; pasture, 12 acres.
Value 40s.

4   BURCOMBE. Haimo holds from him. Before 1066 it paid tax
for 4 hides. Land for 2 ploughs. Of this land 3 hides in
lordship; 1 plough there, with 1 slave.   69 a
>1 villager and 4 smallholders.
>A mill at 10s; meadow, 6 acres; woodland, 10 acres;
>pasture, 20 acres.
The value was £3; now £4.

5   CADENHAM. William holds from him. Before 1066 it paid tax
for 2 hides. Land for 2 ploughs. In lordship 1 hide
of these; 1 plough; 2 slaves;
>8 smallholders with 1 plough.
>Meadow, 5 acres; woodland 2 furlongs long and 1 furlong wide.
The value was 30s; now 40s.

Before 1066 Ednoth the Steward held these five manors.

Idē Cõ ten̄ *FISCARTONE* .7 Haimo de eo . Godric̾ tenuit
T.R.E.7 geldb̄ ꝑ . III . hid̄ . Tra . ē . II . car . In dn̄io ſt . II . hidæ
de hac tra.7 ibi . I . car.7 I . ſeruus . Ibi . III . uilli.7 v . bord̄.
7 molin̄ de . x . ſol.7 xl . ac̄ ꝓti.7 xl . ac̄ paſturæ
Valuit 7 ual . III . lib̄.

.XXIII. TERRA QVÆ FVIT ALBERICI COMITIS.

COMES ALBERICVS tenuit *CONTONE* . T.R.E. geldb̄ ꝑ . VII .
hid̄ . Tra . ē . VI . car̄ . De qua ſuɴ in dn̄io . III . hidæ 7 una v̾
træ.7 ibi . I . car̄.7 VI . ſerui . Ibi . v . uilli 7 v . coſcez . cũ . III. car̄.
Ibi molin̄ de . x . ſol.7 v . ac̄ ꝓti . Paſtura . III . q̂z lḡ.7 una q̂z
lat̄ . Valuit 7 ual . x . lib̄.

DERINTONE geldb̄ T.R.E. ꝑ una hida 7 dim̄ . Tra . ē . I . car̄ .
In dn̄io . ē . I . hida.7 alia tra̅ hn̄t ibi . IIII . coſcez . Ibi . v . ac̄ ꝓti.
In ipſa uilla . ē una hida . Tra . I . car̄ . Hanc tenuit un̄ tain̾
T.R.E. Ibi . ē un̾ bord̄ 7 v . ac̄ ꝓti . Hæ . II . hidæ 7 dim̄ . ual . IIII . lib̄.
WINTRESLEI geldb̄ T.R.E. ꝑ . II . hid̄ . Tra . ē . II . car̄ . Ibi eſt
un̾ uills 7 III . bord̄.7 Silua . I . q̂z lḡ.7 dim̄ q̂z lat̄ . Val . xx . ſol.
ALBOLDINTONE geldb̄ ꝑ . III . hid̄ . Tra . ē . II . car̄ . In dn̄io ſt
II . hidæ de hac tra 7 dimid̄.7 ibi . I . car̄.7 IIII . coſcez . Ibi . xxxv .
ac̄ ꝓti.7 Paſtura . III . q̂z lḡ.7 una q̂z lat̄ . Valet . IIII . lib̄.
CHELTRE geldb̄ T.R.E. ꝑ . VI . hid̄ . Tra . ē . v . car̄ . De hac tra
ſt in dn̄io . III . hidæ.7 ibi . I . car̄.7 IIII . ſerui . Ibi . IIII . uilli 7 II.
bord̄ cũ . II . car̄ . Paſtura . IIII . q̂z lḡ.7 II . q̂z lat̄ . Valuit . IIII . lib̄.
TEDRINTONE geldb̄ T.R.E. ꝑ . II . hid̄ . Tra . ē . II . car̄ ⎰ m̄ . VI . lib̄.
Ibi . ē un̾ uills 7 dimid̄ molin̄ redd̄ xxx . den.7 v . ac̄ ꝓti . Val . xx.
Has . VI . tras tenuit Harding̾ T.R.E.   ⎰ ſolid̄.

6   FISHERTON (Anger). Haimo holds from him. Godric held it
before 1066; it paid tax for 3 hides. Land for 2 ploughs.
In lordship 2 hides of this land; 1 plough there; 1 slave.
    3 villagers and 5 smallholders.
    A mill at 10s; meadow, 40 acres; pasture, 40 acres.
The value was and is £3.

23   LAND WHICH WAS EARL AUBREY'S

1   Earl Aubrey held COMPTON. Before 1066 it paid tax for 7 hides.
Land for 6 ploughs, of which 3 hides and 1 virgate of land
in lordship; 1 plough there; 6 slaves.
    5 villagers and 5 Cottagers with 3 ploughs,
    A mill at 10s; meadow, 5 acres; pasture 3 furlongs long
      and 1 furlong wide.
The value was and is £10.

2   DURRINGTON paid tax for 1½ hides before 1066. Land for 1 plough.
In lordship 1 hide.
    4 Cottagers have the rest of the land.
    Meadow, 5 acres.
    There is also 1 hide in the village. Land for 1 plough.
    A thane held it before 1066.
      1 smallholder.
      Meadow, 5 acres.
Value of these 2½ hides, £4.

3   WINTERSLOW paid tax for 2 hides before 1066. Land for 2 ploughs.
    1 villager and 3 smallholders.
    Woodland 1 furlong long and ½ furlong wide.
Value 20s.

4   ABLINGTON paid tax for 3 hides. Land for 2 ploughs.
In lordship 2½ hides of this land; 1 plough there;
    4 Cottagers.
    Meadow, 35 acres; pasture 3 furlongs long and 1 furlong wide.
Value £4.

5   CHITTERNE paid tax for 6 hides before 1066. Land for 5 ploughs.
Of this land 3 hides in lordship; 1 plough there; 4 slaves.
    4 villagers and 2 smallholders with 2 ploughs.
    Pasture 4 furlongs long and 2 furlongs wide.
The value was £4; now £6.

6   TYTHERINGTON paid tax for 2 hides before 1066. Land for 2 ploughs.
    1 villager.
    ½ mill which pays 30d; meadow, 5 acres.
Value 20s.

Harding held these six lands before 1066.

ALENTONE geldb̄ T.R.E. p̄ . ɪɪɪɪ . hid̄ . Tra . ē . ɪɪ . car̄ . In dn̄io

ſt . ɪɪ . hidæ 7 dim̄ de hac tra . 7 ibi . ē . ɪ . car̄ . 7 ɪɪɪ . ſerui . Ibi . ɪ . uilłs

7 ɪɪɪɪ . coſcez cū . ɪ . car̄ . Ibi molin̄ redd̄ . xx . ſoł . 7 v . ac̄ p̄ti .

Paſtura . ɪɪɪ . q̇ʒ łg . 7 una q̇ʒ łat̄ . Hanc tra tenuit Herald.

in ead uilla ſuꞥ . ɪɪɪɪ . hidæ træ . quas injuſte abſtrax̄ Herald ab

æccła Ambreſberie . teſtimonio tainoʒ ſciræ . M̄ tam̄ ħt æccła.

ELECOME geldb̄ T.R.E. p̄ . xx . hid̄ . 7 vɪɪ . Tra . ē . vɪɪɪ . car̄ .

De hac tra ſt in dn̄io . xxɪɪɪɪ . hidæ . 7 ibi . ɪɪ . car̄ . 7 vɪ . ſerui.

Ibi . ɪɪɪ . uiłti 7 xɪɪɪɪ . bord̄ cū . ɪɪɪ . car̄ . Ibi . ʟx . ac̄ p̄ti . 7 tntd̄ .

paſturæ . 7 xx . ac̄ ſiluæ . Valuit . xxvɪɪ . lib̄ . Modo . xx . lib̄.

STRADFORD . geldb̄ T.R.E. p̄ . xɪɪɪ . hid̄ . Tra . ē . vɪɪ . car̄ .

De hac tra ſt in dn̄io . ɪx . hidæ 7 una v̄ træ . 7 ibi . ɪɪ . car̄ . 7 vɪɪ.

ſerui . Ibi . vɪ . uiłti 7 ɪɪɪɪ . bord̄ 7 x . coſcez . cū . ɪɪɪɪ . car̄.

Ibi . ɪɪ . molini redd̄ . xvɪɪ . ſoł 7 vɪ . den̄ . 7 xv . ac̄ p̄ti . 7 ɪɪ . ac̄

paſture juxta ſlum̄ . 7 alia paſtura . ɪ . łeū łg . 7 vɪ . q̇ʒ łat̄.

In Wiltune . ɪ . burḡſis redd̄ . xx . denar̄ . p̄tin huic ꝋ.

Valet . xx . lib̄.

GESSIC geldb̄ T.R.E. p̄ x . hid̄ . Tra . ē . xɪɪ . car̄ . De hac tra

ſt in dn̄io . ɪɪɪɪ . hidæ 7 dim̄ . 7 ibi . ɪɪ . car̄ . 7 vɪɪɪ . ſerui . Ibi . v . uiłti

7 vɪɪɪ . bord̄ cū . ɪɪɪɪ . car̄ . Ibi . xʟ . ac̄ p̄ti . Paſtura . ɪ . łeū łg.

7 dimid̄ łeū łat̄ . 7 tntd̄ ſiluæ . Valuit . xʟ . lib̄ q̇ Albic̄ recep̄.

Modo . x . lib̄ . H̄ . ɪɪɪ . Maner̄ tenuit Azor . T.R.E.

Tota ħ tra fuit Albici comit̄ . Modo . ē in manu regis.

REDDITVS EDWARDI SARISBER̄.

*E*DWARD uicecom' ħt p̄ ann̄ de denar̄ q̇ p̄tin ad uicecomitat̄ . cxxx . porc̄ .

7 xxxɪɪ . bacons . Frum̄ti . ɪɪ . mod̄ 7 vɪɪɪ . ſextar̄ . 7 tntd̄ braſij.

Auenæ . v . mod̄ 7 ɪɪɪɪ . ſextar̄ . Mellis . xvɪ . ſextar̄ . uel p melle xvɪ . ſolid̄.

Gallinas . cccc . 7 qt tas xx . Oua a 7 ti mille 7 ſexcenta . Caſeos . cen̄t . Agnos .

. ʟ . ɪɪ . Vellera ouiū os . cc . xʟ ta . Annonæ . c . ʟxɪɪ . ac̄s . ɪ . Bled

Habet etiā qt a 7 xx ti . libras ualeꝭ int̄ Rcueland 7 qd̄ inde ħt.

Q̇do p̄poſitis firma deficit . neceſſe . ē Eduuardo reſtaurare de

ꝟ ſuo.

69 a

7   ALLINGTON paid tax for 4 hides before 1066. Land for 2 ploughs. In lordship 2½ hides of this land; 1 plough there; 3 slaves.
> 1 villager and 4 Cottagers with 1 plough.
> A mill which pays 20s; meadow, 5 acres; pasture 3 furlongs long and 1 furlong wide.
> Earl Harold held this land.
> Also in this town are 4 hides of land which Harold wrongfully took away from the Church of Amesbury, according to the evidence of the thanes of the Shire; but now the Church has it.

8   ELCOMBE paid tax for 20 hides and 7 before 1066. Land for 8 ploughs. Of this land 24 hides in lordship; 2 ploughs there; 6 slaves.
> 3 villagers and 14 smallholders with 3 ploughs.
> Meadow, 60 acres; pasture, as much; woodland, 20 acres.
> The value was £27; now £20.

9   STRATFORD (Tony) paid tax for 13 hides before 1066. Land for 7 ploughs. Of this land 9 hides and 1 virgate of land in lordship; 2 ploughs there; 7 slaves.
> 6 villagers, 4 smallholders and 10 Cottagers with 4 ploughs.
> 2 mills which pay 17s 6d; meadow, 15 acres; pasture, 2 acres near to the river; another pasture 1 league long and 6 furlongs wide.
> In Wilton a burgess who pays 20d belongs to this manor.
> Value £20.

10   GUSSAGE paid tax for 10 hides before 1066. Land for 12 ploughs. Of this land 4½ hides in lordship; 2 ploughs there; 8 slaves.
> 5 villagers and 8 smallholders with 4 ploughs.
> Meadow, 40 acres; pasture 1 league long and ½ league wide; woodland, as much.
> The value was £40, when Aubrey acquired it; now £10.

Azor held these three manors before 1066. All this land was Earl Aubrey's; now it is in the King's hands.

24 p   **PAYMENTS OF EDWARD OF SALISBURY**

Edward the Sheriff has, each year, from the money which belongs to the shrievalty, 130 pigs; 32 bacon-pigs; of wheat 2 pecks and 8 sesters; as much malt; of oats 5 pecks and 4 sesters; of honey 16 sesters or, instead of honey, 16s; 480 chickens; 1600 eggs; 100 cheeses; 52 lambs; 240 fleeces; 1 (crop of) standing corn, 162 acres. He also has £80 worth between the Reeveland and what he has from it. When the reeves are short of revenue Edward has to make it up from his own.

TERRA EJVSDEM EDVVARDI SARISB.

.XXII. EDWARD de Sarisberie ten de rege *WILCOTE* . T . R . E . geldb̄
p̄ . xv . hiđ 7 dim̄ . Tra . ē . x . car̄ . De hac tra f̄t in dn̄io . vii .
hidæ . 7 ibi . iii . car̄ . 7 vi . ſerui . Ibi . xviiii . uiłłi 7 vi . borđ 7 xii .
coſcez.　　　　Ibi . xl . ac̄ p̄ti . 7 xx . ac̄ paſturæ . 7 l . ac̄ ſiluæ
minutæ . 7 æccła noua 7 dom obtima 7 uinea bona.
Valuit . xii . lib̄ . Modo . xvi . lib̄ .

Idē Edw̄ . ten *AVLTONE* . T . R . E . geldb̄ p̄ . v . hiđ . Tra . ē . iiii . car̄ .
In dn̄io f̄t . ii . car̄ . 7 iiii . ſerui . Ibi . iii . uiłłi 7 i . borđ . 7 vi . coſcez .
cū . i . car̄ . Ibi molin redđ . x . ſoł . 7 xxv . ac̄ p̄ti . Paſtura . iii . q̃ȝ
lḡ . 7 ii . q̃ȝ lat̄ . Valuit . c . ſoł . Modo . vi . lib̄ .

Idē . Edw ten *ECESATINGETONE* . T . R . E gelđb̄ p̄ . vii . hiđ . Tra . ē
iiii . car̄ . De hac tra f̄t in dn̄io . iiii . hidæ . 7 ibi . iii . car̄ . Ibi . xii .
borđ . 7 vi . cotar̄ . 7 ii . francig tenent . ii . hiđ 7 unā v̄ tre . 7 hn̄t
. ii . car̄ . Ibi . vi . ac̄ p̄ti . 7 l . ac̄ paſturæ . Valuit . vi . lib̄ .
Modo dn̄ium Edw̄ . vi . lib̄ 7 dim̄ . Francig . xl . ſoliđ .

Idē . E . ten *EDINTONE* . T . R . E . geldb̄ p̄ . x . hiđ . Tra . ē . vi . car̄ .
In dn̄io f̄t . iii . car̄ . 7 iiii . ſerui . Ibi . ix . uiłłi 7 ii . cotar̄ . 7 xxiiii .
coſcez . cū . iii . car̄ . Ibi . x . ac̄ p̄ti . 7 viii . ac̄ paſturæ . 7 viii . ac̄
ſiluæ . Valuit . viii . lib̄ . Modo . xii . lib̄ . Herald tenuit .

Idē . E . ten . vi . hiđ in *HVND* de *WRDERVSTESELLE* . 7 p̄ . vi .
hiđ geldb̄ . T . R . E . Tra . ē . iii . car̄ . In dn̄io f̄t . ii . car̄ . 7 iiii . uiłłi
7 ii . coſcez cū . i . car̄ . Ibi molin redđ . xviii . den . 7 xxiiii . ac̄ p̄ti .
7 una q̃ȝ paſturæ . Valuit . c . ſoł . Modo . vi . lib̄ . Briſtric tenuit .
Huarđ ten de Eduuardo .

Idē ten in *ROTEFELD* . i . hiđ . Aluric tenuit T . R . E . 7 p̄ . i . hida
geldb̄ . Herueus ten de Edw̄ . Tra . ē dim̄ car̄ . Ibi . iii . borđ .
7 iiii . ac̄ p̄ti . Paſtura dim̄ q̃ȝ lḡ . 7 tn̄tđ lat̄ . Vał . xv . ſoliđ .

1   Edward of Salisbury holds WILCOT from the King. Before 1066 it paid tax for 15½ hides. Land for 10 ploughs. Of this land 7 hides in lordship; 3 ploughs there; 6 slaves.
     19 villagers, 6 smallholders and 12 Cottagers.....
     Meadow, 40 acres; pasture, 20 acres; underwood, 50 acres;
       a new church; a very good house; a good vineyard.
The value was £12; now £16.

   Edward also holds

2   ALTON (Barnes). Before 1066 it paid tax for 5 hides.
Land for 4 ploughs. In lordship 2 ploughs; 4 slaves.
     3 villagers, 1 smallholder and 6 Cottagers with 1 plough.
     A mill which pays 10s; meadow, 25 acres; pasture 3 furlongs
       long and 2 furlongs wide.
The value was 100s; now £6.

3   ETCHILHAMPTON. Before 1066 it paid tax for 7 hides. Land for 4 ploughs. Of this land 4 hides in lordship; 3 ploughs there.
     12 smallholders, 6 cottagers and 2 Frenchmen who hold 2 hides
       and 1 virgate of land; they have 2 ploughs.
     Meadow, 6 acres; pasture, 50 acres.
The value was £6; now Edward's lordship, £6½;
the Frenchmen's, 40s.

4   HEDDINGTON. Before 1066 it paid tax for 10 hides. Land for 6 ploughs. In lordship 3 ploughs; 4 slaves.
     9 villagers, 2 cottagers and 24 Cottagers with 3 ploughs.
     Meadow, 10 acres; pasture, 8 acres; woodland, 8 acres.
The value was £8; now £12.
     Earl Harold held it.

5   6 hides in the Hundred of HIGHWORTH (at)LUS HILL.
It paid tax for 6 hides before 1066. Land for 3 ploughs.
In lordship 2 ploughs;
     4 villagers and 2 Cottagers with 1 plough.
     A mill which pays 18d; meadow, 24 acres; pasture 1 furlong.
The value was 100s; now £6.
     Brictric held it. Howard holds from Edward.

6   He also holds 1 hide in RATFYN. Aelfric held it before 1066; it paid tax for 1 hide. Hervey holds from Edward. Land for ½ plough.
     3 smallholders.
     Meadow, 4 acres; pasture ½ furlong long and as wide.
Value 15s.

Idē Edw ten *WINTREBVRNE* . Vlueua|tenuit 7 geldꝃ ꝑ.III.
hiđ.Tra.ē.III.caꝵ. Godefrid ten de Edw. De hac tra ten.II.hiđ
in dñio 7 ibi.II.caꝵ.7 IIII.ſerui.Ibi.IIII.uitti 7 IIII.borđ cū.I.caꝵ.
Ibi moliñ redđ.V.ſoliđ.7 VI.ać ꝑti.7 XXX.ać ſiluæ. Paſtura
VI.q̒ƶ lḡ.7 IIII.q̒ƶ laꝱ.Valuit 7 uaꝲ.III.liꝃ.

Idē.E.ten in *WINTREBVRNESTOCH*.I.hiđ 7 dim.7 Walter
ten de eo.Tra.ē.I.caꝵ.quæ ibi.ē.Valet.XXX.ſoliđ.

Idē.E.ten in eađ uilla.I.hiđ.Tra.I.caꝵ.Walter ten de Edw.
Ibi hꝱ.I.caꝵ cū.II.cotaꝵ.7 I.ać ꝑti.7 VI.ać paſturæ.
Valet.XX.ſoꝲ.Aluuius tenuit T.R.E.Cuj uxor ibiđ tenet hiđ
dimiđ de rege.

Idē.E.ten *WINTREBVRNE*.Alric tenuit T.R.E.7 geldꝃ
ꝑ.XIII.hiđ 7 III.virg.Tra.ē.VII.caꝵ.De hac tra ſꝱ in dñio
VII.hidæ.7 ibi.IIII.caꝵ.7 VII.ſerui.Ibi.XII.uitti 7 **v**.borđ
cū.III.caꝵ.Ibi.X.ać ꝑti.Paſtura.I.leū lḡ.7 dim leu laꝲ.
Valuit.VI.liꝃ.Modo.X.liꝃ.

Idē.E.ten *ORCESTONE*.Hugo de eo.Godric tenuit T.R.E.7 geldꝃ
ꝑ.IIII.hiđ 7 dim.Tra.ē.II.caꝵ.In dñio.ē una caꝵ.7 IIII.borđ cū
IIII.ſeruis hñt.I.caꝵ.Ibi paſtura.VIII.q̒ƶ lḡ.7 II.q̒ƶ laꝲ.Valuit
Witts ten de.E.in Orceſtone.II.hiđ.Aluuin tenuit⎰III.liꝃ.ṁ.II.liꝃ.
T.R.E.Tra.ē.I.caꝵ.quæ ibi.ē cū.I.borđ 7 III.ſeruis.7 qt XX.ać
paſturæ.Valuit.XX.ſoꝲ.Modo.XXX.

Ipſe.E.ten *TODOWRDE*.Aluuard tenuit T.R.E.7 geldꝃ ꝑ.IIII.hiđ.
Tra.ē.II.caꝵ.In dñio ſꝱ.III.hidæ de eađ 7 ibi.II.caꝵ.7 III.ſerui.
Ibi.I.uitts 7 II.coſcez.cū dim caꝵ.Paſtura.IIII.q̒ƶ lḡ.7 III.q̒ƶ laꝲ.
Valuit.L.ſoliđ.Modo.LX.ſoliđ.

In Todeuuorde.ē una v̊ træ.quā Croc diratiocinauit ſibi
ꝑtinere deꝃe.Hanc.taṁ ten Eduuard.

Edward also holds

7 SHREWTON. Wulfeva held it before 1066; it paid tax for 3 hides.
Land for 3 ploughs. Godfrey holds from Edward. Of this land
he holds 2 hides in lordship; 2 ploughs there; 4 slaves.
  4 villagers and 4 smallholders with 1 plough.
  A mill which pays 5s; meadow, 6 acres; woodland, 30 acres;
    pasture 6 furlongs long and 4 furlongs wide.
The value was and is £3.

8 in WINTERBOURNE STOKE 1½ hides. Walter holds from him.
Land for 1 plough, which is there.
Value 30s.

9 in the same town 1 hide. Land for 1 plough. Walter holds
from Edward. He has 1 plough, with
  2 cottagers.
  Meadow, 1 acre; pasture, 6 acres.
Value 20s.
  Alfwy held it before 1066; his wife also holds 1½ hides
from the King there.

10 SHREWTON. Alric held it before 1066; it paid tax for 13 hides
and 3 virgates. Land for 7 ploughs. Of this land 7 hides
in lordship; 4 ploughs there; 7 slaves.
  12 villagers and 5 smallholders with 3 ploughs.
  Meadow, 10 acres; pasture 1 league long and ½ league wide.
The value was £6; now £10.

11 ORCHESTON. Hugh holds from him. Godric held it before 1066;
it paid tax for 4½ hides. Land for 2 ploughs. In lordship 1 plough.
  4 smallholders with 4 slaves have 1 plough.
  Pasture 8 furlongs long and 2 furlongs wide.
The value was £3; now £4.

12 William holds 2 hides from Edward in ORCHESTON. Alwin
held them before 1066. Land for 1 plough which is there , with
  1 smallholder and 3 slaves.
  Pasture, 80 acres.
The value was 20s; now 30[s].

13 Edward holds (North) TIDWORTH himself. Alfward held it before
1066; it paid tax for 4 hides. Land for 2 ploughs. In
lordship 3 hides of this (land); 2 ploughs there; 3 slaves.
  1 villager and 2 Cottagers with ½ plough.
  Pasture 4 furlongs long and 3 furlongs wide.
The value was 50s; now 60s.

14 In (North) TIDWORTH 1 virgate of land which Croc proved ought
to belong to him; Edward holds it, however.

Ipſe . E . ten̄ *LITLEGARSELE* . Eluuard tenuit T . R . E . 7 geldƀ ⅋ . I .
hida . Tra . ē . III . car̄ . In dn̄io ſt . II . car̄ . 7 III . ſerui . 7 VIII . coſcez .
cū . I . car̄ . Ibi paſtura . III . q̃ʒ lḡ . 7 una q̃ʒ lat̄ . Silua dim̄ leū
lḡ . 7 II . q̃ʒ lat̄ . Valuit . c . ſolid . Modo . VI . liƀ 7 x . ſol .
Oſmund ten̄ de . E . *AMBRESBERIE* . Vlmer tenuit T . R . E . 7 geldƀ
⅋ . I . hida . Tra . ē . I . car̄ . Ibi ſt . III . coſcez 7 VI . ac̄ p̄ti . Paſtura
. II . q̃ʒ lḡ . 7 dim̄ q̃ʒ lat̄ . Valuit . x . ſol . Modo . xx . ſolid .

69 c

Idē Oſmund ten̄ de . Edw . III . v̄ træ q̄ adjac̄ Ambresƀiæ . Tra
ē . I . car̄ . q̄ ibi . ē cū . II . coſcez 7 III . ſeruis . Vn̄ anglic̄ ten̄ de ead̄
tra . I . virg 7 dim̄ . 7 ibi h̄t dim̄ car̄ . 7 I . coſcet . 7 III . ſeruos .
Tot̄ ual . xL . ſolid . Alric 7 Cole tenuer̄ . T . R . E .
Ipſe . E . ten̄ *DEVREL* . 7 Adelelm̄ de eo . Saulf tenuit T . R . E .
7 geldƀ ⅋ . IIII . hid̄ . Tra . ē . II . car̄ . In dn̄io . II . hidæ 7 dim̄ de ead̄
tra . 7 ibi . II . car̄ . cū . I . ſeruo . Ibi . I . uitts 7 IX . coſcez . cū . I . car̄ .
Ibi . II . ac̄ p̄ti . 7 III . ac̄ ſiluæ . paſtura . III . q̃ʒ lḡ . 7 II . q̃ʒ lat̄ .
Valuit . xL . ſol . Modo . Lx . ſolid .
Ipſe . E . ten̄ *STOCHE* . Stremius tenuit T . R . E . 7 geldƀ ⅋ . xvi .
hid̄ 7 una v̄ . Tra . ē . x . car̄ . De hac ſt in dn̄io . VII . hidæ 7 dim̄ .
7 ibi . IIII . car̄ . 7 II . ſerui . Ibi . VIII . uitti 7 xvi . bord 7 xvi . cotar
★ cū . vi . car̄ . Ibi molin̄ redd . xxx . denar̄ . 7 IIII . ac̄ p̄ti . 7 xx . ac̄
paſturæ . Silua dim̄ leū lḡ . 7 III . q̃ʒ lat̄ . Valuit . vi . liƀ . m̄
Huic m̄ adjac̄ una hida 7 una v̄ træ . ſic diratio ⌐ x . liƀ .
cinati ſt angli . Hanc tram ten̄ Witts de Pinchengi .
Teodric ten̄ de . E . in *SOMREFORDE* . III . virg træ 7 dimid̄ .
7 ⅋ tanto geld̄ . Tra . ē . I . car̄ . q̄ ibi . ē cū . III . bord 7 III . coſcez .

69 b, c

15 Edward holds LUDGERSHALL himself. Alfward held it before 1066; it paid tax for 1 hide. Land for 3 ploughs. In lordship 2 ploughs; 3 slaves;
> 8 Cottagers with 1 plough.
> Pasture 3 furlongs long and 1 furlong wide; woodland ½ league long and 2 furlongs wide.

The value was 100s; now £6 10s.

16 Osmund holds AMESBURY from Edward. Wulfmer held it before 1066; it paid tax for 1 hide. Land for 1 plough.
> 3 Cottagers.
> Meadow, 6 acres; pasture 2 furlongs long and ½ furlong wide.

The value was 10s; now 20s.

17 Osmund also holds from Edward 3 virgates of land which are   69 c attached to Amesbury. Land for 1 plough which is there, with
> 2 Cottagers and 3 slaves.
> An Englishman holds 1½ virgates of this land; he has ½ plough, 1 Cottager and 3 slaves.

Value of the whole, 40s.
> Alric and Cola held it before 1066.

18 Edward holds (Hill) DEVERILL himself, and Aethelhelm from him. Saewulf held it before 1066; it paid tax for 4 hides. Land for 2 ploughs. In lordship 2½ hides of this land; 2 ploughs there, with 1 slave.
> 1 villager and 9 Cottagers with 1 plough.
> Meadow, 2 acres; woodland, 3 acres; pasture 3 furlongs long and 2 furlongs wide.

The value was 40s; now 60s.

19 Edward holds BRADENSTOKE himself. Stremius held it before 1066; it paid tax for 16 hides and 1 virgate. Land for 10 ploughs. In lordship 7½ hides of this; 4 ploughs there; 2 slaves.
> 8 villagers, 16 smallholders and 16 cottagers with 6 ploughs.
> A mill which pays 30d; meadow, 4 acres; pasture, 12 acres; woodland ½ league long and 3 furlongs wide.

The value was £6; now £10.
> 1 hide and 1 virgate of land are attached to this manor, as the Englishmen proved. William of Picquigny holds this land.

20 In SOMERFORD Theodric holds 3½ virgates of land from Edward; it pays tax for as much. Land for 1 plough which is there, with
> 3 smallholders and 3 Cottagers.

Ibi pars molini redđ.xv.deñ.7 v.ac p̃ti.7 vii.ac pasturæ.

In Malmesƀie una dom̃ redđ.xv.deñ.

Valuit.xv.sol̃.Modo.xx.solid̃.Scirold tenuit.T.R.E.

Rotƀt ten de.E.*BLONTESDONE*.Achi tenuit T.R.E.7 geldƀ
p̃.v.hiđ.Tra.ē.iii.car̃.De ea st in dñio.iiii.hidæ 7 dimiđ.
7 ibi.ii.car̃.7 iiii.borđ cū.i.car̃.Ibi moliñ redđ.xxv.deñ
7 xxx.ac p̃ti.7 totiđ pasturæ.Valuit.xl.sol̃.Modo.lx.sol̃.

Ipse.E.ten *CHETRE*.Azor tenuit T.R.E.7 geldƀ p̃.xi.hiđ
7 una v træ.Tra.ē.xiiii.car̃.De ea st in dñio.vi.hide 7 una v
tre.7 ibi.i.car̃.7 iiii.serui.7 xi.coliƀti.7 x.uitti 7 iii.cofcez
cū.v.car̃.Ibi.xviii.ac p̃ti.7 pastura.i.leu lg̃.7 dim̃ leu lat̃.
7 tntđ siluæ.Valuit.xx.liƀ.Modo.xxx.liƀ.

Ipse.E.ten *CHETRE*.Chenuin tenuit T.R.E.7 geldƀ p̃.v.hiđ.
Tra.ē.iiii.car̃.De ea st in dñio.iii.hide.7 ibi.ii.car̃.7 iiii.
serui.7 v.uitti 7 iii.cofcez cū.ii.car̃.Ibi.viii.ac p̃ti.7 pa
stura.v.q̃ʒ lg̃.7 una q̃ʒ lat̃.Valuit.viii.liƀ.Modo.x.liƀ.

Rotƀt ten de.E.*CHETRE*.Vluuen tenuit T.R.E.7 geldƀ
p̃.v.hiđ.Tra.ē.iiii.car̃.De ea st in dñio.iiii.hidæ 7 dimiđ.
7 ibi.ii.car̃.7 iiii.serui.7 iiii.uitti 7 ii.borđ cū.ii.car̃.
Ibi pastura.vi.q̃ʒ lg̃.7 ii.q̃ʒ lat̃.Valuit.lx.sol̃.M.c.sol̃.

Ipse.E.ten *BOIENTONE*.Aluuin tenuit T.R.E.7 geldƀ
p̃.xi.hiđ 7 dimiđ.Tra.ē.vi.car̃.De ea st in dñio.viii.hidæ
7 dimiđ.7 ibi.iii.car̃.7 v.serui.7 vii.uitti 7 v.cofcez.cū.ii.
car̃.Ibi moliñ redđ.xv.sol̃.7 x.ac p̃ti.7 Pastura.iiir.q̃ʒ lg̃.
7 iii.q̃ʒ lat̃.Silua.iii.q̃ʒ lg̃.7 totiđ lat̃.Valuit.viii.liƀ.
Modo.xi.liƀ.7 x.sol̃.

Adelelm ten de.E.*BALLOCHELIE* Winegod tenuit T.R.E.
7 geldƀ p̃ una hiđ.Tra.ē.ii.car̃.quæ ibi st in dñio cū.x.borđ.
Silua.iii.q̃ʒ lg̃.7 una q̃ʒ lat̃.Valuit.xx.sol̃.M.xl.solid̃.

Part of a mill which pays 15d; meadow, 5 acres; pasture,
7 acres; in Malmesbury 1 house which pays 15d.
The value was 15s; now 20s.
Sheerwold held it before 1066.

21   Robert holds BLUNSDON from Edward. Aki held it before 1066;
it paid tax for 5 hides. Land for 3 ploughs, of which 4½
hides are in lordship; 2 ploughs there;
   4 smallholders with 1 plough.
   A mill which pays 25d; meadow, 30 acres; pasture, as many.
The value was 40s; now 60s.

22   Edward holds CHITTERNE himself. Azor held it before 1066;
it paid tax for 11 hides and 1 virgate of land. Land for 14
ploughs, of which 6 hides and 1 virgate of land are in
lordship; 1 plough there; 4 slaves; 11 freedmen;
   10 villagers and 3 Cottagers with 5 ploughs.
   Meadow, 18 acres; pasture 1 league long and ½ league wide;
      woodland, as much.
The value was £20; now £30.

23   Edward holds CHITTERNE himself. Kenwin held it before 1066;
it paid tax for 5 hides. Land for 4 ploughs, of which 3 hides
are in lordship; 2 ploughs there; 4 slaves;
   5 villagers and 3 Cottagers with 2 ploughs.
   Meadow, 8 acres; pasture 5 furlongs long and 1 furlong wide.
The value was £8; now £10.

24   Robert holds CHITTERNE from Edward. Wulfwen held it before 1066;
it paid tax for 5 hides. Land for 4 ploughs, of which 4½ hides
are in lordship; 2 ploughs there; 4 slaves;
   4 villagers and 2 smallholders with 2 ploughs.
   Pasture 6 furlongs long and 2 furlongs wide.
The value was 60s; now 100s.

25   Edward holds BOYTON himself. Alwin held it before 1066;
it paid tax for 11½ hides. Land for 6 ploughs, of which 8½
hides are in lordship; 3 ploughs there; 5 slaves;
   7 villagers and 5 Cottagers with 2 ploughs.
   A mill which pays 15s; meadow, 10 acres; pasture 4 furlongs
      long and 3 furlongs wide; woodland 3 furlongs long and
      as many wide.
The value was £8; now £11 10s.

26   Aethelhelm holds BAYCLIFF from Edward. Winegot held it before 1066;
it paid tax for 1 hide. Land for 2 ploughs which are there,
in lordship, with
   10 smallholders.
   Woodland 3 furlongs long and 1 furlong wide.
The value was 20s; now 40s.

Azelin ten de . E . POLE . Wluuen tenuit T . R . E . 7 geldb
ꝑ . v . hid . Tra . ē . v . car . De ea ſt in dnĩo . III . hidæ 7 ibi . III .
car . 7 vi . ſerui . 7 vi . uiłłi 7 II . bord cū . II . car . Ibi moliñ
redd . x . ſoł . 7 Lx . ac ꝑti . Paſtura . III . q̃ɀ łg . 7 II . q̃ɀ laꞇ .
Silua . I . leu in łg 7 laꞇ . Valuit . c . ſoł . Modo . vi . lib .

Ipſe . E . ten BISCOPESTREV . Edred tenuit T . R . E . 7 geldb
ꝑ . VII . hid . Tra . ē . vi . car . De ea ſt in dnĩo . IIII . hidæ . 7 ibi . III .
car . 7 IIII . ſerui . 7 Ix . uiłłi . 7 vi . bord . 7 II . cotar cū . III . car .
Ibi moliñ redd . xv . ſoł . 7 VIII . ac ꝑti . 7 VIII . ac siluæ . Paſtura
. v . q̃ɀ łg . 7 III . q̃ɀ laꞇ . Valuit . vii . lib . Modo . xi . lib .

Ipſe . E . ten in MIDELTONE . III . virg tr̃æ . Leuuin 7 Alric tenuer̃
T . R . E . 7 ꝑ tanto geldb . Tra . ē . I . car . quæ ibi . ē cū uno uiłło . ſoł .
7 IIII . ac ꝑti . 7 vi . ac paſturæ . 7 ụna ac siluæ . Valuit 7 ual . xxvii .

Gisłebtus ten de . E . TICOODE . Suain tenuit T . R . E . 7 geldb ꝑ . II .
hid . Tra . ē . II . car 7 dim . Ibi ſt . II . car in dnĩo cū . vi . coſcez .
7 III . ac ꝑti . 7 totid paſturæ . Valuit . xxx . ſoł . Modo . xL . ſolid .

69 d

Borel ten de . E . LANGEFEL . Vluui tenuit T . R . E . 7 geldb ꝑ . vii .
hid . Tra . ē . vi . car . De ea ſt in dnĩo . II . hidæ . 7 ibi . II . car .
7 II . ſerui . 7 IIII . uiłłi 7 Ix . cotar . 7 VII . coſcez . cū . III . car .
Ibi . VIII . ac ꝑti . 7 vi . ac siluæ . Valuit . xL . ſoł . modo . IIII . lib .
Idem Vluui ten de ead . tra . I . hid . Valet . x . ſolid .

Borel ten de . E . TERINTONE . Elric tenuit T . R . E . 7 geldb
ꝑ . II . hid . Tra . ē . I . car . quæ ibi . ē . 7 II . ſerui . 7 III . coſcez .
ibi q̃rta pars molini redd . xx . den . 7 vi . ac ꝑti .
Valuit . x . ſoł . Modo . xx . ſolid .

Ipſe . E . ten LACOCH . Eduin tenuit T . R . E . 7 geldb ꝑ . vii .
hid . Tra . ē . Ix . car . De ea ſt in dnĩo . III . hidæ 7 dim . 7 ibi
III . car . 7 VII . ſerui . 7 XII . uiłłi . 7 xvi . coſcez . 7 III . cotar .

27   Azelin holds POOLE (Keynes) from Edward. Wulfwen held it
before 1066; it paid tax for 5 hides. Land for 5 ploughs, of
which 3 hides are in lordship; 3 ploughs there; 6 slaves;
      6 villagers and 2 smallholders with 2 ploughs.
      A mill which pays 10s; meadow, 60 acres; pasture 3 furlongs
          long and 2 furlongs wide; woodland 1 league in length and width.
The value was 100s; now £6.

28   Edward holds BISHOPSTROW himself. Edred held it before 1066;
it paid tax for 7 hides. Land for 6 ploughs, of which 4 hides
are in lordship; 3 ploughs there; 4 slaves;
      9 villagers, 6 smallholders and 2 cottagers with 3 ploughs.
      A mill which pays 15s; meadow, 8 acres; woodland, 8 acres;
          pasture 5 furlongs long and 3 furlongs wide.
The value was £7; now £11.

29   Edward holds 3 virgates of land himself in MIDDLETON.
Leofwin and Alric held them before 1066; they paid tax for
as much. Land for 1 plough which is there, with
      1 villager.
      Meadow, 4 acres; pasture, 6 acres; woodland, 1 acre.
The value was and is 27s.

30   Gilbert holds THICKWOOD from Edward. Swein held it before 1066;
it paid tax for 2 hides. Land for 2½ ploughs. 2 ploughs in
lordship, with
      6 Cottagers.
      Meadow, 3 acres; pasture, as many.
The value was 30s; now 40s.

31   Burghelm holds LANGLEY (Burrell) from Edward. Wulfwy held   69 d
it before 1066; it paid tax for 7 hides. Land for 6 ploughs,
of which 2 hides are in lordship; 2 ploughs there; 2 slaves;
      4 villagers, 9 cottagers and 7 Cottagers with 3 ploughs.
      Meadow, 8 acres; woodland, 6 acres.
The value was 40s; now £4.
      Wulfwy also holds 1 hide of this land; value 10s.

32   Burghelm holds (West) TYTHERTON from Edward. Alric held it
before 1066; it paid tax for 2 hides. Land for 1 plough which
is there; 2 slaves;
      3 Cottagers.
      The fourth part of a mill which pays 20d; meadow, 6 acres.
The value was 10s; now 20s.

33   Edward holds LACOCK himself. Edwin held it before 1066;
it paid tax for 7 hides. Land for 9 ploughs, of which 3½ hides
are in lordship; 3 ploughs there; 7 slaves;
      12 villagers, 16 Cottagers and 3 cottagers.

Ibi . II . molini redd . XVII . ſot 7 VI . den 7 xx . ac p̃ti . 7 dim

ac uineæ . Siluæ . I . leu | inter lg̃ . 7 lat . Valuit 7 uat . VII . lib.

Ipſe . E . ten in *ROCHELIE* . I . hidã . Azor tenuit T . R . E.

    Tra . ē . II . car . In dñio . ē una car . 7 un uitts 7 III . bord

cũ . I . car . 7 XX . ac paſturæ . Valuit 7 uat . XL . ſotid.

Tetbald ten de . E . *WINTREBVRNE* . Aluuard tenuit T . R . E

7 gelde p̃ . III . hid 7 una v̄ træ . 7 IIII . acris . Tra . ē . II . car.

In dñio . ē . I . car . cũ . I . uitto . 7 VI . bord . 7 XIII . ac paſturæ.

Valuit . xxx . ſot . Modo . IIII . lib.

Azelin ten de . E . in *DEPEFORD* . II . hid træ . Oſuuard

7 Goduin teneb T . R . E . 7 p̃ tanto geldb . Tra . ē . II . car . De ea

in dñio . ē hida 7 dim . 7 ibi . II . car . cũ . I . uitto . 7 III . bord . 7 II.

cotar . Ibi moliñ redd . x . ſot . 7 VIII . ac p̃ti . 7 XVI . ac paſturæ.

valuit . xx . ſot . Modo . XL . ſotid . Qui teneb poteran̄ ire q̃ uoteb.

Turchitil ten de . E . in *HERTHA* . I . hid træ . Duo tani tenuer̄

T . R . E . 7 p̃ tanto geldb . Tra . ē . VI . bob . Ibi . ē . I . car . cũ . I . ſeruo.

7 IIII . coſcez . 7 IIII . ac p̃ti . 7 XII . ac paſturæ . 7 III . ac ſiluæ paruæ.

Valuit . x . ſot . Modo . xv . ſotid.

Godefrid ten de . E . *WEROCHESHALLE* . Balduin tenuit T . R . E.

7 geldb p̃ . VII . hid . Tra . ē . IX . car . De ea ſt in dñio . III . hidæ.

7 ibi . IIII . car . 7 III . ſerui . 7 XVI . uitti . 7 v . bord . 7 VI . coſcez . cũ . v.

car . Ibi . II . molini redd . XVIII . ſot . 7 dimid ac p̃ti . Silua . VI . q̃z

lg̃ . 7 IIII . q̃z lat . 7 II . burgſes in Malmeſberie redd . II . ſotid.

Valuit . c . ſot . Modo . VI . lib.

Aiulf ten de . E . *TOLLARD* . Rozo tenuit T . R . E . 7 geldb p̃ . II.

hid 7 dim . Tra . ē totid car . De ea ſt in dñio . II . hidæ 7 dim v̄ træ.

7 ibi . II . car . 7 III . uitti 7 VII . coſcez cũ dim car . Ibi paſtura . II . q̃z lg̃.

7 una q̃z lat . 7 tntd ſiluæ . Valuit . XL . ſot . Modo . L . ſot.

2 mills which pay 17s 6d; meadow, 20 acres; vineyard, ½ acre; woodland, 1 league both in length and width.

The value was and is £7.

34   Edward holds 1 hide in ROCKLEY himself. Azor held it before 1066 and..... Land for 2 ploughs. In lordship 1 plough;
1 villager and 3 smallholders with 1 plough.
Pasture, 20 acres.

The value was and is 40s.

35   Theobald holds SHREWTON from Edward. Alfward held it before 1066; it paid tax for 3 hides, 1 virgate of land and 4 acres.
Land for 2 ploughs. In lordship 1 plough, with
1 villager and 6 smallholders.
Pasture, 13 acres.

The value was 30s; now £4.

36   Azelin holds 2 hides of land in DEPTFORD from Edward.
Osward and Godwin held them before 1066; they paid tax for as much. Land for 2 ploughs, of which 1½ hides are in lordship;
2 ploughs there, with
1 villager; 3 smallholders and 2 cottagers.
A mill which pays 10s; meadow, 8 acres; pasture, 16 acres.

The value was 20s; now 40s.

The holders could go where they would.

37   Thorketel holds 1 hide of land in HARTHAM from Edward. Two thanes held it before 1066; it paid tax for as much. Land for 6 oxen. 1 plough there, with 1 slave;
4 Cottagers.
Meadow, 4 acres; pasture, 12 acres; a small wood, 3 acres.

The value was 10s; now 15s.

38   Godfrey holds (North) WRAXALL from Edward. Baldwin held it before 1066; it paid tax for 7 hides. Land for 9 ploughs, of which 3 hides are in lordship; 4 ploughs there; 3 slaves;
16 villagers, 5 smallholders and 6 Cottagers with 5 ploughs.
2 mills which pay 18s; meadow, ½ acre; woodland 6 furlongs long and 4 furlongs wide.
2 burgesses in Malmesbury who pay 2s.

The value was 100s; now £6.

39   Aiulf holds TOLLARD (Royal) from Edward. Rozo held it before 1066; it paid tax for 2½ hides. Land for as many ploughs, of which 2 hides and ½ virgate of land are in lordship; 2 ploughs there;
3 villagers and 7 Cottagers with ½ plough.
Pasture 2 furlongs long and 1 furlong wide; woodland, as much.

The value was 40s; now 50s.

Petrus teñ de.E.in POERTONE . i . hiđ . God tenuit T.R.E.

Tra.ē.i.car.q̃ ibi.ē cū.i.seruo 7 i.borđ. Ibi moliñ redđ. xxxii.

deñ.7 ii.ac̃ p̃ti. Pastura.L.ouibƺ. Valet.xx.soliđ.

Ipse.E.teñ WINTREBVRNE. Wluuen tenuit T.R.E.7 geldƀ

p̃.vii.hiđ.Tra.ē.vi.car.De ea st in dñio.iii.hidæ.7 ibi.ii.car.

7 viii.serui.7 viii.uitti 7 xii.coscez cū.iii.car.Ibi moliñ

redđ.xv.soł.7 xiii.ac̃ p̃ti.Pastura.v.q̃ƺ lg̃.7 iii.q̃ƺ lat̃.

Valuit.viii.liƀ.Modo.xii.liƀ.

Letard teñ de.E.in LANGEFORDE.i.hidā tre.Azor tenuit

T.R.E.7 p̃ tanto geldƀ.Tra.ē dimiđ car̃.Ibi.ix.ac̃ p̃ti.7 x.

ac̃ pasturæ.Valuit 7 uał.xx.soliđ.Taini diratiocinantur

hanc trā æcclæ Glastingeberie.

.XXV. TERRA ERNVLFI DE HESDING.

ERNVLFVS de HESDING teñ de rege CHIVELE. Brixi tenuit

T.R.E.7 geldƀ p̃.xvi.hiđ.De hac tra st in dñio.vii.hidæ.

Tra.ē
xv.car̃. 7 ibi.vi.car.7 x.serui.7 xviii.uitti.7 xiiii.borđ cū.xii.car̃.

Ibi molini.ii.redđ.Lv.soliđ.7 xvi.ac̃ p̃ti.pastura.iiii.q̃ƺ

lg̃.7 iiii.lat̃.Silua.i.leu lg̃.7 ii.q̃ƺ lat̃.Valet.xxvi.liƀ.

Q̃do recep̃.uałƀ.xx.liƀ.excepta firma.ii.tainoƺ q̃ in mansione

Idē Ern teñ in POTERNE.iii.hiđ 7 unā v̄ træ.   erat.

quæ geldƀ cū Poterne M̃ ep̃i Sarisberiens.T.R.E.Hanc trā cla

mat Osmund ep̃s.Algar qui tenuit T.R.E.ñ poterat ab æccła

separari.Roƀtus tenet de Ernulso.Tra.ē.ii.car.7 st in dñio.

70 a

7 uñ uitts ibi ht̃ dim car.7 vi.serui.7 iii.borđ.Ibi moliñ

redđ.vii.soł 7 vi.deñ.7 xiiii.ac̃ p̃ti.   iii.q̃ƺ lg̃.

7 una q̃ƺ lat̃.Valuit.iiii.liƀ.Modo.c.soliđ.

Lethelin teñ de.Er.CHEVREL.Aluuard tenuit T.R.E.

7 geldƀ p̃.iii.hiđ 7 dim.Tra.ē.iii.car.In dñio st.ii.

car.7 xii.borđ cū.i.car.Ibi dimiđ moliñ redđ.xxx.deñ

7 iii.ac̃ p̃ti.Pastura.x.q̃ƺ lg̃.7 una lat̃.

Valuit.Lx.soliđ.Modo.c.soliđ.

40   Peter holds 1 hide in PORTON from Edward. Goda held it before 1066. Land for 1 plough which is there, with 1 slave.
    1 smallholder.
      A mill which pays 32d; meadow, 2 acres; pasture for 50 sheep. Value 20s.

41   Edward holds WINTERBOURNE (Earls) himself. Wulfwen held it before 1066; it paid tax for 7 hides. Land for 6 ploughs, of which 3 hides are in lordship; 2 ploughs there; 8 slaves;
    8 villagers and 12 Cottagers with 3 ploughs.
      A mill which pays 15s; meadow, 13 acres; pasture 5 furlongs long and 3 furlongs wide.
The value was £8; now £12.

42   Ledhard holds 1 hide of land in LANGFORD from Edward. Azor held it before 1066; it paid tax for as much. Land for ½ plough.
    Meadow, 9 acres; pasture, 10 acres.
The value was and is 20s.
    The thanes adjudge this land to the Church of Glastonbury.

25   LAND OF ARNULF OF HESDIN

1   Arnulf of Hesdin holds KEEVIL from the King. Brictsi held it before 1066; it paid tax for 16 hides. Land for 16 ploughs. Of this land 7 hides in lordship; 6 ploughs there; 10 slaves;
    18 villagers and 14 smallholders with 12 ploughs.
      2 mills which pay 55s; meadow, 16 acres; pasture 4 furlongs long and 4 wide; woodland 1 league long and 2 furlongs wide. Value £26; value when acquired, £20, apart from the revenue of two thanes which was in the place.

2   Arnulf also holds in POTTERNE 3 hides and 1 virgate of land which paid tax with the Bishop of Salisbury's manor of Potterne before 1066. Bishop Osmund claims this land. Algar, who held it before 1066, could not be separated from the church. Robert holds it from Arnulf. Land for 2 ploughs. They are in lordship.
    1 villager has ½ plough; 6 slaves; 3 smallholders.   70 a

r   A mill which pays 7s 6d; meadow, 14 acres; ......3 furlongs long and 1 furlong wide.
The value was £4; now 100s.

3   Lethelin holds CHEVERELL from Arnulf. Alfward held it before 1066; it paid tax for 3½ hides. Land for 3 ploughs. In lordship 2 ploughs;
    12 smallholders with 1 plough.
    ½ mill which pays 30d; meadow, 3 acres; pasture 10 furlongs long and 1 wide.
The value was 60s; now 100s.

In *ECESATINGETONE* st̃ . ii . hidæ . T̃ra . i . car̃ . Edric̃ tenuit
T . R . E . 7 uxor ej ten m̃ de Ernulfo . 7 ibi h̃t . i . car̃ . 7 vii .
bord cũ . i . cotar̃ . Ibi . xii . ac̃ p̃ti . 7 xii . ac̃ pasturæ .
Valuit 7 ual̃ . xl . solid̃ .

Ead̃ uxor Edrici ten de . Er . *CALESTONE* . Vir ej tenuit
T . R . E . 7 geldb̃ p̃ . ii . hid̃ 7 dim̃ . T̃ra . ẽ . iii . car̃ . De ea in
dñio . ẽ . i . hida 7 una v . 7 ibi . i . car̃ . 7 un uilłs 7 x . bord
7 xviii . coscez cũ . i . car̃ . Ibi molin̄ redd xv . sol̃ . 7 xii .
ac̃ p̃ti . 7 vi . ac̃ siluæ . Pastura . iii . q̃ʒ lg̃ . 7 una q̃ʒ lat̃ .
In Calne un burg̃sis redd . xi . denar̃ . Valuit 7 ual̃ . iiii . lib̃ .

~~In *PEVESIE* ten id Er . de rege . ii . hid̃ . T . R . E . teneb̃ eas~~
~~un tain de abbatia Wintoniensi . 7 ñ poterat ab ea sepa~~
~~rari . Valuit 7 ual . xl . solid .~~

Benzelin̄ ten de . Er . *STANDONE* . Brictric tenuit T . R . E .
7 geldb̃ p̃ . ii . hid̃ . T̃ra . ẽ . ii . car̃ . In dñio . ẽ una . 7 molin̄
redd . vi . sol̃ . 7 iiii . ac̃ p̃ti . Pastura . iii . q̃ʒ lg̃ . 7 iii . lat̃ .
Silua . iii . q̃ʒ lg̃ . 7 una q̃ʒ lat̃ . Valet . xl . solid̃ .

Ipse . Er . ten *CALDEFELLE* . Wallef . tenuit T . R . E . 7 geld̃
p̃ . ii . hid̃ 7 dim̃ . T̃ra . ẽ . ii . car̃ . De ea . ẽ in dñio . i . hida
7 dim̃ . 7 ibi . i . car̃ . cũ . i . seruo . 7 iiii . bord . Ibi dim̃ molin̄
redd . xviii . den̄ . 7 vi . ac̃ p̃ti . 7 vi . ac̃ siluæ . 7 viii . ac̃
pasturæ . Valuit . iiii . lib̃ . Modo . l . solid̃ .

Ipse . Er . ten in ead̃ uilla tantd̃ t̃ræ . p uno m̃ . Goduin̄
tenuit T . R . E . Ibi tantd̃ habet̃ q̃tũ in supiori c̃tinet̃ .
7 tntd̃ ap̃ciat̃ .

Id̃e . Er . ten . v . ac̃s t̃ræ in *BVTREMARE* .

Rotb̃t ten de . Er . *SCLIVE* . Chetel tenuit T . R . E . 7 geldb̃ p̃ . iii .
hid̃ . T̃ra . ẽ . ii . car̃ . De ea st̃ in dñio . ii . hidæ 7 dim̃ . 7 ibi . ii . car̃ .
cũ . iiii . coscez . Ibi . xx . ac̃ p̃ti . 7 xv . ac̃ pasturæ . 7 iiii . ac̃
siluæ . Valuit . xxx . sol̃ . Modo . xl . solid̃ .

4   In ETCHILHAMPTON, 2 hides. Land for 1 plough. Edric held them
     before 1066; his wife holds them now from Arnulf; she has 1
     plough and
          7 smallholders with 1 cottager.
          Meadow, 12 acres; pasture, 12 acres.
     The value was and is 40s.

5   Edric's wife also holds CALSTONE (Wellington) from Arnulf.
     Her husband held it before 1066; it paid tax for 2½ hides.
     Land for 3 ploughs, of which 1 hide and 1 virgate are in
     lordship; 1 plough there;
          1 villager, 10 smallholders and 18 Cottagers with 1 plough.
          A mill which pays 15s; meadow, 12 acres; woodland, 6 acres;
              pasture 3 furlongs long and 1 furlong wide.
          In Calne 1 burgess who pays 11d.
     The value was and is £4.

6   *In PEWSEY Arnulf also holds 2 hides from the King. Before 1066*
     a thane held them from Winchester Abbey; he could not be
     separated from it.
     The value was and is 40s.

7   Benzelin holds STANDEN from Arnulf. Brictric held it before 1066;
     it paid tax for 2 hides. Land for 2 ploughs. In lordship 1.
          A mill which pays 6s; meadow, 4 acres; pasture 3 furlongs
              long and 3 wide; woodland 3 furlongs long and 1 furlong wide.
     Value 40s.

8   Arnulf holds CHALFIELD himself. Waltheof held it before 1066;
     it paid tax for 2½ hides. Land for 2 ploughs, of which 1½ hides
     are in lordship; 1 plough there, with 1 slave.
          4 smallholders.
          ½ mill which pays 18d; meadow, 6 acres; woodland, 6 acres;
              pasture, 8 acres.
     The value was £4; now 50s.

9   Arnulf holds as much land himself in this village, as one manor.
     Godwin held it before 1066. As much is recorded as is contained
     in the above; it is assessed at as much.

10   Arnulf also holds 5 acres of land in BUTTERMERE.

11   Robert holds CLYFFE (Pypard) from Arnulf. Ketel held it before 1066;
     it paid tax for 3 hides. Land for 2 ploughs, of which 2½ hides
     are in lordship; 2 ploughs there, with
          4 Cottagers.
          Meadow, 20 acres; pasture, 15 acres; woodland, 4 acres.
     The value was 30s; now 40s.

Roḃt ten de . Er . *BICHENEHILDE* . Chetel tenuit T . R . E . 7 gelđ

ꝑ . I . hida . Tra . ē dimiđ car . q̃ ibi . ē cū . I . coſcet . 7 VI . aͨ ꝑti .

7 IIII . aͨ ſiluæ . Valuit . x . ſol . modo . xv . ſoliđ .

Roḃt ten de . ER . *WIDECOME* . Brictric tenuit T . R . E . 7 gelđb

ꝑ . II . hiđ . Tra . ē . II . car . Ibi . VII . coſcet cū . I . car . 7 XII . aͨ

ꝑti . 7 VI . aͨ paſturæ . 7 XII . aͨ ſiluæ . Valuit . xx . ſol . m̃ . xxx .

Rotḃt ten de . Er . *HELMERINTONE* . Aſchil   ꝼ ſoliđ .

tenuit T . R . E . 7 gelđb ꝑ . I . hida . Tra . ē . I . car . q̃ ibi eſt

cū . III . coſcez . Ibi moliñ redđ . VII . ſol 7 dim̃ . 7 VI . aͨ ꝑti .

7 una aͨ paſturæ . 7 VIII . aͨ ſiluæ . Valuit . xv . ſol . M̊ . xxx .

Vluuard ten de . Er . ad firmã *CELDRINTONE* .   ꝼ ſoliđ .

Ipſe tenuit T . R . E . 7 gelđb ꝑ . I . hida 7 IIII . acris . Tra . ē

. I . car . q̃ ibi . ē in dñio . 7 paſtura . II . q̃ʒ lg̃ . 7 una q̃ʒ lat̃ .

Valuit . xxv . ſol . Modo . XL . ſoliđ .

Ipſe . Er . ten *CELDRINTONE* . Seuui tenuit T . R . E . 7 gelđb

ꝑ . I . hida . Tra . ē . I . car . q̃ ibi . ē . cū . I . coſcet . 7 paſtura

. II . q̃ʒ lg̃ . 7 una q̃ʒ lat̃ . Valuit . xxv . ſol . Modo . XL . ſol .

Godric ten de . Er . In *CELDRINTONE* . I . hidā . Aluuiñ

7 Vluric tenueꞃ T . R . E ꝑ . II . man . 7 ꝑ una hida gelđb .

Tra . ē . I . car 7 dim̃ . 7 tant̃ eſt ibi . cū . II . coſcez . Ibi pa

ſtura . II . q̃ʒ lg̃ . 7 una q̃ʒ lat̃ . Valuit . xx . ſol . M̊ . XL . ſol .

Roḃt ten de . Er . *BECHENEHILDE* . Turgot tenuit T . R . E . 7 gelđ

ꝑ . I . hida . Tra . ē dimiđ car . Ibi . ē uñ coſcet . 7 VI . aͨ ꝑti .

7 VI . aͨ ſiluæ . Valuit . x . ſoliđ . Modo xv . ſoliđ .

Vrſo ten de . Er . *CHENEBVILD* . Vluuid tenuit T . R . E .

7 gelđb ꝑ . II . hiđ 7 dimiđ . Tra . ē . II . car . In dñio . ē una .

70 b

7 II . ſerui . 7 VI . aͨ ꝑti . 7 II . aͨ ſiluæ . Valuit . xx . ſol . Modo . **xxv** . ſoliđ .

12   Robert holds *BICHENEHILDE* from Arnulf. Ketel held it before 1066; it paid tax for 1 hide. Land for ½ plough which is there, with
     1 Cottager.
     Meadow, 6 acres; woodland, 4 acres.
The value was 10s; now 15s.

13   Robert holds WITCOMB from Arnulf. Brictric held it before 1066; it paid tax for 2 hides. Land for 2 ploughs.
     7 Cottagers with 1 plough.
     Meadow, 12 acres; pasture, 6 acres; woodland, 12 acres.
The value was 20s; now 30s.

14   Robert holds HILMARTON from Arnulf. Askell held it before 1066; it paid tax for 1 hide. Land for 1 plough which is there, with
     3 Cottagers.
     A mill which pays 7½s; meadow, 6 acres, pasture, 1 acre;
       woodland, 8 acres.
The value was 15s; now 30s.

15   Wulfward holds CHOLDERTON from Arnulf at a revenue. He held it himself before 1066; it paid tax for 1 hide and 4 acres.
Land for 1 plough which is there, in lordship.
     Pasture 2 furlongs long and 1 furlong wide.
The value was 25s; now 40s.

16   Arnulf holds CHOLDERTON himself. Saewy held it before 1066; it paid tax for 1 hide. Land for 1 plough which is there, with
     1 Cottager.
     Pasture 2 furlongs long and 1 furlong wide.
The value was 25s; now 40s.

17   Godric holds 1 hide in CHOLDERTON from Arnulf. Alwin and Wulfric held it before 1066 as two manors; it paid tax for 1 hide.
Land for 1½ ploughs. As many there, with
     2 Cottagers.
     Pasture 2 furlongs long and 1 furlong wide.
The value was 20s; now 40s.

18   Robert holds *BECHENEHILDE* from Arnulf. Thorgot held it before 1066; it paid tax for 1 hide. Land for ½ plough.
     1 Cottager.
     Meadow, 6 acres; woodland, 6 acres.
The value was 10s; now 15s.

19   Urso holds *CHENEBVILD* from Arnulf. Wulfwy held it before 1066; it paid tax for 2½ hides. Land for 2 ploughs. In lordship 1; 2 slaves. 70 b
     Meadow, 6 acres; woodland, 2 acres.
The value was 20s; now 25s.

Ipſe .Er. ten *CHEIESLAVE* . Vluui tenuit T.R.E.7 geldƀ ꝑ una hida
7 una v̾ 7 dimiđ . Tra.ē.ı.car̄.7 una ac̄ p̄ti 7 dimiđ.7 una ac̄ ſiluæ.
In ead̄ uilla ten un̾ tain̾ de.Er .ıı .v̾ træ 7 dimiđ. ⎰ Val̄.xx.ſoliđ.
Hic.T.R.E . poterat ire ad qué uellet dn̄m.7 T.R.W. ſponte ſe uertit
ad Ern̾ . Val̄ƀ ħ tra . xv . ſot . Modo . xl . den̾.q̄s redđ. Er . de firma.
Vrſo ten̄ de.Er. *DEVREL* . Vlmar̾ tenuit T.R.E.7 geldƀ ꝑ.ıı . hiđ
7 dimiđ.7 dim̄ v̾ træ.Tra.ē. ııı.car̄.De ea ſt in dn̄io .ı . hida 7 dim̄.
7 ibi . ıı . car̄.7 ııı . ſerui.7 ıı . borđ 7 vı . coſcez . cū . ı . car̄.Ibi molin̄
redđ . v . ſoliđ.7 ıı.ac̄ p̄ti . Paſtura dimiđ leu̾ lḡ.7 una q̄ꝛ lat̄.
7 tn̄tđ ſiluæ.Valuit.xxx . ſoliđ.Modo . l . ſoliđ.
Rainbolđ ten̄ de . Er. *OPETONE*.Tous tenuit T.R.E.7 geldƀ ꝑ.ıı.hiđ
7 dimiđ . Tra . ē . ııı . car̄. De ea.ē in dn̄io hida 7 dimiđ.7 ibi.ıı.car̄.
cū . ı.uil̄to 7 v.borđ .Ibi.ııı . ac̄ p̄ti.7 ııı.ac̄ ſiluæ. Valet. xl . ſot.
In hac tra .ē dimiđ hida cōphenſa q̄ geldƀ T.R.E. ſed poſtꝗ rex.W.
in Anglia uenit⸱ geld̄ n̄ reddiđ.
Infra eand̄ tra̅ ten̄ Ernulf̾ de tra Wil̄li de Ow . dimiđ hida̅.7 etia̅
de tra dn̄ica regis tantū qđ ual̄ . ı . hida̅.
Nubolđ ten̄ de.Er.*WINTREBVRNE* . Edric̾ tenuit T.R.E.7 geldƀ
ꝑ.ı.hida 7 ıı.v̾ træ 7 dim̄. Tra . ē . ı|.q ibi.ē cū.ıı.ſeruis.7 vııı.ac̄
paſturæ . Valuit . xx . ſot . Modo . xl . ſoliđ.
Turchil ten̄ de.Er.*HARDENEHVS*. Aluuarđ̾ tenuit T.R.E.7 geldƀ ꝑ.ııı.hiđ
Tra.ē.ıııı.car̄.Ibi ſt.ııı.borđ 7 xıı.ac̄ p̄ti . Silua.ı.q̄ꝛ lḡ.7 ı.q̄ꝛ lat̄.
Valuit . ıııı . lib̄ . Modo . xl . ſoliđ.
Ipſe.Er.ten̾ *ESTONE*.God tenuit T.R.E.7 geldƀ ꝑ.v.hiđ.Tra.ē.ııı.car̄.
In dn̄io ſt.ıı.car̄.cū.ı.ſeruo.7 ııı.borđ.Ibi.x.ac̄ p̄ti.7 xıı.ac̄ paſturæ.
Valuit.lx.ſoliđ.Modo . c . ſoliđ.

20   Arnulf holds CHEDGLOW himself. Wulfwy held it before 1066;
       it paid tax for 1 hide and 1½ virgates. Land for 1 plough.
           Meadow, 1½ acres; woodland, 1 acre.
       Value 20s.

21   In the same village a thane holds 2½ virgates of land from Arnulf.
       Before 1066 he could go to whichever lord he would. After 1066
       he turned to Arnulf of his own accord.
       The value of this land was 15s; now 40d, which he pays to
       Arnulf in revenue.

22   Urso holds DEVERILL from Arnulf. Wulfmer held it before 1066;
       it paid tax for 2½ hides and ½ virgate of land. Land for 3 ploughs,
       of which 1½ hides are in lordship; 2 ploughs there; 3 slaves;
           2 smallholders and 6 Cottagers with 1 plough.
           A mill which pays 5s; meadow, 2 acres; pasture ½ league
               long and 1 furlong wide; woodland, as much.
       The value was 30s; now 50s.

23   Reinbald holds UPTON (Scudamore) from Arnulf. Tholf held it
       before 1066; it paid tax for 2½ hides. Land for 3 ploughs, of
       which 1½ hides are in lordship; 2 ploughs there, with
           1 villager and 5 smallholders.
           Meadow, 4 acres; woodland, 3 acres.
       Value 40s.
           In this land is included ½ hide which paid tax before 1066,
       but after King William came to England it did not pay tax.
           Also within this land, Arnulf holds ½ hide of the land of
       William of Eu, and also as much as is worth 1 hide from the King's
       lordship land.

24   Nubold holds 'WINTERBOURNE' from Arnulf. Edric held it before
       1066; it paid tax for 1 hide and 2½ virgates of land. Land for 1
       plough which is there, with 2 slaves.
           Pasture, 8 acres.
       The value was 20s; now 40s.

25   Thorkell holds HARDENHUISH from Arnulf. Alfward held it
       before 1066; it paid tax for 3 hides. Land for 4 ploughs.
           3 smallholders.
           Meadow, 12 acres; woodland 1 furlong long and 1 furlong wide.
       The value was £4; now 40s.

26   Arnulf holds EASTON (Piercy) himself. Goda held it before 1066;
       it paid tax for 5 hides. Land for 3 ploughs. In lordship 2
       ploughs, with 1 slave;
           3 smallholders.
           Meadow, 10 acres; pasture, 12 acres.
       The value was 60s; now 100s.

Judichel ten de . Er . *Etone* . Duo taini teneɓ T.R.E.7 geldɓ ᵱ.v.hiđ.

Tra.ē.ɪɪɪ.caɼ.De ea ſt in dñio.ɪɪɪ.hidæ 7 dimiđ.7 ibi.ɪɪ.caɼ.7 ɪɪ.uiłłi 7 vɪ.

borđ.7 xx.aͨc p̃ti.7 totiđ paſturæ.7 x.aͨc ſiluæ.Valuit.xxx.ſoł.M̃.ʟ.ſoł.

Hubold ten uñ Man de Ernulfo . Aluric tenuit T.R.E.7 geldɓ ᵱ.ɪ.hida.

Tra.ē.ɪ.caɼ.7 ɪɪɪ.aͨc p̃ti . Valuit . v . ſoliđ . Modo . x . ſoliđ.

.XXVI. Terra Alvredi de Merleberg.

Alvred de Merleberge ten *Adelingtone* . T.R.E. geldɓ

ᵱ xɪ.hiđ 7 dimiđ.7 v.acris træ.Tra.ē.vɪɪ.caɼ.De ea ſt in dñio.vɪɪ.

hidæ 7 dimiđ.7 ibi.ɪɪɪɪ.caɼ.7 vɪɪ.ſerui.7 vɪ.uiłłi 7 vɪɪ.borđ cū.ɪ.caɼ.

Ibi.xx.aͨc p̃ti.Paſtura.vɪ.q̃ʒ l̃g.7 ɪɪɪ.q̃ʒ lat̃.

De hac tra h̃ uñ miles.ɪɪ.hiđ.7 ibi.ɪ.caɼ.Tot̃ ualɓ.xɪɪ.liɓ.m̃.xv.liɓ.

xvɪɪɪ.hiđ. 9   .ɪ.hiđ 9   .ɪ.hiđ.
Willelm 7 Giſłeɓt 7 Vluiet ten de Alur *Rode* . T.R.E.geldɓ

ᵱ.xx.hiđ.Tra.ē.vɪɪɪ.caɼ.In dñio ſt.ɪɪɪɪ.caɼ.7 ɪɪɪɪ.ſerui.7 ɪɪɪɪ.uiłłi

7 vɪɪɪ.borđ.7 xɪ.coſcez.7 pɓr cū.ɪɪɪɪ.caɼ.Ibi.ɪɪ.molini Wiłłi redđ

ɪx.ſoł 7.vɪɪɪ.denaɼ.7 xx.aͨc p̃ti.Silua.vɪ.q̃ʒ l̃g.7 unā q̃ʒ 7 dim lat̃.

Valuit tot̃.vɪ.liɓ.Modo.vɪɪɪ.liɓ.

Ipſe . Al . ten *Tefonte* T.R.E.geldɓ ᵱ.vɪ.hiđ 7 dimiđ.Tra.ē.v.caɼ.

De ea ſt in dñio.ɪɪɪɪ.hidæ.7 ibi.ɪɪ.caɼ.7 ɪx.ſerui.7 ɪɪɪɪ.uiłłi 7 ɪɪɪ.borđ

7 uñ franc cū.ɪɪ.caɼ.Ibi moliñ redđ.x.ſoł.7 vɪ.aͨc p̃ti.7 vɪ.paſture.

7 vɪ.ſiluæ.Valuit 7 uał.vɪ.liɓ.

Hugo ten de.Alu *Crostone* . T.R.E . geldɓ ᵱ.vɪɪɪ.hiđ.Tra.ē.v.

caɼ. De ea ſt in dñio.ɪɪɪ.hidæ.7 ibi.ɪɪɪ.caɼ.7 ɪɪɪ.ſerui.7 ɪɪ.uiłłi 7 v.

coſcez.cū.ɪɪ.caɼ.Ibi moliñ redđ.xxx.ſoł.7 x.aͨc p̃ti.7 paſtura

vɪ.acͨs l̃g.7 totiđ lat̃.Silua.ɪɪɪ.q̃ʒ l̃g.7 una q̃ʒ lat̃.Valuit 7 uał

Ipſe . Alu ten *Newentone* T.R.E. geldɓ ᵱ xɪ.hiđ. ʃvɪɪ.liɓ.

Tra.ē.vɪɪ.caɼ.De ea ſt in dñio.vɪ.hidæ.7.ibi.ɪɪ.caɼ.7 vɪ.ſerui.

27 Judicael holds YATTON (Keynell) from Arnulf. Two thanes held it before 1066; it paid tax for 5 hides. Land for 3 ploughs, of which 3½ hides are in lordship; 2 ploughs there;
 2 villagers and 6 smallholders.
 Meadow, 20 acres; pasture, as many; woodland, 10 acres.
The value was 30s; now 50s.

28 Hubald holds 1 manor from Arnulf. Aelfric held it before 1066; it paid tax for 1 hide. Land for 1 plough.
 Meadow, 3 acres.
The value was 5s; now 10s.

26   LAND OF ALFRED OF MARLBOROUGH

1 Alfred of Marlborough holds ALLINGTON. Before 1066 it paid tax for 11½ hides and 5 acres of land. Land for 7 ploughs, of which 7½ hides are in lordship; 4 ploughs there; 7 slaves;
 6 villagers and 7 smallholders with 1 plough.
 Meadow, 20 acres; pasture 6 furlongs long and 3 furlongs
  wide.
 A man-at-arms has 2 hides of this land; 1 plough there.
The value of the whole was £12; now £15.

2 William, 18 hides, Gilbert, 1 hide and Wulfgeat, 1 hide, hold ROWDE from Alfred. Before 1066 it paid tax for 20 hides. Land for 8 ploughs. In lordship 4 ploughs; 4 slaves;
 4 villagers, 8 smallholders, 11 Cottagers and a priest
  with 4 ploughs.
 2 mills of William's which pay 9s 8d; meadow, 20 acres;
  woodland 6 furlongs long and 1½ furlongs wide.
The value of the whole was £6; now £8.

3 Alfred holds TEFFONT (Evias) himself. Before 1066 it paid tax for 6½ hides. Land for 5 ploughs, of which 4 hides are in lordship; 2 ploughs there; 9 slaves;
 4 villagers, 3 smallholders and 1 Frenchman with 2 ploughs.
 A mill which pays 10s; meadow, 6 acres; pasture, 6; woodland, 6.
The value was and is £6.

4 Hugh holds CROFTON from Alfred. Before 1066 it paid tax for 8 hides. Land for 5 ploughs, of which 3 hides are in lordship; 3 ploughs there; 3 slaves;
 2 villagers and 5 Cottagers with 2 ploughs.
 A mill which pays 30s; meadow, 10 acres; pasture 6 acres
  long and as many wide; woodland 3 furlongs long and
  1 furlong wide.
The value was and is £7.

5 Alfred holds NEWTON (Toney) himself. Before 1066 it paid tax for 11 hides. Land for 7 ploughs, of which 6 hides are in lordship; 2 ploughs there; 6 slaves;

7 vi .uitti 7 iiii .borđ cū .iii .cař .Ibi moliñ redđ .x .soliđ .7 iii .ãc p̃ti.

7 Paſtura .iii .q̃ᷤ lḡ .7 iii .q̃ᷤ lať.

De ead̃ tra h̃t Girard .iii .hiđ .7 ibi .iiii .uitt .7 v .borđ cū .ii .cař.

Valuit .x .liƀ .Modo .xviii .liƀ .Ab anglis ap̃pciať .xii .liƀ.

Eduuard ten de Alu in WINTREBVRNE .i .hidā .Trā .i .cař.

quæ ibi .ē .cū .i .ſeruo .7 i .borđ .Valuit .x .ſol .Modo .xx .ſoliđ.

Ipſe .Alu ten LEDIAR .T.R.E .geldƀ p̃ .vii .hiđ .Tra .ē .vii .cař.

De ea ſt in dñio .iii .hidæ .7 ibi .i .cař .7 iii .ſerui .7 viii .uitti 7 x .coſcez.

cū .iiii .cař .7 xl .ãc p̃ti .7 xxx .ãc paſturæ .Silua .i .leū lḡ .7 dim̃ lať.

Valuit .x .liƀ .Modo .vi .liƀ .In Crichelade .vii .burḡſes redđ .v .ſol.

70 c

Ipſe .Alu .ten in SVINDONE .i .hiđ 7 dimiđ .Tra .vi .bou .Vał .xii .ſol.

Alƀtus ten de .Alu .MORDONE .T.R.E .geldƀ p̃ .vi .hiđ .Tra .ē .iiii .cař.

De ea ſt in dñio .iii .hidæ .7 ibi .ii .cař .7 iii .ſerui .7 iii .uitti 7 v .borđ

cū .ii .cař .Ibi .xxx .ãc p̃ti .Paſtura dimiđ leū lḡ .7 ii .q̃ᷤ lať.

Valuit .c .ſoliđ .Modo .iiii .liƀ.

Gunfrid ten de .Alu WILDEHILLE .T.R.E .geldƀ p̃ .v .hiđ .Tra .ē .iii.

cař .De ea ſt in dñio .iiii .hidæ .7 ibi .ii .cař .7 ii .uitti 7 iiii .borđ cū .i.

cař .Ibi moliñ redđ .xxv .denař .7 xxx .ãc p̃ti .7 totiđ paſturæ.

Valuit .xl .ſol .Modo .lx .ſoliđ.

Radulf ten de .Alu OPETONE .T.R.E .geldƀ p̃ .ix .hiđ .Tra .ē

vi .cař .De ea ſt in dñio .v .hidæ .7 ibi .ii .cař .7 v .ſerui .7 ix .uitti

7 xxii .borđ cū .iiii .cař .Ibi moliñ redđ .xx .ſol .7 v .ãc p̃ti .7 xxx.

ãc paſturæ .Silua .iii .q̃ᷤ lḡ .7 una q̃ᷤ lať .Valuit .viii .liƀ .m̃ .ix .liƀ.

Ipſe .Alu .ten NORTONE .T.R.E .geldƀ p̃ .xi .hiđ .Tra .ē .viii .cař.

De ea ſt in dñio .vi .hidæ .7 ibi .ii .cař .7 ii .ſerui .7 xii .uitti 7 viii.

borđ cū .vi .cař .Ibi .ii .molini redđ .xl .ſol .7 x .ãc p̃ti .Paſtura .iiii .q̃ᷤ

6 villagers and 4 smallholders with 3 ploughs.
A mill which pays 10s; meadow, 3 acres; pasture 3 furlongs
long and 3 furlongs wide.
Gerard has 3 hides of this land.
4 villagers and 5 smallholders with 2 ploughs.
The value was £10; now £18; it is assessed by the English at £12.

6 Edward holds 1 hide in 'WINTERBOURNE' from Alfred. Land for 1
plough, which is there, with 1 slave;
1 smallholder.
The value was 10s; now 20s.

7 Alfred holds LYDIARD (Tregoze) himself. Before 1066 it paid
tax for 7 hides. Land for 7 ploughs, of which 3 hides are
in lordship; 1 plough there; 3 slaves;
8 villagers and 10 Cottagers with 4 ploughs.
Meadow, 40 acres; pasture, 30 acres; woodland 1 league
long and ½ wide.
The value was £10; now £6.
In Cricklade 7 burgesses who pay 5s.

8 Alfred holds 1½ hides in SWINDON himself. Land for 6 oxen. 70 c
Value 12s.

9 Albert holds MOREDON from Alfred. Before 1066 it paid tax
for 6 hides. Land for 4 ploughs, of which 3 hides are in
lordship; 2 ploughs there; 3 slaves;
3 villagers and 5 smallholders with 2 ploughs.
Meadow, 30 acres; pasture ½ league long and 2 furlongs wide.
The value was 100s; now £4.

10 Gunfrid holds WIDHILL from Alfred. Before 1066 it paid tax
for 5 hides. Land for 3 ploughs, of which 4 hides are in
lordship; 2 ploughs there;
2 villagers and 4 smallholders with 1 plough.
A mill which pays 25d; meadow, 30 acres; pasture, as many.
The value was 40s; now 60s.

11 Ralph holds UPTON (Scudamore) from Alfred. Before 1066 it paid
tax for 9 hides. Land for 6 ploughs, of which 5 hides are in
lordship; 2 ploughs there; 5 slaves;
9 villagers and 22 smallholders with 4 ploughs.
A mill which pays 20s; meadow, 5 acres; pasture, 30 acres;
woodland 3 furlongs long and 1 furlong wide.
The value was £8; now £9.

12 Alfred holds NORTON (Bavant) himself. Before 1066 it paid
tax for 11 hides. Land for 8 ploughs, of which 6 hides are
in lordship; 2 ploughs there; 2 slaves;
12 villagers and 8 smallholders with 6 ploughs.
2 mills which pay 40s; meadow, 10 acres; pasture 4 furlongs

lg̅.7 ıı.q̃ƶ lat̅.Silua dimiđ leů lg̅.7 ıııı.q̃ƶ lat̅.

Valuit xxıııı.lıb̅.Modo.xıııı.lıb̅. ⌐Val.vııı.lıb̅.

Ipſe.Al.ten̅ ROCHELIE.T.R.E.geldb̅ ꝑ.x.hiđ.Tra.e̅.vı.car̅.De
ea ſt in dn̅io.vı.hidæ 7 ııı.v tre.7 ibi.ı.car̅.ců.ı.ſeruo.Ibi.vıı.uilti
7 xıı.borđ.ců.ııı.car̅.Ibi.ııı.ac̅ p̃ti.Paſtura dimiđ leů lg̅.7 ıııı.q̃ƶ lat̅. ◦

Ipſe.Alu.ten̅ FIFHIDE.Radulf de eo.T.R.E. geldb̅ ꝑ.v.hiđ.Tra.e̅.ıııı.
car̅.De ea ſt in dn̅io.ııı.hidæ.7 ibi.ı.car̅.7 ııı.ſerui.Ibi.ıx.uilti 7 vı.
borđ ců.ıı.car̅.Ibi.ıı.ac̅ p̃ti.Paſtura dimiđ leů lg̅.7 ıı.q̃ƶ lat̅.Silua
dim̅ leů lg̅.7 dimiđ q̃ƶ lat̅.Valuit.ıııı.lıb̅.Modo.c.ſoliđ. ⌐den.
Ibi.ı.ferraria redđ.xıı.den̅ ꝑ an̅n̅.In Wiltune.ıı.burgſes ređ.xvııı.

Ipſe Alu ten̅ unã v træ in Lacoc.Tra.e̅.ı.car̅.q̃ ibi.e̅ ců.ı.borđ.
7 ıı.ac̅ p̃ti.Valuit.x.ſol.Modo.v.ſoliđ.

Om̅s has p̃ſcriptas t̅ras tenuit Carlo.T.R.E.

Rogeri ten̅ de.Alu.CLIVE.Godric 7 Tedgar 7 Aluric 7 Vluric tenueɼ ꝑ.ıııı. Manerijs
T.R.E.7 geldb̅ ꝑ.ıııı.hiđ.Tra.e̅.ıı.car̅.In dn̅io.e̅ una.car̅.7 ııı.ſerui.
7 ıı.coſcez.Ibi.xxıııı.ac̅ p̃ti.7 xx.ac̅ paſturæ.7 vı.ac̅ ſiluæ.
Valuit.xl.ſoliđ.Modo.l.ſoliđ.

Rob̅t ten̅ de.Alu.in CLIVE.ıı.hiđ 7 dim̅ 7 ꝓ tanto geldb̅ T.R.E.Sigar
7 Carman teneb̅.Tra.e̅.ı.car̅ 7 dimiđ.Ibi ſt.ııı.ſerui.ců.ı.borđ.7 mo
linů redđ.v.ſol.7 xıı.ac̅ p̃ti.7 xx.ac̅ paſture.7 l.ac̅ ſiluæ.
Valuit.xx.ſoliđ.Modo.xxx.ſoliđ.

Siuuard ten̅ de.Alu.SVMREFORD.Alnod tenuit T.R.E.7 geldb̅ ꝑ.ııı.
hiđ.7 xxıııı.acris træ|.De ea ſt in dn̅io.ıı.hidæ.7 ibi.ı.car̅.7 ıı.ſerui. Tra e̅.ııı.car̅.
7 ııı.uilti 7 ıı.borđ 7 vııı.coſcez ců.ıı.car̅.Ibi molin̅ redđ.v.ſoliđ.7 vı.ac̅
p̃ti.Silua.ıı.q̃ƶ lg̅.7 úna q̃ƶ lat̅.Valuit 7 ual.xl.ſoliđ.

long and 2 furlongs wide; woodland ½ league long and
4 furlongs wide.
The value was £24; now £14.

13 Alfred holds ROCKLEY himself. Before 1066 it paid tax for
10 hides. Land for 6 ploughs, of which 6 hides and 3 virgates
of land are in lordship; 1 plough there, with 1 slave.
7 villagers and 12 smallholders with 3 ploughs.
Meadow, 3 acres; pasture ½ league long and 4 furlongs wide.
Value £8.

14 Alfred holds FIFIELD (Bavant) himself, and Ralph from him.
Before 1066 it paid tax for 5 hides. Land for 4 ploughs,
of which 3 hides are in lordship; 1 plough there; 3 slaves.
9 villagers and 6 smallholders with 2 ploughs.
Meadow, 2 acres; pasture ½ league long and 2 furlongs wide;
woodland ½ league long and ½ furlong wide.
The value was £4; now 100s.
1 smithy which pays 12d a year.
In Wilton 2 burgesses who pay 18d.

15 Alfred holds 1 virgate of land in LACOCK himself. Land for
1 plough, which is there, with
1 smallholder.
Meadow, 2 acres.
The value was 10s; now 5s.

Karl held all the above lands before 1066.

16 Roger holds CLEVANCY from Alfred. Godric, Theogar, Aelfric
and Wulfric held it as four manors before 1066; it paid tax for 4
hides. Land for 2 ploughs. In lordship 1 plough; 3 slaves;
2 Cottagers.
Meadow, 24 acres; pasture, 20 acres; woodland, 6 acres.
The value was 40s; now 50s.

17 Robert holds 2½ hides in CLYFFE (Pypard) from Alfred; they
paid tax for as much. Before 1066 Sigar and Carman held them.
Land for 1½ ploughs. 3 slaves there, with
1 smallholder.
A mill which pays 5s; meadow, 12 acres; pasture, 20 acres;
woodland, 50 acres.
The value was 20s; now 30s.

18 Siward holds SOMERFORD from Alfred. Alnoth held it before 1066;
it paid tax for 3 hides and 24 acres of land. Land for 3 ploughs,
of which 2 hides are in lordship; 1 plough there; 2 slaves;
3 villagers, 2 smallholders and 8 Cottagers with 2 ploughs.
A mill which pays 5s; meadow, 6 acres; woodland 2 furlongs
long and 1 furlong wide.
The value was and is 40s.

Eduuard ten de . Alu . in CHEGESLEI . I . hid 7 unā v̄ træ . Tra . ē . I . car.

In dñio . ē dim̄ car . cū . I . feruo . 7 I . cotar . 7 I . ac̄ p̄ti . 7 I . ac̄ filuæ . in lḡ 7 lat̄.

In Malmeſberie dimid̄ dom̄ redd̄ . VI . den̄ . Valuit . XL . fol . Modo . x . fol.

Præt̄ hanc trā ht̄ Durand de Glouuceſtre dimid̄ v̄ træ quā idē Eduuard teneb̄ . T.R.E. Hanc ei abſtulit injuſte Amalric de Dreuues . ut teſtant oms̄

Oſmund ten de Alu in HORNINGHĀ dimid̄ hidā . 7 p̄ tanto ſ taini ſciræ geldb̄ T.R.E. Colſuen teneb̄ . 7 poterat ire q̄ uoleb̄ . Tra . ē . I . car . q̄ ibi . ē cū . IIII . bord̄ . Ibi . VIII . ac̄ filuæ . 7 una leu paſturæ . 7 molin̄ redd̄ . VII . fol 7 VI . denar . Valuit . V . fol . Modo . x . folid̄.

In CHENETE ten Alu . XIII . hid̄ 7 dim̄ 7 II . ac̄s træ . De his ht̄ Nicolaus II . hid̄ . Turſtin . III . hid̄ 7 dimid̄ . Vluiet . II . hid̄ . Leuric . III . hid̄ 7 dimid̄. Vlmar . II . hid̄ 7 dimid̄ . 7 II . ac̄s træ . Tra . ē . VI . car . Ibi ſt̄ . IIII . car . cū . I . uillo 7 xv . bord̄ . Ibi molin̄ redd̄ . XII . fol . 7 XI . ac̄ p̄ti . 7 c . VI . ac̄ paſturæ. 7 VII . ac̄ filuæ . Tot̄ ualb̄ qdo recep̄ . IIII . lib̄ 7 x . fol . Modo . VIII . lib̄ 7 x . fol. Has hid̄ in Chenet T.R.E. tenuer̄ . Vluiet . Alnod̄ . Edmar . Leuric 7 Vlmar.

Wilts dur ten de Alu TEDELINTONE . Vlueua teneb̄ . p̄ . II . Man T.R.E. 7 geldb̄ . p̄ . IIII . hid̄ . Tra . ē . IIII . car . De ea ſt̄ in dñio . II . hidæ . 7 ibi . I . car. 7 II . uilli 7 IIII . bord̄ 7 II . cotar . ⟨⟩ Ibi . II . partes molini redd̄ . XL . den 7 x . ac̄ p̄ti . Valuit 7 ualet . LX . folid̄.

Vlmar ten de Alu . in FIFHIDE . I . hid̄ . Idē teneb̄ T.R.E. Valuit 7 ual . x . fol.

.XXVII. TERRA HVNFRIDI DE INSVLA.

HVNFRIDVS De Inſula ten de rege BROCTONE . Tres taini in parag̃. tenuer̄ . T.R.E. 7 geldb̄ . p̄ . XII . hid̄ . Tra . ē . VIII . car . De ea ſt̄ in dñio . IIII . hidæ 7 dim̄ . 7 ibi . III . car . 7 II . ſerui . 7 XVII . uilli 7 IIII . bord̄ cū . VII . car . Ibi . II . molini redd̄ . IX . folid̄ . 7 XII . ac̄ p̄ti . 7 VIII . ac̄ paſturæ . Silua . I . leu lḡ . 7 II . q̄ʒ lat̄. Valuit . XIII . lib̄ . modo . x . lib̄.

19 Edward holds 1 hide and 1 virgate of land in CHEDGLOW from
Alfred. Land for 1 plough. In lordship ½ plough, with 1 slave;
 1 cottager.
  Meadow, 1 acre; woodland, 1 acre in length and width;
   in Malmesbury ½ house which pays 6d.
The value was 40s; now 10s.
  Besides this land, Durand of Gloucester has ½ virgate of land
which Edward also held before 1066. Amalric of Dreux took it away
from him wrongfully, as all the thanes of the shire testify.

20 Osmund holds ½ hide in HORNINGSHAM from Alfred; it paid
tax for as much. Before 1066 Colswein held it; he could go
where he would. Land for 1 plough, which is there, with
 4 smallholders.
  Woodland, 8 acres; pasture, 1 league; a mill which pays 7s 6d.
The value was 5s; now 10s.

21 In KENNETT Alfred holds 13½ hides and 2 acres of land.
Of these Nicholas has 2 hides, Thurstan 3½ hides, Wulfgeat 2 hides,
Leofric 3½ hides, Wulfmer 2½ hides and 2 acres of land.
Land for 6 ploughs. 4 ploughs there, with
 1 villager and 15 smallholders.
 A mill which pays 12s; meadow, 11 acres; pasture, 106 acres;
  woodland, 7 acres.
Value of the whole when acquired, £4 10s; now £8 10s.
  Wulfgeat, Alnoth, Edmer, Leofric and Wulfmer held these hides
in Kennett before 1066.

22 William Hard holds (West) TYTHERTON from Alfred. Wulfeva and Aelfeva
held it as two manors before 1066; it paid tax for 4 hides. Land
for 4 ploughs, of which 2 hides are in lordship; 1 plough there;
 2 villagers, 4 smallholders and 2 cottagers.
 2 parts of a mill which pay 40d; meadow, 10 acres.
The value was and is 60s.

23 Wulfmer holds 1 hide in FIFIELD (Bavant) from Alfred. He also
held it before 1066.
The value was and is 10s.

27   LAND OF HUMPHREY DE L'ISLE   70 d

1 Humphrey de l'Isle holds BROUGHTON (Gifford) from the King.
Three thanes held it jointly before 1066; it paid tax for 12 hides.
Land for 8 ploughs, of which 4½ hides are in lordship; 3 ploughs
there; 2 slaves;
 17 villagers and 4 smallholders with 7 ploughs.
 2 mills which pay 9s; meadow, 12 acres; pasture, 8 acres;
  woodland 1 league long and 2 furlongs wide.
The value was £13; now £10.

Pagen ten de .H .*CONTONE* .Leuenot tenuit T.R.E.⁊ geldɓ
ꝑ.v.hiđ ⁊ dim.Tra.ē.iiii.caŕ.De ea ſt in dñio.ii.hidæ
⁊ una v̇ træ.⁊ ibi.ii.caŕ.⁊ iiii.ſerui.⁊ iiii.uilli ⁊ iiii.coſcez.
cū.ii.caŕ.Ibi tcia pars.ii.molinoꝝ redđ.x.ſol.⁊ xx.ac
ꝑti.⁊ x.ac paſturæ.⁊ totiđ ſiluæ.Valuit ⁊ ual.iiii.liɓ ⁊ x.ſol.
Ipſe.H.ten *STERTE*.Aluric tenuit T.R.E.⁊ geldɓ ꝑ.v.
hiđ.⁊ una v̇ ⁊ dimiđ cū appenđ.Tra.ē.iii.caŕ.De ea ſt
in dñio.iiii.hidæ.⁊ ibi.iii.caŕ.⁊ vi.ſerui.⁊ xv.borđ.⁊ uñ
Franc hñs unā v̇ ⁊ dim.Ibi.ii.molini redđ.viii.ſoliđ ⁊ xxx.
ac ꝑti.⁊ x.ac paſturæ.⁊ ii.ac ſiluæ.Valuit.c.ſol.M̊.vi.liɓ.
Blacheman ten de.H.*BVRBETC*.Edric tenuit T.R.E.⁊ gelđ
ꝑ.ii.hiđ ⁊ dim.Tra.ē.ii.caŕ ⁊ dim.De ea.ē in dñio hida.
⁊ dim.⁊ ibi.i.caŕ.⁊ ii.uilli ⁊ iii.coſcez cū.i.caŕ.Silua ibi
iii.q̃ꝝ lḡ.⁊ ii.q̃ꝝ lat.Valuit.l.ſol.Modo.xl.ſoliđ.
Pagen ten de.H.*CVBREWELLE*.Leuenot tenuit T.R.E.
⁊ geldɓ ꝑ.iiii.hiđ.Tra.ē.v.caŕ.In dñio ſt.ii.caŕ.cū.i.
ſeruo.⁊ ii.uilli ⁊ iiii.borđ cū.iii.caŕ.Ibi.iiii.ac ꝑti.⁊ v.ac
ſiluæ.Valet.iii.liɓ.De eađ tra h̅ rex.i.hiđ in ſuo dñio
⁊ nil ibi.ē.⁊ Vñ anglic ten dimiđ de rege.Val.viii.ſoliđ.
Gunter ten de.H.*RVSTESELLE*.Vluric tenuit T.R.E.
⁊ geldɓ ꝑ.iiii.hiđ.Tra.ē.ii.caŕ.In dñio.ē una cū.ii.borđ.
⁊ de molino.xii.denar.⁊ viii.ac ꝑti.⁊ dimiđ q̃ꝝ paſturæ.
Valet.xl.ſoliđ.
Roɓt ten de.H.*WERTVNE*.Alnod tenuit T.R.E.⁊ geldɓ
ꝑ.x.hiđ.Tra.ē.iiii.caŕ.De ea ſt in dñio.v.hidæ ⁊ dim.
⁊ ibi.ii.caŕ.⁊ vi.uilli ⁊ ix.borđ cū.ii.caŕ.⁊ ibi uñ franc
ten.ii.hiđ de eađ tra.Ibi moliñ de.xv.deñ.⁊ xxx.ac paſ
turæ.⁊ ii.ac ſiluæ.Valuit ⁊ ual.c.ſoliđ.

2   Payne holds COMPTON (Bassett) from Humphrey. Leofnoth held
it before 1066; it paid tax for 5½ hides. Land for 4 ploughs, of
which 2 hides and 1 virgate of land are in lordship; 2 ploughs
there; 4 slaves;
    4 villagers and 4 Cottagers with 2 ploughs.
    The third part of 2 mills which pays 10s; meadow, 20 acres;
      pasture, 10 acres; woodland, as many.
The value was and is £4 10s.

3   Humphrey holds STERT himself. Aelfric held it before 1066;
it paid tax for 5 hides and 1½ virgates of land with dependencies.
Land for 3 ploughs, of which 4 hides are in lordship; 3 ploughs
there; 6 slaves;
    15 smallholders and 1 Frenchman who has 1½ virgates.
    2 mills which pay 8s; meadow, 30 acres; pasture, 10 acres;
      woodland, 2 acres.
The value was 100s; now £6.

4   Blackman holds BURBAGE from Humphrey. Edric held it before 1066;
it paid tax for 2½ hides. Land for 2½ ploughs, of which 1½ hides
are in lordship; 1 plough there;
    2 villagers and 3 Cottagers with 1 plough.
    Woodland 3 furlongs long and 2 furlongs wide.
The value was 50s; now 40s.

5   Payne holds CUMBERWELL from Humphrey. Leofnoth held it before
1066; it paid tax for 4 hides. Land for 5 ploughs. In lordship
2 ploughs, with 1 slave;
    2 villagers and 4 smallholders with 3 ploughs.
    Meadow, 4 acres; woodland, 5 acres.
Value £3.
    The King has 1 hide of this land in his lordship; nothing
is there. 1 Englishman holds half from the King. Value 8s.

6   Gunter holds LUS HILL from Humphrey. Wulfric held it before
1066; it paid tax for 4 hides. Land for 2 ploughs. In lordship 1,
with
    2 smallholders.
    From a mill, 12d; meadow, 8 acres; pasture, ½ furlong.
Value 40s.

  Robert holds from Humphrey
7   WROUGHTON. Alnoth held it before 1066; it paid tax for 10
hides. Land for 4 ploughs, of which 5½ hides are in lordship;
2 ploughs there;
    6 villagers and 9 smallholders with 2 ploughs. 1 Frenchman
      holds 2 hides of this land.
    A mill at 15d; pasture, 30 acres; woodland, 2 acres.
The value was and is 100s.

Robt ten de .H. *SALTEHARPE* . Vluuin tenuit T.R.E.

7 geldb ꝑ.x. hid. Tra . e . iiii . car . De ea ſt in dnio . viii . hidæ.

7 ibi . ii . car . 7 iii . ſerui . 7 ix . bord cū . i . car . Ibi . xx . ac ꝑti.

7 xxx . ac paſturæ . Valuit . c . ſolid . Modo . iiii . lib.

Robt ten de .H. *CLIVE* . Eduin tenuit T.R.E. 7 geldb ꝑ . viii.

hid . Tra . e . iiii . car . De ea ſt in dnio . vi . hidæ . 7 ibi . ii . car.

7 iiii . ſerui . 7 ii . uilli 7 vii . bord cū . ii . car . Ibi . xx . ac ꝑti.

7 tntd paſturæ . 7 iii . burgſes in crichelade redd . iii . den.

Valuit 7 ual . iiii . lib.

Robt ten de . H. *SVMREFORD* . Eduin tenuit T.R.E. 7 geldb ꝑ . iii.

hid . 7 xxiiii . acris . Tra . e . iii . car . De ea ſt in dnio . ii . hidæ.

Ibi . xvi . coſcez . hnt . ii . car . 7 tcia pars molini redd . viii . ſol.

7 x . ac ꝑti . Paſtura . iii . q̃ lg . 7 una q̃ lat . In Malmeſ

| 7 vii. |
| bord |

berie . i . burgſis redd xii . den . Valuit 7 ual . lx . ſolid.

Elbert ten de . H. *SMITECOTE* . Sauuin tenuit T.R.E.

7 geldb ꝑ . v . hid . Tra . e . iiii . car . De ea ſt in dnio . ii . hidæ

7 dimid . 7 ibi . iii . car . 7 ii . ſerui . 7 iii . uilli 7 iiii . bord.

cū . i . coſcet hnt . ii . car . Ibi molin . v . ſolid . 7 xx . ac ꝑti.

Silua . iiii . q̃ lg . 7 una q̃ lat . 7 un burgſis redd . viii . den.

Valuit . xl . ſolid . Modo . lx . ſolid.

Ilbt ten de . H. *BLVNTESDONE* . Edric tenuit T.R.E.

7 geldb ꝑ . v . hid . Tra . e . ii . car 7 dimid . De ea ſt in dnio . ii.

hidæ 7 dim . 7 ibi . i . car . cū . i . ſeruo . 7 ii . bord cū . i . car 7 dim.

Valuit . xxx . ſolid . Modo . l . ſolid.

Hugo 7 Girald ten de . H. *GRENDEWELLE* . Ordulf tenuit

T.R.E. 7 geldb ꝑ . v . hid . Tra . e . iii . car . De ea ſt in dnio

iiii . hidæ . 7 ibi . ii . car . cū . i . ſeruo . 7 i . uilt 7 ii . bord cū . i . car.

Ibi . xii . ac ꝑti . Valuit . xl . ſolid . Modo . lxx . ſolid.

8   SALTHROP. Wulfwin held it before 1066; it paid tax for 10 hides. Land for 4 ploughs, of which 8 hides are in lordship; 2 ploughs there; 3 slaves;

9 smallholders with 1 plough.

Meadow, 20 acres; pasture, 30 acres.

The value was 100s; now £4.

9   CLYFFE (Pypard). Edwin held it before 1066; it paid tax for 8 hides. Land for 4 ploughs, of which 6 hides are in lordship; 2 ploughs there; 4 slaves;

2 villagers and 7 smallholders with 2 ploughs.

Meadow, 20 acres; pasture, as much.

3 burgesses in Cricklade who pay 3d.

The value was and is £4.

10   SOMERFORD. Edwin held it before 1066; it paid tax for 3 hides and 24 acres. Land·for 3 ploughs, of which 2 hides are in lordship.

16 Cottagers and 7 smallholders have 2 ploughs.

The third part of a mill which pays 8s; meadow, 10 acres; pasture 3 furlongs long and 1 furlong wide.

In Malmesbury 1 burgess who pays 12d.

The value was and is 60s.

11   Albert holds SMITHCOT from Humphrey. Saewin held it before 1066; it paid tax for 5 hides. Land for 4 ploughs, of which 2½ hides are in lordship; 3 ploughs there; 2 slaves.

3 villagers and 4 smallholders, with 1 Cottager, have 2 ploughs.

A mill, 5s; meadow, 20 acres; woodland 4 furlongs long and 1 furlong wide.

1 burgess who pays 8d.

The value was 40s; now 60s.

12   Ilbert holds BLUNSDON from Humphrey. Edric held it before 1066; it paid tax for 5 hides. Land for 2½ ploughs, of which 2½ hides are in lordship; 1 plough there, with 1 slave;

2 smallholders with 1½ ploughs.

The value was 30s; now 50s.

13   Hugh and Gerald hold GROUNDWELL from Humphrey. Ordwulf held it before 1066; it paid tax for 5 hides. Land for 3 ploughs, of which 4 hides are in lordship; 2 ploughs there, with 1 slave;

1 villager and 2 smallholders with 1 plough.

Meadow, 12 acres.

The value was 40s; now 70s.

Roƀt ten de . H . *SCHETONE* . Chenui tenuit T.R.E.

7 gelдƀ ꝑ . vɪ . hiđ . Tra . ē . ɪɪɪɪ . caṟ . De ea ſt in dñio . ɪɪɪ . hidæ.

7 ibi . ɪɪ . caṟ . 7 ɪɪɪ . ſerui . 7 ɪɪɪɪ . uilti 7 ɪɪɪ . coſcez cũ . ɪɪ . caṟ.

Ibi dimiđ moliñ redd . vɪ . ſoł 7 ɪɪɪ . denaṟ . 7 xɪɪ . aͨ ꝑti.

Paſtura . vɪ . q᷑ łg . 7 tñtđ laṭ . Valuit . ɪɪɪɪ . liƀ . Modo . vɪ . liƀ.

Ipſe Hunfrid teñ *WILT* . Aluric tenuit T.R.E . 7 gelдƀ

ꝑ . ɪɪɪ . hiđ . 7 ɪɪɪ . virg . Tra . ē . ɪɪɪɪ ; caṟ . De ea . ē in dñio . ɪ . hida.

7 una v̄ træ . 7 ibi . ɪɪɪ . caṟ . 7 xɪɪ . ſerui . 7 ɪɪ . uilti 7 vɪ . coſcez ;

cũ . ɪ . caṟ 7 dimiđ . Ibi moliñ . xv . ſoliđ . 7 x . aͨ ꝑti . Paſtura

dimiđ leū łg . 7 tñtđ laṭ . Valuit . ɪɪɪ . liƀ . Modo . ɪɪɪɪ . liƀ ;

Ipſe . H . ten *WILRENONE* . Eduiñ tenuit . T.R.E . 7 gelдƀ

ꝑ . ɪɪɪ . hiđ . Tra . ē . ɪɪ . caṟ . De ea ſt in dñio . ɪɪ . hidæ . 7 ibi

una caṟ . 7 ɪɪ . uilti 7 ɪ . coſcet cũ . ɪ . caṟ . Ibi moliñ redd

vɪ . ſoł . 7 v . aͨ ꝑti . 7 vɪɪɪ . aͨ paſturæ . Valuit . xL . ſoł . M̄

Ipſe . H . ten *COLERNE* . Leuenot tenuit T.R.E . ſ Lx . ſoł.

7 gelдƀ ꝑ . x . hiđ . Tra . ē . xɪɪ . caṟ . De ea ſt in dñio . ɪɪɪɪ.

hidæ 7 dimiđ . 7 ibi . ɪɪɪ . caṟ . 7 x . ſerui . 7 xɪɪɪ . uilti 7 v.

coſcez cũ . vɪɪɪ . caṟ . Ibi moliñ redd . xɪɪɪ . ſoł 7 vɪ . deñ.

7 vɪɪɪ . aͨ ꝑti . Silua parua . ɪ . leū łg . 7 alia laṭ.

Valuit 7 uał . x . liƀ.

Ipſe . H . ten *WINTREBVRNE* . Duo tani teneḃ . T.R.E.

7 gelдƀ ꝑ . x . hiđ . Tra . ē . vɪ . caṟ . De ea ſt in dñio . ɪɪɪɪ.

hidæ 7 x . aͨ træ . 7 ibi . ɪɪɪ . caṟ . 7 vɪɪɪ . ſerui . 7 ɪɪɪɪ . uilti

7 vɪɪɪ . borđ cũ . ɪɪɪ . caṟ . Ibi xɪɪɪɪ . aͨ ꝑti . 7 xx . aͨ paſturæ.

Valuit 7 uał . x . liƀ.

Ipſe . H . ten *POLTONE* . Toui tenuit T.R.E . 7 gelдƀ ꝑ . x.

hiđ . Tra . ē . ɪɪɪɪ . caṟ . De ea ſt in dñio . vɪɪɪ . hidæ . 7 ibi . ɪɪ.

caṟ . 7 ɪɪ . ſerui . 7 ɪɪ . uilti 7 vɪɪ . borđ . cũ . ɪ . caṟ . Ibi moliñ

redd . xv . ſoł . 7 ɪɪɪɪ . aͨ ꝑti . 7 x . aͨ paſturæ . 7 vɪɪɪ . aͨ ſiluæ.

Valuit 7 uał . vɪɪɪ . liƀ.

14 Robert holds ASHTON (Gifford) from Humphrey. Kenwin
held it before 1066; it paid tax for 6 hides. Land for 4 ploughs,
of which 3 hides are in lordship; 2 ploughs there; 3 slaves;
    4 villagers and 3 Cottagers with 2 ploughs.
    ½ mill which pays 6s 3d; meadow, 12 acres; pasture 6
       furlongs long and as wide.
The value was £4; now £6.

Humphrey himself holds

15 BATHAMPTON. Aelfric held it before 1066; it paid tax for 3 hides
and 3 virgates. Land for 4 ploughs, of which 1 hide and 1 virgate
of land are in lordship; 3 ploughs there; 12 slaves;
    2 villagers and 6 Cottagers with 1½ ploughs.
    A mill, 15s; meadow, 10 acres; pasture ½ league long
      and as wide.
The value was £3; now £4.

16 BATHAMPTON. Edwin held it before 1066; it paid tax for 3
hides. Land for 2 ploughs, of which 2 hides are in lordship;
1 plough there;
    2 villagers and 1 Cottager with 1 plough.
    A mill which pays 6s; meadow, 5 acres; pasture, 8 acres.
The value was 40s; now 60s.

17 COLERNE. Leofnoth held it before 1066; it paid tax for 10 hides.
Land for 12 ploughs, of which 4½ hides are in lordship; 3 ploughs
there; 10 slaves;
    13 villagers and 5 Cottagers with 8 ploughs.
    A mill which pays 13s 6d; meadow, 8 acres; a small wood
      1 league long and another wide.
The value was and is £10.

18 WINTERBOURNE (Bassett). Two thanes held it before 1066; it paid
tax for 10 hides. Land for 6 ploughs, of which 4 hides and 10
acres of land are in lordship; 3 ploughs there; 8 slaves;
    4 villagers and 8 smallholders with 3 ploughs.
    Meadow, 14 acres; pasture, 20 acres.
The value was and is £10.

19 POULTON. Tovi held it before 1066; it paid tax for 10 hides.
Land for 4 ploughs, of which 8 hides are in lordship; 2 ploughs
there; 2 slaves;
    2 villagers and 7 smallholders with 1 plough.
    A mill which pays 15s; meadow, 4 acres; pasture, 10 acres;
      woodland, 8 acres.
The value was and is £8.

Rannulf⁹ ten de.H. *HANTONE*. Vlgar tenuit T.R.E.

7 geldb ꝓ.x.hid.Tra.ē.iiii.car.De ea ſt in dnio.vi.hidæ.

7 ibi.i.car.cū.i.ſeruo.7 iiii.uilti 7 vi.borđ cū.ii.car.

Ibi.xii.ac p̃ti.7 xiiii.ac paſturæ.Valuit 7 ual.c.ſot.

Turchitil ten de.H. *BEDESTONE*. Aluric tenuit T.R.E.

7 geldb ꝓ.i.hida 7 una v.Tra.ē   Ibi ſt.iiii.coſcez

7 iii.ac p̃ti.7 ii.ac ſiluæ.Valuit.x.ſot.m̃.xx.ſolid.

Hugo ten de.H. *HEORTHAM*. Godric tenuit T.R.E.

7 geldb ꝓ.i.hida.Tra.ē dimiđ car.Ibi ſt.ii.coſcez.

7 ii.ac p̃ti.7 vii.ac paſturæ.7 ii.ac ſiluæ.

Valuit.viii.ſot.Modo.xii.ſolid.

Ipſe.H.ten *COME*. Suain tenuit T.R.E.7 geldb ꝓ.x.hid.

Tra.ē.x.car.De ea ſt in dnio.v.hidæ.una v⁹ min.

7 ibi.iiii.car.7 xiii.ſerui.7 v.uilti 7 vii.borđ 7 v.cotar.

cū.vi.car.Ibi.iii.molini redđ.xxxi.ſot 7 vi.den.

7 xii.ac p̃ti.Silua.i.leu lḡ.7 dimiđ leu lat.

In Wiltune.i.burgſis redđ.v.ſot.7 ii.burgſes in Mal

meſberie redđ.xviii.denar.Valuit 7 ual.x.lib.

Roƀt⁹ ten de.H. *SORESTONE*. Godus tenuit T.R.E.

7 geldb ꝓ.vi.hiđ 7 dimiđ.Tra.ē.v.car.De ea ſt in

dnio.iii.hiđ 7 dimiđ.7 ibi.iii.car.7 ii.ſerui.7 iii.uilti

7 ix.borđ cū.ii.car.Ibi.ii.molini redđ.x.ſoliđ.

7 vi.ac p̃ti.7 x.ac ſiluæ minutæ.Valuit.iii.lib.M̃.iiii.lib.

Ipſe.H.ten *HARDICOTE*. Aluric tenuit T.R.E.7 geldb

ꝓ.iii.hiđ.Tra.ē.iiii.car.De ea ſt in dnio.ii.hidæ.7 ibi

.ii.car.cū.i.ſeruo.7 ii.uilti 7 xii.borđ cū.ii.car.

Ibi moliñ redđ.vi.ſoliđ.7 vi.ac p̃ti.7 viii.ac paſturæ.

Valuit.xl.ſoliđ.Modo.lx.ſolid.

20 Ranulf holds HAMPTON from Humphrey. Wulfgar held it
before 1066; it paid tax for 10 hides. Land for 4 ploughs,
of which 6 hides are in lordship; 1 plough there, with 1 slave;
    4 villagers and 6 smallholders with 2 ploughs.
    Meadow, 12 acres; pasture, 14 acres.
The value was and is 100s.

21 Thorketel holds BIDDESTONE from Humphrey. Aelfric held it
before 1066; it paid tax for 1 hide and 1 virgate. Land for....
    4 Cottagers.
    Meadow, 3 acres; woodland, 2 acres.
The value was 10s; now 20s.

22 Hugh holds HARTHAM from Humphrey. Godric held it before
1066; it paid tax for 1 hide. Land for ½ plough.
    2 Cottagers.
    Meadow, 2 acres; pasture, 7 acres; woodland, 2 acres.
The value was 8s; now 12s.

23 Humphrey holds (Castle) COMBE himself. Swein held it before
1066; it paid tax for 10 hides. Land for 10 ploughs, of which 5
hides, less 1 virgate, are in lordship; 4 ploughs there; 13 slaves;
    5 villagers, 7 smallholders and 5 cottagers with 6 ploughs.
    3 mills which pay 31s 6d; meadow, 12 acres; woodland 1
      league long and ½ league wide.
    In Wilton 1 burgess who pays 5s; 2 burgesses in Malmesbury
      who pay 18d.
The value was and is £10.

24 Robert holds SHERSTON from Humphrey. Gode held it before
1066; it paid tax for 6½ hides. Land for 5 ploughs, of which
3½ hides are in lordship; 3 ploughs there; 2 slaves;
    3 villagers and 9 smallholders with 2 ploughs.
    2 mills which pay 10s; meadow, 6 acres; underwood, 10 acres.
The value was £3; now £4.

25 Humphrey holds HURDCOTT himself. Aelfric held it before 1066;
it paid tax for 3 hides. Land for 4 ploughs, of which 2 hides
are in lordship; 2 ploughs there, with 1 slave;
    2 villagers and 12 smallholders with 2 ploughs.
    A mill which pays 6s; meadow, 6 acres; pasture, 8 acres.
The value was 40s; now 60s.

Ipſe . H . ten *FISTESFERIE* . Edricus tenuit T.R.E. p.III. geldab

hiđ . Tra . ē . IIII . car . De ea ſt in dñio . II . hidæ . 7 ibi . I . car .

7 III . ſerui . 7 IIII . uilti 7 II . borđ . 7 II . colibti cū . III . car . Ibi

XII . ac̄ p̃ti . Silua . II . q̉z̉ lḡ . 7 una q̉z̉ lat . Valuit . XL . ſol . M . L . ſol .

Gozelin ten de . H . in *MELEFORD* dim̄ hiđ træ . 7 p̃ tanto

geldb̄ T.R.E . Sauuold 7 Sauuard teneb̄ . Tra . ē . I . car .

Ibi ſt . VI . cotar 7 III . ac̄ p̃ti . Valuit . XV . deñ . M . VII . ſolid .

Medietas huj træ . ē in foreſta regis

.XXVIII. TERRA MILONIS CRISPIN.

71 b

MILO CRISPIN ten de rege *WODETONE* . Leueñod tenuit T.R.E.

7 geldb̄ p̃ . XII . hiđ . Tra . ē . XII . car . De ea ſt in dñio . VI . hidæ . 7 ibi . III . car .

7 V . ſerui . 7 XI . uilti 7 XIIII . borđ cū . VI . car . Ibi moliñ redđ . XXX . denar .

7 . XXIIII . ac̄ p̃ti . 7 XXXIII . ac̄ paſturæ . Silua . II . leu lḡ . 7 una leu lat .

In Malmeſbie una dom̄ redđ XIII . deñ . Valuit . X . lib . Modo . IX . lib .

Rainalđ ten de . M . *CILLETONE* . Herald tenuit T.R.E . 7 geldb̄ p̃ . X . hiđ .

Tra . ē . XII . car . De ea ſt in dñio . VI . hidæ 7 dimiđ . 7 ibi . II . car . 7 II . ſerui .

7 VII . uilti 7 X . coſcet . cū . V . car . Ibi . II . molini redđ . XL . ſol . 7 p̃tū . II . q̉z̉ lḡ .

7 una q̉z̉ lat . 7 tñtđ paſturæ . Silua . I . leu lḡ . 7 II . q̉z̉ lat .

Valuit . XII . lib . Modo . X . lib .

Hunfriđ ten de . M . *CLIVE* . Herald tenuit T.R.E . 7 geldb̄ p̃ . V . hiđ . Tra . ē

II . car . De ea ſt in dñio . III . hidæ 7 dim̄ . 7 ibi . I . car . cū . I . ſeruo . Ibi . III . uilti

7 IIII . borđ . 7 I . cotar cū dim̄ car . Ibi . XX . ac̄ p̃ti . 7 XII . ac̄ paſturæ .

Valuit . XXX . ſol . Modo . L . ſolid .

In eađ *CLIVE* ten Milo . I . hiđ . Tra dim̄ car . Val . VI . ſol . Qui teneb̄ T.R.E .

poterat ire ad que̅ dñm uoleb̄ .

26 Humphrey holds 'FRUSTFIELD' himself. Edric held it before 1066;
    it paid tax for 3 hides. Land for 4 ploughs, of which 2 hides
    are in lordship; 1 plough there; 3 slaves;
        4 villagers, 2 smallholders and 2 freedmen with 3 ploughs.
        Meadow, 12 acres; woodland 2 furlongs long and 1 furlong wide.
    The value was 40s; now 50s.

27 Jocelyn holds ½ hide of land in MILFORD from Humphrey; it paid
    tax for as much. Before 1066 Saewold and Saeward held it.
    Land for 1 plough.
        6 cottagers.
        Meadow, 3 acres.
    The value was 15d; now 7s.
        Half of this land is in the King's Forest.

28   **LAND OF MILES CRISPIN**   71 b

1   Miles Crispin holds WOOTTON (Bassett) from the King. Leofnoth
    held it before 1066; it paid tax for 12 hides. Land for 12 ploughs,
    of which 6 hides are in lordship; 3 ploughs there; 5 slaves;
        11 villagers and 14 smallholders with 6 ploughs.
        A mill which pays 30d; meadow, 24 acres; pasture, 33 acres;
            woodland 2 leagues long and 1 league wide; in Malmesbury
            1 house which pays 13d.
    The value was £10; now £9.

2   Reginald holds CHILTON (Foliat) from Miles. Earl Harold held
    it before 1066; it paid tax for 10 hides. Land for 12 ploughs,
    of which 6½ hides are in lordship; 2 ploughs there; 2 slaves;
        7 villagers and 10 Cottagers with 5 ploughs.
        2 mills which pay 40s; meadow 2 furlongs long and 1 furlong
            wide; pasture, as much; woodland 1 league long and
            2 furlongs wide.
    The value was £12; now £10.

3   Humphrey holds CLYFFE (Pypard) from Miles. Harold held it before
    1066; it paid tax for 5 hides. Land for 2 ploughs, of which 3½
    hides are in lordship; 1 plough there, with 1 slave.
        3 villagers, 4 smallholders and 1 cottager with ½ plough.
        Meadow, 20 acres; pasture, 12 acres.
    The value was 30s; now 50s.

4   Also in CLYFFE (Pypard) Miles holds 1 hide. Land for ½ plough.
    Value 6s.
        The holder before 1066 could go to whichever lord he would.

Turchetil teñ de. M. *LITLECOTE*. Godric tenuit T.R.E. 7 ꝑ una hida 7 una geldƀ. Tra. ē dim car̃. q̃ ibi. ē cū. I. borđ. Ibi. IIII. ac̃ pti. 7 totiđ pasturæ 7 totiđ spineti. Valet. x. soliđ.

* Rainbald teñ de. M. in *WALECOTE*. II. hiđ 7 dimiđ. Alnod tenuit. T.R.E. 7 ibiđ. III. virg træ. q̃s tenuit Leuenot T.R.E. Tot̃ ualet. XXIII. soliđ.

Rainald teñ de. M. *DRACOTE*. Leuenot tenuit T.R.E. 7 geldƀ ꝑ. x. hiđ. Tra. ē. VI. car. De ea sť in dnio. v. hidæ. 7 ibi. II. car̃. cū. I. seruo. 7 IIII. uitti 7 VII. borđ cū. III. car̃. Ibi. XVIII. ac̃ pti. 7 XL. ac̃ pasturæ. Valuit 7 uał. c. sol

Hunfrid teñ de. M. *BRENCHEWRDE*. Tochi tenuit T.R.E. 7 geldƀ ꝑ. v. hiđ. Tra. ē. III. car. De ea sť in dnio. IIII. hide. 7 ibi. I. car̃. Ibi. VIII. borđ 7 VIII. coscez cū. I. car. Ibi. XXIIII. ac̃ pti. 7 III. ac̃ pasture. Silua IIII. q̃z lg. 7 tntđ lat. Valuit 7 uał. L. soliđ. Iste Tochi poterat ire q̃ uoleƀ.

Rainold teñ de. M. *REDBORNE*. Wigot tenuit T.R.E. 7 geldƀ ꝑ. v. hiđ. Tra. ē. IIII. car. De ea sť in dnio. II. hidæ Ibi. III. uitti 7 v. borđ 7 I. seru cū. III. car. ptū. VI. q̃z lg. 7 II. q̃z lat̃. Pastura. II. q̃z lg. 7 tntđ lat. Valuit. c. soliđ. Modo. IIII. liƀ.

Vn tain (Siuuard) teñ de. M. *CHESESLAVE*. Duo taini tenuer̃. T.R.E. 7 geldƀ ꝑ. I. hida. 7 vna v 7 dim. Tra. ē. VI. bou. qui ibi sť arantes 7 I. cotar 7 uno seruo. Ibi. I. ac̃ pti 7 una v 7 dim. 7 I. ac̃ siluæ. Valuit 7 uał. x. soliđ. Qui teneƀ T.R.E. poterant ire quo uoleƀ.

Præt hanc trã hť durand dimiđ v træ quã teneƀ Siuuard T.R.E. Hanc abstulit ei injuste Amalric de Dreuues. ut dicunt taini sciræ.

Ipse Milo teñ *OGHEBVRNE*. Herald (com) tenuit T.R.E. 7 geldƀ ꝑ. x. hiđ. Tra. ē. VIII. car. De ea sť in dnio. VI. hidæ. 7 ibi. III. car. 7 IIII. serui.

5   Thorketel holds LITTLECOTT from Miles. Godric held it before 1066; it paid tax for 1 hide and 1 virgate. Land for ½ plough, which is there, with
> 1 smallholder.
> Meadow, 4 acres; pasture, as many; spinney, as many.

Value 10s.

6   Reginald holds 2½ hides in WALCOT from Miles. Alnoth held them before 1066. Also 3 virgates of land there which Leofnoth held before 1066.

Value of the whole 23s.

7   Reginald holds DRAYCOT (Foliat) from Miles. Leofnoth held it before 1066; it paid tax for 10 hides. Land for 6 ploughs, of which 5 hides are in lordship; 2 ploughs there, with 1 slave;
> 4 villagers and 7 smallholders with 3 ploughs.
> Meadow, 18 acres; pasture, 40 acres.

The value was and is 100s.

8   Humphrey holds BRINKWORTH from Miles. Toki held it before 1066; it paid tax for 5 hides. Land for 3 ploughs, of which 4 hides are in lordship; 1 plough there.
> 8 smallholders and 8 Cottagers with 1 plough.
> Meadow, 24 acres; pasture, 3 acres; woodland 4 furlongs
> > long and as wide.

The value was and is 50s.
> Toki could go where he would.

9   Reginald holds RODBOURNE from Miles. Wigot held it before 1066; it paid tax for 5 hides. Land for 4 ploughs, of which 2 hides are in lordship.....
> 3 villagers, 5 smallholders and 1 slave with 3 ploughs.
> Meadow 6 furlongs long and 2 furlongs wide; pasture 2
> > furlongs long and as wide.

The value was 100s; now £4.

10   A thane, Siward, holds CHEDGLOW from Miles. Two thanes held it before 1066; it paid tax for 1 hide and 1½ virgates. Land for 6 oxen, which are there, ploughing.
> 1 cottager and 1 slave.
> Meadow, 1 acre and 1½ virgates; woodland, 1 acre.

The value was and is 10s.
> The holders before 1066 could go where they would.
> Besides this land Durand has ½ virgate of land which Siward held before 1066. Amalric of Dreux took it away from him wrongfully, as the thanes of the Shire state.

11   Miles holds OGBOURNE himself. Earl Harold held it before 1066; it paid tax for 10 hides. Land for 8 ploughs, of which 6 hides are in lordship; 3 ploughs there; 4 slaves;

7 xi.uilti 7 iiii.borđ cū.iii.caŕ.Ibi moliñ redđ.xxx.ſoliđ.7 viii.āc p̄ti.
Paſtura dimiđ leū l̄g.7 t̄ntđ laŕ.Valuit 7 ual.xv.lib̄.

Rainalđ ten de.M.*MANETVNE*.Wigot tenuit T.R.E.7 geldb̄ p̄.iii.
hiđ.Tra.ē.iii.caŕ.De ea.ē in dñio.i.hida.7 ibi.i.caŕ.7 ii.ſerui.7 v.
uilti.7 v.borđ.cū.ii.caŕ.Ibi.iiii.āc p̄ti.7 xl.āc paſture.7 totiđ ſiluæ.
Valuit 7 ual.iii.lib̄.

Rainalđ ten de.M.*HASEBERIE*.Leuenot tenuit T.R.E.7 geldb̄ p̄.v.
hiđ.Tra.ē.v.caŕ.De ea.ē in dñio.i.hida.7 ibi.ii.caŕ.7 ii.ſerui.7 v.uilti
7 xiii.coſcez.7 ii.cotaŕ cū.iii.caŕ.Ibi.ii.molini redd.xxxv.ſoliđ.
7 xxii.āc p̄ti.7 Silua.ii.q̄z̄ l̄g.7 una q̄z̄ laŕ.Valuit 7 ual.vi.lib̄.

.XXIX. TERRA GISLEBERTI DE BRETEVILE.

Gislebert de Breteuile ten de rege *CHESEBERIE*.Edric tenuit T.R.E.
7 geldb̄ p̄.v.hiđ.Tra.ē.ix.caŕ.In dñio ſt.iiii.caŕ.7 vii.ſerui.7 xii.uilti
7 iii.borđ.7 xiiii.coſcez cū.v.caŕ.Ibi.ii.molini redd.xx.ſoliđ.7 xv.āc p̄ti.
7 xl.āc ſiluæ.Paſtura.xv.q̄z̄ l̄g.7 iii.q̄z̄ laŕ.Valuit.viii.lib̄.Modo.xii.lib̄.
Idē.G.ten in *BECHENHALLE*.v.hiđ.Hacun tenuit T.R.E.Tra.ē.ii.caŕ.
De ea ſt in dñio.iiii.hidæ.7 ibi.i.caŕ.7 iiii.ſerui.7 i.uilts 7 iii.borđ cū.i.caŕ.
Ibi.x.āc p̄ti.7 xii.āc paſturæ.7 iiii.āc ſiluæ.Valuit.xl.ſol.Modo.l.ſol.
In eađ uilla.ii.hiđ una v̄ miñ tenuit Toli T.R.E.Tra.vi.boū.Ibi h̄t Giſlebt
uñ uiltm.Valet.xviii.ſolid.
In eađ uilla.iii.hiđ 7 una v̄ tre teneɫ Saul 7 Aluuiñ T.R.E.Tra.ē.x.boū.
Ibi h̄t Giſlebt.ii.uittos.7 iiii.acs p̄ti.7 vi.acs paſturæ.Valb̄ xx.ſol.M̊.xxvii.ſol.

11 villagers and 4 smallholders with 3 ploughs.
A mill which pays 30s; meadow, 8 acres; pasture ½ league
  long and as wide.
The value was and is £15.

12 Reginald holds MANTON from Miles. Wigot held it before 1066;
it paid tax for 3 hides. Land for 3 ploughs, of which 1 hide is
in lordship; 1 plough there; 2 slaves;
  5 villagers and 5 smallholders with 2 ploughs.
  Meadow, 4 acres; pasture, 40 acres; woodland, as many.
The value was and is £3.

13 Reginald holds HAZELBURY from Miles. Leofnoth held it
before 1066; it paid tax for 5 hides. Land for 5 ploughs, of
which 1 hide is in lordship; 2 ploughs there; 2 slaves;
  5 villagers, 13 Cottagers and 2 cottagers with 3 ploughs.
  2 mills which pay 35s; meadow, 22 acres; woodland 2 furlongs
    long and 1 furlong wide.
The value was and is £6.

29   LAND OF GILBERT OF BRETEUIL

1 Gilbert of Breteuil holds CHISBURY from the King. Edric held
it before 1066; it paid tax for 5 hides. Land for 9 ploughs.
In lordship 4 ploughs; 7 slaves.
  12 villagers, 3 smallholders and 14 Cottagers with 5 ploughs.
  2 mills which pay 20s; meadow, 15 acres; woodland, 40 acres;
    pasture 15 furlongs long and 3 furlongs wide.
The value was £8; now £12.

2 Gilbert also holds 5 hides in BINCKNOLL. Hakon held them
before 1066. Land for 2 ploughs, of which 4 hides are in
lordship; 1 plough there; 4 slaves;
  1 villager and 3 smallholders with 1 plough.
  Meadow, 10 acres; pasture, 12 acres; woodland, 4 acres.
The value was 40s; now 50s.

3 In the same village Toli held 2 hides, less 1 virgate,
before 1066. Land for 6 oxen. Gilbert has
  1 villager.
Value 18s.

4 In the same village Saul and Alwin held 3 hides and 1 virgate
of land before 1066. Land for 10 oxen. Gilbert has
  2 villagers and
  meadow, 4 acres; pasture, 6 acres.
The value was 20s; now 27s.

Ipſe.G.ten̄ *CLIVE*.Aluric 7 Burgel 7 Godeue tenueř T.R.E.7 geldb̄ ꝑ.xvi.hid̄
una v̄ min.Tra.ē.vii.cař.De ead̄ tra h̄t Ansfrid.xi.hid̄ de Giſleƀto.7 ibi
iii.cař in dñio.7 vii.ſeruos.7 iii.uiłłos.7 ii.bord̄.7 x.coſcez cū.ii.cař 7 dimid̄.
Ibi moliñ redd̄.v.ſoł.7 L.ac̄ ṗti.7 Lxx.ac̄ paſturæ.7 xviii.ac̄ ſiluæ.
De his.xi.hid̄ eſt una in *TORNELLE*.q̄ jaceƀ in Cliue.T.R.E.

Ibi in Cliue ſt̄.ii.bord̄ 7 ii.ſerui.7 xvi.ac̄ ṗti.7 xvii.ac̄ paſturæ ſub Giſleƀto
hoc ualet.xxxv.ſoł.Qd̄ Ansfrid ten̄:ualet.vi.liƀ.

Turſtin̄ ten̄ de.G.*MORTVNE*.Vlgar tenuit T.R.E.7 geldb̄ ꝑ.iii.hid̄
una v̄ min.Tra.ē.ii.cař.De ea ſt̄ in dñio.i.hida 7 una v̄ træ.7 ibi.i.cař.
7 ii.uiłłi 7 iiii.bord̄ cū.ii.cař.Ibi.xx.ac̄ ṗti.7 q̄t xx.ac̄ paſturæ.
Valuit 7 ual.xL.ſolid̄.

Ipſe.G.ten̄ *HENTONE*.Vlgar tenuit T.R.E.7 geldb̄ ꝑ.xi.hid̄ 7 una v̄.
Tra.ē.v.cař.De ea ſt̄ in dñio.ix.hidæ 7 una v̄ træ.7 ibi.ii.cař.7 iiii.
uiłłi 7 v.bord̄ cū.ii.cař.Ibi.xvi.ac̄ ṗti.7 xxx.ac̄ paſturæ.Valuit.c.ſoł.

Ansfrid ten̄ de.G.*BACHENTVNE*.Edric tenuit T.R.E. ſ Modo.vii.lib.
7 geldb̄ ꝑ.ii.hid̄.Tra.ē.iii.cař.De ea.ē in dñio.i.hida.7 ibi.ii.cař.
7 iiii.uiłłi 7 vii.bord̄ 7 iii.cotař cū.ii.cař.Ibi.viii.ac̄ ṗti.7 xL.ac̄ paſturæ.
Valuit 7 ual.vi.liƀ.

Ansfrid ten̄ de.G.*STAMERE*.Bruning tenuit T.R.E.7 geldb̄ ꝑ.ii.
hid̄ 7 dim.Tra.ē.ii.cař.De ea ſt̄ in dñio.ii.hidæ.7 ibi.i.cař.7 ii.ſerui.
7 un uiłłs 7 iii.bord̄.cū dimid̄ cař.   Valuit.xx.ſolid̄.Modo.xL.ſoł.

.XXX. TERRA DVRANDI DE GLOWECESTRE.

Dvrandvs de Glowecestre·ten̄ de rege *CERITONE*.Almarus
tenuit T.R.E.7 geldb̄ ꝑ.x.hid̄.Tra.ē.v.cař.De ea ſt̄ in dñio.vii.
hidæ.cū.i.cař 7 dim.7 vii.uiłłi 7 x.bord̄ cū.ii.cař.Ibi molin̄ redd̄
.x.ſolid̄.7 xxx.ac̄ ṗti.Paſtura dimid̄ leū lḡ.7 iii.q̄ƶ lař.
Valuit.xi.lib.Modo.x.liƀ.

5 Gilbert holds CLYFFE (Pypard) himself. Aelfric, Burghelm and
Godiva held it before 1066; it paid tax for 16 hides, less 1
virgate. Land for 7 ploughs. Ansfrid has 11 hides of this
land from Gilbert; 3 ploughs there, in lordship; 7 slaves and
   3 villagers, 2 smallholders and 10 Cottagers with 2½ ploughs.
   A mill which pays 5s; meadow, 50 acres; pasture, 70 acres;
      woodland, 18 acres.
   Of these 11 hides, 1 is in Thornhill; it lay in (the lands of)
   Clyffe (Pypard) before 1066. In Cliffe (Pypard)   71 c
      2 smallholders and 2 slaves.
      Meadow, 16 acres; pasture, 17 acres.
Value of this under Gilbert, 35s; value of what Ansfrid holds £6.

6 Thurstan holds MOREDON from Gilbert. Wulfgar held it before
1066; it paid tax for 3 hides, less 1 virgate. Land for 2 ploughs,
of which 1 hide and 1 virgate of land are in lordship; 1 plough there;
   2 villagers and 4 smallholders with 2 ploughs.
   Meadow, 20 acres; pasture, 80 acres.
The value was and is 40s.

7 Gilbert holds (Broad) HINTON himself. Wulfgar held it before 1066;
it paid tax for 11 hides and 1 virgate. Land for 5 ploughs, of which
9 hides and 1 virgate of land are in lordship; 2 ploughs there;
   4 villagers and 5 smallholders with 2 ploughs.
   Meadow, 16 acres; pasture, 30 acres.
The value was 100s; now £7.

8 Ansfrid holds BECKHAMPTON from Gilbert. Edric held it before
1066; it paid tax for 2 hides. Land for 3 ploughs, of which 1 hide
is in lordship; 2 ploughs there;
   4 villagers, 7 smallholders and 3 cottagers with 2 ploughs.
   Meadow, 8 acres; pasture, 40 acres.
The value was and is £6.

9 Ansfrid holds STANMORE from Gilbert. Browning held it before
1066; it paid tax for 2½ hides. Land for 2 ploughs, of which 2
hides are in lordship; 1 plough there; 2 slaves;
   1 villager and 3 smallholders with ½ plough.
The value was 20s; now 40s.

30   **LAND OF DURAND OF GLOUCESTER**

1 Durand of Gloucester holds CHIRTON from the King. Aelmer held
it before 1066; it paid tax for 10 hides. Land for 5 ploughs,
of which 7 hides are in lordship, with 1½ ploughs;
   7 villagers and 10 smallholders with 2 ploughs.
   A mill which pays 10s; meadow, 30 acres; pasture ½ league
      long and 3 furlongs wide.
The value was £11; now £10.

Rogeri ten de . D . *Tocheha̅* . Dodo tenuit T . R . E . de æcc̄la Malmeſ
berienſi . 7 n̄ poterat ab ea ſeparari . 7 geldb̄ ꝑ . v . hid . Tra . e̅

In dn̄io . e̅ dimid.　　　　　7 ibi . ii . car̄ . cu̅ . i . ſeruo . 7 vii . uilti 7 iii . bord̄
cu̅ . ii . car̄ . Ibi moli̅n redd̄ ꓶ ꓶ . denar̄ . 7 xii . ac̄ p̄ti . 7 iiii . ac̄ paſturæ .
7 ii . ac̄ ſiluæ . Valuit . xl . ſolid̄ . Modo . iiii . lib̄ .

Id̅e ten in *Vfecote* . i . hid̄ 7 dimid̄ . Tra . e̅ . i . car̄ . H̄ eſt in dn̄io . Valuit
7 uat̄ . xv . ſot̄ . Almar tenuit T . R . E .

Ipſe . D . ten *Segrete* . Duo taini tenuer̄ T . R . E . 7 geldb̄ ꝑ . v . hid̄ .
Tra . e̅ . iiii . car̄ . De ea ſt̄ in dn̄io . ii . hidæ . 7 ibi . i . car̄ . 7 iii . uilti 7 ii . bord̄
cu̅ . iii . car̄ . Ibi . xl . ac̄ p̄ti . Valuit . xl . ſot̄ . Modo . l . ſolid̄ . Duo milites
ten de Durando . Qui teneb̄ T . R . E . poterant ire quó uoleb̄ .

Ipſe . D . ten *Esselie* . Eldred tenuit T . R . E . 7 geldb̄ . ꝑ . v . hid̄ una v
min . Tra . e̅ . iiii . car̄ . De his ſt̄ in dn̄io . iii . hidæ . 7 ibi . ii . car̄ . 7 iii . ſerui .
7 v . uilti 7 iii . bord̄ cu̅ . ii . car̄ . 7 ii . cotar̄ . Ibi . v . ac̄ p̄ti . 7 v . ac̄ ſiluæ .
Valuit 7 uat̄ . iiii . lib̄ . Vna̅ v træ in ipſa uilla calu̅niat un miles Milon̄ꜛ.

Ipſe . D . ten *Locherige* . Elmar tenuit T . R . E . 7 redd̄ geld̄ ꝑ . ii . hid̄ .
Tra . e̅ . i . car̄ . De hac e̅ in dn̄io . i . hida . Ibi . i . uilts . 7 ii . bord̄ cu̅ . i . ſeruo .
7 una ac̄ p̄ti . 7 xii . ac̄ paſturæ . 7 vi . ac̄ ſiluæ . Valuit . xl . ſot̄ . M̊ . xxx . ſot̄ .

Herman ten de . D . *Lochintone* . Herald tenuit T . R . E . 7 geldb̄
ꝑ . iiii . hid̄ . Tra . e̅ . v . car̄ . De ea ſt̄ in dn̄io . ii . hidæ . 7 ibi . ii . car̄ . cu̅ . i . ſeruo .
7 vi . uilti 7 viii . bord̄ cu̅ . ii . car̄ . Ibi moli̅n redd̄ . v . ſolid̄ . 7 x . ac̄ p̄ti .
7 viii . ac̄ paſturæ . 7 iiii . ac̄ ſiluæ . Valuit . c . ſolid̄ . Modo . iiii . lib̄ .

2 Roger holds TOCKENHAM from Durand. Doda held it before 1066
from Malmesbury Church; he could not be separated from it.
It paid tax for 5 hides. Land for ....[ploughs.] In lordship ½ [hide];
2 ploughs there, with 1 slave;
> 7 villagers and 3 smallholders with 2 ploughs.
> A mill which pays 50d; meadow, 12 acres; pasture, 4 acres;
> woodland, 2 acres.

The value was 40s; now £4.

3 He also holds 1½ hides in UFFCOTT. Land for 1 plough; it is
in lordship.
The value was and is 15s.
> Aelmer held it before 1066.

4 Durand holds SEAGRY himself. Two thanes held it before 1066;
it paid tax for 5 hides. Land for 4 ploughs, of which 2 hides
are in lordship; 1 plough there;
> 3 villagers and 2 smallholders with 3 ploughs.
> Meadow, 40 acres.

The value was 40s; now 50s.
> Two men-at-arms hold from Durand. The holders before 1066

could go where they would.

5 Durand holds ASHLEY himself. Aldred held it before 1066; it paid
tax for 5 hides, less 1 virgate. Land for 4 ploughs, of which 3
hides are in lordship; 2 ploughs there; 3 slaves;
> 5 villagers and 3 smallholders with 2 ploughs; 2 cottagers.
> Meadow, 5 acres; woodland, 5 acres.

The value was and is £4.
> A man-at-arms of Miles Crispin's claims 1 virgate of land in

this village.

6 Durand holds LOCKERIDGE himself. Aelmer held it before 1066;
it paid tax for 2 hides. Land for 1 plough, of which 1 hide
is in lordship.
> 1 villager and 2 smallholders with 1 slave.
> Meadow, 1 acre; pasture, 12 acres; woodland, 6 acres.

The value was 40s; now 30s.

7 Herman holds LUCKINGTON from Durand. Earl Harold held it
before 1066; it paid tax for 4 hides. Land for 5 ploughs,
of which 2 hides are in lordship; 2 ploughs there, with 1 slave;
> 6 villagers and 8 smallholders with 2 ploughs.
> A mill which pays 5s; meadow, 10 acres; pasture, 8 acres;
> woodland, 4 acres.

The value was 100s; now £4.

.XXXI. TERRA WALTERIJ GIFARD.

WALTERIVS GIFARD ten de rege *BRADELIE* . Tofti tenuit T.R.E.

7 p . x . hiđ fe defenđ . Tra . ē . x . cař . De ea ſt in dñio . iiii . hidæ.

7 ibi . ii . cař . 7 iiii . ſerui . 7 vi . uiłłi 7 xiii . borđ cū . vi . cař . Ibi . ii . mo

lini redđ . xii . ſoliđ 7 vi . den . 7 x . ač p̃ti . Paſtura dimiđ leu lḡ.

7 ii . q̃ʒ laŧ . Silua . i . leu lḡ . 7 una laŧ . Valuit . xii . liŧ . Modo . x . liŧ.

.XXXII. TERRA WILLELMI DE OW.

WILLELM De . Ow . ten de rege *DIARNEFORD* . T.R.E. gelđŧ p . xvi.

hiđ . Tra . ē . xiiii . cař . De ea ſt in dñio . iiii . hidæ . 7 ibi . ii . cař.

7 ii . ſerui . 7 xxvi . uiłłi 7 xxxvii . borđ cū . xii . cař . Ibi . iii . molini redđ

xxiiii . ſoliđ 7 vi . den . 7 xxx . ač p̃ti . Paſtura . x . q̃ʒ lḡ . 7 ii . q̃ʒ laŧ.

Silua . iiii . q̃ʒ lḡ . 7 ii . q̃ʒ laŧ . In Wiltone . iiii . dom redđ . iiii . ſoliđ.

Valuit 7 uał . xxiiii . liŧ.

Wiłłs de Aldrie ten de . W . *LITELTONE* . T.R.E. gelđŧ p . vi . hiđ

7 una v træ . Tra . ē . vi . cař . In dñio ſt . ii . cař . cū . i . ſeruo . 7 iii . uiłłi

7 xxi . borđ cū . iii . cař . Ibi . ii . molini redđ . xxx . ſoł . 7 xii . ač p̃ti.

Paſtura . x . q̃ʒ lḡ . 7 ii . q̃ʒ laŧ . Valuit . x . liŧ . Modo . viii . liŧ.

Hæc tra fuit T.R.E. tainlande æcclæ Sariſberiæ Aleſtan tenuit.

71 d

Iđē . W . ten de . W . *CONTONE* . T.R.E. gelđŧ p . vi . hiđ.

Tra . ē . iiii . cař . In dñio ſt . ii . cař . 7 v . ſerui . 7 iii . uiłłi

7 xi . borđ cū . ii . cař . Ibi tcia pars . ii . molinoʒ redđ

. x . ſoliđ . 7 xxiiii . ač p̃ti . 7 x . ač paſturæ . 7 totiđ filuæ.

Valuit 7 uał . c . ſoliđ.

Wiłłs de Mara ten de . W . *BREVRESBROC* . T.R.E. gelđŧ p . ii . hiđ

7 dimiđ . Tra . ē . ii . cař . De ea . ē in dñio . i . hida 7 dim . 7 ibi . ii . cař.

7 ii . ſerui . 7 i . uiłłs 7 viii . borđ . Valuit 7 uał . xxx . ſoliđ.

LAND OF WALTER GIFFARD

1   Walter Giffard holds (Maiden) BRADLEY from the King. Earl Tosti
held it before 1066; it answered for 10 hides. Land for 10
ploughs, of which 4 hides are in lordship; 2 ploughs there; 4 slaves;
    6 villagers and 13 smallholders with 6 ploughs.
    2 mills which pay 12s 6d; meadow, 10 acres; pasture ½ league
        long and 2 furlongs wide; woodland 1 league long and 1 wide.
The value was £12; now £10.

32   **LAND OF WILLIAM OF EU**

1   William of Eu holds DURNFORD from the King. Before 1066 it
paid tax for 16 hides. Land for 14 ploughs, of which 4 hides
are in lordship; 2 ploughs there; 2 slaves;
    26 villagers and 37 smallholders with 12 ploughs.
    3 mills which pay 24s 6d; meadow, 30 acres; pasture 10
        furlongs long and 2 furlongs wide; woodland 4 furlongs
        long and 2 furlongs wide; in Wilton 4 houses which pay 4s.
The value was and is £24.

2   William of Audrieu holds LITTLETON (Pannell) from William.
Before 1066 it paid tax for 6 hides and 1 virgate of land.
Land for 6 ploughs. In lordship 2 ploughs, with 1 slave;
    3 villagers and 21 smallholders with 3 ploughs.
    2 mills which pay 30s; meadow, 12 acres; pasture 10 furlongs
        long and 2 furlongs wide.
The value was £10; now £8.
    Before 1066 this land was thaneland of Salisbury Church;
Alstan (of) Boscombe held it.

3   William also holds COMPTON (Bassett) from William. Before   71 d
1066 it paid tax for 6 hides. Land for 4 ploughs. In lordship 2
ploughs; 5 slaves;
    3 villagers and 11 smallholders with 2 ploughs.
    The third part of 2 mills which pays 10s; meadow, 24 acres.
        pasture, 10 acres; woodland, as many.
The value was and is 100s.

4   William Delamere holds BEVERSBROOK from William. Before 1066
it paid tax for 2½ hides. Land for 2 ploughs, of which 1½
hides are in lordship; 2 ploughs there; 2 slaves;
    1 villager and 8 smallholders.
The value was and is 30s.

Hugo teñ de . W . *CERLETONE* . T . R . E . geldb̃ p̄ . v . hid̃ . Tra . ē . vii . car̃ . De ea st̃ in dn̄io . iiii . Hidæ 7 dim̃ . 7 ibi . i . car̃ . 7 ii . uitti 7 vii . bord̃ cū dimid̃ car̃ . Ibi . ii . molini redd̃ . viii . sol̃ . 7 iiii . den̄ . 7 xv . ac̃ p̃ti . Pastura . iiii . qz̃ lḡ . 7 una qz̃ lat̃ . Silua . vi . qz̃ lḡ . 7 iii . qz̃ lat̃ . Valuit 7 ual̃ . c . solid̃.

Idē H . teñ de . W . *GRAFTONE* . T . R . E . geldb̃ p̄ una h̃ . Tra . ē . i . car̃ 7 dim̃ . Ibi st̃ . iii . bord̃ . pastura . ii . qz̃ lḡ . 7 una qz̃ lat̃ . Valuit . lx . solid̃ . Modo . xl . solid̃.

Eduuard teñ de . W . *BOSCVBE* . T . R . E geldb̃ p̄ . vii . hid̃ . Tra . ē . iiii . car̃ . De ea st̃ in dn̄io . iiii . hidæ 7 dim̃ . 7 ibi . ii . car̃ . 7 ibi . ii . serui . 7 iii . uitti 7 iiii . coscez . cū . i . car̃ 7 dim̃ . Ibi vi . ac̃ p̃ti . Pastura . xii . qz̃ lḡ . 7 totid̃ lat̃ . Valet . x . lib̃.

Bernard teñ *CELDRETONE* . T . R . E . geld̃ p̄ . iii . hid̃ 7 dimid̃ iiii . acris min̄ . Tra . ē . ii . car̃ . De ea st̃ in dn̄io . iii . hidæ 7 ibi ii . car̃ . 7 ii . serui . 7 v . bord̃ . 7 ii . coscez . Ibi pastura . vi . qz̃ lḡ . 7 v . qz̃ lat̃ . Valuit . c . solid̃ . Modo . ix . lib̃.

Radulf teñ de . W . *ADHELMERTONE* . T . R . E . geldb̃ p̄ . ix . hid̃ . Tra . ē . viii . car̃ . De ea st̃ in dn̄io . iii . hidæ . 7 ibi . ii . car̃ . 7 vii . uitti 7 x . bord̃ cū . vi . car̃ . Ibi molin̄ redd̃ . vii . sol̃ . 7 l . ac̃ p̃ti . 7 xl . ac̃ pasturæ . Valuit 7 ual̃ . vii . lib̃.

Bernard teñ de . W . *COTEFORD* . T . R . E . geldb̃ p̄ . i . hida 7 dim̃ . Tra . ē . ii . car̃ . De ea in dn̄io . i . hida 7 ibi . i . car̃ . cū . i . seruo . 7 ii . coscez cū . i . car̃ . Ibi . x . ac̃ p̃ti . 7 q̃rta pars molini redd̃ . iii . sol̃ . pastura . iiii . qz̃ lḡ . 7 ii . qz̃ lat̃ . Valuit . iiii . lib̃ . Modo . iii . lib̃.

Warner teñ de . W . *DIGERIC* . T . R . E . geldb̃ p̄ . i . hida 7 iii . v̄ træ . Tra . ē . i . car̃ . q̄ ibi . ē in dn̄io . 7 ii . uitti 7 iiii . coscez . Ibi dimid̃

5   Hugh holds 'CHARLTON' from William. Before 1066 it paid tax
     for 5 hides. Land for 7 ploughs, of which 4½ hides are in
     lordship; 1 plough there;
    2 villagers and 7 smallholders with ½ plough.
    2 mills which pay 8s 4d; meadow, 15 acres; pasture 4
      furlongs long and 1 furlong wide; woodland 6 furlongs
      long and 3 furlongs wide.
     The value was and is 100s.

6   Hugh also holds GRAFTON from William. Before 1066 it paid
     tax for 1 hide. Land for 1½ ploughs.
    3 smallholders.
    Pasture 2 furlongs long and 1 furlong wide.
     The value was 60s; now 40s.

7   Edward holds BOSCOMBE from William. Before 1066 it paid tax
     for 7 hides. Land for 4 ploughs, of which 4½ hides are in
     lordship; 2 ploughs there; 2 slaves there;
    3 villagers and 4 Cottagers with 1½ ploughs.
    Meadow, 6 acres; pasture 12 furlongs long and as many wide.
     Value £10.

8   Bernard holds CHOLDERTON. Before 1066 it paid tax for 3½
     hides, less 4 acres. Land for 2 ploughs, of which 3 hides are in
     lordship; 2 ploughs there; 2 slaves;
    5 smallholders and 2 Cottagers.
    Pasture 6 furlongs long and 5 furlongs wide.
     The value was 100s; now £9.

9   Ralph holds HILMARTON from William. Before 1066 it paid tax
     for 9 hides. Land for 8 ploughs, of which 3 hides are in
     lordship; 2 ploughs there;
    7 villagers and 10 smallholders with 6 ploughs.
    A mill which pays 7s; meadow, 50 acres; pasture, 40 acres.
     The value was and is £7.

10   Bernard holds CODFORD from William. Before 1066 it paid tax
     for 1½ hides. Land for 2 ploughs, of which 1 hide is in
     lordship; 1 plough there, with 1 slave;
    2 Cottagers with 1 plough.
    Meadow, 10 acres; the fourth part of a mill which pays 3s;
      pasture 4 furlongs long and 2 furlongs wide.
     The value was £4; now £3.

11   Warner holds DITTERIDGE from William. Before 1066 it paid tax
     for 1 hide and 3 virgates of land. Land for 1 plough, which
     is there, in lordship;
    2 villagers and 4 Cottagers.

moliñ redd.v.folid.7 vii.ac̄ p̄ti.7 xv.ac̄ paſturæ.7 xvii.

ac̄ filuæ minutæ.Valet.xxx.fol.De hac t̄ra.i.hid p̄reſtitit

Aleſtano q̄dā abb̄ malmesbienſis.

Radulf⁹ teñ de.W.*LACHAM*.T.R.E.geldb̄ p̄.vii.hid 7 dim.

T̄ra.ē.x.car̄.De ea in dñio.ē.i.hida 7 dim.7 ibi.ii.car̄.

7 ii.ferui.7 x.uilli 7 iiii.bord 7 xxiiii.cofcez cū.viii.car̄.

Ibi.ii.molini redd.xxx.fol.7 xv.ac̄ p̄ti.Silua.i.leu lḡ.7 tñtd

lat̄.Valuit.vi.lib̄.Modo fimilit̄.

Wilts teñ de.W.*SEVAMENTONE*.T.R.E.geldb̄ p̄.x.hid.

T̄ra.ē.vii.car̄.De ea ſt in dñio.iiii.hidæ 7 ibi.ii.car̄.7 x.uilli

7 v.bord.cū.v.car̄.Ibi.xx.ac̄ p̄ti.Silua.ii.q̄z lḡ.7 una

q̄z lat̄.Valuit.vi.lib̄.Modo.vii.lib̄.

Vn Anglic⁹ teñ de.W.*GETONE*.T.R.E geldb̄ p̄ una v̄ t̄ræ.

T̄ra.ē dim car̄.q̄ ibi.ē.Redd.v.folid.

Has oms p̄ſcriptas t̄ras Wilti de ow.tenuit Aleſtan de Boſcube.

Hugo teñ de.W.*SOPEWORDE*.Aluric tenuit T.R.E.7 geldb̄

p̄.v.hid.T̄ra.ē.vi.car̄.De ea ſt in dñio.iii.hide 7 dimid.

7 ibi.ii.car̄.7 vi.ferui.7 iii.uilli 7 v.bord cū.iii.car̄.

Valuit.vi.lib̄.Modo.iiii.lib̄.

Idē.W.teñ *TOLLARD*.Toli tenuit T.R.E.p̄ uno ᷁.7 geldb̄ p̄.i.

hida.T̄ra.ē.i.car̄.Ibi ſt   cofcez.7 v.ac̄ p̄ti.7 una q̄rent

filuæ.Valuit 7 ual.xx.folid.

Ansfrid⁹ teñ de.W.*OPETONE*.Toli tenuit T.R.E.7 geldb̄

p̄.iii.hid.T̄ra.ē.ii.car̄ 7 dim.De ea ſt in dñio.ii.hidæ.

7 ibi.i.car̄.7 ii.uilli 7 v.bord cū.i.car̄.Ibi moliñ red.v.fol.

7 iiii.ac̄ p̄ti.Silua.ii.q̄z lḡ.7 una q̄z lat̄.7 xx.ac̄ paſturæ.

Valuit.xv.fol.Modo.lx.folid.

p̄ dimid hida ñ reddid geld poſtq̄.W.rex uenit in angliā.

7 Hernulf⁹ de Eſding teñ injuſte dimid hid in ipfa uilla.

½ mill which pays 5s; meadow, 7 acres; pasture, 15 acres; underwood, 17 acres.

Value 30s.

An Abbot of Malmesbury leased 1 hide of this land to Alstan.

12 Ralph holds LACKHAM from William. Before 1066 it paid tax for 7½ hides. Land for 10 ploughs, of which 1½ hides are in lordship; 2 ploughs there; 2 slaves;
   10 villagers, 4 smallholders and 24 Cottagers with 8 ploughs.
   2 mills which pay 30s; meadow, 15 acres; woodland 1 league long and as wide.
   The value was £6; now the same.

13 William holds SEVINGTON from William. Before 1066 it paid tax for 10 hides. Land for 7 ploughs, of which 4 hides are in lordship; 2 ploughs there;
   10 villagers and 5 smallholders with 5 ploughs.
   Meadow, 20 acres; woodland 2 furlongs long and 1 furlong wide.
   The value was £6; now £7.

14 An Englishman holds YATTON (Keynell) from William. Before 1066 it paid tax for 1 virgate of land. Land for ½ plough, which is there. It pays 5s.

Alstan of Boscombe held all the above lands of William of Eu.

15 Hugh holds SOPWORTH from William. Aelfric held it before 1066; it paid tax for 5 hides. Land for 6 ploughs, of which 3½ hides are in lordship; 2 ploughs there; 6 slaves;
   3 villagers and 5 smallholders with 3 ploughs.
   The value was £6; now £4.

16 William also holds TOLLARD (Royal). Toli held it before 1066 as 1 manor; it paid tax for 1 hide. Land for 1 plough.
   .....Cottagers.
   Meadow, 5 acres; woodland, 1 furlong.
   The value was and is 20s.

17 Ansfrid holds UPTON (Scudamore) from William. Toli held it before 1066; it paid tax for 3 hides. Land for 2½ ploughs, of which 2 hides are in lordship; 1 plough there;
   2 villagers and 5 smallholders with 1 plough.
   A mill which pays 5s; meadow, 4 acres; woodland 2 furlongs long and 1 furlong wide; pasture, 20 acres.
   The value was 15s; now 60s.
   It did not pay tax for ½ hide after King William came to England. Arnulf of Hesdin wrongfully holds ½ hide in this village.

.XXXII. TERRA WILLI DE BRAIOSE.

Wills De Braiose ten de rege *ESSAGE*. Aluuin tenuit
T.R.E.7 geldb p̄.II.hid 7 una v træ.│Tra.e̅.I.car 7 dimid.
De ea st in dn̄io.II.hidæ.Ibi.I.uilts 7 II.bord cū dimid car.
Ibi.XL.ac̄ pasturæ.7 Silua.I.leu lḡ.7 III.q̊ lat.
Valuit.X.solid.Modo.XX.solid.Robt ten de Willo.

XXXIIII. TERRA WILLI DE MOIVN.

Wills De Moivn ten de rege.*SVTONE*.7 Walter de eo.
Colo tenuit T.R.E.7 geldb p̄.V.hid.Tra.e̅.IIII.car.De ea
st in dn̄io.III.hidæ 7 una v træ.7 ibi.II.car.7 III.serui.
7 III.uilti 7 VI.bord.cū.II.car.Ibi molin redd.IIII.solid.
7 IIII.ac̄ p̄ti.7 II.ac̄ siluæ.Pastura dimid leu lḡ.7 unā lat.
Valuit.IIII.lib.Modo.c.solid.

.XXXV. TERRA WILLI DE FALEISE.

Wills de Faleise ten de rege dimid hid in *STANINGES*
7 Aluuard de eo.Tra.e̅ dimid car.q̄ ibi.e̅.7 IIII.ac̄ p̄ti.
Valuit.XX.solid.Modo redd.X.solid.Leuing tenuit T.R.E.

XXXVI. TERRA WALSCINI DE DOWAI.

Walscinvs De Dwai ten de rege *CELDEWELLE*.7 Go
descal de eo.Alsi tenuit T.R.E.7 geldb p̄.V.hid.Tra.e̅
III.car.De ea st in dn̄io.III.hidæ 7 III.v træ.7 ibi.I.car.
cū.I.seruo.7 I.uilto 7 VI.bord cū dim car.Ibi.X.ac̄ p̄ti.
7 VII.ac̄ pasturæ.7 VIII.ac̄ siluæ.Valuit 7 uat.III.lib.
Radulf ten de.W.*STORTONE*.Aluuacre tenuit T.R.E.
7 geldb p̄.VIII.hid.Tra.e̅.VI.car.De ea st in dn̄io.V.
hidæ 7 ibi.II.car.cū.I.seruo.7 VI.uitti 7 XIII.coscez.7 VIII.
cotar cū.IIII.car.Ibi.II.molini redd.XX.denar.7 LX.ac̄
pasturæ.Silua.I.leu lḡ.7 una lat.Valuit.IIII.lib.m̄.VII.lib.

33   LAND OF WILLIAM OF BRAOSE

1   William of Braose holds SHAW from the King. Alwin held it
before 1066; it paid tax for 2 hides and 1½ virgates of land.
Land for 1½ ploughs, of which 2 hides are in lordship.
    1 villager and 2 smallholders with ½ plough.
    Pasture, 40 acres; woodland 1 league long and 3 furlongs wide.
The value was 10s; now 20s.
    Robert holds from William.

34   LAND OF WILLIAM OF MOHUN

1   William of Mohun holds SUTTON (Veny) from the King, and
Walter from him. Cola held it before 1066; it paid tax
for 5 hides. Land for 4 ploughs, of which 3 hides and 1 virgate
of land are in lordship; 2 ploughs there; 3 slaves;   47
    3 villagers and 6 smallholders with 2 ploughs.   a1
    A mill which pays 4s; meadow, 4 acres; woodland, 2 acres;
       pasture ½ league long and 1 wide. 1 cob; 300 sheep.
The value was £4; now 100s.

35   LAND OF WILLIAM OF FALAISE

1   William of Falaise holds ½ hide in STANDLYNCH from the King,
and Alfward from him. Land for ½ plough, which is there.
    Meadow, 4 acres.
The value was 20s; now it pays 10s.
    Leofing held it before 1066.

36   LAND OF WALSCIN OF DOUAI

1   Walscin of Douai holds *CELDEWELLE* from the King, and Godescal
from him. Alfsi held it before 1066; it paid tax for 5 hides.
Land for 3 ploughs, of which 3 hides and 3 virgates of land
are in lordship; 1 plough there, with 1 slave and
    1 villager and 6 smallholders with ½ plough.
    Meadow, 10 acres; pasture, 7 acres; woodland, 8 acres.
The value was and is £3.

2   Ralph holds STOURTON from Walscin. Alwaker held it before 1066;
it paid tax for 8 hides. Land for 6 ploughs, of which 5 hides
are in lordship; 2 ploughs there, with 1 slave;
    6 villagers, 13 Cottagers and 8 cottagers with 4 ploughs.
    2 mills which pay 20d; pasture, 60 acres; woodland 1 league
      long and 1 wide.
The value was £4; now £7.

WALERANN ten de rege *COTEFORD*. Erlebald tenuit
T.R.E. 7 geldb p. vi. hid. Tra. e̅. vi. car̅. De ea ſt in dn̅io
iii. hide. 7 ibi. ii. car̅. 7 iii. ſerui. 7 vii. uilli 7 vi. borđ cu̅. iii.
car̅. Ibi moliñ redđ. x. ſoł. 7 x. ac̅ pti. Paſtura dim̅ leu̅
lg̅. 7 v. q̅ꝫ lat̅. Valuit x. lib. Modo. xii. lib.

WAlter ten de. W. *ANESTIGE*. Aluric 7 Vluuard ten̅
T.R.E. 7 geldb p. vii. hid. Tra. e̅. iiii. car̅. De ea ſt in dn̅io
. v. hidæ. 7 una v træ. 7 ibi. ii. car̅. 7 ii. ſerui. 7 vi. uilli 7 iiii.
borđ cu̅. ii. car̅. Ibi moliñ redđ. v. ſoł. 7 xvi. ac̅ pti. 7 xv. ac̅
ſiluæ. Paſtura dim̅ leu̅ lg̅. 7 iii. q̅ꝫ lat̅. Valuit 7 uał. c. ſoł.

Azelin ten de. W. *BVTREMARE*. Octo taini tenuer̅ T.R.E.
7 geldb p. i. hida 7 una v træ. Tra. e̅. ii. car̅. Valet. xx. ſoliđ.

Ipſe. W. ten. i. hidā in *STANINGES*. Colo tenuit T.R.E. Tra. e̅
dimiđ car̅. Ibi ſt. vi. ac̅ pti. Valuit. v. ſoł. Modo. x. ſoł.

Ricarđ ten de. W. *CHENETE*. Leueclai tenuit T.R.E. 7
7 geldb p una hida 7 dim̅. 7 una v træ. Tra. e̅. i. car̅. q̅ ibi. e̅
cu̅. i. ſeruo. 7 ii. borđ. 7 una ac̅ pti. 7 iiii. ac̅ paſturæ. Valuit 7 uał

Azelin ten de. W. *STANLEGE*. Seleuuin tenuit   ⌐ xx. ſoł.
T.R.E. 7 geldb p una hida 7 iii. v træ. Tra. e̅. i. car̅.
Ibi ſt. iii. uilli 7 iii. borđ. 7 x. ac̅ pti. Valuit. xv. ſoł. m̅ xxx. ſoł.

Ipſe Waler̅ ten *LANGEFORD*. Oſulf tenuit T.R.E. 7 geldb
p x. hiđ. Tra. e̅. v. car̅. De ea ſt in dn̅io. v. hidæ. 7 ibi. ii.
car̅. 7 v. ſerui. 7 viii. uilli 7 iiii. borđ. cu̅. iii. car̅. Ibi moliñ
redđ. xv. ſoł. 7 xxx. ac̅ pti. Paſtura dim̅ leu̅ lg̅. 7 ii. q̅ꝫ lat̅.
Valuit 7 uał. x. lib.

LAND OF WALERAN HUNTER

1   Waleran holds CODFORD from the King. Erlebald held it before 1066; it paid tax for 6 hides. Land for 6 ploughs, of which 3 hides are in lordship; 2 ploughs there; 3 slaves;
> 7 villagers and 6 smallholders with 3 ploughs.
> A mill which pays 10s; meadow, 10 acres; pasture ½ league long and 5 furlongs wide.

The value was £10; now £12.

2   Walter holds ANSTY from Waleran. Aelfric and Wulfward held it before 1066; it paid tax for 7 hides. Land for 4 ploughs, of which 5 hides and 1 virgate of land are in lordship; 2 ploughs there; 2 slaves;
> 6 villagers and 4 smallholders with 2 ploughs.
> A mill which pays 5s; meadow, 16 acres; woodland, 15 acres; pasture ½ league long and 3 furlongs wide.

The value was and is 100s.

3   Azelin holds BUTTERMERE from Waleran. Eight thanes held it before 1066; it paid tax for 1 hide and 1 virgate of land. Land for 2 ploughs.
Value 20s.

4   Waleran holds 1 hide in STANDLYNCH himself. Cola held it before 1066. Land for ½ plough.
> Meadow, 6 acres.

The value was 5s; now 10s.

5   Richard holds KENNETT from Waleran. Leofday held it before 1066; it paid tax for 1½ hides and 1 virgate of land. Land for 1 plough, which is there, with 1 slave;
> 2 smallholders.
> Meadow, 1 acre; pasture, 4 acres.

The value was and is 20s.

6   Azelin holds STANLEY from Waleran. Selwin held it before 1066; it paid tax for 1 hide and 3 virgates of land. Land for 1 plough.
> 3 villagers and 3 smallholders.
> Meadow, 10 acres.

The value was 15s; now 30s.

7   Waleran holds LANGFORD himself. Oswulf held it before 1066; it paid tax for 10 hides. Land for 5 ploughs, of which 5 hides are in lordship; 2 ploughs there; 5 slaves;
> 8 villagers and 4 smallholders with 3 ploughs.
> A mill which pays 15s; meadow, 30 acres; pasture ½ league long and 2 furlongs wide.

The value was and is £10.

Erenburgis teñ de.W.*LANGEFORD*.Norman tenuit
T.R.E.7 geldƀ ꝑ.v.hiđ.Tra.ē.ii.caṙ.De ea ſt in dñi
hidæ.7 ibi.i.caṙ.cū.i.ſeruo.7 i.uiłło.7 v.borđ cū ᴄ
Ibi dimiđ moliñ redđ.xxx.deñ.7 xx.ac̄ ꝑti.Paſtura.ii
q̃ƶ lḡ.7 una q̃ƶ lat̄.Valuit 7 uał.c.ſoliđ.
Engenold teñ de.W.dimiđ hiđ in *BEREFORD*.7
T.R.E.Bolle tenuit.Tra.ē dim̃ caṙ.Ibi ſt.ii.b
ꝑti.Valuit 7 uał.vii.ſoliđ.
Roƀt teñ de.W.in *WITFORD*.iii.v̄ træ.7 ꝑ tanto geldƀ
T.R.E.Bolle tenuit.Tra.ē dimiđ caṙ.Ibi ſt.ii.borđ.7 iiii.
ac̄ ꝑti.Valuit 7 uał.x.ſoliđ.

72 b

Herƀt teñ de.W.*GREMESTEDE*.Agemund tenuit T.R.E.7 geldƀ
ꝑ.iii.hiđ.Tra.ē.iii.caṙ.De ea.ē in dñio.i.hida 7 dim̃.7 ibi.i.caṙ.
7 ii.ſerui.7 v.uiłłi.7 vii.coſcez cū.iii.caṙ.Ibi.x.ac̄ ꝑti.Silua.v.q̃ƶ
lḡ.7 ii.q̃ƶ lat̄.Valuit 7 uał.lx.ſoliđ.
Engenulf teñ de.W.*WATEDENE*.Bolle tenuit T.R.E.7 geldƀ
ꝑ.ii.hiđ.Tra.ē.i.caṙ 7 dim̃.De ea in dñio.ē hida 7 dim̃.7 ibi.i.caṙ.
7 iiii.coſcez cū dimiđ caṙ.Ibi.vii.ac̄ ꝑti.Siluæ.ii.q̃ƶ lḡ.7 dim̃ q̃ƶ lat̄.
Valuit.xv.ſoł.Modo.xxv.ſoliđ.
In *WATEDENE* teñ.ii.milites.iii.v̄ træ 7 dimiđ.ii.ac̄s miñ.T.R.E.
teneƀ.iiii.taini.q̃ poterant ire q̃ uoleƀ.Tra.ē dimiđ caṙ.q̃ ibi.ē
cū.ii.coſcez.7 iiii.ac̄ ꝑti 7 dimiđ.Valet.xii.ſoliđ.
Engenulf teñ de.W.unā v̄ træ in *ALWARBERIE*.7 ibi hƚ.i.coſcet.
Valet.ii.ſoliđ.Bode tenuit T.R.E.

8   Ernburgis holds LANGFORD from Waleran. Norman held
it before 1066; it paid tax for 5 hides. Land for 2 ploughs, of
which 4 hides are in lordship; 1 plough there, with 1 slave and
     1 villager and 5 smallholders with ½ plough.
     ½ mill which pays 30d; meadow, 20 acres; pasture 4 furlongs
       long and 1 furlong wide.
The value was and is 100s.

9   Engenold holds ½ hide in BARFORD from Waleran; it paid
tax for as much. Before 1066 Bolla held it. Land for ½ plough.
     2 smallholders.
     Meadow, 3 acres.
The value was and is 7s.

10   Robert holds 3 virgates of land in WISHFORD from Waleran; it paid
tax for as much. Before 1066 Bolla held it. Land for ½ plough.
     2 smallholders.
     Meadow, 4 acres.
The value was and is 10s.

11   Herbert holds GRIMSTEAD from Waleran. Agemund held it   72 b
before 1066; it paid tax for 3 hides. Land for 3 ploughs, of
which 1½ hides are in lordship; 1 plough there; 2 slaves;
     5 villagers and 7 Cottagers with 3 ploughs.
     Meadow, 10 acres; woodland 5 furlongs long and 2 furlongs wide.
The value was and is 60s.

12   Engenwulf holds WHADDON from Waleran. Bolla held it before 1066;
it paid tax for 2 hides. Land for 1½ ploughs, of which 1½ hides
are in lordship; 1 plough there;
     4 Cottagers with ½ plough.
     Meadow, 7 acres; woodlands 2 furlongs long and ½ furlong wide.
The value was 15s; now 25s.

13   In WHADDON 2 men-at-arms hold 3½ virgates of land, less 2 acres.
Before 1066 four thanes held them; they could go where they would.
Land for ½ plough, which is there, with
     2 Cottagers.
     Meadow, 4½ acres.
Value 12s.

14   Engenwulf holds 1 virgate of land in ALDERBURY from Waleran; he has
     1 Cottager.
Value 2s.
     Boda held it before 1066.

Ipſe Waler teñ *DVENE* . Godric tenuit T.R.E. 7 geldb p̄.II. hid

7 una v̄ træ . Tra . ē . III . car̄ . De ea . ē in dñio . I . hida . 7 ibi car̄ 7 dim̄ .

7 II . ſerui . 7 uñ uilłs 7 x . coſcez cū car̄ 7 dim̄ . Ibi moliñ 7 dimid .

redd . xvi . ſolid . 7 v . āc p̄ti . Silua . I . q̃ʒ int lḡ 7 lat̄ .

Valuit 7 ual̄ . lx . ſolid .

In *HERDICOTE* teñ dimid hid . Tra . ē dim̄ car̄ . Ibi h̄t dimid

moliñ redd . vi . ſol̄ . Tot̄ ualet . xx . ſolid . Ednod tenuit . T.R.E.

.XXXVIII.   TERRA WILLI FILIJ WIDONIS.

Wiłłs filius Widonis teñ de rege *SVTONE* . Aluuold 7 ſoror

ej tenuer̄ T.R.E. 7 geldb p̄. viii . hid . Tra . ē . vi . car̄ . De ea ſt in

dñio . IIII . hidæ . 7 ibi . II . car̄ . 7 IIII . ſerui . 7 vi . uiłłi 7 viii . bord

cū . IIII . car̄ . Ibi . II . partes molini redd . xiii . ſolid . 7 IIII . denar̄ .

7 vi . āc p̄ti . Paſtura . I . leu lḡ . 7 II . q̃ʒ lat̄ . 7 tñtd ſiluæ .

Valuit . viii . lib . Modo . x . lib .

.XXXIX.   TERRA HENRICI DE FERIERES.

Henricvs de Fereires teñ de rege *STANDENE* . Godric tenuit

T.R.E. 7 geldb p̄. I . hida . Tra . ē . v . car̄ . In dñio ſt . IIII . 7 IIII . ſerui .

7 viii . āc p̄ti . 7 x . āc paſturæ 7 vi . āc ſiluæ . Valet . c . ſolid .

Ibi . ē ſilua p̄tiñ ad *BEDVINE* . T.R.E.

Idē teñ *CLIVE* . Godric tenuit T.R.E. 7 geldb p̄. v . hid una v̄ min .

Tra . ē . III . car̄ . De ea ſt in dñio . IIII . hidæ 7 una v̄ . 7 ibi . III . car̄ . 7 vi .

ſerui . 7 v . bord . 7 xxx . āc p̄ti . 7 xii . āc paſturæ . Valuit 7 ual̄ . IIII . lib .

.XL.   TERRA RICARDI FILIJ GISLEBERTI.

Ricard fili Giſlebti teñ de rege *SVTONE* . 7 Berenger de eo .

Vluuard tenuit T.R.E. 7 geldb p̄. x . hid . Tra . ē . vi . car̄ . De ea ſt

72 b

15 Waleran holds (West) DEAN himself. Godric held it before 1066; it paid tax for 2 hides and 1 virgate of land. Land for 3 ploughs, of which 1 hide is in lordship; 1½ ploughs there; 2 slaves;
    1 villager and 10 Cottagers with 1½ ploughs.
    1½ mills which pay 16s; meadow, 5 acres; woodland 1 furlong in both length and width.
The value was and is 60s.

16 In HURDCOTT [...] holds ½ hide. Land for ½ plough. He has
    ½ mill which pays 6s.
Value of the whole 20s.
    Ednoth held it before 1066.

38   LAND OF WILLIAM SON OF GUY

1 William son of Guy holds SUTTON (Veny) from the King. Alfwold and his sister held it before 1066; it paid tax for 8 hides.
Land for 6 ploughs, of which 4 hides are in lordship; 2 ploughs there; 4 slaves;
    6 villagers and 8 smallholders with 4 ploughs.
    2 parts of a mill which pay 13s 4d; meadow, 6 acres; pasture 1 league long and 2 furlongs wide; woodland, as much.
The value was £8; now £10.

39   LAND OF HENRY OF FERRERS

1 Henry of Ferrers holds STANDEN from the King.
Godric held it before 1066; it paid tax for 1 hide.
Land for 5 ploughs. In lordship 4; 4 slaves.
    Meadow, 8 acres; pasture, 10 acres; woodland, 6 acres.
Value 100s.
    A wood which belonged to Bedwyn before 1066.

2 He also holds CLYFFE (Pypard). Godric held it before 1066; it paid tax for 5 hides, less 1 virgate. Land for 3 ploughs, of which 4 hides and 1 virgate are in lordship; 3 ploughs there; 6 slaves;
    5 smallholders.
    Meadow, 30 acres; pasture, 12 acres.
The value was and is £4.

40   LAND OF RICHARD SON OF GILBERT

1 Richard son of Count Gilbert holds SUTTON (Mandeville) from the King, and Berengar from him. Wulfward held it before 1066; it paid tax for 10 hides. Land for 6 ploughs, of which 7 hides

in dñio.vii.hidæ.7 ibi.iii.car.7 v.ſerui.7 vi.uilli 7 ix.borð cũ.iii.

car.Ibi moliñ redð.x.ſol.7 xii.ac pti.7 iii.ac ſiluæ.Paſtura.

vi.q̃ʒ lg̃.7 iii.q̃ʒ lat.7 v.burgſes redð.l.denar.

Valuit 7 ual.vi.lib.

.XLI.   TERRA RADVLFI DE MORTEMER

RADVLFVS DE MORTEMER ten de rege *HVNLAVINTONE*.Herald

tenuit.7 geldb p.xx.hið.Tra.ē.xiiii.car.De ea ſt in dñio.xiiii.

hidæ.7 ibi.iiii.car.7 viii.ſerui.7 xix.uilli 7 viii.coſcez cũ.vi.car.

Ibi.xii.ac pti.7 x.ac paſture.7 viii.ac ſiluæ.Valuit 7 ual.xii.lib.

Oidelard ten de Rað *TOCHEHA*.⌐In Malmeſbie una dom reð.xii.den.

Aluuin tenuit T.R.E.7 geldb p.ii.hið 7 dimið.Tra.ē.iii.car.

De ea ſt in dñio.ii.hidæ.7 ibi.ii.car.cũ.i.ſeruo.7 i.uillo.7 iii.coſcez

cũ dimið car.Ibi.xii.ac pti.7 totið paſturæ.7 ii.ac ſiluæ.

Valuit.xxx.ſolið.Modo.l.ſolið.

Eduuard ten de Rað *BRADEFELDE*.Briſtuui 7 Eluui tenueꝛ T.R.E

7 geldb p.ii.hið 7 dimið.Tra.ē.ii.car.De ea.ē in dñio.i.hida 7 dimið.

7 ibi.ii.car.7 iii.uilli.7 ii.coſcez.7 xii.ac pti.Valuit 7 ual.xxx.ſolið.

In *HIWI*.ten Rað.i.hið.7 ibi ht.i.borð.7 iiii.acs pti.Val.xv.ſol.

Toti emit eā T.R.E.de æccla Malmeſbienſi.ad etatē triũ hõum.7 infra

hc tminũ poterat ire cũ ea ad quē uellet dñm.

Ipſe Rað ten *CLATFORD*.Aluuin tenuit T.R.E.7 geldb p.v.hið.Tra.ē.iii.

car.De ea ſt in dñio.iii.hidæ 7 ibi.ii.car.cũ.i.ſeruo.7 i.uillo.7 vii.borð

cũ.i.car.Ibi moliñ redð.xx.ſol.7 v.ac pti.Paſtura.dim leũ lg̃.7 iii.q̃ʒ

lat.Silua dimið leũ lg̃.7 tntð lat.Valuit 7 ual.c.ſolið.

are in lordship; 3 ploughs there; 5 slaves;
   6 villagers and 9 smallholders with 3 ploughs.
   A mill which pays 10s; meadow, 12 acres; woodland, 3 acres;
     pasture 6 furlongs long and 3 furlongs wide.
   5 burgesses who pay 50d.
The value was and is £6.

41   LAND OF RALPH OF MORTIMER

1   Ralph of Mortimer holds HULLAVINGTON from the King. Earl
Harold held it; it paid tax for 20 hides. Land for 14 ploughs,
of which 14 hides are in lordship; 4 ploughs there; 8 slaves;
   19 villagers and 8 Cottagers with 6 ploughs.
   Meadow, 12 acres; pasture, 10 acres; woodland, 8 acres.
The value was and is £12.
   In Malmesbury 1 house which pays 12d.

2   Odilard holds TOCKENHAM from Ralph. Alwin held it before 1066;
it paid tax for 2½ hides. Land for 3 ploughs, of which 2 hides
are in lordship; 2 ploughs there, with 1 slave and
   1 villager and 3 Cottagers with ½ plough.
   Meadow, 12 acres; pasture, as many; woodland, 2 acres.
The value was 30s; now 50s.

3   Edward holds BRADFIELD from Ralph. Brictwy and Alfwy held it
before 1066; it paid tax for 2½ hides. Land for 2 ploughs,
of which 1½ hides are in lordship; 2 ploughs there;
   3 villagers and 2 Cottagers.
   Meadow, 12 acres.
The value was and is 30s.

4   In HIGHWAY Ralph holds 1 hide; he has
   1 smallholder and
   meadow, 4 acres.
Value 15s.
   Toti bought it before 1066 from Malmesbury Church for the
lifetimes of three men; within this term he could go with it to
whichever lord he would.

5   Ralph holds CLATFORD himself. Alwin held it before 1066; it paid
tax for 5 hides. Land for 3 ploughs, of which 3 hides are in
lordship; 2 ploughs there, with 1 slave and
   1 villager and 7 smallholders with 1 plough.
   A mill which pays 20s; meadow, 5 acres; pasture ½ league long
     and 3 furlongs wide; woodland ½ league long and as wide.
The value was and is 100s.

Ipſe Rađ ten _IMEMERIE_ . Aluuin tenuit T.R.E.7 geldƀ ꝑ. ii . hiđ. Tra.ē
ii.caꝛ.In dūio.ē.i.caꝛ.7 ii.ſerui.7 i.uitts 7 iiii.borđ.Ibi paſtura.iii.q̄ꝙ lḡ.
7 ii . q̄ꝙ lat̄ . Valuit . iii . liƀ . Modo . iiii . liƀ.

Ricarđ ten de Rađ _SIRENDONE_ . Aluui tenuit T.R.E .7 geldƀ ꝑ.v.hiđ.
Tra.ē.vi.caꝛ. De ea ſt in dūio. ii.hidæ 7 dimiđ.7 ibi.ii.caꝛ.7 iiii.ſerui.7 xii.
uitti 7 iiii.borđ cū.iiii.caꝛ.Ibi.vii.ac̄ pti.Valuit 7 uat̄.vii.liƀ.

Rogeri ten de Rađ _CHINTONE_.Aluuin tenuit T.R.E.7 geldƀ ꝑ.i.hida 7 dim̄.
Tra.ē.i.caꝛ.ꝗ ibi.ē in dūio.cū.i.ſeruo.7 ii.borđ.Ibi molin redđ.ii.ſoliđ.
7 iiii.ac̄ pti.7 vi.ac̄ ſiluæ.Valuit.xx .ſoliđ.Modo.xxx.ſoliđ.

Hic Aluuin teneƀ hanc tꝛa de æccla Glaſtingeberie.7 n̄ poterat ab ea ſepa
rari .7 inde ſeruiebat abƀi.

Ricarđ ten de Rađ.iii.hiđ in _ALDRITONE_.7 Walter.i.hidā.ten ibiđe.
Alric Goduin Algar 7 Godric|tenueꝛ T.R.E.7 geldƀ ꝑ.iiii.hiđ.Tra.ē.iiii.caꝛ.
Ibi ſt.iiii.uitti 7 v.borđ 7 ii.ſerui.7 Molenđ de xxxvii.den 7 xxv.ac̄ pti.
In Malmeſƀie . i . burḡſis redđ . vii . den . Valuit 7 uat̄ . lx . ſoliđ.

Eduuarđ ten de Rađ _LOCHINTONE_ . Aluuarđ tenuit T.R.E.7 geldƀ
ꝑ.iii.hiđ.Tra.ē.iiii.caꝛ.De ea ſt in dūio.ii.hidæ una v̄ min.7 ibi.ii.car.
7 ii.uitti 7 iiii.borđ cū.ii.caꝛ.Ibi.viii.ac̄ pti.7 iiii.ac̄ ſiluæ . Valuit 7 uat̄

XLII. TERRA ROBERTI FILIJ GIROLDI. ⌠ iii.liƀ.

Roƀertvs fiłi GIROLD ten de rege _WITEBERGE_.Saulf tenuit T.R.E.
7 geldƀ ꝑ.x.hiđ.Tra.ē.v.caꝛ.De ea ſt in dūio.vii.hidæ.7 ibi.iiii.
caꝛ.7 v.ſerui.7 v.uitti.7 xi.cozez.cū.i.borđ hn̄t.i.car.Ibi molin redđ
xii.ſoliđ.7 vi.den.7 l.ac̄ pti.7 l.ac̄ paſturæ.7 x.ac̄ ſiluæ minutæ.
Valuit.vii.liƀ.Modo.x.liƀ.Gozelin ten de Roƀto.

6   Ralph holds IMBER himself. Alwin held it before 1066; it paid
tax for 2 hides. Land for 2 ploughs. In lordship 1 plough;
2 slaves;
    1 villager and 4 smallholders.
    Pasture 3 furlongs long and 2 furlongs wide.
The value was £3; now £4.

7   Richard holds SURRENDELL from Ralph. Alfwy held it before   72 c
1066; it paid tax for 5 hides. Land for 6 ploughs, of which
2½ hides are in lordship; 2 ploughs there; 4 slaves;
    12 villagers and 3 smallholders with 4 ploughs.
    Meadow, 7 acres.
The value was and is £7.

8   Roger holds KINGTON (St. Michael) from Ralph. Alwin held it
before 1066; it paid tax for 1½ hides. Land for 1 plough,
which is there, in lordship, with 1 slave;
    2 smallholders.
    A mill which pays 2s; meadow, 4 acres; woodland, 6 acres.
The value was 20s; now 30s.
    Alwin held this land from Glastonbury Church; he could not
be separated from it; he served the Abbot from it.

9   Richard holds 3 hides in ALDERTON from Ralph; Walter also
holds 1 hide there. Alric, Godwin, Algar and Godric held it
jointly before 1066; it paid tax for 4 hides. Land for 4 ploughs.
    4 villagers, 5 smallholders and 2 slaves.
    A mill at 37d; meadow, 25 acres.
    In Malmesbury 1 burgess who pays 7d.
The value was and is 60s.

10 Edward holds LUCKINGTON from Ralph. Alfward held it before 1066;
it paid tax for 3 hides. Land for 4 ploughs, of which 2 hides,
less 1 virgate, are in lordship; 2 ploughs there;
    2 villagers and 4 smallholders with 2 ploughs.
    Meadow, 8 acres; woodland, 4 acres.
The value was and is £3.

42   LAND OF ROBERT SON OF GERALD

1   Robert son of Gerald holds WOODBOROUGH from the King. Saewulf
held it before 1066; it paid tax for 10 hides. Land for 5 ploughs,
of which 7 hides are in lordship; 4 ploughs there; 5 slaves.
    5 villagers and 11 Cottagers with 1 smallholder have 1 plough.
    A mill which pays 12s 6d; meadow, 50 acres; pasture, 50 acres;
      underwood, 10 acres.
The value was £7; now £10.
    Jocelyn holds from Robert.

Raineri ten de Robto *FISTESBERIE*. Vitel tenuit T.R.E. 7 geldb ᵱ.x. hiđ. Tra. ē. v. caŕ. De ea s̄t in dn̄io. vi. hiđæ. 7 ibi. ii. caŕ. 7 ii. ſerui. 7 vii. uilłi 7 ii. borđ cū. i. caŕ 7 dim. Ibi paſtura. v. q̃ʒ lg̃. 7 iii. q̃ʒ lat̃. Silua dim̃ leu lg̃. 7 iii. q̃ʒ lat̃. Valuit 7 uał. c. ſoliđ.

Rainer ten de. Ro. *FOSTESBERGE*. Aluuin̄ tenuit T.R.E. 7 geldb ᵱ. ii. hiđ. Tra. ē. ii. caŕ. Ibi s̄t. iii. borđ cū. i. caŕ. Paſtura. ii. q̃ʒ lg̃. 7 una q̃ʒ 7 dim lat̃. Silua. ii. q̃ʒ lg̃. 7 ii. q̃ʒ lat̃. Valuit. xv. ſoł. Modo. xxx. ſoliđ.

Robt ten *BEDESDENE*. Coolle tenuit T.R.E. 7 geldb ᵱ una v træ. Tra. ē. i. caŕ. q ibi. ē. cū. i. uilło. 7 ii. borđ. 7 iiii. ſeruis. 7 Paſtura. ii. q̃ʒ lg̃. 7 una lat̃

Robt ten de. Ro. *BRISMARTONE*. Briſmar te Reddit. xxx. ſoliđ. nuit T.R.E. 7 geldb ᵱ. iiii. hiđ. Tra. ē. ii. caŕ. q ibi s̄t in dn̄io. cū xi. borđ. Ibi molin̄ redđ. xii. ſoł. 7 x. āc p̃ti. Paſtura. xii. q̃ʒ lg̃. 7 iiii. q̃ʒ lat̃. Valuit. x. ſoł. Modo. iiii. lib.

Idē Robt ten de. Ro. *MILDESTONE*. Briſmar tenuit T.R.E. 7 geldb ᵱ hida 7 dimiđ. Tra. ē. i. caŕ q ibi cū. ii. ſeruis. 7 iiii. coſcez. Ibi molin̄ redđ. xviii. ſoliđ. 7 iiii. āc p̃ti. Paſtura. xii. q̃ʒ lg̃. 7 una q̃ʒ lat̃. Valuit. xx. ſoł. M̃. xxx. ſoł.

Hugo ten de. Ro. *WIFLESFORD*. Toui tenuit T.R.E. 7 geldb ᵱ. i. hida. Tra. ē. i. caŕ. q ibi. ē cū. i. uilło. 7 iii. coſcez. Ibi molin̄ redđ. x. ſoł. 7 vi. āc p̃ti. Paſtura. ix. q̃ʒ lg̃. 7 ii. q̃ʒ lat̃. Valuit. xxx. ſoł. Valet. lx. ſoliđ.

Rainer ten de. Ro. *VITELETONE*. Vitel tenuit T.R.E. 7 geldb ᵱ. x. hiđ. Tra ē. xii. caŕ. De ea s̄t in dn̄io. v. hidæ 7 un v træ. 7 ibi. iii. caŕ. 7 vi. ſeruł. 7 vi. uilłi 7 xii. borđ cū. iii. caŕ. Ibi molin̄ redđ. xxii. ſoł. 7 vi. den. 7 iii. āc p̃ti. Paſtura. i. leū lg̃. 7 dim leu lat̃. Valuit 7 uał. xii. lib.

2 Rainer holds FOSBURY from Robert. Vitalis held it before 1066; it paid tax for 10 hides. Land for 5 ploughs, of which 6 hides are in lordship; 2 ploughs there; 2 slaves;
    7 villagers and 2 smallholders with 1½ ploughs.
    Pasture 5 furlongs long and 3 furlongs wide; woodland
       ½ league long and 3 furlongs wide.
The value was and is 100s.

3 Rainer holds FOSBURY from Robert. Alwin held it before 1066; it paid tax for 2 hides. Land for 2 ploughs.
    3 smallholders with 1 plough.
    Pasture 2 furlongs long and 1½ furlongs wide; woodland
       2 furlongs long and 2 furlongs wide.
The value was 15s; now 30s.

4 Robert holds BIDDESDEN. Cuthwulf held it before 1066; it paid tax for 1 virgate of land. Land for 1 plough, which is there, with
    1 villager, 2 smallholders and 4 slaves.
    Pasture 2 furlongs long and 1 wide.
It pays 30s.

5 Robert holds BRIGMERSTON from Robert. Brictmer held it before 1066; it paid tax for 4 hides. Land for 2 ploughs, which are there, in lordship, with
    11 smallholders.
    A mill which pays 12s; meadow, 10 acres; pasture 12 furlongs
       long and 4 furlongs wide.
The value was 10s; now £4.

6 Robert also holds MILSTON from Robert. Brictmer held it before 1066; it paid tax for 1½ hides. Land for 1 plough, which (is) there, with 2 slaves.
    4 Cottagers.
    A mill which pays 18s; meadow, 4 acres; pasture 12 furlongs
       long and 1 furlong wide.
The value was 20s; now 30s.

7 Hugh holds WILSFORD from Robert. Tovi held it before 1066; it paid tax for 1 hide. Land for 1 plough, which is there, with
    1 villager and 3 Cottagers.
    A mill which pays 10s; meadow, 6 acres; pasture 9 furlongs
       long and 2 furlongs wide.
The value was 30s; the value is 60s.

8 Rainer holds FITTLETON from Robert. Vitalis held it before 1066; it paid tax for 10 hides. Land for 12 ploughs, of which 5 hides and 1 virgate of land are in lordship; 3 ploughs there; 6 slaves;
    6 villagers and 12 smallholders with 3 ploughs.
    A mill which pays 22s 6d; meadow, 3 acres; pasture 1 league
       long and ½ league wide.
The value was and is £12.

Hugo ten de.R. *SCAGE*. Cudulf tenuit T.R.E.7 geldb̄ .p. II. hiđ.7 una v̄ 7 dimiđ.

Tra.ē. I. car̄. Ibi. ē un uiłłs 7 II. ferui.7 xxx. ac̄ pafturæ. Silua. I. leu̇ lḡ.7 una

q̃ʒ lat̄. Valuit xx. fol. Modo. xL. fol.

Robt̄ ten de.R. *EBLESBORNE*. Aluuarđ 7 Fitheus tenuer̄ T.R.E. .p. II. ᴔ.

7 geldb̄ .p. XIIII. hiđ. Tra.ē. x. car̄. De ea s̄t in dn̄io. x. hidæ.7 ibi. VI. car̄.

7 IIII. ferui.7 XVIII. uiłłi 7 VII. borđ cū. IIII. car̄. Ibi. xIIII. ac̄ p̃ti. Paftura

xIIII. q̃ʒ lḡ.7 IIII. q̃ʒ lat̄. Silua. II. leu̇ int lḡ.7 lat̄. Valuit. xII. lib̄. M̄. xII.

.XLIII. TERRA ROBERTI FILIJ ROLF.   ⌐ lib̄.

ROBERT fili Rolf ten in *MORDONE*. I. hiđ 7 una v̄ træ. Vlgar tenuit

T.R.E.7 geldb̄ .p. v. virg træ. Tra.ē. I. car̄. q̃ ibi.ē in dn̄io. cū. I. feruo 7 I. uiłło.

7 x. ac̄ p̃ti.7 xL. ac̄ pafturæ. Valuit 7 uał. xx. foliđ.

Robt̄ fili Rolf ten *HANTONE*. Vlgar tenuit T.R.E.7 geldb̄ .p. IX. hiđ

una v̄ min. Tra.ē. v. car̄. De ea s̄t in dn̄io. VI. hidæ.7 ibi. II. car̄. cū. I. feruo.

7 v. uiłłi 7 VI. borđ. Ibi. xII. ac̄ p̃ti. paftura. I. q̃ʒ lḡ.7 tn̄tđ lat̄. Valuit 7 uał. VI. lib̄

.XLII ROGERIJ DE CORCELLES.

ROGERIVS de CVRCELLE ten de rege *FISERTONE* Bondi tenuit T.R.E.

7 geldb̄ .p. x. hiđ. Tra.ē. x. car̄. De ea s̄t in dn̄io. v. hidæ 7 dimiđ.7 ibi. III.

car̄.7 xVI. uiłłi 7 xII. borđ 7 xIIII. cotar̄. cū. VII. car̄. Ibi moliñ. xx. fol red.

7 xII. ac̄ p̃ti.7 x. ac̄ filuæ. Paftura dim leu̇ lḡ.7 tn̄tđ lat̄. Valuit 7 uał. x̄xv.

.XLV. ROGERIJ DE BERCHELAI.   ⌐ lib̄.

ROGERIVS de Berchelai ten de rege *FOXELEGE* . Æltret tenuit T.R.E.

7 geldb̄ .p. II. hiđ. Tra.ē. IIII. car̄. De ea s̄t in dn̄io. I. hida 7 ibi. II. car̄.7 III. ferui.

7 IIII. uiłłi.7 III. cofcez. cū. III. car̄. Ibi moliñ. VII. fol 7 VI. deñ.7 IIII. ac̄ p̃ti.7 VIII.

ac̄ pafturæ.7 una dom in Malmeſbie.   Valuit 7 uał. xL. fol.

9   Hugh holds SHAW from Robert. Cuthwulf held it before 1066; it paid
tax for 2 hides and 1½ virgates. Land for 1 plough.
> 1 villager and 2 slaves.
>
> Pasture, 30 acres; woodland 1 league long and 1 furlong wide.

The value was 20s; now 40s.

10   Robert holds EBBESBORNE (Wake) from Robert. Alfward and Vitalis
held it before 1066 as two manors; it paid tax for 14 hides.
Land for 10 ploughs, of which 10 hides are in lordship; 6 ploughs
there; 4 slaves;
> 18 villagers and 7 smallholders with 4 ploughs.
>
> Meadow, 14 acres; pasture 14 furlongs long and 4 furlongs wide;
>   woodland 2 leagues in both length and width.

The value was £12; now £14.

43   LAND OF ROBERT SON OF ROLF

1   Robert son of Rolf holds 1 hide and 1 virgate of land in MOREDON.
Wulfgar held it before 1066; it paid tax for 5 virgates of land.
Land for 1 plough, which is there, in lordship, with 1 slave and
> 1 villager.
>
> Meadow, 10 acres; pasture, 40 acres.

The value was and is 20s.

2   Robert son of Rolf holds HAMPTON. Wulfgar held it before 1066;
it paid tax for 9 hides, less 1 virgate. Land for 5 ploughs,
of which 6 hides are in lordship; 2 ploughs there, with 1 slave;
> 5 villagers and 6 smallholders.
>
> Meadow, 12 acres; pasture 1 furlong long and as wide.

The value was and is £6.

44   [LAND] OF ROGER OF COURSEULLES

1   Roger of Courseulles holds FISHERTON (de la Mere) from the King.
Bondi held it before 1066; it paid tax for 10 hides. Land for 10
ploughs, of which 5½ hides are in lordship; 3 ploughs there;
> 16 villagers, 12 smallholders and 14 cottagers with 7 ploughs.
>
> A mill which pays 20s; meadow, 12 acres; woodland, 10 acres;
>   pasture ½ league long and as wide.

The value was and is £25.

45   [LAND] OF ROGER OF BERKELEY

1   Roger of Berkeley holds FOXLEY from the King. Aldred held it
before 1066; it paid tax for 2 hides. Land for 4 ploughs,
of which 1 hide is in lordship; 2 ploughs there; 3 slaves;
> 4 villagers and 3 Cottagers with 3 ploughs.
>
> A mill, 7s 6d; meadow, 4 acres; pasture, 8 acres;
>   1 house in Malmesbury.

The value was and is 40s.

Idē.Ro.ten̄.ı.hiď dimiď v̄ min⁹ de dn̄ica firma de Cepehā.Celein⁹ tenuit T.R.E.

Ipſe.Ro.ten̄ Estone.Aluui tenuit T.R.E.7geldb̄ ꝑ.ııı.hiď ⌠ꝓreſtū Edrici uicecom̄.
dimiď v̄ min.Traē.ııı.caŕ.De ea ſt.ıı.hidæ in dn̄io.7 ibi.ıı.caŕ.7 ıııı.ſerui.7 ıı.uiłłi
7 ıııı.borď cū.ı.caŕ.Ibi moliñ redd.vı.ſoł.Valuit.xxx.ſoliď.Modo.xl.ſoliď.

72 d

.XLVI. Bᴇʀɴᴀʀᴅ ᴾᵃⁿᶜᵉᵛᵒˡᵗ ten⁹ Fᴇʀsᴛᴇsꜰᴇʟᴅ.Goduin⁹ tenuit T.R.E.7 geldb̄
ꝑ una v̄ tre 7 dimiď.Tra.ē dim caŕ Valet.v.ſoliď.

.XLVII   Tᴇʀʀᴀ Bᴇʀᴇɴɢᴇʀ Gɪꜰᴀʀᴅ.

Bᴇʀᴇɴɢᴇʀ Gifard ten de rege Fᴏɴᴛᴇʟ.Euing tenuit T.R.E.
7 geldb̄ ꝑ.v.hiď.Tra.ē.vıı.caŕ.De ea.ē in dn̄io.ı.hida.
7 ibi.ııı.caŕ.7 ıııı.ſerui.7 vı.uiłłi 7 xvı.borď cū.ıııı.caŕ.
Ibi moliñ redd.v.ſoliď.7 vıı.āc p̄ti.Paſtura dim leū lḡ.
7 ııı.q̇ɺ lat.Silua.ıııı.q̇ɺ lḡ.7 ıı.q̇ɺ lat.Valuit.c.ſoł.M̄

Idē ten.ı.hiď in Bᴇʀᴇꜰᴏʀᴅ.Herald tenuit ᶜᵒⁱ̄ᵐ ⌠ vı.lib.
T.R.E.7 ꝑ tanto geldb̄.Tra.ē.ı.caŕ.Ibi ſt.vı.borď.7 vı.
āc p̄ti.Valuit.lx.ſoł.Modo.xx.ſoliď.

.XLVIII.   Tᴇʀʀᴀ Osʙᴇʀɴɪ Gɪꜰᴀʀᴅ.

Osʙᴇʀɴ Gifard ten⁹ de rege Wɪɴᴛʀᴇʙᴠʀɴᴇ.Domne te
nuit T.R.E.7 geldb̄ ꝑ.xı.hiď.Tra.ē.vı.caŕ.De ea ſt ıx
dn̄io.ıx.hidæ.7 ibi.ıııı.caŕ.7 v.ſerui.7 ıııı.uiłłi 7 v.borď
cū.ıı.caŕ.Ibi.vı.āc p̄ti.7 paſtura.ıx.q̇ɺ lḡ.7 vı.q̇ɺ lat.
Valuit.vıı.lib.Modo.ıx.lib.

Idē.O.ten.ıı.hiď in Wɪɴᴛʀᴇʙᴠʀɴᴇ.Tra.ē.ı.caŕ.
Ibi.ıı.āc p̄ti.7 ııı.āc paſturæ.Valuit.xxx.ſoł.M̄.xl.ſoł.

2   Roger also holds 1 hide, less ½ virgate, of the lordship revenue of
CHIPPENHAM. Ceolwin held it before 1066 on lease from Edric
the Sheriff.

3   Roger holds EASTON (Grey) himself. Alfwy held it before 1066;
it paid tax for 3 hides, less ½ virgate. Land for 3 ploughs,
of which 2 hides are in lordship; 2 ploughs there; 4 slaves;
    2 villagers and 3 smallholders with 1 plough.
    A mill which pays 6s.
The value was 30s; now 40s.

46   [LAND OF BERNARD PANCEVOLT]   72d

1   Bernard Pancevolt holds 'FRUSTFIELD'. Godwin held it before 1066;
it paid tax for 1½ virgates of land. Land for ½ plough.
Value 5s.

47   LAND OF BERENGAR GIFFARD

1   Berengar Giffard holds FONTHILL (Gifford) from the King.
Ewing held it before 1066; it paid tax for 5 hides.
Land for 7 ploughs, of which 1 hide is in lordship;
3 ploughs there; 4 slaves;
    6 villagers and 16 smallholders with 4 ploughs.
    A mill which pays 5s; meadow, 7 acres; pasture ½ league long and
      3 furlongs wide; woodland 4 furlongs long and 2 furlongs wide.
The value was 100s; now £6.

2   He also holds 1 hide in BARFORD (St. Martin). Earl Harold held
it before 1066; it paid tax for as much. Land for 1 plough.
    6 smallholders.
    Meadow, 6 acres.
The value was 60s; now 20s.

48   LAND OF OSBERN GIFFARD

1   Osbern Giffard holds ELSTON from the King. Dunn held it
before 1066; it paid tax for 11 hides. Land for 6 ploughs,
of which 9 hides are in lordship; 4 ploughs there; 5 slaves;
    4 villagers and 5 smallholders with 2 ploughs.
    Meadow, 6 acres; pasture 9 furlongs long
      and 6 furlongs wide.
The value was £7; now £9.

2   Osbern also holds 2 hides in ELSTON. Land for 1 plough.
    Meadow, 2 acres; pasture, 3 acres.
The value was 30s; now 40s.

Idē.O.ten.III.hiđ 7 dim̃ in ORCESTONE.Vlmar 7 Aluuin
tenuer.T.R.E.Tra.ē.II.car.q̃ ibi ſt in dñio.7 III.ſerui.
Paſtura dimiđ leu 7 XL.ac lḡ.7 lat.Valuit XL.ſol.M.L.ſol.

Ipſe.O.ten STANTONE.Briĉtric tenuit T.R.E.7 geldb̃ p xviii.
hiđ.Ibi ht.II.car in dñio.in IX.hiđ.7 ibi.VII.ſerui.7 IX.uilli.
7 III.coſcez cū.VI.car.Ibi.VI.ac pti.Paſtura.I.leu lḡ.7 I.lat.
Silua.I.leu lḡ.7 III.q̃z lat.Valuit.IX.lib.Modo.VIII.lib.

Æccła Ş Stefani de Fontened ten de.O.II.hiđ 7 una v træ in
MIDELTONE.Domno tenuit T.R.E.7 p tanto geldb̃.Tra.ē.II.
car.q̃ ibi ſt in dñio cū.I.ſeruo 7 II.borđ.Ibi.V.ac pti.7 xx.
ac paſturæ.7 una ac ſiluæ.Valuit.XX.ſol.Modo.L.ſoliđ.

Ipſe.O.ten COTEFORD.Aluric tenuit T.R.E.7 geldb̃ p una
hida 7 dim̃.Tra.ē.II.car.De ea.ē in dñio.I.hida.7 ibi.I.
car 7 dim̃.7 II.ſerui.7 VI.coſcez 7 I.cotar cū dim̃ car.Ibi
.IIII.pars molini redđ.III.ſol.7 III.obolos.7 X.ac pti.paſtura
IIII.q̃z lḡ.7 una q̃z lat.Valeb̃.L.ſoliđ.Modo.LX.ſoliđ.

Ipſe.O.ten ORCHESTONE.Traſemund tenuit T.R.E.
7 geldb̃ p.V.hiđ.Tra.ē.III.car.De ea ſt in dñio.IIII.hidæ.
7 ibi.II.car.7 III.ſerui.7 IIII.uilli 7 III.coſcez 7 V.cotar.
cū.I.car 7 dimiđ.Ibi paſtura.III.q̃z lḡ.7 una q̃z lat.
Valuit.IIII.lib.Modo.C.ſoliđ.

Ipſe.O.ten DEVREL.Smail tenuit T.R.E.7 geldb̃ p.III.
hiđ.7 dim̃ v træ.Tra.ē.III.car.De ea ſt in dñio.II.hidæ.
7 ibi.II.car.cū.I.ſeruo.7 IX.coſcez 7 III.borđ.
Ibi molin̄ redđ.XXX.den.7 II.ac pti.7 paſtura.II.q̃z lḡ.
7 una q̃z lat.Silua dimiđ leu lḡ.7 tntđ lat.Valuit.XL.ſol.

3   Osbern also holds 3½ hides in ORCHESTON. Wulfmer and
    Alwin held it before 1066. Land for 2 ploughs, which are
    there, in lordship; 3 slaves.
       Pasture ½ league and 40 acres long and wide.
    The value was 40s; now 50s.

4   Osbern holds STANTON (St. Quintin) himself. Brictric held it
    before 1066; it paid tax for 18 hides. He has 2 ploughs in
    lordship on 9 hides; 7 slaves there;
       9 villagers and 3 Cottagers with 6 ploughs.
       Meadow, 6 acres; pasture 1 league long and 1 wide; woodland
          1 league long and 3 furlongs wide.
    The value was £9; now £8.

5   St. Stephen's Church of Fontenay holds 2 hides and 1 virgate
    of land in MIDDLETON from Osbern. Dunn held it before 1066; it
    paid tax for as much. Land for 2 ploughs, which are there, in
    lordship, with 1 slave;
       2 smallholders.
       Meadow, 5 acres; pasture, 20 acres; woodland, 1 acre.
    The value was 20s; now 50s.

   Osbern himself holds

6   CODFORD. Aelfric held it before 1066; it paid tax for 1½ hides.
    Land for 2 ploughs, of which 1 hide is in lordship; 1½ ploughs
    there; 2 slaves;
       6 Cottagers and 1 cottager with ½ plough.
       The fourth part of a mill which pays 3s and 3 halfpence;
          meadow, 10 acres; pasture 4 furlongs long and 1 furlong wide.
    The value was 50s; now 60s.

7   ORCHESTON. Thrasemund held it before 1066; it paid tax
    for 5 hides. Land for 3 ploughs, of which 4 hides are in lordship;
    2 ploughs there; 3 slaves;
       4 villagers, 3 Cottagers and 5 cottagers with 1½ ploughs.
       Pasture 3 furlongs long and 1 furlong wide.
    The value was £4; now 100s.

8   (Hill) DEVERILL. Small held it before 1066; it paid tax
    for 3 hides and ½ virgate of land. Land for 3 ploughs, of which
    2 hides are in lordship; 2 ploughs there, with 1 slave;
       9 Cottagers and 3 smallholders.
       A mill which pays 30d; meadow, 2 acres; pasture 2 furlongs long
          and 1 furlong wide; woodland ½ league long and as wide.
    The value was 40s; now 60s.

Ipſe.O.ten ⁷TERINTONE.Dōno tenuit T.R.E.⌐Modo.LX.ſol.

7 geldb ᵱ.x.hiđ.⁷Tra.ē.vi.caⁿ.De ea ſⁿt in dⁿio.ix.

hidæ.7 ibi.iii.caⁿ.7 iiii.ſerui.7 ii.uiłłi 7 iiii.coſcez.7 iii.borđ

cū.iii.caⁿ.Ibi.x.ăc p̃ti.Valuit.iiii.lib.Modo.c.ſoliđ.

Ipſe.O.ten ⁷SCARENTONE.Algar tenuit T.R.E.7 geldb

ᵱ.v.hiđ.Tra.ē.ii.caⁿ 7 dīm.De ea ſⁿt in dⁿio.iiii.hidæ

7 dīm.7 ibi.ii.caⁿ.7 v.ſerui.7 ii.uiłłi cū dīm caⁿ.Ibi dīm

molīn redđ.vii.ſol.7 vi.den.7 vi.ăc p̃ti.7 LX.ăc paſturæ.

7 XL.ăc ſiluæ.Valuit.iiii.lib.Modo.c.ſoliđ.

Ipſe.O.ten ⁷SCARENTONE.Smalo tenuit T.R.E.7 geldb

ᵱ.v.hiđ.Tra.ē.ii.caⁿ 7 dīm.De ea ſⁿt in dⁿio.iiii.hidæ

7 dimiđ.7 ibi.ii.caⁿ.7 v.ſerui.7 ii.uiłłi cū dīm caⁿ.Ibi

dīm molīn redđ.vii.ſol 7 vi.den.7 vi.ăc p̃ti.7 LX.ăc paſturæ.

7 XL.ăc ſiluæ.7 in Wiltune.i.burgſis redđ.iii.ſoliđ.

Valuit.iiii.lib.Modo.c.ſoliđ.

Gunduin⁹ ten ⁷de.O.OGEFORD.Ednⁿod tenuit T.R.E.7 gelđ

ᵱ.ii.hiđ 7 dīm.Tra.ē.i.caⁿ.q̃ ibi.ē.cū.i.ſeruo.7 i.borđ.

Ibi molīn redđ.iiii.ſol.7 iiii.ăc p̃ti.7 x.ăc paſturæ.

Valuit.xxx.ſol.Modo.XL.ſoliđ.   ⌐recupauit Ednⁿod⁹.

Hanc trā abſtulit Goduin⁹ comes Ŝ MARIÆ Wiltun⁹.7 t̃c eā

TERRA DROGONIS FILIJ PONZ.

.XLIX Drogo.F.ponz ten⁷ de rege SEGRIE.Wiſłet tenuit

T.R.E.7 geldb ᵱ.v.hiđ.Tra.ē.iiii.caⁿ.De ea ſⁿt in dⁿio.ii.hidæ.

Rogerivs ^{de Laci} & Turſtin ^{fili'Rolf⁹} 7 Wiłłs ^{Leuric} ten⁷.i.hiđ in COLESELLE.

Tres taini teneb T.R.E.Pars om̃iū ual.iiii.lib.

7 ibi.i.caⁿ.7 v.uiłłi 7 vi.borđ 7 v.coſcez cū.i.caⁿ.Ibi.ii.mo

lini redđ.xxii.ſoł 7 iiii.denaⁿ.7 xxx.ăc p̃ti.In Malmesbie

una dom⁹ redđ.ix.denaⁿ.Valuit.LX.ſoł.Modo.LXX.ſoł.

9   TYTHERTON (Kellaways). Dunn held it before 1066; it paid tax
for 10 hides. Land for 6 ploughs, of which 9 hides are
in lordship; 3 ploughs there; 4 slaves;
> 2 villagers, 4 Cottagers and 3 smallholders with 3 ploughs.
> Meadow, 10 acres.

The value was £4; now 100s.

10   SHERRINGTON. Algar held it before 1066; it paid tax for 5 hides.
Land for 2½ ploughs, of which 4½ hides are in lordship; 2 ploughs
there; 5 slaves;
> 2 villagers with ½ plough.
> ½ mill which pays 7s 6d; meadow, 6 acres; pasture, 60 acres;
>   woodland, 40 acres.

The value was £4; now 100s.

11   SHERRINGTON. Small held it before 1066; it paid tax for 5 hides.
Land for 2½ ploughs, of which 4½ hides are in lordship; 2 ploughs
there; 5 slaves;
> 2 villagers with ½ plough.
> ½ mill which pays 7s 6d; meadow, 6 acres; pasture, 60 acres;
>   woodland, 40 acres.
> In Wilton 1 burgess who pays 3s.

The value was £4; now 100s.

12   Gundwin holds UGFORD from Osbern. Ednoth held it before 1066;
it paid tax for 2½ hides. Land for 1 plough, which is there,
with 1 slave.
> 1 smallholder.
> A mill which pays 4s; meadow, 4 acres; pasture, 10 acres.

The value was 30s; now 40s.
> Earl Godwin took this land away from St. Mary's of Wilton;

then Ednoth recovered it.

49   LAND OF DROGO SON OF POYNTZ

1   Drogo son of Poyntz holds SEAGRY from the King. Wiflet held it
before 1066; it paid tax for 5 hides. Land for 4 ploughs, of
which 2 hides are in lordship;

Misplaced entry. No transposition signs to show its proper place. See notes.

1a   Roger of Lacy, Thurstan son of Rolf and William Leofric hold 1
hide in COLESHILL. Three thanes held it before 1066.
Value of the part of all of them, £4.

49,1   continued   73 a
> 1 plough there;
> 5 villagers, 6 smallholders and 5 Cottagers with 1 plough.
> 2 mills which pay 22s 4d; meadow, 30 acres; in Malmesbury
>   1 house which pays 9d.

The value was 60s; now 70s.

Gislebt ten de Drog ESTONE. Osuuard tenuit T.R.E.
7 geldb ꝑ.v.hid.Tra.ē.III.car.De ea st in dnio.IIII.hidæ.
7 ibi.II.car.7 II.ferui.7 un uitts 7 IIII.bord 7 II.cofcez.
Ibi.x.ac pti.Silua.II.q̓꜔ lg̅.7 II.q̓꜔ lat.
Valuit.xL.folid.Modo.L.folid.

Hugo ten de.D.ALDRINTONE.Edric tenuit T.R.E.7 geld
ꝑ.III.hid.Tra.ē.III.car.De ea st in dnio.II.hidæ 7 III.v
træ.7 ibi.I.car.cū.I.feruo.7 II.bord.De parte molini
.xxII.denar.7 xv.ac pti.Valuit 7 uat.Lx.folid.

TERRA HVGONIS LASNE.

.L. H͞vgo ten.I.hid træ 7 III.v de rege in SCALDEBVRNE.
7 Witts ten de eo.Vn tain tenuit de rege.E.7 ꝑ tanto
geldb.Tra.ē.II.car.Ibi.ē un uitts 7 IIII.cofcez.cū.I.car.
Ibi.I.arpenn pti.7 II.ac filuæ.Valet.xxx.fot.

Herald ten de.H.WICHELESTOTE.Leuric tenuit T.R.E.
7 geldb ꝑ.v.hid.Tra.ē.II.car.De ea st in dnio.IIII.hidæ.
7 ibi.I.car 7 dim.cū.I.feruo.7 III.uitti 7 vi.bord cū dim
car.Ibi molin redd.v.fot.7 xxv.ac pti.7 xxx.ac pafturæ.

Ipfe.H.ten in CLIVE.II.hid.Godeua ᚠ Valut 7 uat.xL.fot.
tenuit ꝑ uno M̅.Tra.ē.I.car.Ibi.ē un cofcet 7 xII.ac pti.

Witts ten de.H.CORTITONE.Dene tenuit ᚠ Valet xII.fot.
T.R.E.7 geldb ꝑ.vi.hid.Tra.ē.IIII.car.De ea st in dnio
IIII.hidæ.7 ibi.I.car 7 dim.7 II.ferui.7 IIII.bord cū dim
car.Ibi molin redd.xx.folid.7 vi.ac pti.Paftura.III.q̓꜔
lg̅.7 II.q̓꜔ lat.7 tntd filuæ.Valuit.c.folid.Modo.vi.lib

2 Gilbert holds EASTON from Drogo. Osward held it
before 1066; it paid tax for 5 hides. Land for 3 ploughs,
of which 4 hides are in lordship; 2 ploughs there; 2 slaves;
  1 villager, 4 smallholders and 2 Cottagers.
  Meadow, 10 acres; woodland 2 furlongs long and 2 furlongs wide.
The value was 40s; now 50s.

3 Hugh holds ALDERTON from Drogo. Edric held it before 1066; it
paid tax for 3 hides. Land for 3 ploughs, of which 2 hides and 3
virgates of land are in lordship; 1 plough there, with 1 slave;
  2 smallholders.
  From part of a mill, 22d; meadow, 15 acres.
The value was and is 60s.

50   LAND OF HUGH DONKEY

1 Hugh Donkey holds 1 hide of land and 3 virgates in SHALBOURNE
from the King, and William holds from him. A thane held it
from King Edward; it paid tax for as much. Land for 2 ploughs.
  1 villager and 4 Cottagers with 1 plough.
  Meadow, 1 *arpent;* woodland, 2 acres.
Value 30s.

2 Harold holds WESTLECOTT from Hugh. Leofric held it before 1066;
it paid tax for 5 hides. Land for 2 ploughs, of which 4 hides
are in lordship; 1½ ploughs there, with 1 slave;
  3 villagers and 6 smallholders with ½ plough.
  A mill which pays 5s; meadow, 25 acres; pasture, 30 acres.
The value was and is 40s.

3 Hugh holds 2 hides in CLYFFE (Pypard) himself. Godiva held it
as one manor. Land for 1 plough.
  1 Cottager.
  Meadow, 12 acres.
Value 12s.

4 William holds CORTON from Hugh. Dene held it before 1066; it
paid tax for 6 hides. Land for 4 ploughs, of which 4 hides are
in lordship; 1½ ploughs there; 2 slaves;
  4 smallholders with ½ plough.
  A mill which pays 20s; meadow, 6 acres; pasture 3 furlongs
   long and 2 furlongs wide; woodland, as much.
The value was 100s; now £6.

Æcclā Ṣ Mariæ Winton ten de . H . *Chenete* . ᵽ filia ej.

Honeuuin tenuit T.R.E. 7 geldb ᵽ . ıı . hıd una v̊ min.

Tra . ē . ı . car̄ . q̊ ibi . ē in dñio cū . ıı . bord 7 una aċ p̄ti.

☞ 7 vı . aċ pasturæ . Valuit . x . ſol . Modo . xx . ſolid.

HVNFRIDI CAMERARIJ.

.LII. **H**camerar' Vnfrid ten de rege *Schernecote* . Aluuard tenuit

T.R.E. 7 geldb ᵽ . v . hıd Tra . ē . ıııı . car̄ . De ea st in dñio . ıı .

hidæ 7 dim . 7 ibi . ıı . car̄ . 7 ııı . ſerui . 7 vııı . uitti cū . ıı . car̄ .

Ibi . l . aċ p̄ti . 7 paſtura . ıı . q̊z̧ lḡ . 7 una q̊z̧ lat̄ .

Valuit . xl . ſolid . Modo . lx . ſolid.

.LIII. TERRA GVNFRIDI MALDOITH.

Gvnfrid Malduit ten de rege *Calestone* . Agar

tenuit T.R.E. 7 geldb ᵽ . ıı . hıd 7 una v̊ træ . Tra . ē . ıı . car̄ .

De ea st in dñio . v . uirg træ . 7 ibi . ıı . car̄ . 7 ııı . ſerui . 7 vı .

bord cū dim car̄ . Ibi moliñ redd . xv . ſol . 7 vııı . aċ p̄ti .

Paſtura . ıı . q̊z̧ lḡ . 7 una q̊z̧ lat̄ . Valuit . xl . ſol . M̊ . l . ſol.

Idē Gunf ten *Witelie* . Appe tenuit T.R.E. 7 geldb

ᵽ una hida . Tra . ē . ıı . car̄ . q̊ ibi st in dñio . cū . ı . ſeruo.

7 vı . bord . Ibi . vııı . aċ p̄ti . Silua . ııı . q̊z̧ lḡ . 7 una q̊z̧ lat̄ .

Valuit . xl . ſol . Modo . l . ſolid.

TERRA ALVREDI ISPANIENSIS.

.LII. **A**lvred de Iſpania ten de rege *Etesberie* . Aluui

tenuit T.R.E. 7 geldb ᵽ . v . hıd . Tra . ē . ıııı . car̄ . De ea st

in dñio . ııı . hidæ 7 dim̄ . 7 ibi . ıı . car̄ . 7 ıı . ſerui . 7 vıı . bord.

7 un miles cū . ı . car̄ . Ibi . xx . aċ paſturæ . Valuit . ııı . lib.

.LV. **AIVLFI VICECOMITIS** Ϝ Modo . ıııı . lib.

Auicecom̄ Ivlfvs ten de rege . v . hıd in *Tollard* . 7 dimid hidā.

Quinq̧ taini tenuer̄ T.R.E. 7 ᵽ . v . hıd 7 dim geldb.

5   St. Mary's Church, Winchester holds KENNETT from
Hugh for his daughter. Hunwine held it before 1066; it paid tax.
for 2 hides, less 1 virgate. Land for 1 plough which is there,
in lordship, with
    2 smallholders.
    Meadow, 1 acre; pasture, 6 acres.
The value was 10s; now 20s.

† *Ch. 51, written across the bottom of cols. 73 a, b and directed to its proper place by*
transposition signs, is entered here after 56,1.

52   [LAND] OF HUMPHREY THE CHAMBERLAIN

1   Humphrey the Chamberlain holds SHORNCOTE from the King.
Alfward held it before 1066; it paid tax for 5 hides. Land for 4
ploughs, of which 2½ hides are in lordship; 2 ploughs there; 3 slaves;
    8 villagers with 2 ploughs.
    Meadow, 50 acres; pasture 2 furlongs long and 1 furlong wide.
The value was 40s; now 60s.

53   LAND OF GUNFRID MAWDITT

1   Gunfrid Mawditt holds CALSTONE (Wellington) from the King. Algar
held it before 1066; it paid tax for 2 hides and 1 virgate of land.
Land for 2 ploughs, of which 5 virgates of land are in lordship; 2
ploughs there; 3 slaves.
    6 smallholders with ½ plough.
    A mill which pays 15s; meadow, 8 acres; pasture 2 furlongs
       long and 1 furlong wide.
The value was 40s; now 50s.

2   Gunfrid also holds WHITLEY. Ape held it before 1066; it paid tax
for 1 hide. Land for 2 ploughs, which are there, in lordship,
with 1 slave;
    6 smallholders.
    Meadow, 8 acres; woodland 3 furlongs long and 1 furlong wide.
The value was 40s; now 50s.

54   LAND OF ALFRED OF 'SPAIN'

1   Alfred of 'Spain' holds YATESBURY from the King. Alfwy held it
before 1066; it paid tax for 5 hides. Land for 4 ploughs, of
which 3½ hides are in lordship; 2 ploughs there; 2 slaves;
    7 smallholders and 1 man-at-arms with 1 plough.
    Pasture, 20 acres.
The value was £3; now £4.

55   [LAND] OF AIULF THE SHERIFF

1   Aiulf the Sheriff holds 5 hides and ½ hide in TOLLARD (Royal) from
the King. Five thanes held it before 1066; it paid tax for 5½ hides.

Tra.ē.ıııı.caɼ.De ea sͭ in dñio.ıııı.hidæ.7 ibi.ıı.caɼ.
7 ıı.ſerui.7 ııı.uiłłi.7 xıııı.borđ.Ibi.ıı.arpenni uineæ.
7 xx.aͨc paſturæ.7.ıııı.aͨc ſiluæ.Valuit.ıııı.liɓ.M̊.vı.liɓ.
Idē.A.teñ dim hiđ in BERMENTONE.Tra.ē dim caɼ.
Redđ.xıı.ſolid.Radulf⁹ tenuit T.R.E.

TERRA NIGELLI MEDICI.

.LVI NıGELLVS medicus teñ de rege STRATONE T.R.E.
geldɓ ₚ.xxx.hiđ.Tra.ē.xıııı.caɼ.De ea sͭ in dñio.v.
hidæ.7 ibi.ııı.caɼ.7 ıı.ſerui.7 xxıııı.uiłłi 7 xvııı.borđ
cū.xıı.caɼ.Ibi moliñ redđ.ıı.ſoł.7 ꝑtū.vııı.q̃ɀ lͭg.7 v.q̃ɀ
laͭt.Paſtura.ı.leū lͭg.7 v.q̃ɀ laͭt.Valuit.xvııı.liɓ.M̊.xvı.liɓ.

TERRA HVGON̅ FILIJ BALDRICI.

☞ LI.
Hvoo.F.Baldrici teñ MERESDENE.7 Walteri de eo.Weneſi tenuit T.R.E.
7 geldɓ ₚ x.hiđ.Tra.ē.vııı.caɼ.In dñio sͭ.ıı.caɼ.7 ıııı.ſerui.7 ıx.uiłłi
7 xıııı.coſcez.7 ıı.borđ cū.v.caɼ.Ibi moliñ redđ.vıı.ſoł 7 dimid.7 xxıııı.aͨc ꝑti.
Paſtura.ııı.q̃ɀ iͫ lͭg.7 ıı.q̃ɀ laͭt.In Wiltuͫe.ı.đₒ̈ıı̇ redđ.ı.x.denaɼ.Valuit.vıı.liɓ.
Modo.x.liɓ.

73 b
Idē:Nlg.teñ CHESIGEBERIE.T.R.E.geldɓ ₚ.vııı.hiđ.Tra.ē.v.caɼ.De
ea sͭ in dñio.ıııı.hiđ 7 dim.7.ibi.ıı.caɼ 7 dim.7 ıı.ſerui.7 vııı.uiłłi 7 xıı.
borđ.cū.ıı.caɼ.Ibi moliñ redđ.vıı.ſoł 7 dim.7 xx.aͨc ꝑti.7 paſtura
ıı.leū lͭg.7 v.q̃ɀ laͭt.Valuit 7 uał.xııı.lib.
Idē.N.teñ.ı.hiđ in NIGRAVRE.7 Durand de eo.Tra.ē.ı.caɼ.Ibi sͭ
ııı.borđ cū dim caɼ.7 vı.aͨc ꝑti.Paſtura.ıııı.q̃ɀ lͭg.7 ıı.q̃ɀ laͭt
Valuit 7 uał.ııı.liɓ.Hec.ııı.Man ꝑtiñ ad æccłɑm de Nigrauræ.

Land for 4 ploughs, of which 4 hides are in lordship; 2 ploughs
there; 2 slaves;
3 villagers and 14 smallholders.
Vineyard, 2 *arpents;* pasture, 20 acres; woodland, 4 acres.
The value was £4; now £6.

2   Aiulf also holds ½ hide in BEMERTON. Land for ½ plough.
It pays 12s.
Ralph held it before 1066.

56   LAND OF NIGEL THE DOCTOR

1   Nigel the doctor holds STRATTON (St. Margaret) from the King.
Before 1066 it paid tax for 30 hides. Land for 14 ploughs,
of which 5 hides are in lordship; 3 ploughs there; 2 slaves;
24 villagers and 18 smallholders with 12 ploughs.
A mill which pays 2s; meadow 8 furlongs long and 5 furlongs
wide; pasture 1 league long and 5 furlongs wide.
The value was £18; now £16.

† *Misplaced entry, directed to its proper place by transposition signs.*

51   LAND OF HUGH SON OF BALDRIC

1   Hugh son of Baldric holds MARDEN, and Walter his son-in-law from
him. Wenesi held it before 1066; it paid tax for 10 hides.
Land for 8 ploughs. In lordship 2 ploughs; 4 slaves;
9 villagers, 14 Cottagers and 2 smallholders with 5 ploughs.
A mill which pays 7½ s; meadow, 24 acres; pasture 3 furlongs
in length and 2 furlongs wide; in Wilton 1 house which pays 10d.
The value was £7; now £10.

,2   Nigel also holds CHISENBURY. Before 1066 it paid tax for 8   73 b
hides. Land for 5 ploughs, of which 4½ hides are in lordship;
2½ ploughs there; 2 slaves;
8 villagers and 12 smallholders with 2 ploughs.
A mill which pays 7½ s; meadow, 20 acres; pasture 1 league
long and 5 furlongs wide.
The value was and is £13.

3   Nigel also holds 1 hide in NETHERAVON, and Durand from him.
Land for 1 plough.
3 smallholders with ½ plough.
Meadow, 6 acres; pasture 4 furlongs long and 2 furlongs wide.
The value was and is £3.

These three manors belong to Netheravon Church.

Idē.N.teñ.IIII.hiđ in *SVDTONE*.7 ᵽ tanto geldᵬ T.R.E.Tra.ē.III.cař.

S MARIA de Monteburg teñ de Nig.De hac ᵗra sᵗ iñ dñio.II.hidæ.
7 ibi.I.cař.7 III.ſerui.7 v.uilti 7 v.borđ cū.II.cař.Ibi tcia pars molini
redđ.vi.ſot 7 VIII.deñ.7 III.āc ᵽti.Paſtura dim̄ leū lḡ.7 I.q̊ᵹ lat.
Silua.I.leū lḡ.7 I.q̊ᵹ lat.Valuit.IIII.lib.Modo.c.ſolid.
Hæc.IIII.ᴍ̃ tenuit Spirtes ᵽᵬr T.R.E.

NIGEL teñ dim̄ hiđ in *BEVRESBROC*.7 ᵽ tanto geldᵬ T.R.E.Ibi hᵗ.I.uillm̄
7 uñ borđ.7 ſilua.I.q̊ᵹ lḡ.7 dim̄ q̊ᵹ lat.Valet.VII.ſolid.

Idē.N.teñ *HASEBERIE*.T.R.E.geldᵬ ᵽ una v træ.Tra.ē.vi.boū.
Ibi sᵗ.III.borđ 7 III.āc ᵽti.Paſtura.IIII.q̊ᵹ lḡ.7 una q̊ᵹ lat.Valet.x.ſot
Has.II.ᵗras tenuit Alſi ᵽᵬr T.R.E.

.LVII.   TERRA OSBERNI PᴿᴮI

OSBERN ᵽᵬr teñ *HVMITONE*.Alſi tenuit T.R.E.7 geldᵬ ᵽ.II.hiđ.Tra.ē
.I.cař.Ibi sᵗ.II.coſcez.7 III.āc ᵽti.7 vi.āc paſturæ.Valet.xxx.ſolid.

.LVIII.   TERRA RICARDI PVINGIANT.

RICARD teñ de rege *CALESTONE*.Gunnar tenuit T.R.E.7 geldᵬ ᵽ.IIII.
hiđ una v min Tra.ē.IIII.cař.De ea sᵗ in dñio.II.cař.7 una v.7 ibi.III.
cař.7 II.ſerui.7 xvi.coſcez.7 III.borđ cū.I.cař.Ibi.II.molini redđ.xxxIII.
ſolid.7 vi.deñ.7 xv.āc ᵽti.7 totiđ paſturæ.Silua.III.q̊ᵹ lḡ.7 II.q̊ᵹ lat.
7 in Calne.II.burḡſes redđ xx.deñ.Valuit.IIII.lib.Modo.c.ſolid.
Idē.Ri.teñ *TROI*.T.R.E.geldᵬ ᵽ.vii.hiđ 7 dim̄.Tra.ē.IIII.cař.De ea
sᵗ in dñio.v.hidæ.7 ibi.III.cař.Ibi sᵗ.III.uilti cū.I.cař.7 II.āc ᵽti.Paſtura

4   Nigel also holds 4 hides in SUTTON (Veny); it paid tax for as much
before 1066. Land for 3 ploughs. St. Mary's of Montebourg holds
from Nigel. 2 hides of this land are in lordship; 1 plough
there; 3 slaves;
>5 villagers and 5 smallholders with 2 ploughs.
>The third part of a mill which pays 6s 8d; meadow, 3 acres;
>>pasture ½ league long and 1 furlong wide; woodland 1 league
>>long and 1 furlong wide.

The value was £4; now 100s.

Spirtes the priest held these four manors before 1066.

5   Nigel holds ½ hide in BEVERSBROOK ; it paid for as much
before 1066. He has
>1 villager and 1 smallholder.
>Woodland 1 furlong long and ½ furlong wide.

Value 7s.

6   Nigel also holds HAZELBURY. Before 1066 it paid tax for 1 virgate
of land. Land for 6 oxen.
>3 smallholders.
>Meadow, 3 acres; pasture 4 furlongs long and 1 furlong wide.

Value 10s.

Alfsi the priest held these two lands before 1066.

57   LAND OF OSBERN THE PRIEST

1   Osbern the priest holds HOMINGTON. Alfsi held it before 1066;
it paid tax for 2 hides. Land for 1 plough.
>2 Cottagers.
>Meadow, 3 acres; pasture, 6 acres.

Value 30s.

58   LAND OF RICHARD POYNANT

1   Richard Poynant holds CALSTONE (Wellington) from the King.
Gunnar held it before 1066; it paid tax for 4 hides, less 1
virgate. Land for 4 ploughs, of which 2 [hides?] and 1 virgate
are in lordship; 3 ploughs there; 2 slaves;
>16 Cottagers and 3 smallholders with 1 plough.
>2 mills which pay 33s 6d; meadow, 15 acres; pasture, as many;
>>woodland 3 furlongs long and 2 furlongs wide.
>In Calne 2 burgesses who pay 20d.

The value was £4; now 100s.

2   Richard also holds TROW. Before 1066 it paid tax for 7½ hides.
Land for 4 ploughs, of which 5 hides are in lordship; 3 ploughs there.
>3 villagers with 1 plough.

IIII.q̃ʒ lḡ.7 III.q̃ʒ laꝥ. Silua . VI . q̃ʒ lḡ.7 III . q̃ʒ laꝥ. Valuit . c . ſoꝉ. Ṁ.VII .liꝺ.

Hanc trã teneꝺ S MARIA de Wiltune T.R.E.7 ñ poterat ab æccla ſeparari.

.LIX.   ## TERRA ROBERTI MARESCAL.

R︦OBERTVS ten de rege *LAVENTONE* . Eddid regina tenuit.7 geldꝺ

.p . XV . hiꝺ . Tra . ē . X . caꝛ. De ea ſꝥ in dño . VII . hidæ .7 ibi . IIII.caꝛ.7 VIII

ſerui .7 XIIII.uitti 7 XVII . borꝺ cũ . V . caꝛ . Ibi . II . molini redꝺ . XVI . ſoliꝺ.

7 IIII . den .7 XX . ãc p̃ti .7 XII . ãc ſiluæ . Paſtura . I . leũ lḡ.7 tñtꝺ laꝥ.

Valuit 7 uaꝉ . XX . liꝺ.

Idē.Ro. ten *GARE*. Oſuuard tenuit T.R.E.7 geldꝺ .p . III. hiꝺ . Tra . ē . III.

caꝛ. De ea ſꝥ in dño . II . hidæ 7 ibi . II . caꝛ .7 VI . ſerui .7 III . uitti 7 I . borꝺ

cũ . I . caꝛ.7 XL . ãc paſturæ . valuit . XXX . ſoliꝺ . Modo . L . ſoliꝺ.

.LX. R︦OBERTVS ten de rege *LAVENTONE* . Achi tenuit T.R.E.7 geldꝺ .p . X.

hiꝺ . Tra . ē . VII . caꝛ . De ea ſꝥ in dño . I . hida 7 una v̄.7 ibi . I . caꝛ.

Duo generi ej ten de eo . VII . hiꝺ 7 una v̄.7 ibi hñt.V . caꝛ cũ hõibʒ ſuis.

Ibi molin redꝺ . V . ſoꝉ.7 paſtura. I . leũ 7 dim lḡ .7 IIII . q̃ʒ laꝥ.

Valuit . XV . liꝺ . Modo . XII . liꝺ.   ## TERRA RICARDI STVRMID.

.LXI. R︦ICARD ten de rege *CVVLESTONE* . Aluric tenuit T.R.E.7 geldꝺ .p . II.

hiꝺ . Tra . ē . II . caꝛ . De ea . ē in dño . I . hida.7 ibi . I . caꝛ .7 II . uitti 7 VIII.

coſcez cũ . II . caꝛ . Ibi paſtura . II . q̃ʒ lḡ.7 una q̃ʒ laꝥ .7 tñtꝺ ſiluæ.

Valuit . XV . ſoliꝺ . Modo . XXX . ſoliꝺ.   ## RAINALDI CANVT.

.LXII. R︦AINALD ten de rege . I . hiꝺ in *CHIPEHA* Tochi tenuit T . R . E . Tra . ē . I . caꝛ.

Ibi . II . borꝺ hñt dim caꝛ.7 XX . ãc p̃ti .7 dimiꝺ molin redꝺ . XV . ſoꝉ. Toꞇ ualuit 7 uaꝉ

ꝉ XX . ſoliꝺ.

Meadow, 2 acres; pasture 4 furlongs long and 3 furlongs wide; woodland 6 furlongs long and 3 furlongs wide.
The value was 100s; now £7.

St. Mary's of Wilton held this land before 1066; it could not be separated from the church.

59 LAND OF ROBERT MARSHALL

1 Robert Marshall holds LAVINGTON from the King. Queen Edith held it; it paid tax for 15 hides. Land for 10 ploughs, of which 7 hides are in lordship; 4 ploughs there; 7 slaves;
   14 villagers and 17 smallholders with 5 ploughs.
   2 mills which pay 16s 4d; meadow, 20 acres; woodland, 12 acres; pasture 1 league long and as wide.
The value was and is £20.

2 Robert also holds GORE. Osward held it before 1066; it paid tax for 3 hides. Land for 3 ploughs, of which 2 hides are in lordship; 2 ploughs there; 6 slaves;
   3 villagers and 1 smallholder with 1 plough.
   Pasture, 40 acres.
The value was 30s; now 50s.

60 [LAND OF ROBERT BLUNT]

1 Robert Blunt holds LAVINGTON from the King. Aki held it before 1066; it paid tax for 10 hides. Land for 7 ploughs, of which 1 hide and 1 virgate are in lordship; 1 plough there. His two sons-in-law hold 7 hides and 1 virgate from him; they have 5 ploughs with their men.
   A mill which pays 5s; pasture 1½ leagues long and 4 furlongs wide.
The value was £15; now £12.

61 LAND OF RICHARD STURMY

1 Richard Sturmy holds COWESFIELD from the King. Aelfric held it before 1066; it paid tax for 2 hides. Land for 2 ploughs, of which 1 hide is in lordship; 1 plough there;
   2 villagers and 8 Cottagers with 2 ploughs.
   Pasture 2 furlongs long and 1 furlong wide; woodland, as much.
The value was 15s; now 30s.

62 [LAND] OF REGINALD CANUTE

1 Reginald Canute holds 1 hide in CHIPPENHAM from the King. Toki held it before 1066. Land for 1 plough.
   2 smallholders have ½ plough.
   Meadow, 20 acres; ½ mill which pays 15s.
The value of the whole was and is 20s.

.LXI. **M**ACI de Moretania teñ de rege *WINTREBVRNE* . Vluuard
tenuit T.R.E.7 geldb p.IIII.hid . Tra.e.II.car . De ea st in dñio .II.hide.
7 ibi.I.car. cu.I.feruo.7 II.uilti 7 IIII.bord cu.I.car.Ibi paftura.IIII.q̃ʒ lg.
7 tñtd lat.Valuit.XL.fot.Modo.LX.folid. **GOZELINI RIVEIRE.**

.LX **G**OZELIN teñ de rege *SELE* . Almar tenuit T.R.E.7 geldb p.II.hid 7 dimid.
Tra.e.III.car . In dñio.e.I.car.7 II.ferui.7 V.uitti 7 III.cofcez cu.II.car.
Ibi molin.XL.den redd.7 III.ac pti.Paftura.III.q̃ʒ lg.7 III.lat . Silua dimid
leu lg.7 tñtd lat . Valuit 7 uat.XXX.folid. **GODESCALLI.**

.LXV **G**ODESCAL teñ de rege *WINTREBVRNE*. Aluui tenuit T.R.E.7 geldb p.II.
hid . Tra.e.II.car . In dñio.e.I.car.7 III.ferui.7 IIII.bord.7 V.cofcez.
Ibi dimid molin redd.III.fot 7 IX.den.7 dimid ac pti.Silua.II.q̃ʒ lg.7 tñtd
lat.Valuit.XXX.fot.Modo.XL.folid. Valet.XII.fot.

Ide.Go.teñ dimid hid q Gudmund tenuit T.R.E.7 p tanto geldb.Ibi.e.I.cofcet.

SERVIENT
REGIS.

.LXVI **H**ERMAN teñ de rege *ETONE*.Edric tenuit T.R.E.7 geldb p.II.hid.Tra.e.II.car.
In dñio.e.I.car.7 II.bord 7 II.cofcez 7 I.uitt cu.I.car.Ibi.II.ac pti.Silua.I
q̃ʒ lg.7 una q̃ʒ lat.Valuit 7 uat.XXX.folid.

73 c
AMELRIC teñ de rege *MANIFORD*.Godric tenuit T.R.E.7 geldb p.III.hid
7 dimid.Tra.e.I.car 7 dim.Ibi st.IIII.bord.7 tcia pars molini redd.L.
denar.7 XII.ac pti.Paftura.IIII.q̃ʒ lg.7 una q̃ʒ 7 dim lat.Valuit XXX.fot.

Modo.LX.fot.

63   LAND OF MATTHEW OF MORTAGNE

1   Matthew of Mortagne holds MADDINGTON from the King. Wulfward
held it before 1066; it paid tax for 4 hides. Land for 2 ploughs,
of which 2 hides are in lordship; 1 plough there, with 1 slave;
    2 villagers and 4 smallholders with 1 plough.
    Pasture 4 furlongs long and as wide.
The value was 40s; now 60s.

64   [LAND] OF JOCELYN RIVERS

1   Jocelyn Rivers holds ZEALS from the King. Aelmer held it
before 1066; it paid tax for 2½ hides. Land for 3 ploughs. In
lordship 1 plough; 2 slaves;
    5 villagers and 3 Cottagers with 2 ploughs.
    A mill which pays 40d; meadow, 3 acres; pasture 3 furlongs long
        and 3 wide; woodland ½ league long and as wide.
The value was and is 30s.

65   [LAND] OF GODESCAL

1   Godescal holds WINTERBOURNE from the King. Alfwy held it
before 1066; it paid tax for 2 hides. Land for 2 ploughs. In
lordship 1 plough; 3 slaves;
    4 smallholders and 5 Cottagers.
    ½ mill which pays 3s 9d; meadow, ½ acre; woodland 2 furlongs
        long and as wide.
The value was 30s; now 40s.

2   Godescal also holds ½ hide, which Godmund held before 1066;
it paid tax for as much.
    1 Cottager.
Value 12s.

66 [LAND OF HERMAN AND OTHER] SERVANTS OF THE KING   ψ

1   Herman of Dreux holds (Castle) EATON from the King. Edric held it
before 1066; it paid tax for 2 hides. Land for 2 ploughs.
In lordship 1 plough;
    2 smallholders, 2 Cottagers and 1 villager with 1 plough.
    Meadow, 2 acres; woodland 2 furlongs long and 1 furlong wide.
The value was and is 30s.

2   Amalric of Dreux holds MANNINGFORD from the King. Godric   73c
held it before 1066; it paid tax for 3½ hides. Land for 1½ ploughs.
    4 smallholders.
    The third part of a mill which pays 50d; meadow, 12 acres;
        pasture 4 furlongs long and 1½ furlongs wide.
The value was 30s; now 60s.

Acoqus Ansgervs ten *Helprintone*. Tres taini tenuer parrit' T.R.E.

7 geldb p. IIII. hid 7 una v 7 VI. acris. Tra e III. car. q ibi st in dnio.

eu. I. seruo. 7 IX. coscez. Ibi. XII. ac pti. 7 XX. ac pasturae.

Valuit. IIII. lib. Modo. X. solid min.

Wills Corniole ten de rege *Helprintone*. Quattuor taini tenuer parif T.R.E.

7 geldb p. V. hid 7 una v træ. Tra e. V. car. In dnio st. II. car. 7 un uitls

cu. I. car. 7 XII. ac pti. 7 XX. ac pasturae. Reddit. XL. solid.

Fvlchered ten. III. v træ in *Gelingeha*. Algar tenuit T.R.E. Tra e

. II. car. q ibi st. cu. I. bord. Valuit 7 ual. XV. solid.

Stefan carpentari ten. I. hid 7 una v træ in *Ardescote*. Odo tenuit

T.R.E. Tra e. II. car. q ibi st cu. I. seruo. 7 III. uittis. 7 II. bord. Ibi. XXX.

ac pti. 7 VIII. ac pasturæ. 7 In Crichelade un ortu redd. II. denar.

Valuit. XXX. sot. Modo. LX. solid.

Ide Stefan ten. III. hid. Achil tenuit T.R.E. Tra e. I. car. q ibi. e

cu. I. uitto. 7 IIII. bord. Ibi pastura dimid leu lg. 7 III. qz lat.

Valuit. XX. solid. Modo. XL. solid.

Osmvnd ten. I. hida in *Ponberie*. Alnod tenuit T.R.E. Tra e. I. car.

q ibi. e in dnio. Valuit. V. sot. Modo. X. solid.

.LXVII. **Terra Odonis & Alioʒ Tainoʒ Regis.**

Odo De Wincestre ten de rege *Colecote*. Ibi st. V. hidæ. T.R.E. geldb

p dim hida. Tra e. III. car. De ea st in dnio. IIII. hide 7 dim.

Ibi. I. uitts 7 IIII. bord cu. I. seruo hnt. I. car. 7 LX. ac pti. In Crichelade

III. burgses redd. XXI. denar. Valet. IIII. lib.

Brictric ten de rege *Covelestone*. T.R.E. geldb p. V. hid. Tra e. IIII.

car. In dnio st. II. car. 7 VI. serui. 7 V. uitti 7 III. bord cu. II. car. Ibi

molin redd. X. sot. 7 XXX. ac pti. 7 V. qrent pasturæ. Valet. C. solid.

3 Ansger Cook holds HILPERTON. Three thanes held it jointly
before 1066; it paid tax for 4 hides, 1 virgate and 6 acres.
Land for 3 ploughs, which are there, in lordship, with 1 slave;
    9 Cottagers.
    Meadow, 12 acres; pasture, 20 acres.
The value was £4; now 10s less.

4 William Cornelian holds HILPERTON from the King. Four thanes
held it jointly before 1066; it paid tax for 5 hides and 1 virgate
of land. Land for 5 ploughs. In lordship 2 ploughs;
    1 villager with 1 plough.
    Meadow, 12 acres; pasture, 20 acres.
It pays 40s.

5 Fulcred holds 3 virgates of land in GILLINGHAM. Algar held them
before 1066. Land for 2 ploughs, which are there, with
    1 smallholder.
The value was and is 15s.

6 Stephen Carpenter holds 1 hide and 1 virgate of land in EARLSCOURT.
Odo held it before 1066. Land for 2 ploughs, which are there,
with 1 slave and
    3 villagers and 2 smallholders.
    Meadow, 30 acres; pasture, 8 acres; in Cricklade 1 garden
        which pays 2d.
The value was 30s; now 60s.

7 Stephen also holds 3 hides. Aki held them before 1066.
Land for 1 plough, which is there with
    1 villager and 4 smallholders.
    Pasture ½ league long and 3 furlongs wide.
The value was 20s; now 40s.

8 Osmund holds 1 hide in POMEROY. Alnoth held it before 1066.
Land for 1 plough, which is there, in lordship.
The value was 5s; now 10s.

67   LAND OF ODO AND OTHER THANES OF THE KING

1 Odo of Winchester holds CALCUTT from the King. 5 hides.
Before 1066 it paid tax for ½ hide. Land for 3 ploughs, of
which 4½ hides are in lordship.
    1 villager and 4 smallholders with 1 slave have 1 plough.
    Meadow, 60 acres.
    In Cricklade 3 burgesses who pay 21d.
Value £4.

2 Brictric holds COULSTON from the King. Before 1066 it paid tax
for 5 hides. Land for 4 ploughs. In lordship 2 ploughs; 6 slaves;
    5 villagers and 3 smallholders with 2 ploughs.
    A mill which pays 10s; meadow, 30 acres; pasture, 5 furlongs.
Value 100s.

Bᴙɪᴄᴛʀɪᴄ ten .ɪ. hiđ in *Svaloclive*.7 unā v́ træ 7 dimiđ . Tra . ē . ɪ . cař.
q̊ ibi . ē cū . ɪɪ . uiłlis . Valet . xv . soliđ.　　　　　　Ⅎ x . soliđ.

Bᴙɪᴄ́ᴛʀɪᴄ ten .ɪ. hiđ in *Trole* ; Tra . ē . ɪ . cař . q̊ ibi . ē cū . ɪ . uiłto . Valet

Bᴙɪᴄ́ᴛʀɪᴄ ten *Farlege* .7 fř ej de eo . T.R.E. gelđɓ ꝓ . v . hiđ . Tra . ē ,ɪɪɪɪ .
cař . In dn̄io . ē . ɪ . cař . 7 ɪɪɪɪ . serui . 7 v . uiłti 7 ɪɪɪ . borđ cū . ɪɪɪ . cař.
Ibi . xx . ac̃ pasturæ . 7 ɪɪɪ . ac̃ siluæ . Valet . ʟxx . soliđ.

Bᴙɪᴄᴛʀɪᴄ ten *Wochesie* . Pat ej tenuit T.R.E. 7 gelđɓ ꝓ . x . hiđ.
Tra . ē . vɪ . cař . In dn̄io st̄ . ɪɪ . cař . 7 x . serui . 7 vɪ . uiłti . 7 xɪɪ . coscez
cū . ɪɪɪɪ . cař . Ibi molin̄ . v . sol redđ . 7 xʟ . ac̃ p̃ti . 7 xxx . ac̃ pasturæ .
Silua . ɪ . leu lg̃ . 7 dim̄ leu lat̄ . Valuit . vɪɪɪ . liɓ . Modo . vɪ . liɓ.

Bᴙɪᴄᴛʀɪᴄ ten *Strabvrg* . Pat ej tenuit T.R.E. 7 gelđɓ ꝓ . x . hiđ.
Tra . ē . ɪx . cař . In dn̄io st̄ . ɪɪ . cař . 7 vɪɪ . serui . 7 xɪ . uiłti 7 vɪ . coscez
cū . vɪɪ . cař . Ibi molin̄ . x . sol redđ . 7 x . ac̃ p̃ti . 7 xɪɪ . ac̃ pasturæ .
Silua . v . q̊℈ lg̃ . 7 ɪɪɪ . q̊℈ lat̄ . Valuit . ɪɪɪɪ . liɓ . Modo . vɪɪɪ . liɓ.

Bᴙɪᴄᴛʀɪᴄ ten *Stavretone* . Pat ej tenuit T.R.E. 7 gelđɓ ꝓ . v . hiđ.
Tra . ē . ɪɪɪ . cař . In dn̄io st̄ . ɪɪ . cař . 7 vɪɪ . serui . 7 ɪɪɪ . uiłti 7 ɪɪ . coscez cū . ɪ .
cař . Ibi molin̄ redđ . xx . sol . 7 xx . ac̃ p̃ti . 7 xx . ac̃ pasturæ . Valet . ʟxx . soliđ.

Bᴙɪᴄᴛʀɪᴄ ten *Odestote* . Pat ej tenuit T.R.E. 7 gelđɓ ꝓ . xɪɪ . hiđ.
Tra . ē . vɪ . cař . In dn̄io . ē . ɪ . cař . 7 ɪɪɪ . serui . 7 ɪx . uiłti . 7 xvɪ . coscez
cū . ɪɪ . cař 7 dim̄ . Ibi molin̄ redđ . vɪɪ . sol 7 vɪ . denař . 7 xʟ . ac̃ p̃ti .
Pastura . ɪ . leu lg̃ . 7 ɪɪɪ . q̊℈ lat̄ . 7 in alia parte . v . ac̃ pasturæ . Silua
ɪɪɪ . q̊℈ lg̃ . 7 ɪɪɪ . q̊℈ lat̄ . In Wiltune . ɪ . burg̃sis redđ . xɪɪ . denař.

Bᴙɪᴄᴛʀɪᴄ 7 Aluui fř ej ten *Colesfeld* . T.R.E. Ⅎ Valet . x . liɓ.
gelđɓ ꝓ . ɪ . hida 7 dimiđ . Tra . ē . ɪ . cař . q̊ ibi . ē cū . ɪɪɪ . coscez.
Ibi . ɪɪ . q̊rent siluæ minutæ . Valet . x . soliđ.

Brictric holds

3   in SWALLOWCLIFFE 1 hide and 1½ virgates of land. Land for 1 plough, which is there, with
      2 villagers.
    Value 15s.

4   in TROWLE 1 hide. Land for 1 plough, which is there, with
      1 villager.
    Value 10s.

5   (Monkton) FARLEIGH. His brother holds from him. Before 1066 it paid tax for 5 hides. Land for 4 ploughs. In lordship 1 plough; 4 slaves;
      5 villagers and 3 smallholders with 3 ploughs.
      Pasture, 20 acres; woodland, 3 acres.
    Value 70s.

6   OAKSEY. His father held it before 1066; it paid tax for 10 hides. Land for 6 ploughs. In lordship 2 ploughs; 10 slaves;
      6 villagers and 12 Cottagers with 4 ploughs.
      A mill which pays 5s; meadow, 40 acres; pasture, 30 acres;
        woodland 1 league long and ½ league wide.
    The value was £8; now £6.

7   TROWBRIDGE. His father held it before 1066; it paid tax for 10 hides. Land for 9 ploughs. In lordship 2 ploughs; 7 slaves;
      11 villagers and 6 Cottagers with 7 ploughs.
      A mill which pays 10s; meadow, 10 acres; pasture, 12 acres;
        woodland 5 furlongs long and 3 furlongs wide.
    The value was £4; now £8.

8   STAVERTON. His father held it before 1066; it paid tax for 5 hides. Land for 3 ploughs. In lordship 2 ploughs; 7 slaves;
      3 villagers and 2 Cottagers with 1 plough.
      A mill which pays 20s; meadow, 20 acres; pasture, 20 acres.
    Value 70s.

9   ODSTOCK. His father held it before 1066; it paid tax for 12 hides. Land for 6 ploughs. In lordship 1 plough; 3 slaves;
      9 villagers and 16 Cottagers with 2½ ploughs.
      A mill which pays 7s 6d; meadow, 40 acres; pasture 1 league long
        and 3 furlongs wide; elsewhere pasture, 5 acres; woodland
        3 furlongs long and 3 furlongs wide.
      In Wilton 1 burgess who pays 12d.
    Value £10.

10   Brictric and his brother Alfwy hold COWESFIELD. Before 1066 it paid tax for 1½ hides. Land for 1 plough, which is there, with
      3 Cottagers.
      Underwood, 2 furlongs.
    Value 10s.

Alward ten . iii . hiđ in *POTERNE* . T.R.E. gelđb eū Maner epi.
Tra . ē . iii . car . In đnio . ē una . 7 iii . uilti 7 iiii . borđ cū . ii . car.

★ Ibi   iiii . q̃z̃ lg̃ . 7 iii . q̃z̃ lat . Valet . lxx . fot . Eps Ofmund calūniat.
Aluuard ten . i . hiđ in *TIDVLFHIDE* . Tra . ē . i . car . q̃ ibi . ē . 7 i . q̃rent

★ Aluuard ten *SVALOCLIVE* . T.R.E. 7 gelđb   ſ pafturæ Valet . xx . fot.
p̃ . iii . hiđ . dim v min . Tra . ē . i . car 7 dimiđ . vilti teneꝗ . Valet . xxx. ſolid.
Aluuard ten *CVNVCHE* . T.R.E. gelđb p̃ . iiii . hiđ . Tra . ē . iii . car.

In đnio . ē una car . 7 iii . ſerui . 7 iiii . uilti 7 iii . borđ cū . ii . car.
Ibi moliñ redđ . xv . ſolid . 7 v . ac p̃ti . Paftura dimiđ leū lg̃ . 7 una
q̃z̃ lat . Valet . iiii . lib.

73 d

Alvric ten de rege *WIVLESFORD* . Brifmar tenuit T.R.E.
7 gelđb p̃ . v . hiđ . Tra . ē . ii . car 7 dimiđ . quæ ibi ſt cū . x . borđ.
Ibi . viii . ac p̃ti . Paftura . v . q̃z̃ lg̃ . 7 una q̃z̃ lat.
Valuit . c . fot . Modo . viii . ſolid . Edmuard ten in uadimonio.

Alvric ten *FARLEGE* . Brifmar tenuit T.R.E. 7 gelđb p̃ . v.
hiđ . Tra . ē . iiii . car . In đnio . ē . i . car . 7 iiii . ſerui . 7 v . uilti
7 iii . borđ cū . iii . car . Ibi . xx . ac pafturæ . 7 iii . ac ſiluæ.
Valet . lxx . ſolid.

Aluric ten *WADONE* . Ipfe tenuit T.R.E. 7 gelđb p̃ . iii . hiđ.
Tra . ē . ii . car . In đnio . ē una . 7 iii . ſerui . 7 iii . coſcez.
Ibi moliñ redđ . v . ſolid . 7 viii . ac p̃ti . Vna q̃z̃ pafturæ in lg̃ 7 lat.

Alvric ten . ii . v træ 7 dim in *TIDVLFHIDE* .   ſ Valet . xx . fot.
Tra . ē dimiđ car . Valet . vii . fot 7 vi . denar.

Ide ten . i . hiđa in *HELMERTVNE* . Tra . ē . i . car . 7 ibi ht
uñ feruū . Valet . xv . ſolid.

11 Alfward holds 3 hides in POTTERNE. Before 1066 it paid tax with
the Bishop's manor. Land for 3 ploughs. In lordship 1;
    3 villagers and 4 smallholders with 2 ploughs.
    .... 4 furlongs long and 3 furlongs wide.
Value 70s.
    Bishop Osmund claims it.

12 Alfward holds 1 hide in TILSHEAD. Land for 1 plough, which is there.
    Pasture, 1 furlong.
Value 20s.

13 Alfward holds SWALLOWCLIFFE. Before 1066 it paid tax for 3 hides,
less ½ virgate. Land for 1½ ploughs. The villagers hold (them?).
Value 30s.

14 Alfward Colling holds KNOOK. Before 1066 it paid tax for 4 hides.
Land for 3 ploughs. In lordship 1 plough; 3 slaves;
    4 villagers and 3 smallholders with 2 ploughs.
    A mill which pays 15s; meadow, 5 acres; pasture ½ league long
      and 1 furlong wide.
Value £4.

15 Aelfric of Melksham holds WILSFORD from the King. Brictmer held   73d
it before 1066; it paid tax for 5 hides. Land for 2½ ploughs,
which are there, with
    10 smallholders.
    Meadow, 8 acres; pasture 5 furlongs long and 1 furlong wide.
The value was 100s; now 8s.
    Edward holds it in pledge.

16 Aelfric holds (Monkton) FARLEIGH. Brictmer held it before 1066;
it paid tax for 5 hides. Land for 4 ploughs. In lordship 1 plough;
4 slaves;
    5 villagers and 3 smallholders with 3 ploughs.
    Pasture, 20 acres; woodland, 3 acres.
Value 70s.

17 Aelfric holds WHADDON. He held it himself before 1066; it paid
tax for 3 hides. Land for 2 ploughs. In lordship 1; 3 slaves;
    3 Cottagers.
    A mill which pays 5s; meadow, 8 acres; pasture, 1 furlong
      in length and width.
Value 20s.

18 Aelfric Small holds 2½ virgates of land in TILSHEAD. Land for ½ plough.
Value 7s 6d.

19 He also holds 1 hide in HILMARTON. Land for 1 plough. He has 1 slave.
Value 15s.

Idē ten̄ . I . hiđ in *TOCHEHA* . 7 ꝑ tanto geldb̄ . Tra ̄ē . I . car̄.

Ibi . VI . ac p̄ti . 7 VI . ac pasturæ . Valet . XIII . foliđ.

Idē ten̄ . II . hiđ una v̄ miñ quas . II . taini tenuer̄ T.R.E.

Tra . ē . VI . bou̅ . Valet . XV . foliđ.

A̅LWINVS ten̄ *SVMREFORD* . T.R.E geldb̄ ꝑ . II . v̄ træ 7 dim̄.

Tra . ē dimiđ car̄ . Ibi st̄ . II . cofcez . 7 I . cotar̄ . 7 pars molini

redđ . XV . denar̄ . 7 IIII . ac p̄ti . 7 IIII . ac pasturæ . Valet . XI . fot.

In eađ uilla ten̄ Aluuius . II . v̄ træ 7 dim̄ . 7 ꝑ tanto geldb̄

T.R.E. Tra . ē dim̄ car̄ . Ibi st̄ . II . cofcez . 7 pars molini . XV . den̄.

7 IIII . ac p̄ti . 7 IIII . ac pasturæ . Valuit 7 uat . VIII . foliđ.

In eađ uilla ten̄ Eduuard dimiđ hiđ . Tra . ē dimiđ car̄.

In eađ uilla ten̄ Saieua . II . v̄ træ 7 dim̄ . Valet . XL . den̄.

Tra . ē dim̄ car̄ . Ibi . ē un̄ cofcet 7 I . cotar̄ . Pars molini redđ

XV . den̄ . 7 IIII . ac p̄ti . 7 IIII . ac pasturæ . Valet . XI . foliđ.

A̅LWI . ten̄ dimiđ hiđ in *STANINGES* . Tra . ē dimiđ car̄.

Ibi . IIII . ac p̄ti . Valet . V . foliđ.

A̅LRIC ten̄ dimiđ hiđ in *TOCHEHA* . Tra . ē dim̄ car̄ . Ibi . III.

ac p̄ti . 7 III . ac pasturæ . Valet . VII . foliđ.

A̅ZOR ten̄ . II . hiđ in *BERRELEGE* . Dōne tenuit T.R.E. Tra . ē . IIII.

car̄ . In dn̄io st̄ . II . car̄ . cū . I . borđ 7 II . uittis . Valuit 7 uat . XL . fot.

A̅LESTAN ten̄ dimiđ hiđ træ in *TIDVLFHIDE* . Valet . V . foliđ.

A̅LMAR . ten̄ . II . v̄ træ 7 dimiđ in *TIDVLFHIDE* . Valet . V . foliđ.

A̅LGAR ten̄ . I . hiđ in *TOCHEHA* . Tra . ē . I . car̄ . Ibi ht̄ dim̄ car̄.

cū . I . borđ . 7 VI . ac p̄ti . 7 totiđ pasturæ . Valet . XIII . foliđ.

20 He also holds 1 hide in TOCKENHAM; it paid tax for as much.
Land for 1 plough.
   Meadow, 6 acres; pasture, 6 acres.
Value 13s.

21 He also holds 2 hides, less 1 virgate, which two thanes held
before 1066. Land for 6 oxen.
Value 15s.

22 Alwin the priest holds SOMERFORD. Before 1066 it paid tax
for 2½ virgates of land. Land for ½ plough.
   2 Cottagers and 1 cottager.
   Part of a mill which pays 15d; meadow, 4 acres; pasture, 4 acres.
Value 11s.

23 In the same village Alfwy holds 2½ virgates of land; it paid tax
for as much before 1066; Land for ½ plough.
   2 Cottagers.
   Part of a mill, 15d; meadow, 4 acres; pasture, 4 acres.
The value was and is 8s.

24 In the same village Edward holds ½ hide. Land for ½ plough.
Value 40d.

25 In the same village Saeva holds 2½ virgates of land. Land for ½ plough.
   1 Cottager and 1 cottager.
   Part of a mill which pays 15d; meadow, 4 acres; pasture, 4 acres.
Value 11s.

26 Alfwy son of Thurber holds ½ hide in STANDLYNCH. Land for ½ plough.
   Meadow, 4 acres.
Value 5s.

27 Alric holds ½ hide which pays tax in TOCKENHAM. Land for ½ plough.
   Meadow, 3 acres; pasture, 3 acres.
Value 7s.

28 Azor holds 2 hides in 'BARLEY'. Dunn held them before 1066.
Land for 4 ploughs. In lordship 2 ploughs, with
   1 smallholder and 2 villagers.
The value was and is 40s.

29 Alstan holds ½ hide of land in TILSHEAD.   Value 5s.

30 Aelmer holds 2½ virgates of land in TILSHEAD.   Value 5s.

31 Algar holds 1 hide which pays tax in TOCKENHAM. Land for 1 plough.
He has ½ plough, with
   1 smallholder.
   Meadow, 6 acres; pasture, as many.
Value 13s.

Aʟᴠɪᴇᴅ ten *Sᴇʟᴀ*. T.R.E. geldɓ ꝑ. ɪɪ. hiđ 7 dim . Tra . ē. ɪɪɪ. caĩ.

In dñio . ē . ɪ . caĩ . 7 ɪɪɪɪ . ſerui . 7 ᴠɪɪɪ . uiɫɫi 7 ɪx . borđ cū . ɪɪ . caĩ.

Ibi moliñ redđ . ɪɪɪ . ſoliđ 7 ɪɪɪɪ . aĩc ꝓti . 7 xʟ . aĩc paſturæ.

Silua dimiđ leū lḡ . 7 dimiđ leū laĩ . Valet . xxx . ſoliđ.

Aᴢᴏʀ ten . ɪ . hiđ in *Cᴏʀsᴇʟɪᴇ*. Tra . ē . ɪ . caĩ . q̃ ibi . ē in dñio

cū . ɪɪɪɪ . borđ . Ibi moliñ redđ . xʟ . denaĩ . 7 Silua . ɪ . q̃ɀ lḡ.

7 dimiđ q̃ɀ laĩ . Valet . xx . ſoliđ.

Aʟᴅʀᴇᴅ ten *Bɪᴍᴇʀᴛᴏɴᴇ*. Ipſe tenuit T.R.E. 7 geldɓ ꝑ. ɪɪ.

hiđ . Tra . ē . ɪɪ . caĩ . Ibi . ē . ɪ . uiɫɫs 7 ɪɪɪ . borđ 7 ɪɪɪɪ . aĩc ꝓti.

7 moliñ redđ . xɪɪ . ſoɫ 7 ᴠɪ . denaĩ . Valet . xʟ . ſoliđ.

Aʟᴅʀᴇᴅ ten *Fᴇʀsᴛᴇsғᴇʟᴅ*. Ipſe tenuit T.R.E. 7 geldɓ ꝑ una

hida Tra . ē . ɪɪ . caĩ . Ibi . ē . ɪ . caĩ cū . ɪ . uiɫɫo 7 ɪɪɪ . coſcez.

Ibi paſtura . ɪ . q̃ɀ lḡ . 7 una laĩ . Silua . ɪɪ . q̃ɀ lḡ . 7 una q̃ɀ laĩ.

Aʟᴅʀᴇᴅ ten *Wɪɴᴛʀᴇʙʏʀɴᴇ*. Goduin tenuit Ꞁ Valet . x . ſoliđ.

T.R.E. 7 geldɓ ꝑ. ɪ . hida 7 dim . Tra . ē . ɪ . caĩ . Ibi . ē dim caĩ cū

uno uiɫɫo 7 ɪ . borđ . 7 pars **molini redđ** . xxɪɪ . denaĩ 7 obolū.

Paſtura . ɪɪ . q̃ɀ lḡ . 7 tñtđ laĩ . Valet . xxx . ſoliđ.

Cᴠᴅᴠʟғ ten *Wɪɴᴛʀᴇʙʏʀɴᴇ*. Ipſe tenuit T.R.E. Ibi habt . ᴠɪ . hiđ.

Tra . ē . ɪɪɪ . caĩ . In dñio ſt . ɪɪ . caĩ . 7 ᴠ . ſerui . cū . ɪ . uiɫɫo 7 ɪɪ . borđ

hñt . ɪ . caĩ . Ibi . ɪɪɪɪ . aĩc ꝓti . 7 dimiđ leū paſturæ . Valet . ɪɪɪ . liɓ.

Cʜᴇᴛᴇʟ ten . ɪ . hiđ in *Mᴀʟᴍᴇsʙᴇʀɪᴇ* . Goduin tenuit T.R.E.

Tra . ē . ɪ . caĩ . q̃ ibi . ē cū . ɪɪ . borđ . Ibi . ᴠɪ . aĩc ꝓti . Paſtura . ɪɪɪ . q̃ɀ

lḡ . 7 dimiđ q̃ɀ laĩ . Valet . xx . ſoliđ.

32 Alfgeat holds ZEALS. Before 1066 it paid tax for 2½ hides.
Land for 3 ploughs. In lordship 1 plough; 4 slaves;
    8 villagers and 9 smallholders with 2 ploughs.
      A mill which pays 3s; meadow, 4 acres; pasture, 40 acres;
        woodland ½ league long and ½ league wide.
Value 30s.

33 Azor holds 1 hide in CORSLEY. Land for 1 plough, which is there,
in lordship, with
    4 smallholders.
      A mill which pays 40d; woodland 1 furlong long
        and ½ furlong wide.
Value 20s.

34 Aldred holds BEMERTON. He held it himself before 1066; it paid
tax for 2 hides. Land for 2 ploughs.
    1 villager and 3 smallholders.
    Meadow, 4 acres; a mill which pays 12s 6d.
Value 40s.

35 Aldred holds ALDERSTONE. He held it himself before 1066; it paid
tax for 1 hide. Land for 2 ploughs. 1 plough there, with
    1 villager and 3 Cottagers.
    Pasture 1 furlong long and 1 wide; woodland 2 furlongs
      long and 1 furlong wide.
Value 10s.

36 Aldred holds WINTERBOURNE. Godwin held it before 1066; it paid
tax for 1½ hides. Land for 1 plough. ½ plough there, with
    1 villager and 1 smallholder.
    Part of a mill which pays 22½d; pasture 2 furlongs long
      and as wide.
Value 30s.

† *67,37-38 written across the bottom of cols. 73c,d and entered here after 67,42.*

39 Cuthwulf holds 'WINTERBOURNE'. He held it himself before 1066. He
has 6 hides. Land for 3 ploughs. In lordship 2 ploughs; 5 slaves, with
    1 villager; 2 smallholders have 1 plough.
    Meadow, 4 acres; pasture, ½ league.
Value £3.

40 Ketel holds 1 hide in MALMESBURY. Godwin held it before 1066.
Land for 1 plough, which is there, with
    2 smallholders.
    Meadow, 6 acres; pasture 3 furlongs long and ½ furlong wide.
Value 20s.

Cheping ten HASEBERIE . Ipſe tenuit T.R.E.7 geldb p una v
træ.Tra.ē.ı.caɼ.q̄ ibi.ē.7 Silua.ıı.q̄ɀ lḡ.7 una q̄ɀ laɫ. Valet.vıı.

Cola ten GRAMESTEDE . Pat ej tenuit T.R.E.7 geldb ⌐ſoliɗ.
p.ı.hida 7 dim.Tra.ē.ı.caɼ.Ibi ſt.ıııı.uiɫɫı.Valet.xv.ſoliɗ.

☞ Aldred ten in ANESTIGE.ııı.hiɗ.Tra.ē.ıı.caɼ.quæ ibi ſt cũ.ı.ſeruo 7 ı.uiɫɫo.7 ııı.borɗ.
Ibi moliñ reddɫ.xxv.den̄.7 v.ac ſiluæ 7 v.ac pti.7 ıı.q̄ɀ paſturæ.Vaɫ.xxx.

Aldred ten jn WERVETONE.x.hiɗ.Tra.ē.ıııı.caɼ.q̄ ibi ſt cũ.v.ſeruis.7 ııı.uiɫɫ
7 ııı.borɗ.Valuit 7 uaɫ.c.ſoɫ.Has.ıı.tras tenueɼ Bricnoɫ 7 Aluuin T.R.E.

Grimbald ten MANIFORD . Eduuard tenuit T.R.E.7 geldb
p.vı.hid 7 dimid.Tra.ē.ıııı.caɼ.In dn̄io ſt.ıı.caɼ.7 un uiɫɫs.
7 x.coſcez 7 ıı.borɗ cũ.ı.caɼ.Ibi.ıı.partes molini redɗ.xıı.
ſoliɗ 7 vı.denaɼ.7 xx.ac pti.Paſtura.xıı.q̄rent in lḡ 7 laɫ.
Valuit.c.ſoliɗ.Modo.vı.liɓ.

Idē.G.ten STANTONE.Lange tenuit T.R.E.7 geldb p.x.hiɗ.
Tra.ē.vı.caɼ.In dn̄io ſt.ıı.caɼ.7.ıı.ſerui.7 ıııı.uiɫɫi.7 x.
coſcez cũ.ııı.caɼ.Ibi.ııı.ac pti.Paſtura.vı.q̄ɀ lḡ.7 ıııı.laɫ.

Godric ten unā v træ in MERA.Tra.ē dim caɼ.⌐ Valet.xıı.liɓ.
Ibi hɼ.ı.coſcet 7 dimiɗ acm pti.Valet.v.ſoliɗ.

Godric ten HERTHA.Pat ej tenuit T.R.E.7 geldb p.ııı.virg 7 dim.
Tra.ē dim caɼ.Ibi.ıı.ac pti.7 ııı.ac paſturæ.Valet.x.ſoliɗ.

Godvin ten unā v tre in HELPERITVNE.Valet.ıı.ſolid.

41 Chipping holds HAZELBURY. He held it himself before 1066; it paid tax for 1 virgate of land. Land for 1 plough, which is there.
    Woodland 2 furlongs long and 1 furlong wide.
Value 7s.

42 Cola holds GRIMSTEAD. His father held it before 1066; it paid tax for 1½ hides. Land for 1 plough.
    4 villagers.
Value 15s.

† *Misplaced entries 67, 37-38. See notes.*

37 Aldred holds 3 hides in ANSTY. Land for 2 ploughs which are there, with 1 slave and
    1 villager and 3 smallholders.
    A mill which pays 25d; woodland, 5 acres; meadow, 5 acres;
        pasture, 2 furlongs.
Value 30s.

38 Aldred holds 10 hides in WROUGHTON. Land for 4 ploughs which are there, with 5 slaves.
    3 villagers and 3 smallholders.
The value was and is 100s.

Brictnoth and Alwin held these two lands before 1066.

43 Grimbald Goldsmith holds MANNINGFORD. Edward held it   74a
before 1066; it paid tax for 6½ hides. Land for 4 ploughs.
In lordship 2 ploughs;
    1 villager, 10 Cottagers and 2 smallholders with 1 plough.
    2 parts of a mill which pays 12s 6d; meadow, 20 acres;
        pasture 12 furlongs in length and width.
The value was 100s; now £6.

44 Grimbald also holds STANTON (Fitzwarren). Lang held it before 1066; it paid tax for 10 hides. Land for 6 ploughs.
In lordship 2 ploughs; 2 slaves;
    4 villagers and 10 Cottagers with 3 ploughs.
    Meadow, 3 acres, pasture 6 furlongs long and 4 wide.
Value £12.

45 Godric Hunter holds 1 virgate of land which pays tax in MERE.
Land for ½ plough. He has
    1 Cottager and
    meadow, ½ acre.
Value 5s.

46 Godric holds HARTHAM. His father held it before 1066; it paid tax for 3½ virgates. Land for ½ plough.
    Meadow, 2 acres; pasture, 3 acres.
Value 10s.

47 Godwin Clack holds 1 virgate of land in HILPERTON.
Value 2s.

GODE ten . I . hid in STOTEÇOME . Ipſa tenuit T.R.E. Tra . ē . III . caſ .

In dñio . ē . I . caſ . 7 II . uilli 7 v . borđ cū . II . caſ . Ibi molin đe . xv .

ſoliđ . 7 L . ac̃ ſiluæ . Valet . L . ſoliđ .

ERLECHING ten unã v træ 7 dim in ECHESATINGETONE .

Tra . ē . II . boũ . Valet . VII . ſoliđ 7 VI . denaſ .   Ł ſoliđ .

EDRIC ten . I . hidã in PEVESIE . Tra . ē . I . caſ 7 dim . Valet . xx .

EDVIN ten CHIGELEI . Ipſe tenuit T.R.E. 7 gelđb p una v træ

7 dimiđ . Tra . ē dimiđ caſ . q̃ ibi . ē . Valet . III . ſoliđ .

EDGAR ten dimiđ hiđ in DEVREL . Algar tenuit T.R.E. 7 p tanto

gelđb . Tra . ē dim caſ . Ibi hɫ . II . coſcez . paſtura . III . q̃z l͠g . 7 una laſ .

EDRIC ten HERTHÃ . Ipſe tenuit T.R.E. 7 gelđb   Ł Valet . XII . ſol .

p una v træ . Tra . ē . II . boũ . qui ibi sɫ .   Valet . xxx . denaſ .

EDWARD ten WIDETONE . Paɫ ej tenuit T.R.E. 7 gelđb p . III . hiđ .

Tra . ē . III . caſ . In dñio . ē . I . caſ . 7 IIII . uilli 7 v . coſcez 7 III . borđ

cū . I . caſ . Ibi molin redđ . x . ſoɫ . 7 xx . ac̃ p̃ti . 7 III . q̃z ſiluæ .

Valuit . III . liƀ . Modo . IIII . liƀ .

EDMVND ten dimiđ v træ in BRAMESSAGE . Valet . xxx . den .

EDMVND ten PLEITEFORD . Algar tenuit T.R.E. 7 gelđb p una

virg træ . Tra . ē dim caſ . q̃ ibi . ē cū . II . borđ 7 II . coſcez .

Ibi molin redđ . x . den . Silua . III . q̃z l͠g . 7 una q̃z laſ .

IDE . Ed . ten una v træ . in qua hɫ dimiđ caſ . 7 IIII . borđ 7 II .

cotaſ . Hæ duæ træ ſimul ualent . XL . ſoliđ .   Ł 7 VI . den .

EDMVND filius Aiulf ten . I . hiđ in BREDFORD . Redđ . XII . ſoliđ .

Filius Aiulf ten GRAMESTEDE . Paɫ ej tenuit T.R.E. 7 gelđb

p una hida 7 dim . Tra . ē . II . caſ . In dñio . ē . I . caſ . cū . I . uilɫo .

7 II . coſcez 7 II . cotaſ . Ibi molin redđ . x . ſoɫ . 7 XIIII . ac̃ p̃ti . 7 IIII .

q̃rent paſturæ . Silua q̃z IIII . l͠g . 7 IIII . q̃z laſ . Valet . XL . ſoliđ .

48   Goda holds 1 hide in STITCHCOMBE. She held it herself before 1066.
Land for 3 ploughs. In lordship 1 plough;
    2 villagers and 5 smallholders with 2 ploughs.
    A mill at 15s; woodland, 50 acres.
Value 50s.

49   Erlechin holds 1½ virgates of land in ETCHILHAMPTON.   Land for 2 oxen.
Value 7s 6d.

50   Edric holds 1 hide in PEWSEY. Land for 1½ ploughs.
Value 20s.

51   Edwin holds CHEDGLOW. He held it himself before 1066; it paid
tax for 1½ virgates of land. Land for ½ plough, which is there.
Value 3s.

52   Edgar the priest holds ½ hide in DEVERILL. Algar held it before 1066;
it paid tax for as much. Land for ½ plough. He has
    2 Cottagers.
    Pasture 3 furlongs long and 1 wide.
Value 12s.

53   Edric Blind holds HARTHAM. He held it himself before 1066; it paid
tax for 1 virgate of land. Land for 2 oxen, which are there.
Value 30d.

54   Edward holds WITHERINGTON. His father held it before 1066; it paid
tax for 3 hides. Land for 3 ploughs. In lordship 1 plough;
    4 villagers, 5 Cottagers and 3 smallholders with 1 plough.
    A mill which pays 10s; meadow, 20 acres; woodland, 3 furlongs.
The value was £3; now £4.

55   Edmund holds ½ virgate of land in BRAMSHAW.
Value 30d.

56   Edmund holds PLAITFORD. Algar held it before 1066; it paid tax
for 1 virgate of land. Land for ½ plough, which is there, with
    2 smallholders and 2 Cottagers.
    A mill which pays 10d; woodland 3 furlongs long
      and 1 furlong wide.

57   Edmund also holds 1 virgate of land on which he has ½ plough and
    4 smallholders and 2 cottagers.
Value of these two lands together, 40s.

58   Edmund son of Aiulf holds 1 hide in BRITFORD.
It pays 12s 6d.

59   Aiulf's son holds GRIMSTEAD. His father held it before 1066; it paid
tax for 1½ hides. Land for 2 ploughs. In lordship 1 plough, with
    1 villager, 2 Cottagers and 2 cottagers.
    A mill which pays 10s; meadow, 14 acres; pasture, 4 furlongs;
      woodland 4 furlongs long and 4 furlongs wide.
Value 40s.

Harding ten de rege WENISTETONE . Ipſe tenuit T.R.E.7 gelđ
p . xi . hiđ . Tra . e̅ . vi . car . In dn̅io s̅t . ii . car .7 vi . ſerui .7 vii . uiłłi
7 vi . coſcez cu̅ . iii . car . Ibi moli̅n redđ . x . ſolid .7 xx . a̅c p̅ti .
Paſtura . xii . q̊ꝝ lg̅ .7 iii . q̊ꝝ laꞇ . Valet . xi . liƀ .

Harding ten FISGLEDENE . Ipſe tenuit T.R.E.7 gelđƀ p . xi . hiđ
7 dimiđ . Tra . e̅ . v . car . In dn̅io . e̅ . i . car . 7 vi . ſerui .7 vii . uiłłi
7 viii . borđ cu̅ . iiii . car . Ibi moli̅n redđ . xv . ſolid .7 xx.iiii . a̅c p̅ti .
Paſtura . xii . q̊ꝝ laꞇ .7 iii . q̊ꝝ laꞇ . Valet . ix . liƀ .
De hac tra habuit A̅l̅bicus . iiii . hiđ 7 dim . Modo ten rex .

Harding ten OCHEBVRNE . Ipſe tenuit T.R.E.7 gelđƀ p . v . hiđ .
Tra . e̅ . iii . car . Ibi dn̅io . e̅ . i . car . cu̅ . i . ſeruo .7 iii . uiłłi 7 iiii . borđ
cu̅ . i . car . Ibi . ii . a̅c p̅ti . Paſturæ . ii . q̊ꝝ lg̅ .7 una q̊ꝝ laꞇ . Valet

Tvrchil ten in CONTONE . Ipſe tenuit T.R.E.7 gelđƀ ꜰ iiii . liƀ .
p . vi . hiđ . Tra . e̅ . iiii . car . In dn̅io . e̅ . i . car .7 iiii . ſerui .7 v . uiłłi
7 x . coſcez .7 iii . borđ . cu̅ . ii . car . Ibi tcia pars . ii . molinoꝝ
redđ . x . ſolid .7 xxiiii . a̅c p̅ti .7 x . a̅c paſturæ .7 x . a̅c ſiluæ .

Vlf ten . i . hiđ in BODEBERIE . Tra . e̅ . i . car . ꜰ Valet . c . ſolid .
Ibi s̅t . iiii . borđ 7 iii . ſerui .7 iii . a̅c ſiluæ . Valet . x . ſolid .

Ulvric ten . i . hiđ 7 una v̅ træ in SCALDEBVRNE̅ . Orduuold
tenuit T.R.E.7 p tanto gelđƀ . Tra . e̅ . i . car .7 dim .7 ibi s̅t
iii . borđ . Valet . xx . ſolid .

Vlvric ten . iii . v̅ træ in WINTRESLEI .7 una v̅ træ in TVDER
LEGE . Pat ej tenuit T.R.E.7 p una hida gelđƀ . Tra . e̅ . i . car .
Hanc hn̅t ibi . iiii . ruſtici . Silua . iiii . q̊ꝝ lg̅ .7 una q̊ꝝ laꞇ .

                                    ꜰ Valet . xx . ſoł .

60   Harding holds KNIGHTON from the King. He held it himself
before 1066; it paid tax for 11 hides. Land for 6 ploughs.
In lordship 2 ploughs; 6 slaves;
   7 villagers and 6 Cottagers with 3 ploughs.
   A mill which pays 10s; meadow, 20 acres; pasture 12 furlongs
      long and 3 furlongs wide.
Value £11.

61   Harding holds FIGHELDEAN. He held it himself before 1066; it paid
tax for 11½ hides. Land for 5 ploughs. In lordship 1 plough; 6 slaves;
   7 villagers and 8 smallholders with 4 ploughs.
   A mill which pays 15s; meadow, 24 acres; pasture 12 furlongs long
      and 3 furlongs wide.
Value £9.
   Earl Aubrey had 4½ hides of this land; now the King holds them.

62   Harding holds OGBOURNE. He held it himself before 1066; it paid
tax for 5 hides. Land for 3 ploughs. In lordship 1 plough,
with 1 slave;
   3 villagers and 4 smallholders with 1 plough.
   Meadow, 2 acres; pastures 2 furlongs long and 1 furlong wide.
Value £4.

63   Thorkell holds [....] in COMPTON (Bassett). He held it himself
before 1066; it paid tax for 6 hides. Land for 4 ploughs.
In lordship 1 plough; 4 slaves;
   5 villagers, 10 Cottagers and 3 smallholders with 2 ploughs.
   The third part of 2 mills which pays 10s; meadow, 24 acres;
      pasture, 10 acres; woodland, 10 acres.
Value 100s.

64   Ulf holds 1 hide in BUDBURY. Land for 1 plough.
   4 smallholders and 3 slaves.
   Woodland, 3 acres.
Value 10s.

  Wulfric holds

65   in SHALBOURNE 1 hide and 1 virgate of land. Ordwold held it
before 1066; it paid tax for as much. Land for 1½ ploughs.
   3 smallholders.
Value 20s.

66   in WINTERSLOW 3 virgates of land and in TYTHERLEY 1 virgate of land.
His father held them before 1066; they paid tax for 1 hide.
Land for 1 plough.
   4 countrymen have it there.
   Woodland 4 furlongs long and 1 furlong wide.
Value 20s.

Vᴌᴠʀɪᴄ ten . ɪɪɪ . hiđ 7 dim in *Vʟꜰᴇᴄᴏᴛᴇ*.

Pat ej tenuit T.R.E.Tra . ē . ɪ . car 7 dimiđ . Valet . xxx . ſoliđ.

Vᴌᴠʀɪᴄ ten *Mᴇʀᴀ* . Allic tenuit T.R.E.7 geldɓ p una v træ
7 dimiđ . Tra . ē dimiđ cař . q̃ ibi . ē cũ . ɪɪɪɪ . borđ . 7 dimiđ ač p̃ti .
7 una ač paſturæ . Valet . ᴠɪɪ . ſoliđ 7 ᴠɪ . denar.

74 b

Vᴌᴠʀɪᴄ ten . ɪ . hiđ 7 unā v træ in *Sᴘɪɴᴅᴏɴᴇ* . Tra . ē dimiđ car. ꜰ Valet . ᴠɪɪ . ſol.

Vᴌᴠʀɪᴄ ten . ɪ . hiđ in *Bʀᴇᴅꜰᴏʀᴅ* . Tra . ē dim cař . Val . xɪɪ . ſoł 7 ᴠɪ . deñ.

Vᴌᴠʀɪᴄ ten . ɪ . hiđ in *Fʀɪsᴛᴇsꜰᴇʟᴅ* . 7 ibi hɫ . ᴠɪ . borđ . Valet . xx . ſoł.

Vᴌᴠʀɪᴄ ten *Pᴏʀᴛᴏɴᴇ* . Pat ej tenuit . T.R.E.7 geldɓ p . ɪɪ . hiđ .
Tra . ē . ɪɪ . cař . In dñio . ē una cař . cũ . ɪ . ſeruo . 7 ɪɪ . uiłłi 7 ɪɪɪ . coſceʒ
cũ . ɪ . cař . Ibi . ᴠɪ . ač p̃ti . 7 ɪɪɪ . q̃rent paſturæ . Valet . xʟ . ſoliđ.

Uʟᴡᴀʀᴅ ten . ɪɪɪɪ . hiđ in *Wɪɴᴛʀᴇsʟᴇɪ* . Tra . ē . ɪɪɪ . cař . In dñio
ē . una cař . 7 ɪɪ . ſerui . 7 ɪ . uiłłs 7 ɪɪɪ . borđ . Silua . ɪɪɪ . q̃ɋ lḡ . 7 una q̃ɋ lať .

Vʟᴡᴀʀᴅ p̃bendari regis ten . ɪɪ . hiđ in *Sᴘɪɴᴅᴏɴᴇ* ꜰ Valet . xʟ . ſoliđ .
Tra . ē . ᴠɪ . boũ . Valet . xᴠ . ſoliđ.

Vᴌᴠʀɪᴄ ᵂᵃᵘˡᵃ ten dimiđ hiđ in *Cʟɪᴠᴇ* . Tra . ē dim car . Valet . ɪɪɪɪ . ſoliđ.

Vᴌɴᴏᴅ ten . ɪ . hiđ in *Mᴇʀᴇ* . 7 p tanto geldɓ T.R.E. Tra . ē . ɪ . cař . q̃ ibi . ē
cũ . ᴠɪ . cotar . 7 ɪɪɪɪ . ač p̃ti . 7 una ač paſturæ . Valet . xx . ſoliđ.

Vᴌᴠɪᴇᴛ ᵘᵉⁿᵃᵗᵒʳ ten *Lᴀɴɢᴇꜰᴏʀᴅ* . T.R.E. geldɓ p . ɪɪɪɪ . hiđ . Tra . ē . ɪɪ . cař .
In dñio . ē . ɪ . cař . cũ . ɪ . ſeruo . 7 ɪɪ . uiłłi 7 ᴠɪ . borđ 7 ɪɪɪ . cotar .
Ibi moliñ redđ . ᴠ . ſoliđ . 7 xx . ač p̃ti . Paſtura . ᴠ . q̃ɋ lḡ . 7 ɪɪ . q̃ɋ lať .

Vᴌɴᴏᴅ ten dim hiđ in *Bʀᴀᴍᴇssᴀɢᴇ* . ꜰ Valet . ʟx . ſoliđ.

Pat ej tenuit . Tra . ē dim cař . Valet . x . ſoliđ.

67 in UFFCOTT 3½ hides. His father held them before 1066.
    Land for 1½ ploughs.
    Value 30s.

68 MERE. Aellic held it before 1066; it paid tax for 1½ virgates
    of land. Land for ½ plough, which is there, with
        4 smallholders.
        Meadow, ½ acre; pasture, 1 acre.
    Value 7s 6d.

69 in SWINDON 1 hide and 1 virgate of land. Land for ½ plough.   74b
    Value 7s.

70 in BRITFORD 1 hide. Land for ½ plough.
    Value 12s 6d.

71 in 'FRUSTFIELD' 1 hide. He has
        6 smallholders.
    Value 20s.

72 PORTON. His father held it before 1066; it paid tax for 2 hides.
    Land for 2 ploughs. In lordship 1 plough, with 1 slave;
        2 villagers and 3 Cottagers with 1 plough.
        Meadow, 6 acres; pasture, 3 furlongs.
    Value 40s.

73 Wulfward holds 4 hides in WINTERSLOW. Land for 3 ploughs.
    In lordship 1 plough; 2 slaves;
        1 villager and 3 smallholders.
        Woodland 3 furlongs long and 1 furlong wide.
    Value 40s.

74 Wulfward the King's purveyor holds 2 hides in SWINDON. Land for 6 oxen.
    Value 15s.

75 Wulfric Waula holds ½ hide in CLYFFE (Pypard). Land for ½ plough.
    Value 4s.

76 Wulfnoth holds 1 hide in MERE; it paid tax for as much before 1066.
    Land for 1 plough, which is there, with
        6 cottagers.
        Meadow, 4 acres; pasture, 1 acre.
    Value 20s.

77 Wulfgeat Hunter holds LONGFORD. Before 1066 it paid tax for 4 hides.
    Land for 2 ploughs. In lordship 1 plough, with 1 slave;
        2 villagers, 6 smallholders and 3 cottagers.
        A mill which pays 5s; meadow, 20 acres; pasture 5 furlongs long
            and 2 furlongs wide.
    Value 60s.

78 Wulfnoth holds ½ hide which pays tax in BRAMSHAW. His father
    held it. Land for ½ plough.
    Value 10s.

Vᴌᴠɪᴇᴛ ten dimiɗ hiɗ in *Mᴇʟᴇꜰᴏʀᴅ* . Ťra . ē . ɪɪ . boū . Valet . ɪɪ . ſoł.

Dimidia h̄ tra . ē in foreſta.

Wᴇɴᴇsɪɪ uxor ten *Tɪᴛɪᴄᴏᴍᴇ* . Vir ej tenuit T.R.E. ⁊ geldƀ p̄ . ɪɪ . hiɗ . Ťra ē ɪɪɪ . caŕ . In dn̄io . ē . ɪ . caŕ . cū . ɪ . ſeruo . ⁊ ɪɪ . uiłłi ⁊ ᴠɪ . borɗ cū . ɪɪ . caŕ . Ibi mo lin̄ redɗ . xᴠ . ſoł . ⁊ ɪɪɪɪ . ãc ſiluæ . Paſtura . ᴠ . q̊ꝗ lḡ . ⁊ ɪɪ . q̊ꝗ lať . Valet . ʟxx . ſoł.

Wᴀᴅᴏ ten . ɪ . hiɗ in *Bᴇʀᴇꜰᴏʀᴅ* . Ipſe tenuit T . R . E . Ťra . ē . ɪ . caŕ ꝗ ibi . ē cū . ɪ . borɗ . ⁊ ᴠɪ . ãc p̄ti . Valet . xᴠ . ſoliɗ.

Osɢᴏᴛ ten̄ dim hiɗ in *Sᴄᴀʟᴅᴇʙᴠʀɴᴇ* . Ťra . ē dim caŕ . Valet . ᴠ . ſoliɗ.

Oᴅᴏʟɪɴᴀ ten . ɪ . hiɗ in *Mᴀʀᴛᴏɴᴇ* . Ťra . ē . ɪ . caŕ ⁊ dim . Ibi . xxx . ãc int p̄tū ⁊ paſturā . Valet . xʟ . ſoliɗ.

Sᴀᴠʟꜰ ten . ɪ . hiɗ| ᵍᵉˡᵈᵃⁿᵗᵉ in *Gᴀᴛᴇɢʀᴀ̄* . Pat ej tenuit . Ťra . ē dim caŕ . Valet . x . ſoł.

Tᴠʀᴄʜɪʟ ten . ɪɪ . hiɗ in *Oᴄʜᴇʙᴠʀɴᴇ* . Pat ej tenuit . Ťra . ē . ɪ . caŕ . Ibi . xxx . ãc paſturæ . Valet . x . ſoliɗ.

Lᴇᴠɪᴇᴛ ten *Cᴠɴᴠᴄʜᴇ* . Vir ej tenuit T.R.E. ⁊ geldƀ p̄ . ɪɪɪ . hiɗ ⁊ dimiɗ . Ťra . ē . ɪɪ . caŕ . ⁊ dim . ꝗ ibi ſt cū . ɪ . ſeruo . ⁊ ɪɪɪɪ . uiłłi ⁊ ɪɪɪɪ . borɗ . Ibi molin̄ redɗ . xᴠ . ſoliɗ . ⁊ ᴠ . ãc p̄ti . Paſtura dim leū lḡ . ⁊ una q̊ꝗ lať . Valet . ɪɪɪ . liƀ. H̄ Leuiede fecit ⁊ facit aurifriſiū regis ⁊ reginæ.

Aʟꜰɪʟᴅɪs ten *Hᴇᴏʀᴛʜᴀ̄* . Vir ej tenuit T . R . E . ⁊ geldƀ p̄ . ɪ . ᴠ . Ťra . ē dim caŕ . ꝗ ibi . ē . ⁊ una ãc p̄ti . Valet . ɪɪɪ . ſoliɗ.　　　　ſ Valet . ɪɪɪ . ſoł.

Sᴀɪᴇᴠᴀ ten unā ᴠ træ . ᵍᵉˡᵈᵇ Aluui tenuit T . R . E . Ťra . ē . ɪɪ . boƀ . Ibi . ɪ . ãc p̄ti.

79 Wulfgeat holds ½ hide in MILFORD. Land for 2 oxen.
Value 2s.
  Half of this land is in the Forest.

80 Wenesi's wife holds TIDCOMBE. Her husband held it before 1066;
it paid tax for 2 hides. Land for 3 ploughs. In lordship 1 plough,
with 1 slave;
  2 villagers and 6 smallholders with 2 ploughs.
  A mill which pays 15s; woodland, 4 acres; pasture 5 furlongs long
    and 2 furlongs wide.
Value 70s.

81 Wado holds 1 hide in BARFORD (St. Martin). He held it himself
before 1066. Land for 1 plough, which is there, with
  1 smallholder.
  Meadow, 6 acres.
Value 15s.

82 Osgot holds ½ hide in SHALBOURNE. Land for ½ plough.
Value 5s.

83 Odolina holds 1 hide in MARTEN. Land for 1½ ploughs.
Both meadow and pasture, 30 acres.
Value 40s.

84 Saewulf holds 1 hide which pays tax in *GATEGRAM*. His father held it.
Land for ½ plough.
Value 10s.

85 Thorkell holds 2 hides in OGBOURNE. His father held them.
Land for 1 plough.
  Pasture, 30 acres.
Value 10s.

86 Leofgeat holds KNOOK. Her husband held it before 1066; it paid tax
for 3½ hides. Land for 2½ ploughs, which are there, with 1 slave;
  4 villagers and 4 smallholders.
  A mill which pays 15s; meadow, 5 acres; pasture ½ league long
    and 1 furlong wide.
Value £3.
  Leofgeat made and makes the King's and Queen's gold fringe.

87 Alfhild holds HARTHAM. Her husband held it before 1066; it paid
tax for 1 virgate. Land for ½ plough, which is there.
  Meadow, 1 acre.
Value 3s.

88 Saeva holds 1 virgate of land which pays tax. Alfwy held it
before 1066. Land for 2 oxen.
  Meadow, 1 acre.
Value 3s.

LꞮsᴇᴍᴀɴ teñ.ɪɪɪ.hiđ in *Mᴇʟᴄʜᴇsʜᴀ̄*.Ipſe tenuit T.R.E.⁊ ᵱ tanto
geldɓ.Tra.ē.ɪɪ.caꞃ ⁊ dim̃.In dñio.ē.ɪ.caꞃ.⁊ ɪɪɪɪ.uiłłi ⁊ ɪɪɪ.borđ ⁊ ɪɪɪ.cotar
cū.ɪ.caꞃ.Ibi.x.ac̃ p̃ti.⁊.v.ac̃ paſturæ.⁊ v.ac̃ ſiluæ.Valet.xxx.ſoliđ.

EʟᴅꞮʟᴅ teñ.ɪ.hiđ ⁊ vɪ.ac̃s træ in *HᴇʟᴘᴇʀꞮɴᴛᴏɴᴇ*.Vir ej tenuit T.R.E.
Tra.ē.ɪ.caꞃ.Ibi.ē.ɪ.borđ ⁊ ɪɪɪɪ.ac̃ p̃ti.Valet.vɪɪɪ.ſoliđ. ꬳſoliđ.⁊ vɪ.den

Osᴡᴀʀᴅ teñ.ɪ.hiđ, ⁱⁿ geldᵒ *Bʀᴇᴛꜰᴏʀᴅ*.Tra.ē dim caꞃ.Pat ej tenuit.Valet.xɪɪ.

Oᴛʜᴏ teñ *Lᴀɴɢᴇꜰᴏʀᴅ*.Pat ej tenuit T.R.E.⁊ geldɓ ᵱ.ɪɪ.hiđ.Tra.ē.ɪɪ.
caꞃ.Ibi ſt̃.vɪ.borđ.⁊ moliñ redđ.xx.denaꞃ.Ibi paſtura.ɪ.leū l̄g.⁊ dim̃
leu lat̃.Silua.ɪɪɪɪ.q̃ꝝ l̄g.⁊ ɪɪɪɪ.q̃ꝝ lat̃.Valet.xv.ſoliđ.

Sʙᴇʀɴ teñ unā v̄ træ in *CʀꞮsᴛᴇsꜰᴇʟᴅ*.Valet.xv.den.

SvᴀꞮɴ teñ *Sᴛᴀᴘʟᴇꜰᴏʀᴅ*.Pat ej tenuit T.R.E.⁊ geldɓ ᵱ.x.hiđ.⁊ dim̃.Tra.ē
.x.caꞃ.In dñio ſt̃.ɪɪ.caꞃ.cū.ɪ.ſeruo.⁊ xvɪɪ.uiłłi ⁊ x.borđ cū.vɪɪɪ.caꞃ.
Ibi.ɪɪ.molinꞇ redđ.xxx.ſoliđ.⁊ xʟ.ac̃ p̃ti.Paſtura dim̃ leū l̄g.⁊ tñtđ lat̃.
Silua.ɪ.leū l̄g.⁊ dimiđ leū lat̃.Valet.xɪɪ.liɓ.

SᴀʀꞮᴄ teñ *WꞮɴᴛʀᴇʙvʀɴᴇ*.Aluuiñ tenuit T.R.E.⁊ geldɓ ᵱ.ɪ.hida ⁊ dim̃.
Tra.ē.ɪ.caꞃ.q̃ ibi.ē in dñio.cū.ɪ.uiłło ⁊ ɪɪɪɪ.coſcez.Ibi pars molini.redđ
xxɪɪ.den ⁊ obolū.Silua.ɪɪ.q̃ꝝ l̄g.⁊ una q̃ꝝ lat̃.Valet.xxx.ſoliđ.

SᴀʀꞮᴄ teñ *Lᴀvᴇʀᴛᴇsᴛᴏᴄʜᴇ*.Geſt fr ej tenuit T.R.E.⁊ geldɓ ᵱ dim̃ hida.
Tra.ē dim car q̃ ibi.ē Valet.x.ſoliđ.

Sᴀᴡᴀʀᴅ teñ.ɪɪɪ.hiđ in *Bʀᴏᴄᴛvɴᴇ*.Aluuold tenuit T.R.E.Tra.ē.ɪɪ.caꞃ
quæ ibi ſt̃.Valet.xʟ.ſoł.

89   Liseman holds 3 hides in MELKSHAM. He held it himself before 1066;
it paid tax for as much. Land for 2½ ploughs. In lordship 1 plough;
    4 villagers, 3 smallholders and 3 cottagers with 1 plough.
    Meadow, 10 acres; pasture, 5 acres; woodland, 5 acres.
Value 30s.

90   Ealdhild holds 1 hide and 6 acres of land in HILPERTON. Her husband
held them before 1066. Land for 1 plough.
    1 smallholder.
    Meadow, 4 acres.
Value 8s.

91   Osward holds 1 hide which pays tax in BRITFORD. Land for ½ plough.
His father held it.
Value 12s 6d.

92   Otho holds LANDFORD. His father held it before 1066; it paid tax
for 2 hides. Land for 2 ploughs.
    6 smallholders.
    A mill which pays 20d; pasture 1 league long and ½ league wide;
      woodland 4 furlongs long and 4 furlongs wide.
Value 15s.

93   Esbern holds 1 virgate of land in 'FRUSTFIELD'.
Value 15d.

94   Swein holds STAPLEFORD. His father held it before 1066; it paid
tax for 10½ hides. Land for 10 ploughs. In lordship 2 ploughs,
with 1 slave;
    17 villagers and 10 smallholders with 8 ploughs.
    2 mills which pay 30s; meadow, 40 acres, pasture ½ league long
      and as wide; woodland 1 league long and ½ league wide.
Value £12.

95   Saeric holds WINTERBOURNE. Alwin held it before 1066; it paid tax
for 1½ hides. Land for 1 plough, which is there, in lordship, with
    1 villager and 4 Cottagers.
    Part of a mill which pays 22½d; woodland 2 furlongs long and
      1 furlong wide.
Value 30s.

96   Saeric holds LAVERSTOCK. Gest, his brother, held it before 1066;
it paid tax for ½ hide. Land for ½ plough, which is there.
Value 10s.

97   Saeward holds 3 hides in BROUGHTON (Gifford). Alfwold held it
before 1066. Land for 2 ploughs, which are there.
Value 40s.

Rainbvrgis teñ uñ Maner̃ q̃ Godric tenuit T.R.E.7 geldb̃ p̃.v.hiđ.
Tra.ē.iii.cař.q̃ ibi st̃.7 v.ſerui.7 vi.uilti 7 i.borđ.7 iiii.ac̃ p̃ti.Paſtura
.v.q̃ɺ l̃g.7 ii.q̃ɺ lat̃.Valuit.iiii.lib̃.Modo.c.ſoliđ.

Forestarij Regis teñ.i.hiđ 7 dim̃ in foreſta de Grauelinges.Val.xxx.ſoliđ.

Lanch tenuit de rege.E.Blonteſdone.7 deſdb̃ ſe p̃.ii.hiđ.M̃ teñ Edward
in manu regis.7 ibi st̃.iii.borđ.Valuit.xx.ſol.M̃.vii.ſol.

LXVIII. TERRA SERVIENTIVM REGIS.

Hervevs de Wiltvnè teñ de rege.i.hiđ in *EDENDONE*.
Oſuuard tenuit T.R.E.Tra.ē.i.cař.Ibi st̃.iii.borđ.7 tant̃
p̃ti 7 paſturæ q̃tũ c̃uenit.i.hidæ.Valet.xxx.ſoliđ.

Herueus teñ.i.hiđ 7 dimiđ.Hanc tenuit Eduin T.R.E.Tra.ē
.i.cař.Ibi st̃.iiii.ac̃ paſturæ.Valuit 7 ual.xxx.ſol.H̃.ē in *NIGRA*

Ricard teñ.i.hiđ 7 unā v træ 7 dim in *IWIS*.Tra.ē.iii.cař ʃ *AVRA*.
In dñio.ē una cař.7 iiii.ſerui.7 iii.uilti 7 iiii.coſcez.cũ.ii.cař.
Ibi.iiii.c̈ p̃ti.7 Silua.i.leũ l̃g.7 iiii.q̃ɺ lat̃.Valuit.xxx.ſol.m̃.lx.

Idē.R.teñ *BVBERGE*.7 Wilts de eo.Aluric tenuit T.R.E. ʃ ſoliđ.
7 geldb̃ p̃.ii.hiđ 7 dim.Tra.ē.ii.cař.q̃ ibi st̃ cũ.i.ſeruo.7 i.uilto
7 iiii.coſcez.Ibi.ii.arpenz p̃ti.7 Silua.iiii.q̃ɺ l̃g.7 ii.q̃ɺ lat̃.

Iđ teñ in *GRASTONE*.i.hiđ.Valet.xx.ſoliđ. ʃ Valet.xxx.ſoliđ.

Iđ teñ in *HAREDONE*.i.hiđ 7 dimiđ.7 Rob̃t de eo.Aluric tenuit
T.R.E.Tra.ē.i.cař.q̃ ibi.ē in dñio.Valet.x.ſoliđ.

98   Reinburg holds 1 manor, which Godric held before 1066; it paid tax
for 5 hides. Land for 3 ploughs, which are there; 5 slaves.
>6 villagers and 1 smallholder.
>Meadow, 4 acres; pasture 5 furlongs long and 2 furlongs wide.

The value was £4; now 100s.

99   The King's Foresters hold 1½ hides in GROVELY WOOD.
Value 30s.

100   Lang held BLUNSDON from King Edward; it answered for 2 hides.
Now Edward the Sheriff holds it in the King's hands.
>3 smallholders.

The value was 20s; now 7s.

68   LAND OF [HERVEY AND OTHER] SERVANTS OF THE KING 74c

1   Hervey of Wilton holds 1 hide in EDINGTON from the King. Osward
held it before 1066. Land for 1 plough.
>3 smallholders.
>Meadow and pasture, as much as is enough for 1 hide.

Value 30s.

2   Hervey holds 1½ hides. Edwin held them before 1066.
Land for 1 plough.
>Pasture, 4 acres.

The value was and is 30s.
>This is in NETHERAVON.

3   Richard Sturmy holds 1 hide and 1½ virgates of land in HUISH.
Land for 3 ploughs. In lordship 1 plough; 4 slaves;
>3 villagers and 4 Cottagers with 2 ploughs.
>Meadow, 4 acres; woodland 1 league long and 4 furlongs wide.

The value was 30s; now 60s.

4   Richard also holds BURBAGE, and William from him. Aelfric held it
before 1066; it paid tax for 2½ hides. Land for 2 ploughs, which
are there, with 1 slave and
>1 villager and 4 Cottagers.
>Meadow, 2 *arpents;* woodland 4 furlongs long and
>2 furlongs wide.

Value 30s.

5   He also holds 1 hide in GRAFTON.
Value 20s.

6   He also holds 1½ hides in HARDING, and Robert from him.
Aelfric held them before 1066. Land for 1 plough, which
is there, in lordship.
Value 10s.

Iđ teñ in *SALDEBORNE* . I . hiđ 7 III . v́ træ . Orduuolđ tenuit T.R.E.

7 p̃ tanto geldb̄ . Tra . ē . III . cař . In dñio st̄ . II . cař . 7 IIII . ſerui . 7 III . uilłi

7 III . coſcez cū . I . cař . Ibi . III . arpenz p̃ti . 7 Silua . IIII . q̃z̃ lḡ . 7 II . q̃z̃ lat̄.

R̃OBERT ^{F.Radulf 9} teñ in *GRASTONE* . I . hiđ 7 II . v́ træ 7 dim̄ ⎰ Valet . XL . ſoliđ.

Vlmar tenuit T.R.E . Tra . ē . II . cař . q̃ ibi st̄ in dñio . cū . I . ſeruo . 7 v.

coſcez . 7 II . arpenz ſiluæ . Valet . xxx . ſoliđ.

R̃ADVLFVS ^{de haluile} teñ in *GRASTONE* . III . hiđ 7 dimiđ . Aluuiñ 7 Aluuolđ

7 Leuuiñ 7 Celeſtan tenueŕ T.R.E . de eo . Tra . ē . IIII . cař 7 dimiđ.

In dñio st̄ . III . cař . 7 III . ſerui . 7 IIII . coſcez cū . I . cař 7 dimiđ . Ibi

Paſtura . II . q̃z̃ lḡ . 7 dimiđ q̃z̃ lat̄ . Valet . VII . lib̄.

Iđ . R . teñ in *MERTONE* . I . hiđ . Duo taini teneb̄ T.R.E . Tra . ē . I . cař.

q̃ ibi . ē in dñio cū . II . ſeruis . 7 II . coſcez . Ibi . II . arpenz p̃ti . 7 II . ãc pa

Iđ . R . teñ in *BVRBED* . II . hiđ 7 unā v́ træ . ⎰ ſturæ . Val̄ . XL . ſol.

Alric tenuit T.R.E . Tra . ē . II . cař . q̃ ibi st̄ cū . I . ſeruo . 7 II . uilłi 7 I . borđ.

Silua . III . q̃z̃ lḡ . 7 II . q̃z̃ lat̄ . Valet . xxx . ſoliđ.

In *VLFELA* habet . IIII . hiđ . Turolđ 7 Aluuiñ teneb̄ T.R.E.

7 p̃ tanto geldb̄ . Tra . ē . III . cař . 7 nil pecuniæ . Ibi moliñ redđ . XVI.

ſoliđ . 7 IIII . uilłi 7 IIII . coſcez . Silua . II . q̃z̃ lḡ . 7 tñtđ lat̄ . Valet . xxx.

TVRBERT teñ in *MERTONE* . I . hiđ . Leuuiñ tenuit ⎰ ſoliđ.

T.R.E . 7 p̃ tanto geldb̄ . Tra . ē . I . cař . Ibi st̄ . II . coſcez . 7 VI . ãc p̃ti.

7 x . ãc paſturæ . Valuit 7 ual̄ . XL . ſoliđ.

7   He also holds 1 hide and 3 virgates of land in SHALBOURNE. Ordwold held them before 1066; they paid tax for as much. Land for 3 ploughs. In lordship 2 ploughs; 4 slaves;
    3 villagers and 3 Cottagers with 1 plough.
    Meadow, 3 *arpents*; woodland 4 furlongs long and 2 furlongs wide.
    Value 40s.

8   Robert son of Ralph holds 1 hide and 2½ virgates of land in GRAFTON. Wulfmer held them before 1066. Land for 2 ploughs, which are there, in lordship, with 1 slave;
    5 Cottagers.
    Woodland, 2 *arpents*.
    Value 30s.

9   Ralph of Hauville holds 3 hides and 1½ virgates of land in GRAFTON. Alwin, Alfwold, Leofwin and Ceolstan held them from him before 1066. Land for 4½ ploughs. In lordship 3 ploughs; 3 slaves;
    4 Cottagers with 1½ ploughs.
    Pasture 2 furlongs long and ½ furlong wide.
    Value £7.

10 Ralph also holds 1 hide in MARTEN. Two thanes held it before 1066. Land for 1 plough, which is there, in lordship, with 2 slaves;
    2 Cottagers.
    Meadow, 2 *arpents*; pasture, 2 acres.
    Value 40s.

11 Ralph also holds 2 hides and 1 virgate of land in BURBAGE. Alric held them before 1066. Land for 2 ploughs, which are there, with 1 slave;
    2 villagers and 1 smallholder.
    Woodland 3 furlongs long and 2 furlongs wide.
    Value 30s.

12 In WOLF HALL [...] has 4 hides. Thorold and Alwin held them before 1066; they paid tax for as much. Land for 3 ploughs.
    No livestock. A mill which pays 16s.
    4 villagers and 4 Cottagers.
    Woodland 2 furlongs long and as wide.
    Value 30s.

13 Thorbert holds 1 hide in MARTEN. Leofwin held it before 1066; it paid tax for as much. Land for 1 plough.
    2 Cottagers.
    Meadow, 6 acres; pasture, 10 acres.
    The value was and is 40s.

CROC ten TODEWRDE . Tres taini tenuer̄ T.R.E.7 geldb̄ p̄ . III . hid̄.
7ra . ē . I . car̄ 7 dimid̄ . De ea ten Croc . III . v̄ træ.7 un miles ej̄ . II . hid̄.
Ibi . ē . I . car̄.7 . II . bord̄ 7 un̄ uitt̄s.7 paſtura . II . q̂ʒ lḡ.7 una q̂ʒ lat̄.
Valuit . xx . ſolid̄ . Modo . L . ſolid̄ . Eduuard ten unā v̄ træ . q̄ ptin
uicecom̄

HERVEVS ten ROTEFELDE . Herald tenuit T.R.E.   𝘛his . III . hid̄.
7 geldb̄ p̄ . II . hid̄ . 7ra . ē . I . car̄ . q̄ ibi . ē in dn̄io.7 v̄ . bord̄ . Ibi . VIII . ac̄
p̄ti.7 Paſtura . II . q̂ʒ lḡ.7 una q̂ʒ lat̄ . Valuit . xxx . ſot . Modo . xL . ſot.

TETBALD 7 Hunfrid ten WIDEHILLE . Rob̄t . F . Wimarc tenuit
7 geldb̄ p̄ . v̄ . hid̄ . 7ra . ē . v̄ . car̄ . In dn̄io ſt̄ . II . car̄.7 II . ſerui.7 vI . bord̄
Ibi . L . ac̄ p̄ti.7 Lx . ac̄ paſturæ . Valuit . xx . ſolid̄ . Modo . xL . ſot.

ANSCHITIL ten BVTREMERE . Goduin tenuit T.R.E.7 geldb̄ pro
dimid̄ v̄ træ . 7ra . ē . II . bou . Valet . xL . denar̄.

JOH̄S hoſtiari ten ELTONE . Godric 7 Bollo tenuer̄ T.R.E.7 geldb̄
p̄ . v̄ . hid̄ . 7ra . ē . IIII . car̄ . In dn̄io ſt̄ . II . car̄.7 III . ſerui.7 IIII . uitt̄i.7 II.
cotar̄ cū dimid̄ car̄ . Ibi . VIII . ac̄ p̄ti.7 Paſtura . III . q̂ʒ lḡ.7 II . q̂ʒ lat̄.
De hac 7ra ten Turſtin . I . hid̄.7 Frauuin̄ . I . hid̄ . Ibi . ē . un bord̄.7 I . cotar̄
cū dimid̄ car̄.7 II . ac̄ p̄ti . Paſtura . IIII . q̂ʒ lḡ.7 II . q̂ʒ lat̄ . Tot ualet . c . ſot.

ID̄E ten dimid̄ hid̄ in BEREFORD . Aluric tenuit T.R.E. 7ra . ē . I . car̄.
Ibi . ē un bord̄ cū . I . ſeruo.7 VIII . ac̄ p̄ti . Valuit 7 ualet . x . ſolid̄.

WILL̄S Scudet ten WESBERIE . Vluuard tenuit T.R.E.7 geldb̄ p̄ . IIII.
hid̄ 7 dimid̄ . 7ra . ē . vII . car̄ . In dn̄io ſt̄ . IIII . car̄.7 IIII . ſerui.7 xx . bord̄
cū . III . car̄ . Ibi . xx . ac̄ p̄ti.7 IIII . ac̄ ſiluæ.7 II . molini redd̄ . xxv . ſolid̄.
Valuit 7 ualet . vI·II . lib̄.

14   Croc holds (North) TIDWORTH. Three thanes held it before 1066;
it paid tax for 3 hides. Land for 1½ ploughs, of which Croc
holds 3 virgates of land, and one of his men-at-arms 2 hides.
1 plough there;
>2 smallholders and 1 villager.
>Pasture 2 furlongs long and 1 furlong wide.

The value was 20s; now 50s.
>Edward the Sheriff holds 1 virgate of land which belongs to
these 3 hides.

15   Hervey holds RATFYN. Earl Harold held it before 1066; it paid
tax for 2 hides. Land for 1 plough, which is there, in lordship;
>5 smallholders.

>Meadow, 8 acres; pasture 2 furlongs long and 1 furlong wide.

The value was 30s; now 40s.

16   Theobald and Humphrey hold WIDHILL. Robert son of Wymarc
held it; it paid tax for 5 hides. Land for 5 ploughs. In lordship 2
ploughs; 2 slaves;
>6 smallholders.

>Meadow, 50 acres; pasture, 60 acres.

The value was 20s; now 40s.

17   Ansketel holds BUTTERMERE. Godwin held it before 1066; it paid
tax for ½ virgate of land. Land for 2 oxen.
Value 40d.

18   John the Usher holds ALTON. Godric and Bolla held it
before 1066; it paid tax for 5 hides. Land for 4 ploughs.
In lordship 2 ploughs; 3 slaves;
>4 villagers and 2 cottagers with ½ plough.

>Meadow, 8 acres; pasture 3 furlongs long and 2 furlongs wide.

Of this land Thurstan holds 1 hide and Frawin 1 hide.
>1 smallholder and 1 cottager with ½ plough.

>Meadow 2 acres; pasture 4 furlongs long and 2 furlongs wide.

Value of the whole, 100s.

19   He also holds ½ hide in BARFORD (St. Martin). Aelfric held it
before 1066; Land for 1 plough.
>1 smallholder with 1 slave.

>Meadow, 8 acres.

The value was and is 10s.

20   William Shield holds WESTBURY. Wulfward held it before 1066;
it paid tax for 4½ hides. Land for 7 ploughs. In lordship 4
ploughs; 4 slaves;
>20 smallholders with 3 ploughs.

>Meadow, 20 acres; woodland, 4 acres; 2 mills which pay 25s.

The value was and is £8.

Goisfrid teñ *Draicote*. Edric tenuit T.R.E. 7 gelde ꝓ.v.hid.Tra.ē
v.cař.In dñio st.ii.cař.7 iiii.serui.7 vii.uilli 7 x.coscez.cū.iii.cař.
Ibi moliñ redd.v.solid.7 xl.ac pti.Pastura.ii.q̷Ꝫ lg.7 una q̷Ꝫ lat.
Silua.iiii.q̷Ꝫ lg.7 ii.q̷Ꝫ lat.7 uñ burgeñs redd.xii.den.Valet.c.solid.
Wills.F.Ansculf teñ *Tornvele*.Strami tenuit T.R.E.7 geldb ꝓ.vii.
hid 7 dimid.Tra.ē.v.cař.In dñio st.ii.cař.7 v.uilli 7 v.bord.7 v.coscez
cū.iii.cař.Ibi moliñ redd.v.solid.7 xi.ac pti.7 x.ac siluæ.7 pastura
.ii.q̷Ꝫ lg.7 ii.lat.Valuit 7 ual.c.solid.

74 d

Wills teñ.ii.hid ꝓpe istas.vii.hid supdictas.Vna ptinet
ad Bradeñestoch ⓜ Eduuardi uicecoñ.7 altera ad Cliue ⓜ Gilleberti de breteuile.
scdm testimoniū tainoꝻ.Valent.xx.solid.
Wibert teñ *Clive*.H fuit de tra Vlueuæ betestau.7 geldb T.R.E.
ꝓ.v.hid 7 una v træ.Tra.ē.iii.cař.In dñio st.ii.cař.7 iii.uilli
7 i.bord 7 i.coscez cū.i.cař.In Crichelade una dom redd.iii.den
Ibi.xlii.ac pti.7 dimid.7 qt xx 7 iiii.ac pasturæ.7 xxiiii.ac
siluæ.Valuit.xx.solid.Modo.iii.lib 7 x.solid.
Odinvs Camerari teñ *Svindone*.Torbert tenuit T.R.E.
7 geldb ꝓ.xii.hid.Tra.ē.vi.cař.In dñio st.ii.cař.7 ii.serui.
7 vi.uilli.7 viii.bord cū.iii.cař.Ibi moliñ redd.iiii.solid.7 xxx.
ac pti.7 xx.ac pasturæ.Valuit.lx.solid.Modo.c.solid.
De hac tra teñ Milo crispin.ii.hid.7 ibi ht.i.cař.Odin eas caluniat.
Tvrstin camerari teñ *Clive*.Aluuin tenuit T.R.E.7 geldb ꝓ.iiii.hid.
Tra.ē.i.cař 7 dimid.In dñio.ē.i.cař.cū.i.seruo.7 iiii.coscez.
Ibi moliñ redd.v.solid.7 xii.ac pti.7 viii.ac pasturæ.Valet.l.sol.

21 Geoffrey holds DRAYCOT (Cerne). Edric held it before 1066;
it paid tax for 5 hides. Land for 5 ploughs. In lordship 2
ploughs; 4 slaves;
 7 villagers and 10 Cottagers with 3 ploughs.
 A mill which pays 5s; meadow, 40 acres; pasture 2 furlongs
  long and 1 furlong wide; woodland 4 furlongs long
  and 2 furlongs wide.
 A burgess who pays 12d.
Value 100s.

22 William son of Ansculf holds THORNHILL. Stremius held it before 1066;
it paid tax for 7½ hides. Land for 5 ploughs. In lordship 2 ploughs;
 5 villagers, 5 smallholders and 5 Cottagers with 3 ploughs.
 A mill which pays 5s; meadow, 11 acres; woodland 10 acres;
  pasture 2 furlongs long and 2 wide.
The value was and is 100s.

23 William holds 2 hides near the said 7 hides. 1 belongs to Edward 74d
the Sheriff's manor of BRADENSTOKE, and the other to Gilbert of
Breteuil's manor of CLYFFE (Pypard), according to the witness
of the thanes.
Value 20s.

24 Wibert holds CLYFFE (Pypard). It was (part) of Wulfeva Beteslau's
land; it paid tax before 1066 for 5 hides and 1 virgate of land.
Land for 3 ploughs. In lordship 2 ploughs;
 3 villagers, 1 smallholder and 1 Cottager with 1 plough.
 In Cricklade 1 house which pays 3d. Meadow, 42½ acres; pasture,
  84 acres; woodland, 24 acres.
The value was 20s; now £3 10s.

25 Odin the Chamberlain holds SWINDON. Thorbert held it before 1066;
it paid tax for 12 hides. Land for 6 ploughs. In lordship 2
ploughs; 2 slaves;
 6 villagers and 8 smallholders with 3 ploughs.
 A mill which pays 4s; meadow, 30 acres; pasture, 20 acres.
The value was 60s; now 100s.
 Miles Crispin holds 2 hides of this land; he has 1 plough.
Odin claims them.

26 Thurstan the Chamberlain holds CLYFFE (Pypard). Alwin held it
before 1066; it paid tax for 4 hides. Land for 1½ ploughs.
In lordship 1 plough, with 1 slave;
 4 Cottagers.
 A mill which pays 5s; meadow, 12 acres; pasture, 8 acres.
Value 50s.

A̅LBERICVS ten *SMALEBROC* . Mainard tenuit T.R.E. 7 geldͨ

ꝓ . II . hiđ . T̅ra . e̅ . III . car̅ . In dn̅io . e̅ . I . car̅ . 7 un̅ uiłts 7 XII . borđ

cu̅ . II . car̅ . Ibi . VI . ac̅ pti . 7 IX . ac̅ filuæ . Valuit . XXX . fot . M̊ . XL . fot .

A̅LBERICVS ten *DEVREL* . Duo taini tenuer̅ T.R.E. 7 geldͨ ꝓ . I .

hida . T̅ra . e̅ . I . car̅ . Ibi ſt . VIII . cofcez cu̅ . I . car̅ . 7 molin̅ redđ . IIII .

foliđ . 7 una ac̅ pti . Paſtura . IIII . q̊ʒ lg̅ . 7 II . q̊ʒ łat̅ . Silua . V . q̊ʒ

lg̅ . 7 una q̊ʒ łat̅ . Valuit . XL . foliđ . Modo . XXIX . fot .

G̅VNDVINVS ten *WITECLIVE* . Aluui tenuit T.R.E. 7 geldͨ ꝓ . II .

hiđ . T̅ra . e̅ . I . car̅ . q̅ ibi . e̅ in dn̅io cu̅ . I . feruo . 7 I . cofcet .

Ibi . II . ac̅ pti . 7 Paſtura . IIII . q̊ʒ lg̅ . 7 una q̊ʒ łat̅ . Silua . I . q̊ʒ lg̅ .

7 altera łat̅ . Valuit . XX . foliđ . Modo . XXXV . foliđ .

W̅ARINVS ten *CELEWRDE* . Edric tenuit T.R.E. 7 geldͨ ꝓ . II .

hiđ . T̅ra . e̅ . II . car̅ . In dn̅io . e̅ . I . car̅ . cu̅ . IIII . borđ . Ibi . VIII . ac̅ pti .

7 X . ac̅ filuæ . Valuit 7 uał . XL . foliđ .

C̅ROC ten dimiđ hiđ in *STOCHE* . T̅ra . e̅ dimiđ car̅ . Valet . X . fot .

W̅ills ten *WICHEFORD* . Auitius tenuit T.R.E. 7 geldͨ ꝓ . II .

hiđ . T̅ra . e̅ . II . car̅ . Ibi ſt . III . uiłłi 7 III . borđ cu̅ . I . car̅ . 7 molin̅

redđ . XV . foliđ . Ibi . VIII . ac̅ pti . Valuit 7 uał . XL . foliđ .

E̅DWARD ten una̅ v̅ tre in *ALWARBERIE* . Bode tenuit T.R.E.

Valet . XL . denar̅ .

27   Aubrey the Chamberlain holds SMALLBROOK. Maynard held it before 1066; it paid tax for 2 hides. Land for 3 ploughs.
In lordship 1 plough;
    1 villager and 12 smallholders with 2 ploughs.
    Meadow, 6 acres; woodland, 9 acres.
The value was 30s; now 40s.

28   Aubrey the Chamberlain holds DEVERILL. Two thanes held it before 1066; it paid tax for 1 hide. Land for 1 plough.
    8 Cottagers with 1 plough.
    A mill which pays 4s; meadow, 1 acre; pasture 4 furlongs long and
      2 furlongs wide; woodland 5 furlongs long and 1 furlong wide.
The value was 40s; now 29s.

29   Gundwin the keeper of the granaries holds WHITECLIFF.
Alfwy held it before 1066; it paid tax for 2 hides.
Land for 1 plough which is there, in lordship, with 1 slave;
    1 Cottager.
    Meadow, 2 acres; pasture 4 furlongs long and 1 furlong wide;
      woodland 1 furlong long and another wide.
The value was 20s; now 35s.

30   Warin Bowman holds CHELWORTH. Edric held it before 1066; it paid tax for 2 hides. Land for 2 ploughs. In lordship 1 plough, with
    4 smallholders.
    Meadow, 8 acres; woodland, 10 acres.
The value was and is 40s.

31   Croc holds ½ hide in BRADENSTOKE. Land for ½ plough.
Value 10s.

32   William Cornelian holds WISHFORD. Aefic held it before 1066; it paid tax for 2 hides.
Land for 2 ploughs.
    3 villagers and 3 smallholders with 1 plough.
    A mill which pays 15s. Meadow, 8 acres.
The value was and is 40s.

33   Edward holds 1 virgate of land in ALDERBURY. Boda held it before 1066.
Value 40d.

WILTSHIRE HOLDINGS
ENTERED ELSEWHERE IN THE SURVEY

The Latin text of these entries is given in the county volumes concerned.
Exon. references and entries are given in small type.

In BERKSHIRE

1   LAND OF THE KING

E 1   The King holds in lordship
        in KINTBURY Hundred...   57 c

   27   SHALBOURNE. King Edward held it. 6½ hides. Land for 10 ploughs.
        In lordship 3 ploughs;
           14 villagers and 13 smallholders with 6 ploughs.
           3 slaves; a mill at 10s; meadow, 8 acres; woodland for fencing.
        Value before 1066 and later £12; now £20.
          Of this manor 2½ hides were put in Henry's manor; one hide
       was Reeve's land, the other was the villagers'; the half-hide was of
       the King's revenue, but in the time of Godric the Sheriff it was put
       outside. This the whole Shire confirms.

21   LAND OF HENRY OF FERRERS

E 2   Henry also holds
        in KINTBURY Hundred   60 c

   6   BAGSHOT. Godric held it from King Edward as a manor. 2 hides.
        They did not pay tax because they were of the King's revenue;
        they are claimed for the King's work. Land for 4 ploughs.
          9 villagers and 10 smallholders with 4 ploughs.
          3 slaves; a mill at 11s; meadow, 8 acres; woodland for fencing.
        The value was 30s; now 40s.

In SOMERSET

23
E 3   LAND OF WALTER GIFFARD   95 a

   1   Walter Giffard holds YARNFIELD from the King, and William
        from him. Ernebald held it before 1066; it paid tax for 2 hides.
        Land for 3 ploughs. In lordship 2 ploughs &1 hide & 2½ virgates,
        with 1 slave;
          5 smallholders with 1 plough &1½ virgates.   447
          Pasture, 20 acres; woodland, 60 acres.   2 cows; 25 pigs; 124 sheep.   a 4
        The value was 40s; now 30s.

1   LAND OF THE KING

E 4   The King holds   86 c
   9   BRUTON   90

                                                    b3

From this manor ½ hide in KILMINGTON has been taken away.
Serlo of Burcy holds it; value 10s. It had been part of the   91
lordship revenue.   a2

37   LAND OF SERLO OF BURCY
E 5

   7   St. Edward's Church holds KILMINGTON from Serlo for his   98 a
daughter who is there. Alfsi held it before 1066. 5 hides there,
but it paid tax for 1 hide. Land for 5 ploughs. In lordship 1 plough
& 4 hides & 1 virgate.
      4 villagers and 3 smallholders with 4 ploughs & 3 virgates.   453
      Woodland, 1 league in length and 3 furlongs wide.   a 1
         14 cattle; 15 pigs; 137 sheep.
(Value) formerly 30s; now 40s.

Exon. Extra Information and Discrepancies

1,9   FROM THIS MANOR .. Also in 520 a 4.

37,7   SERLO. 'Serlo of Burcy gave it to St. Edward's Abbey with his daughter'.
       BUT IT PAID TAX FOR 1 HIDE. 'but it did not pay tax, except for 1 hide'.

NOTES

ABBREVIATIONS used in the notes. DB...Domesday Book. DG...H. C. Darby and G.R. Versey *Domesday Gazetteer* Cambridge 1975. DGSW...H.C. Darby and R. Welldon Finn *The Domesday Geography of South-West England* Cambridge 1967. EHR...English Historical Review. EPNS... English Place-name Society Survey, xvi, 1939. Exon...Exeter Book. FA...*Inquisitions and Assessments Relating to Feudal Aids with Other Analogous Documents preserved in the Public Records Office AD 1284-1431* HMSO 1899-1920, 6 vols. Fees...*Book of Fees* HMSO 1920-31. FF...E.A. Fry *A Calendar of the Feet of Fines Relating to the County of Wiltshire 1195-1272*, Devizes 1930. Finn...R. Welldon Finn *An Introduction to Domesday Book* London 1963. GF...*Feodary of Glastonbury Abbey* Somerset Record Society vol. 26, 1910. Jones...W. Jones *Domesday for Wiltshire* Bath 1865. MS...Manuscript. NV...F. Palgrave '*Nomina Villarum*' in *Parliamentary Writs* vol. ii, Div. 3, p.346-9. OE...Old English. OEB...G. Tengvik *Old English Bynames* Uppsala 1938. OED...E. Ekwall *Contributions to the Study of Old English Dialects*, Lund 1917. OFr...Old French. PNDB...O. von Feilitzen *Pre-Conquest Personal Names of Domesday Book* Uppdala 1937. RH...*Rotuli Hundredorum* vol.ii. VCH...Victoria County History (Wiltshire vol. ii, 1955).

References are to VCH vol. ii, unless stated, and therein to the section numbers of the Domesday translation, unless prefixed p.

Text, translation and commentary on the Exon Tax Returns appear in VCH vol. ii, p.178ff.

The manuscript is written on leaves, or folios, of parchment (sheepskin), measuring about 15 by 11 inches (38 by 28 cms.), on both sides. On each side, or page, are two columns, making four to each folio. The folios were numbered in the 17th century, and the four columns of each are here lettered a, b, c, d. The manuscript emphasises words and usually distinguishes chapters and sections by the use of red ink. Underlining here indicates deletion.

WILTSHIRE. In red, across the top of the page, spread above both columns, *WILTESCIRE.*

M 1   DWELLING. *Masura* (= *mansura*) possibly a group of houses. See Notts. B8 for a similar statement of houses within residences *(mansiones)*.
43s 6d. 51 dwellings at 10d is 42s 6d. Probably a figure error. DB uses the old English currency system which lasted for a thousand years until 1971. The pound contained 20 shillings, each of 12 pence, abbreviated as £(ibrae), s(olidi) and d(enarii). DB often gives smaller sums in multiples of pence (e.g., in 1,21, 32d for 2s 8d) and of shillings rather than in pounds, as here.

M 3   COTTAGERS. *Coscet* singular, *coscez, cozets* plural, represent Anglo-Norman versions of OE *cot-seta* sg., *cot-seta(n)* pl. 'a cottage-dweller; cottage holder' (OE *cot, saeta,* see *English Place-Name Elements* s.v. *cot-saeta,* OED s.v. *cotset*): the Anglo-Norman letter *z* represents the sound *ts* and the spelling *sc* a miscopied *st* representing metathesis of *ts,* so *coscet = cotset, coscez* and *cozets = cotsets*. The OE plural *cot-seta(n)* would be reflected in the plural *coscet* (=*cotset*) 25,13 and 28,2. The Plural in -*s* represented by *cozets* (=*cotsets*) is the result of either a French adaptation, or an Old English change of inflexion, and is the form used in ch. 1,1-15.
'Cottagers' are almost entirely confined to the South-West counties, Wiltshire providing about 80% of the total entries. In Wiltshire, except in four cases, they are listed after villagers and smallholders, and usually before the cottagers, *cotarii.* Very little is known about their status and economic position, though as can be seen from 24,15 and 32,10 they did have at least part of a plough. See Jones p.1ix.

M 7   DURAND. Sheriff of Gloucestershire.

M 12 GEOFFREY MARSHALL. See 68,21 note below.

M 15 EDRIC'S WIFE. *Uxor Edric;* no genitive indicated, as sometimes happens with personal names.

M 16 ROGER OF BERKELEY. See 45,1.
INJUDICIOUSLY. *Incaute;* perhaps 'without security'.
THESE TWO. 'Dwellings' is meant.

L 34 *WILLELMUS DE MOIUN.* Rendered as William of Mohun in deference to the more regular 13th century spelling of the English form of the surname; but the place of origin was Moyon (La Manche) and the DB spelling is *Moion, Moiun,* etc. Exon *Moione, Mouin;* see OEB 98.

L 55   AIULF. On the form of the personal-name see 55,1 note.

L 60   BLUNT. *Flavus,* 'fair'; elsewhere *Blundus,* 'blond' and *Albus,* 'white'.

L 61   STURMY. *Sturmid.* Occurs as *Sturmi, Sturmy* in Fees; Tengvik, OEB 345 cites Godefroy *Dictionnaire de l'ancienne langue française* Paris 1898-1902 vol.III 627 'OFr *estormi "étourdi, troublé, accablé"*. Dr. Morris (Surrey 8,18) rendered this s.n. according to the sense *étourdi,* (cp. the English s.n. Sturdy OFr *Estordit* 'stunned, dazed, reckless, violent'), but a better rendering would be 'turbulent, ready for battle'.

L 62   *RAINALDUS CANUD.* 'Reginald Canute'. The surname *Canud, Canutus* is ambiguous. It can represent either the OScand personal name *Knutr* or the OFr adjective *chanu* (Lat. *canutus*) 'grey-haired' as in the French surnames *(le)Chanu, (le) Chenu;* see OEB 215.

L 65   GODESCAL. OFr. *Godescal,* (Lat. *Godescallus*), OE *Godesscalc,* are forms of the Old German personal name and byname *Godassalc, Godscalc,* 'God's warrior' (modern German surname *Gottschalk,* anglicized *Gosschalk*), see T. Forssner *Continental-Germanic Personal-Names in England* (Uppsala 1916) 121. The Old German name was not used or adopted by the English, so there is no modern or equivalent form. Mod: Eng. *Gosschalk* is an adaptation of the modern immigrant surname *Gottschalk.* The best way to represent this personal name in a Modern English translation would seem to be in the OFr. *Godescal.*

B 2   FOR A HAWK. *Pro;* perhaps 'instead of', an example of rents in kind being commuted.
ORA. Literally an ounce. A unit of currency still in use in Scandinavia; reckoned at either 16d or 20d. See Economic History Review, 1967, p,221 ff.

B 4   THIRD PENNY. A third of a borough's total revenues, to which the King was entitled. See J.H. Round *The Tertius Denarius* in EHR xxxiv (1919).
OF BATH. See Somerset 1,31 (col. 87b): 'Edward pays £11 of the third penny of this Borough (Bath)'. It was probably included here because Edward of Salisbury was responsible for its collection.
INCREASE. 'A premium paid by the sheriff in excess of the regular ferm for the privilege of farming the shire', W.A. Morris *The Medieval English Sheriff* p.64. Also occurs in Oxfordshire 154 d, ch.1,12.

B 5   EXCEPT FOR the first line, this entry is written across the bottom of cols. 64c, d, in three lines, the beginning of each being here exdented, in the Latin text.
HUSSEY. OFr *hosed* 'provided with hose; wearing hose', OEB 370.
TWO PARTS OF THE BOROUGH. The King's two-thirds of the revenue of Malmesbury.
ACRE. *agr,* which could either abbreviate *agrum* from *ager,* 'field', or, more likely, *agram* from *agra,* the regular word in Exon for 'acre'. *Acra* is the usual DB word for 'acre'. *Agri* for *acrae* occurs also in Somerset 1,9 (col. 86c). As the payment here is rather large for only an acre, perhaps the word is being used more loosely as an area of land. OE *aecer* means 'a plot of arable or cultivated land' as well as the particular local measure 'one acre'.
BOATMEN. Probably 'seamen-warriors'; see P. Vinogradoff *English Society in the 11th century,* p.20.

1,1   THE KING HOLDS. Repeated at the beginning of sections 1,1-22.
HIDES ARE THERE. *Sint,* subjunctive. The subjunctive and indicative are interchangeable in indirect questions in Medieval Latin. But see J.H. Round *Feudal England* p.109. *Sint* occurs regularly in the same formula in Somerset ch.1, where Exon. generally has *sunt.*
ONE NIGHT'S REVENUE. Many royal manors, especially in the South-West had to pay this revenue, which took the place of the normal tax payment, the manors not being assessed in hides. Originally this meant the amount of food needed to support the King and his household for one night, though by the 11th century these food rents were generally commuted. £80 is a probable figure before 1066, and £100 after, for one night's revenue. Lat. *firma* here = OE *feorm* 'a food rent', see OED *farm* sb.i. See R.L. Poole *The Exchequer in the Twelfth Century* p.29.
BURGESSES. Probably written in error in the middle of the manor's resources; their usual place is with 'villagers' etc. or as a separate entry before the 'value' statement.
FURLONGS...ACRES. *Quarentina,* 'furlong', a fourth part or quarter, commonly used in DB for measurements of length, as a quarter of a league, but also as a measurement of area, each side being 1 furlong, as in 24,5. 67,59 etc. *Acra,* 'acre', is also used both as a linear measure, as in 26,4;19 etc., and as an area measure, as here. See DB Oxfordshire 18,1 note.
ALFRED OF 'SPAIN'. Epaignes, in the département of Eure, France, OEB 92. Latin *Hispania* is a kind of word play.
5 HIDES. Possibly in Yatesbury, 54,1.

1,2   WOOD. See 39,1.
HENRY...IT. MS and Farley have *eū,* (*eum,* 'it'), but the facsimile has not reproduced the line over the *eu.*

1,3   LAND FOR 40 PLOUGHS. The detail amounts to 39 ploughs. Unlike in some other counties, the lordship and villagers' ploughs in Wiltshire do not always add up to the ploughs in the assessment; often, as here, they fall short, sometimes, as in 1,4, they exceed the estimate.

On the frequent artificiality of the numbers in the plough assessment, see R. Welldon Finn p. 97ff. of *The Teamland of the Domesday Inquest* in EHR 1xxxiii (1968).

THIS MANOR... The gap of about 4 letters in the MS is caused by an ink blot, which appears to cover an erased word, possibly *redd'* (*reddit*, 'pays').

EARL WILLIAM. Probably William FitzOsbern, Earl of Hereford and 'regent' during some of King William's absences; he was killed in battle in 1071. See also 1,21.

KING EDWARD...ABBESS OF WILTON. Wilton Abbey was richly endowed and rebuilt in stone by Queen Edith, Edward's wife, and consecrated in 1065. One of her brother Harold's daughters, Gunnild, was a nun there; see *Vita Wulfstani* ed. Darlington, p. 34.

EARL WILLIAM...REVENUE. Transposition signs in the MS indicate that this sentence should precede the one about the Abbess of Wilton.

THANELANDS. Or perhaps singular, '(part) of the thaneland'. Thaneland was land reserved by a lord, commonly a church, for the maintenance of a thane, armed and mounted; it was usually inalienable and not automatically heritable. See Finn p. 28-9, 138-9.

ISLE OF WIGHT LAND. That is, Bowcombe. See also DB Hants. 1,31 (col. 39a).

1,5 BISHOP OSBERN. Of Exeter 1072-1103. Brother of William FitzOsbern, Earl of Hereford.

ONE LAND. *Una terra*, not classified as a manor.

RECORDED. *Habetur;* see also 25,9 and Beds. 12,1, (col. 211a).

1,6 12 VILLAGERS. In the MS 7 is written under the *x* of *xii*, in error.

1,9 GYTHA. Probably Countess Gytha, mother of Earl Harold, as this holding, and also 1,10; 13, are said to have been Harold's (and, for 1,13, Queen Edith's) in the Exon Tax Returns for Swanborough, Thornhill and Calne Hundreds respectively.

1,10 GYTHA. See 1,9 note above.

1,11 EARL TOSTI. Brother of Earl Harold and Queen Edith, and Earl of Northumbria; killed in 1066.

DEPENDENCIES. *Appendic'* in MS; Farley misprints *append'*.

ASSESS. The facsimile has not reproduced the line over the second *p* in *apƥciant*.

ST. STEPHEN'S OF CAEN. Founded by Duke William in 1064 and consecrated in 1066. Lanfranc, afterwards Archbishop of Canterbury, was the first Abbot.

1,12 ASSESS. *Apƥciant'* (*appreciantur*, passive) in the MS and Farley, in error for the active *appreciant*, as in 1,11.

1,13 GYTHA. See 1,9 note above.

60 ACRES. So MS; Farley misprints '40 acres'.

1,16 POTTERS. *Potarii*. Possibly a scribal mistake for *porcarii*, 'pigmen', DGSW p. 29n.

A MINOR CLERK HOLDS IT. Written above 'Value of the church', with transposition signs to indicate its correct place.

WILLIAM SHIELD. OEB 372; and see 68,20 and 2,4 note below.

1,17 ABBOT. *Abb'*, perhaps abbreviating *abbatia*, 'abbey'.

1,18 HERVEY. See 68,2. Probably Hervey of Wilton; see VCH p. 75;106. NIGEL. See 56,3.

[VILLAGERS]. In MS *car'*, 'plough', in error.

TITHE. The only reference to tithe in Wiltshire.

1,21 EARL WILLIAM. See 1,3 note above.

1,22 THE GAP of about 16 letters in the MS was probably for the later addition of TRE holder.

1,23c REINBALD THE PRIEST. There is a gap of about 4 letters after this in the MS, not reproduced by Farley.

1,23h BISHOP OSMUND. Of Salisbury 1078-1099.

2,1 IN THE MS *Fac.* is written in the left margin level with the chapter number; not reproduced by Farley.

100 HIDES LESS 3. The reason for the scribe writing the number like this, rather than 97, is explained here, but this is not so in every case, such as the '100 villagers less 8' in 1,12.

BISHOP WALKELIN. Of Winchester 1070-1098.

2,2 THE BISHOP ALSO HOLDS. Repeated at the beginning of sections 2,2-7 and 2,9-12.

2,3 MONKS' SUPPLIES. The monks of the Benedictine monastery which was connected with Winchester Cathedral. The tenants of the estates detailed below had to provide a certain amount of food for the monks.

2,4 WILLIAM SHIELD. One of King William's cooks, according to a charter (*Calendar of Charter Rolls* iii, 345) in which the Bishop of Winchester, at the King's request, granted to William Shield, his cook, land held by Wulfward 'Belgisone' in 'Alwolditon' (Alton Priors); it was to revert to the monks on the cook's death.

2,8 OF THIS LAND. Capital *d* for *de* in the MS, not reproduced by Farley.

2,9 THE BISHOP ALSO HOLDS. See 2,2 note.

2,10	10 HIDES IN LORDSHIP. In the MS *st (sunt)*; Farley has unusually extended it to *sunt*; the reverse happens in Somerset 1,10 (col. 86c), and 3,1 (col. 87d).
2,11	...VILLAGERS. Space is left in the MS for the insertion of the number of villagers, with *rq'* (= *require*, 'enquire') in the left margin. Omitted in Farley.
2,12	VALUE 100s AND 10s. Either 110s is meant, or *x sol'* is a MS error for *x den'*, '10d'. See Sussex 3,1 (col. 16d) for an identical case, and Beds. 27,1 (col. 215b) for *val' c sol' 7 x.* There are many instances in DB of corrections of *sol'* to *den'* and vice versa.
3,1	BISHOP HERMAN. Bishop of Ramsbury and Sherborne 1045-1078; the see was then moved to Salisbury where Herman's successor was Osmund.
	ALFWARD...3 HIDES. See 67,11 and note. ARNULF. See 25,2.
	1 VIRGATE. MS and Farley have an abbreviation mark over the *v* for virgate; the facsimile has not reproduced it.
	BISHOP CLAIMS THEM. *Eas,* probably referring just to Arnulf's holding, as can be gathered from 25,2. However, Bishop Osmund was also claiming Alfward's 3 hides (67,11).
3,2	3 VILLAGERS...4 PLOUGHS. In the MS *ii*, with *ii* written over it to make *iiii. car'.*
4,1	BISHOP OF BAYEUX. Odo, half brother of King William, and Earl of Kent; he was 'regent' during some of King William's absences.
4,4	ROBERT. Possibly Robert the Bursar of the Exon Tax Returns for Branch Hundred.
5,1	BISHOP OF COUTANCES. Geoffrey of Mowbray, one of King William's chief justices.
5,2	THE BISHOP ALSO HOLDS. Repeated at the beginning of sections 5,2-7.
5,6	ABBOT OF GLASTONBURY. See 7,10.
6,1	BISHOP OF LISIEUX. Gilbert Maminot, King William's doctor and chaplain.
7,1	(THE LANDS). Plural *appreciantur,* although the subject grammatically is *totum manerium,* 'the whole manor'; possibly a scribal error.
	MEN. Probably the jurors who were called together to give information to the DB commissioners as to the extent and value of the several estates; Jones p. 28.
7,2	LIFETIMES OF THREE MEN. That is, the purchaser of the 3 hides and his two succeeding heirs.
7,4	EDWARD. Possibly Edward of Salisbury; see Places notes below.
	THANELAND. See 1,3 note above. An example of the holders not being able to dispose of their land.
7,5	6 ACRES. In the MS above and between *vi* and *acs'* there is an ink blot shaped rather like *i*, which Farley reproduces as a figure, perhaps believing it was an intended correction of the *vi* to *vii*. However, it is not in quite the usual place for a correction and there is no underlining. Also, 7 acres would not add up with the 4 to make the 10 acres mentioned, and Osbern Gifford is stated as having 6 acres of meadow in 48,4.
	ALFWARD. Probably the same Alfward as in 5,6. BISHOP GEOFFREY. Of Coutances.
7,6	THE CHURCH ITSELF HOLDS. Repeated at the beginning of sections 7,6-11.
7,10	BISHOP OF COUTANCES. See 5,6.
7,12	EDWARD. Of Salisbury; see Places notes below.
7,13	EDWARD. Of Salisbury; see 24,42.
	TO THE ABBEY AS THANELAND. *Abbatiae ad tainlande;* or perhaps 'to the thaneland of the Abbey', reading *abbatiae* as genitive rather than dative. See 1,3 note above for thaneland.
8,2	THE CHURCH ITSELF HOLDS. Repeated at the beginning of sections 8,2-13.
8,6	RANULF FLAMBARD. Bishop of Durham 1099-1128. Abbreviated *Rā* here, *Rān* in the the 'value' paragraph, and simply *R.* in 8,9. Such abbreviations occur throughout DB for personal names.
8,9	RANULF FLAMBARD. See 8,6 note above.
	RALPH. *Radulfus.* VCH 79 has 'Ralf (*recte* Ranulf)', but two different people must be meant because of the statement 'value of what the men hold'.
8,12	OF THIS (LAND). In the MS there is a gap of about 5 letters due to an erasure, but no sign of the original word can be seen; perhaps the scribe intended to write some such word as *terra*.
	WILLIAM OF EU. See 32,11, Ditteridge, which is at the other end of the Hundred from Bremhill. 32,14 makes clear that this is Alstan of Boscombe.
8,13	21½ HIDES. *st xxi hida 7 dim'.* The singular *hida* is usual in DB with the number *xxi* (see 12,6 note below), but *est*, 'is', should be the verb here.
9	IN THE MS the words *Petrus Westmonast'* are blurred and appear to have been written on top of an erasure.
9,1	THIRD PENNY. See B 4 note above.
10,2	THE CHURCH ITSELF HOLDS. Repeated at the beginning of sections 10,2-5.
	THANELAND. See 1,3 note above.
10,3	ARNULF OF HESDIN. See 25,6, an entry underlined for deletion; the value of the 2 hides there, however, is stated as 40s.

12,2 THE CHURCH ITSELF HOLDS. Repeated at the beginning of sections 12,2-6.
FROM THE ABBEY. In the MS *de abb'ia;* Farley misprints *de abb'a;* the *i* is very faint, however. *Abbia* is the normal abbreviation for *abbatia,* 'Abbey', whereas *abba* is unusual, both as an abbreviation for *abbatia,* and for *abbatissa,* 'Abbess'.

12,4 SESTERS. The sester is a measure, sometimes of liquid, as here, sometimes dry, as in ch. 24p; of uncertain and probably variable size, reckoned at 32 oz. for honey.
ARPENT. A French measure of uncertain and probably variable size, usually applied in DB to vineyards, as here and in 55,1, but to meadow in 50,1. 68,4;7;10 and to woodland in 68,8.

12,6 21 VILLAGERS. *Vill(anu)s,* singular, for *vill(an)i,* plural, as elswhere with 21, 31, etc. in DB. But see 13,1 *xxi coscez,* rather than *xxi coscet.*

13,2 THE CHURCH ITSELF HOLDS. Repeated at the beginning of sections 13,2-14;16-20.
10 PLOUGHS CAN PLOUGH. An unusual phrase in Wilts. In Exon it is the regular formula for DB's 'Land for so many ploughs'.
RICHARD STURMY. Possibly at Huish, 68,3.

13,3 SERVED AS A THANE. Possibly rendering military service.
6 OXEN IN THE LORD'S PLOUGH. Unusually exact. Exon regularly gives the number of oxen actually there, but DB generally rounds the oxen at work up or down to the nearest ½ plough, at 8 oxen to a plough. See 28,20 note below. The formula 'Land for so many oxen' is more common, however.

13,9 RICHARD POYNANT...5 PLOUGHS. See 58,2; there are 4 ploughs there, however.
SERVING AS VILLAGERS. Presumably this means they rendered the same services as are due from villagers.

13,10 THE VALUE of South Newton is placed at the end of the next entry, with signs in the MS to indicate its correct position.

13,18 (REPAIRING). Probably as in 13,10, although 'building' could be meant.

13,21 FROM THEM. The two hides.

15,1 21 VILLAGERS. See 12,6 note above.
WILLIAM. Shield. He restored to Romsey Abbey his holdings here and at Ashton (15,2) when two of his daughters became nuns there; see the charter of Henry 1 confirming this restoration, in W. Farrer *An Outline Itinerary of King Henry 1,* no. 173, in EHR xxxiv (1919). See also 2,4 note above.
HERVEY. Probably Hervey of Wilton; see VCH p. 75; 106.

15,2 WILLIAM. Shield; see 15,1 note above.

16,3 ALLINGTON. See 23,7.

16,5 THE CHURCH. In the MS signs next to this entry and to 20,6 indicate that this holding was at Winterslow.
COUNT OF MORTAIN. The half brother of King William, and a large landholder in the South-West, especially Cornwall; he had wrongful possession of numerous holdings.

17,1 QUEEN MATILDA. Wife of King William; she died in 1083.

19 THE CANONS OF LISIEUX. This heading applies only to the first entry in this chapter.

20,2 30[s]. Probably *sol'* omitted in error in the MS after *xxx*; also occurs with *xxx* in 24,12.

20,3 CLYFFE PYPARD. Often no population is recorded in small holdings, but rarely in one of this size; the omission may be accidental. See also 25,7;19. 48,2-3.

20,5 ½ MILL. See 37,8 for the other half.

20,6 ABBESS. See 16,5.

21,1 EARL ROGER. Roger of Montgomery, Earl of Shrewsbury.

22,1 EARL HUGH. Hugh of Avranches, Earl of Chester and nephew of King William.

22,2 THE EARL ALSO HOLDS. Repeated at the beginning of sections 22,2-6.

22,5 OF THESE. *De his,* referring to the 2 hides paying tax. *De ea,* referring to *terra,* the land in the plough assessment, or *De hac terra* is the usual formula here.

23,1 EARL AUBREY. Probably Aubrey of Coucy, formerly Earl of Northumbria. His estates were forfeited to the King when he resigned. But see Jones p. 61 and H. Ellis *A General Introduction To Domesday Book,* i, p. 367 for a different identification, i.e. Aubrey de Vere. As far as can be seen A. de Vere is never referred to as *comes* Earl.

23,2 REST OF THE LAND. *Aliam terram.* This phrase is very common in Exon, where the villagers' holding of land, as well as of ploughs, is regularly given. This is its only occurrence in Wilts. DB and, apart perhaps from 24,3 and 67,13 (see notes below), the only occasion there where the villagers' holding is mentioned.

23,7 ALSO IN THIS TOWN. In the MS a capital *i* for *In eadem villa,* not reproduced by Farley.
4 HIDES. See 16,3.

23,9 PASTURE...RIVER. River Ebble, a tributary of the Wiltshire Avon.

24p 1 (CROP OF) STANDING CORN, 162 ACRES. *Annonae clxii ācs,* with *.i. Bled* written above *Annonae.* The *.i.* may not be a number, but the abbreviation for *id est,* making

Bled (= *bladi*, 'corn before the harvest', Ducange) a gloss on *annonae*, which can mean variously produce, corn-rents, or the grain itself. VCH 163 interprets the *.i.* as *scilicet*, 'namely', and DGSW p. 61 as *vel*, 'or'.

REEVELAND. Its meaning is uncertain, perhaps land held by the Sheriff during his term of office; see P. Vinogradoff *English Society in the 11th Century*, p.372ff.

FROM HIS OWN. *De suo* cannot grammatically refer to *firma*, 'revenue'; it probably means Edward's estates, resources, generally.

24,1 COTTAGERS. There is a gap in the MS of about 9 letters after this, probably for the later addition of the villagers' ploughs, though there is no *rq'* (for *require*, 'enquire') in the margin, as in 2,11. 25,2. and 67,11.

24,2 EDWARD ALSO HOLDS. Repeated at the beginning of sections 24,2-5;7-11.

24,3 2 HIDES AND 1 VIRGATE. Perhaps a rare instance of the villagers' land being given, but it is more likely that the *tenent'* refers only to the 2 Frenchmen, as in 27,3. See 23,2 note above.

24,5 HIGHWORTH (AT) LUS HILL. The scribe mistakenly wrote the Hundred name and the place-name as one word, instead of two with a preposition between them.

24,6 HERVEY. Of Wilton; see VCH p. 75;106.

24,9 1½ HIDES. *hid' dimid'*. Either the scribe omitted *7* in error at the end of the line, or, possibly, the two words were mistakenly transposed, '½ hide' being intended (VCH 172 and Jones p.66). There are a number of cases (e.g. 24,36), however, where the number *i* has been omitted before *hida 7 dim'*.

24,12 30[s]. See 20,2 note above.

24,13 IN THE MS, in the right margin next to the first 2 lines of this entry. *TODEWORTH* is written in large and ornate capitals in a late 13th century hand. Farley does not reproduce it.

24,14 CROC...EDWARD. See 68,14.

24,19 10 PLOUGHS. The MS has *x. . car'* with a gap of about 2 letters between the full-stops, due to an erasure. It would seem that originally a number larger than *x* had been written in error. Farley does not reproduce the gap.

PASTURE, 12 ACRES. Farley misprints '20 acres'.

ENGLISHMEN. Called 'thanes' in 68,23.

PROVED. *Diratiocinati sunt* is more probably deponent (cf. classical Latin *ratiocinari*) than passive, despite the active *diratiocinavit* in 24,14. The deponent form is also found in 24,42. In the Middle Ages there was some confusion between the deponent and the active forms of a verb, both forms occurring together, as here.

WILLIAM OF PICQUIGNY. The same person as William, son of Ansculf of Picquigny in Picardy. He was an important man in the Midlands and was lord of Dudley Castle. See 68,22-23.

24,20 PART OF A MILL. See 67,22;23;25 and Places notes below.

24,32 THE FOURTH PART OF A MILL. 26,22 has '2 parts of a mill which pay 40d'. There is no other mention of a ¼ mill under other holdings in Tytherton or nearby places; either it is missing (possibly from 48,9 Tytherton Kellaways) or the '2 parts' represent ¾ of a mill, or perhaps the reading should be *Ibi tercia pars* for *Ibi quarta pars*. The MS has a capital *i* for *Ibi*, which Farley does not reproduce.

24,34 BEFORE 1066 AND... In the MS there is *7* after *TRE*, omitted by Farley, with a gap of about 4 letters following it, then another gap of about 5 letters at the beginning of the next line before *Terra est.*. The gaps are due to erasures, but do not seem to be large enough for words such as *pro tanto geldb'* ('it paid tax for as much'), which one would expect here; see 24,36-37.

24,40 PASTURE, 50 SHEEP. The only mention in Wiltshire of sheep.

24,42 ADJUDGE. *Diratiocinantur*, deponent; see 24,19 note above.

CHURCH OF GLASTONBURY. See 7,13.

25,1 LAND FOR 16 PLOUGHS. Written in the left margin. Farley misprints '15 ploughs'.

25,2 POTTERNE. See 3,1.

BISHOP OF SALISBURY..1066. Anachronistic; there was not in fact a Bishop of Salisbury itself until 1078; see 3,1 note above.

...3 FURLONGS. There is a gap of about 7 letters in the MS with *r* (for *require*, 'enquire') in the left margin to remind the scribe to find out whether pasture or wood-land was so described; the *r* is not reproduced by Farley or the facsimile. It is interesting to note that for two out of the three entries for Potterne (see 67,11) the scribe was unsure of the nature of part of the land measured.

25,6 PEWSEY. This entry is lined through in black for deletion because it had appeared already as part of 10,3. See 10,3 note above.

25,7 STANDEN. See 20,3 note above.

25,9 RECORDED. See 1,5 note above.

ABOVE. The manor of Chalfield, 25,8.

25,13	7 COTTAGERS. See M 3 note above.

25,13 7 COTTAGERS. See M 3 note above.

25,19 *CHENEBUILD.* See 20,3 note above.

25,23 THOLF. See PNDB 388.

ARNULF..½ HIDE. See 32,17.

AS MUCH AS IS WORTH. This holding was probably from the King's land at nearby Warminster, which was not hidated (see 1,4), hence the unusual expression here.

26,3 PASTURE, 6. Probably *acrae* understood.

26,4 2 PLOUGHS. In the MS there is a gap of about 2 letters due to an erasure between *ii* and *căr,* which Farley does not reproduce.

26,6 LAND. *T'r̄a* (=*terram,* accusative) in the MS, a mistake for the usual *t'ra* (=*terra,* nominative).

26,9 PASTURE, ½ LEAGUE. The MS and Farley have the abbreviation mark over *leu* (=*leuua/ leuca,* 'league'), but it is not reproduced in the facsimile.

26,13 VALUE. Written in darker ink at the end of 26,12 with transposition signs to indicate its correct place.

26,15 SAID LANDS. 26,1-15.

26,17 BEFORE 1066. As *TRE* is written between *geldb'* and *Sigar,* with no punctuation or 7, it could equally well be translated 'they paid tax for as much before 1066. Sigar and Carman held them' (so Jones p. 83). Also occurs in 26,20. 27,27 and 37,9-10.

26,19 DURAND OF GLOUCESTER. See 28,10 and note.

TESTIFY. Unless it is a scribal error, *testant'* (=*testantur*) is more likely to be deponent (as it is in classical Latin) than passive. See 24,19 note above.

26,20 BEFORE 1066. See 26,17 note above.

26,22 2 PARTS OF A MILL. See 24,32 and note.

27,2 THE THIRD PART OF 2 MILLS. See 32,3 and 67,63 for the other two-thirds of these mills.

27,7 ROBERT HOLDS FROM HUMPHREY. Repeated at the beginning of sections 27,7-10.

27,10 AND 7 SMALLHOLDERS. Written in the left margin, but with no signs to show its correct place in the text.

27,14 ½ MILL. See 32,10 and 48,6 and Places notes below for the other parts of the mill.

27,15 HUMPHREY HIMSELF HOLDS. Repeated at the beginning of sections 27,15-19.

27,21 LAND FOR.. In the MS there is a gap of about 4 letters, presumably for the scribe to fill in the amount of land when available.

27,26 HELD. *ten'uit* in the MS and Farley; the scribe seems to have written *ten'* (the usual abbreviation for *tenet,* 'holds') first, and then added *uit* and not removed the abbreviation mark.

27,27 BEFORE 1066. See 26,17 note above.

28,2 10 COTTAGERS. See M 3 note above.

28,6 REGINALD. *Rainald* in MS; Farley misprints *Rainbald.*

28,9 REGINALD. Reginald Canute; see Exon Tax Returns for Shippen Hundred.

LORDSHIP.. In the MS there is a gap of about 7 letters after this; probably intended for the ploughs in lordship when their number was available.

28,10 6 OXEN..THERE, PLOUGHING. See 13,3 note above. As 8 oxen normally formed a plough-team, perhaps 2 were borrowed from a neighbouring manor. As to whether there were smaller teams in the South-West, see R. Lennard in EHR 1x (1945) p. 217ff. and in EHR 1xxxi (1966) p. 770ff., and H.P.R. Finberg in EHR 1xvi (1951) p. 67ff.

1 COTTAGER AND 1 SLAVE. *i. cotar(ius) 7 uno servo.* Either a mistake for *..7 unus servus* or for *.. cum uno servo.*

MEADOW..1½ VIRGATES. Either the 1½ virgates are part of the meadow measurement, or *pastura* was omitted in error before it.

DURAND. Of Gloucester; see 26,19. Edward is stated there to have held this ½ virgate before 1066. Perhaps Siward held it from Edward (or vice versa), or the scribe misread one of the names in the returns, or the return was itself faulty.

29,5 THORNHILL. See 68,23.

IT LAY. *Quae,* referring to the hide, not Thornhill.

30,2 LAND FOR.. There is a gap of about 4 letters in the MS after this; 4 ploughs may have been intended, as Exon 531 a 1 gives the total number of assessed ploughs in Durand's Wiltshire holding as 24, and in DB they total 20 apart from the number omitted here. ½[HIDE]. There is a gap of about 4 letters in the MS due to an erasure; *hida* was probably intended and this fits in with the total of 32 hides 3 virgates given in Exon 531 a 1 as Durand's holding in Wiltshire.

30,3 HE. Grammatically *Idem* refers to Roger (30,2), but as *de D(urando)* has been omitted (perhaps in error), Durand may have held these 1½ hides himself. The Exon summary of Durand's holdings in Wiltshire (531 a 1) is no help because the 1½ hides would be counted as part of Durand's total holding whether Roger held from him or not.

30,5 A MAN-AT-ARMS..1 VIRGATE. Miles Crispin holds the adjacent Chedglow (28,10), on which the holding of this man-at-arms may have encroached.

31,1 WALTER GIFFARD. Created Earl of Buckingham in 1100/1101.

32,2 THANELAND. See 1,3 note above.

32,3 MILLS. See 27,2 and 67,63 for the other two parts.

32,10 MILL. See 27,14 and 48,6 for the other two parts of the mill.

32,11 ALSTAN. Alstan of Boscombe; see 8,12.

32,14 ABOVE LANDS. 32,1-14.

32,16 ...COTTAGERS. In the MS there is a gap of about 3 letters before Cottagers; the figure was probably not to hand at the time of writing.

32,17 TAX FOR ½ HIDE. In the MS the *p* of *P(ro) dimid' hida* is a capital and is emphasised in red ink; Farley does not reproduce this. The *H* of *Hernulf* is similarly emphasised. See 25,23 for both these statements.

33,1 ROBERT. Robert *debraiosa* ('of Braose') in Exon 14 b 6, the Tax Return for Selkley Hundred; probably a mistake, as in the other two Wiltshire Tax Return texts (2 a 5 and 8 b 4) he is plain Robert, holding 2 hides from William of Braose.

34,1 WILLIAM OF MOHUN. His holding is the only one in Wiltshire DB which appears in Exon (47 a 1). The extra information given there is included, either in small type in the translation or below.
WALTER. Exon has *W. Hosat(us)*: Hussey, OEB 370-1.
VILLAGERS. Exon 'They have 2 hides, less 1 virgate'. The term *villani* is general and includes the smallholders.
MILL..4s. Exon *per annum*, 'a year', as almost always with present values.
PASTURE. Exon '½ league long and 1 furlong wide'. Perhaps the DB scribe omitted *q(uarentena)* before the *lat'* here, otherwise '1 league' is implied.

37,5 LEOFDAY. The MS has *Leueclai* for *Leuedai* through the common confusion between *cl* and *d*. PNDB 311, note 4.
BEFORE 1066. The MS has two 7 signs after *TRE*, one at the end of the first line, the other at the beginning of the next, in error.

37,8 ½ MILL. See 20,5 for the other half.

37,9-10 BEFORE 1066. See 26,17 note above.

37,12 OF WHICH..LORDSHIP. In the MS there is a gap of about 2 letters (possibly *st* erased) between *De ea* and *in dn̄io*, not reproduced by Farley.

37,16 [...]. No holder is actually named; probably Waleran was intended.

38,1 2 PARTS OF A MILL. See 56,4 for the other part.

39,1 WOOD. See 1,2.

40,1 COUNT GILBERT. Of Brionne (département Eure, France).

41,4 LIFETIMES OF THREE MEN. See 7,2 note above.

42,1 COTTAGERS. *Cozez* for *cozets, coscez*, the usual plural forms. See M 3 note above.

42,4 CUTHWULF. *Coolle;* see PNDB 220.

42,6 (IS). *E(st)* omitted in error in MS.

42,8 1 VIRGATE. In the MS *un* for *una*; an ink blot appears to have been erased after it.

42,10 VITALIS. *Fitheus;* see PNDB 405-6.

43,2 PASTURE 1 FURLONG. MS and Farley have *pastura i. q';* the facsimile has a line over the *i.*

44 [LAND]. *Terra* omitted in error in the MS; also in the heading for chs. 45,52,55,62,64, 65,66. The whole heading is omitted in chs. 46 and 60.

45,1 (IS). In MS *sunt* for *est.* 1 HOUSE IN MALMESBURY. See M 16.

45,2 ON LEASE FROM. *p'restū,* more likely to be *per prest(it)um,* 'on lease from', than *perprest(ur)um,* 'as a purpresture' (VCH 378).'Purpresture' - an encroachment on waste. See Jones p. 115.
EDRIC THE SHERIFF. Sheriff of Wiltshire; Edward of Salisbury's predecessor.

46,1 PANCEVOLT. 'Paunch-face', OEB 324-5.

48,4 MEADOW, 6 ACRES. See 7,5 and note.

48,6 OSBERN HIMSELF HOLDS. Repeated at the beginning of sections 48,6-11.
MILL. See 27,14 and 32,10 for the other parts of the mill.

48,10 ½ MILL. See 48,11 for the other half.

49,1a ROGER...£4. This entry is written in darker ink at the bottom of col. 72d, but extending some 3 letters' width into the left margin, though this is not shown by Farley. It is not part of 49,1 though written in the middle of it, nor part of Osbern Giffard's lands. It may have been written earlier than some, or all, of col. 72d, because there seems no other reason why the scribe should stop in the middle of 49,1 two lines up from the end of the column. See Berks. 14,1 (col. 59d); 28,1 (col. 61b) and 55,1 (col. 63a) for the rest of the Coleshill manor; also VCH 395n. ROGER OF LACY. Lassy, département of Calvados.

50,1 ARPENT. See 12,4 note above.

55,1 AIULF. Sheriff of Dorset. The personal name is the Anglo-Norman form for OE Athulf - Æthelwulf, PNDB 191.

51 THIS CHAPTER is written in two lines across the bottom of cols. 73a, b with signs indicating its correct position in the text. The beginning of the second line is here exdented in the Latin text.
HUGH SON OF BALDRIC. Sheriff of Notts. and Derby.

51,1 WALTER. Probably Walter *de Rivera;* ('Rivers'); MS A of the Exon Tax Returns (1 a 6) for Swanborough Hundred has 'Walter de Rivera, 5 hides, which Hugh gave to his daughter', probably as a dowry.

56,3 NIGEL. See 1,18.

56,4 ST. MARY'S OF MONTEBOURG. In the diocese of Coutances in Normandy.
MILL. See 38,1 for the other two-thirds of this mill.
SPIRTES THE PRIEST. A wealthy churchman who held a total of nearly 80 hides in Somerset, Hants., Wilts., Herefordshire and Shropshire. In Shrops. (Col. 252d) he is described as one of the twelve canons of St. Mary's, Shrewsbury.

58,1 [HIDES?]. In the MS *car'*. Although this could be an abbreviation for *carucatae,* 'carucates', it is more likely to be a mistake for *hidae;* not 'ploughs' as they are mentioned next.

58,2 RICHARD. See 13,9 and note.

59,1 SLAVES. The MS and Farley have *serui 7 xiiii vill(an)i,* but the facsimile has not reproduced the 7, which is rather faint.

60,1 HOLDS. The facsimile has not reproduced the abbreviation mark over *ten',* which is in the MS and Farley.
TWO SONS-IN-LAW. William of Audley and Robert of Aumale, according to the Exon Tax Returns for Rowborough Hundred. They were given their holding in this Hundred by Robert Blunt (*Blondus*) from his lordship; presumably the 4 hides mentioned there were a dowry as they were given to each 'with his daughter'.

65,1 ½ MILL. See 67,36 and 67,95 for the probable other half of this mill.

66,1 MARGINAL SIGN. See 58,1 note below.
1 VILLAGER. It is unusual for the villagers to be placed after the smallholders and Cottagers; also occurs at 67,28 and 68,14.
WOODLAND 2 FURLONGS. So MS; Farley misprints '1 furlong'.

66,2 THIRD PART OF A MILL. See 67,43 for the other 2 parts.

67,1 TAX. It would seem from these figures that the lordship land did not pay tax. This is not always the case, as can be seen from the Exon Tax Returns.

67,2-10 BRICTRIC. A Norman rendering of OE Brihtric (= Beorhtric).

67,3 BRICTRIC HOLDS. Repeated at the beginning of sections 67,3-9.

67,9 ODSTOCK. In the MS *ch* is written above the second *t* in the place-name, altering it from *Odestote* to *Odestoche;* the scribe omitted to underline the *t* for deletion.

67,11 BISHOP'S MANOR. Bishop Herman; see 3,1 and note.
4 FURLONGS. There is a gap of about 4 letters in the MS with *r* (for *require,* 'enquire') in the margin next to it, to remind the scribe to find out what was being thus described. Farley does not reproduce the *r*. See 25,2 note above.
BISHOP OSMUND. Of Salisbury. He is presumably claiming the 3 hides because Wulfward White, the purchaser, had died and they were then due to revert to the bishopric by the terms of the purchase; see 3,1.

67,13 BEFORE 1066. The MS has *TRE geldb';* Farley misprints *TRE 7 geldb'*.
THE VILLAGERS HOLD (THEM?). *vill(an)i tenent.* There is no way of telling from the Latin whether the land or the ploughs are the object. However, except for 23,2 and possibly 24,3, the villagers' land holding is not given in Wilts., whereas their ploughs almost invariably are. Cf. 1,23a and 23,2 ("thane...it").

67,15 8s. Perhaps a mistake for £8, as this is rather a large drop in value.

67,22;23;25 MILL. See 24,20 note above.

67,28 2 VILLAGERS. See 66,1 note above.

67,36 MILL. See 65,1 note above.

67,39 IN LORDSHIP...1 PLOUGH. The Latin is ambiguous, with two main verbs (*sunt* and *habent*); it could also be translated "In lordship 2 ploughs. 5 slaves with 1 villager and 2 smallholders have 1 plough", although in DB slaves do not usually have ploughs.

67,41 CHIPPING. *Cheping.* See OEB 177, PNDB 221 (s.v. *Cypping*).

67,37-38 THESE ENTRIES are written in two lines across the bottom of col. 73c,d, with a sign beside them but no corresponding one in the columns to indicate their correct position. However, they naturally belong with Aldred's other holdings. The second line is here exdented in the Latin text.

67,43 MILL. See 66,2 for the other part. One would expect the payment for the 2 parts of the mill to be twice that for the one-third in 66,2, but it is three times it, which suggests that the scribe may have given the payment for the whole mill here, in error. See DGSW p. 46.

67,53 EDRIC BLIND. See OEB 299.

67,57 1 VIRGATE. The MS has *unā* (=*unam*, accusative); Farley misprints *una*, nominative.

67,63 COMPTON BASSETT. No gap is left in the MS for the insertion of the amount of land held there by Thorkell, so perhaps the *in* is a scribal error.
MILLS. See 27,2 and 32,3 for the other 2 parts.

67,65 WULFRIC HOLDS. Repeated at the beginning of sections 67,65-72.
WULFRIC. Called 'Hunter' in the Exon Tax Returns for Kinwardstone Hundred. Also possibly in 67,70 in the Return for Cawdon Hundred, though he holds 1½ hides jointly with a relative there.

67,66 4 COUNTRYMEN HAVE IT. Referring to the plough, not the land. This is the only occurrence of the term *rustici* in Wilts. DB. They were probably less prosperous villagers, VCH p. 55.

67,70 1 HIDE. See 67,65 note above.

67,93 15d. Possibly *xx* changed to *xv*, or vice versa, in the MS.

67,95 MILL. See 65,1 note above.

67,100 LANG. *Lanch;* see OEB 320.

68,1 IN THE MS there is a sign in the left margin beside this entry, with a corresponding one in the right margin above the marginal heading *SERVIENT' REGIS* in col. 73b. It could indicate that the ½ hide held by Godescal (65,2) lay in Edington, or it could just be meant to draw attention to other holdings of the King's servants.

68,2 HERVEY. See 1,18 and note.

68,3 MEADOW, 4 ACRES. *Ac (acrae)* is visible under an ink blot in the MS.

68,4 ARPENTS. Also 68,7;8;10. See 12,4 note above.

68,9 HAUVILLE. In the département of Eure, France; OEB 91.
3 HIDES AND 1½ VIRGATES. In the MS *7 unā v' t'rae* is written above *7 dimid'*, the tail of the 7 extending down between *hid'* and 7, indicating where the scribe intended it to go. When the 3 hides and 1½ virgates are added to the 1 hide and 2½ virgates of the other Grafton entry (68,8) a 5-hide estate is formed (VCH p. 166 n), which would not be the case if 3½ hides and 1 virgate were read.

68,12 [...]. No holder is actually named; probably Ralph (of Hauville) was intended.

68,14 1 VILLAGER. See 66,1 note above.
EDWARD THE SHERIFF. See 24,14.

68,15 HERVEY. Of Wilton; see VCH p. 75;106.

68,16 THEOBALD AND HUMPHREY. Called respectively the doctor and the cook in the Exon Tax Returns for Shippen Hundred.

68,20 WILLIAM SHIELD. See 1,16.

68,21 GEOFFREY. Called Geoffrey 'Marshall' (*mariscalc', marescal*) in the Exon Tax Returns for Startley Hundred. Perhaps the same person as the Geoffrey Marshall in M 12.

68,22 WILLIAM SON OF ANSCULF. See 24,19 note above.
STREMIUS. *Strami.* Perhaps the same person as the Stremius in 24,19, who held Edward the Sheriff's manor of Bradenstoke before 1066, of which William held 1 hide and 1 virgate in 1086.

68,23 WILLIAM. William of Picquigny, son of Ansculf; see 24,19 for his holding at Bradenstoke, which is stated as 1 hide and 1 virgate. For his holding at Clyffe Pypard see 29,5.

68,24 BETESLAU. The identification of Round (VCH Hants. i. 429) of *Beteslau* as "of Beslow" (Shropshire) is questioned by von Feilitzen in *Winchester in the Early Middle Ages (Winchester Studies, 1)* ed. M. Biddle, p.207-8. Wulfeva Beteslau also appears in Hants. 6,12 (col. 43 b).
1 COTTAGER. In the MS *i coscez*, plural, but an attempt seems to have been made to change the *z* to a *t*, making the singular *coscet*. See M3 note above.

68,32 AEFIC. *Avitius;* see PNDB 172.

Notes on Place Name Identifications

The secure identification of places in the five south-western counties is less straightforward than for much of the country, and Wiltshire presents particular problems. With the exception of Lus Hill (24,5) the text of DB does not give Hundred headings. Moreover, several modern places often share the same DB name; sometimes these are widely separated like the Somerfords, and Langford, Landford and Longford (DB *Langeford*); sometimes they are adjacent places distinguished now by East and West, St Mary and St Peter. This lack of Hundred headings can in part be made good by evidence from the Exon Tax Return, which it is hoped to publish in a supplementary volume. It lists the holdings of major landowners by Hundreds but without placenames, although most entries can be located. Identification is sometimes possible where an uncertain place comes in the text of DB between places in the same or adjacent hundreds. But Wiltshire DB does not generally list the places in Hundred groups, unlike the text of Exon Domesday in the other south western counties. Exon Domesday is represented for Wiltshire only by one entry (47a1). Unless the Tax Return has evidence, identification of the different Suttons, Lydiards and Eastons *etc.*, should be treated with caution.

Placenames research involves also a full study of later surveys and of family and manorial history, outside the scope of this edition. The notes below draw attention to some of the problems and cite some of the early evidence to enable places of the same basic name to be separated. Sometimes these may represent sub-divisions of a holding that are later than 1086. It is by no means clear for example that the separate Codfords or Deverills existed at the time of the Survey. The text generally prints these separate identifications only to distinguish places of the same basic name in different hundreds, e.g. Littleton *Pannell* and *Drew*. Usually only the basic name appears in the text, and the problem is discussed in a note. Of these adjacent places, only the larger, or the one for which there is good evidence, is mapped.

The pioneering work of W.H. Jones *Domesday for Wiltshire*, London and Bath 1865, is still valuable. His identifications are largely reproduced by VCH (Vol II 1955), by EPNS (1939) and by DG, often omitting his evidence and his hesitations and queries. The EPNS volume does not give exact DB references, but its identifications are followed, except where noted below.

DEVERILL. The old name for the upper Wylye is given in DB to various settlements on its banks in the Hundreds of Mere (Kingston and Monkton Deverill), and Heytesbury (Hill, Brixton and Longbridge Deverill). The Tax Return enables most to be allocated to their Hundreds, but individual identities are sometimes uncertain.

WINTERBOURNE. The old name for the Rivers Bourne and Till and probably for the Kennet is used in DB for a number of villages on their banks. Only Winterbourne Stoke (24,8-9) is separately identified by DB. Of the Till settlements (Dole Hundred), it is possible to distinguish Addestone, Maddington, Shrewton, Winterbourne Stoke, Elston and possibly Berwick St. James, usually on the basis of later evidence. EPNS (235) would also include Rolleston. Of the Bourne settlements (Dauntsey, Earls, Gunner), only Winterbourne Earls is certain. The two Kennett Winterbournes, (Monkton and Bassett in Selkley Hundred) can be separated. In some cases, the Tax Return allows a Winterbourne to be assigned to a particular Hundred, but the holding at 26,6 cannot even be identified in this way.

B3-4 SALISBURY. The DB site was Old Sarum, the cathedral and the town being moved to the present site (GR 14 29) in the 13th Century.

1,3 CHEVERELL. Probably Great Cheverell, VCH X.42.

1,14 BROMHAM. The Tax Return for Calne Hundred gives the name. Queen Edith, the 1066 holder in the Tax Return, perhaps names St Edith's Marsh, EPNS 255.

1,15 WOOTTON (Rivers). This Wootton is required by the Tax Return for Kinwardstone Hundred.

1,17 WINTERBOURNE (Stoke). The Tax Return for Dole Hundred records that the King's reeve of *Winterburnestoca* retained tax of 2 hides and 1 virgate, the amount for which this DB Winterbourne paid tax.

1,19 COLLINGBOURNE (Ducis). Named from the Dukes of Lancaster to whom the royal holding later passed, EPNS 342-3. See 10,2 note.

1,20 (East) KNOYLE. Formerly Knoyle Regis, EPNS x1.

1,21 LYDIARD (Millicent). Required by the Tax Return for Chippenham Hundred, later in Staple.

Chapter 2. Many of these holdings are later in the hands of the Priory of St Swithin's, Winchester.

2,1 DOWNTON. The forest is mentioned in the Tax Return (2 b 7, 9 a 5, 15 b 3) and is probably Melchet rather than the New Forest. See DGSW 37.

2,3 FYFIELD. The Bishop of Winchester later holds Fifield in Enford, EPNS x1, RH II 258 a. But St Swithin's holds *Fifhide* with Overton (see 2,11), in Selkley Hundred, RH II 234b. See Fees 748, NV 348a. "Five Hides" is the taxable land in DB, EPNS 295.

2,4 ALTON (Priors) EPNS 317.

2,7 WROUGHTON. This holding is *Nether Werston'* RH II 243b. See 27,7 note.

2,8 BUSHTON. Bishop's Tun EPNS 266-7. Fees 737. See 20,3 note.

2,11 (East) OVERTON. EPNS 305 n1. See 13,8 note.

3,5 SHIPLEY. Possibly the place in Aldbourne, EPNS 293, but not necessarily in Wilts.

4,1 (North) TIDWORTH. EPNS 370. South Tidworth is just in Hampshire, (GR 23 47), and the holdings at North Tidworth 12 hides in all probably straddled the border. See 24,14 note.

5,1 DRAYCOT (Fitzpayne). This Draycot is required by the Tax Return for Swanborough Hundred.

5,2 'WITTENHAM' EPNS 123, lost in Wingfield.

5,6 LITTLETON (Drew). The same place as 7,5 since Alfward held from Glastonbury before 1066. This is probably Littleton Drew as in 7,5 it is listed with Stanton St Quintin. EPNS 241.

6,1 YATTON (Keynell). EPNS (23-24) identifies *Etune*, with Castle Eaton (see 21,1), but a holding of the Bishop is required in the Tax Return for Chippenham Hundred. See 25,27 and 66,1 notes.

6,2 SOMERFORD (Keynes). Held in Fees 738 by William de Kaignes, who probably inherited indirectly from the Bishop. Jones 234, VCH 56.

7,3 DEVERILL. This entry and 7,16 refer to two Glastonbury holdings each of 10 hides, with 5 hides in Lordship. The Tax Return allows one to be identified as Longbridge Deverill in Heytesbury EPNS 166, (*Dēvel Lungpunt* Fees 732), and the other as Monkton Deverill in Mere (EPNS 174), but it is impossible to say which is which. The land was granted by Athelstan, and it is clear from the Glastonbury Feodary (xxiv and 19) that it was regarded as one holding of 20 hides. The sub-tenancies given in the Feodary do not help with identification. The second DB entry refers to woodland 2 leagues long and ½ league wide. The modern Longbridge Deverill has extensive woodland in the neighbourhood of Shear Water.

7,4 CHRISTIAN MALFORD. Edward is possibly Edward the Sheriff whose successors held *Aven* (= Avon), probably the village in Christian Malford (GR 95 86) Fees 720.

7,5 STANTON (St. Quintin). Required by the Tax Return for Startley Hundred. See 5,6 note.

7,11 (Kington) LANGLEY. EPNS 101. The Glastonbury holding (with Nettleton and Grittleton) is *Kinkton* in Fees (732). It seems to have been in Thorngrove Hundred (Tax Return). The Church in fact held the manor of Kington St Michael, of which Kington Langley is a hamlet. GF xxiii, 13.

7,12 LANGFORD. Edward's holding is mentioned in 24,42. The Salisbury land was at *Parva Langeford*, FA V 243. See GF xxv.

7,14 IDMISTON. DB *Eunestetone*, not the same name as Idmiston (EPNS 380), although possibly the same place, is a difficult form. It appears to represent a compound of OE *tun*, 'farm, village' with either the superlative (*-este*) of the adjective *efn* 'level, smooth', or, more likely, metathesis of OE *efnetes*, genitive singular of *efnet* 'a smooth or level place' Nonetheless, the Tax Return places this holding in Alderbury Hundred, and there was a Glastonbury holding at *Idemeston* in Fees 746. See NV 346a, VCH p96, GF xxvi.

7,15 WINTERBOURNE. Probably on the River Bourne, as it appears to be required by the Tax Return for Alderbury Hundred. The 5 hide holding here, added to the 10 hides of *Eunestetone* accounts for the 15 hides of *Idemeston* in GF xxvi.

7,16 DEVERILL. See 7,3 note.

8,3 SOMERFORD. The Abbot of Malmesbury holds *Som'ford Mauduth* (= Little Somerford) RH II 272a. EPNS 73.

8,5 NORTON. Required by the Tax Return for Startley Hundred.

8,9 CHARLTON. Required by the Tax Return for Chedglow Hundred.

8,12 BREMHILL. Gilbert's 2 hides are at Thickwood (24,30) and William of Eu's holding is Ditteridge (32,11). Both are adjacent to each other, but must have been outliers of Bremhill.

Chapter 10. These holdings later belong to the Abbey of Hyde, Winchester.

10,2 COLLINGBOURNE (Kingston). Earlier Collingbourne Abbatis, EPNS 342-3. See 1,19 note.

10,4 ADDESTONE. "Abbot's Tun", EPNS 233.

11,2 DAMERHAM. The single hide is perhaps Hyde Farm, (grid reference SU 08 14). See EPNS 401.

12,6 DINTON. Later a detached part of Warminster Hundred, and included in its Tax Return. See 44,1 note.

13,1 STANTON (St. Bernard). Identified from the Tax Return for Swanborough Hundred. See RH II 274b.

13,7 (West) KNOYLE. Also Little Knoyle and Knoyle Hodierne. The 10 hides here contrast with the 30 at East Knoyle. See 1,20 note FA V 267.

13,8 (West) OVERTON. A Wilton Holding, EPNS 305 n1. See 2,11 note.

13,9 CHALKE. Gerard's holding is represented by Gurston in Broad Chalke (GR 02 25) EPNS 205. The DB holding no doubt included Broad and Bower Chalke, Berwick and Semley NV 347a.

13,10 (South) NEWTON. EPNS 228 only identifies North Newnton in DB. The evidence of the Tax Return for Branch Hundred is unsatisfactory, but the Abbess of Wilton holds both in Fees 739.
MELCHET FOREST. If the modern wood represents the DB site, it is fourteen miles away, whereas Grovely Wood is 2½m. (67,99). See 13,18 note.

13,11 WYLYE. A river name, probably like Winterbourne applied to several settlements. Bathampton 27,15-16 can be separately identified.

13,12 WISHFORD. The Wilton holding is Little Wishford, FA V 202,243. NV 347a.

13,13 LANGFORD. Little Langford FA V 243. The boundaries of the grant of land are in J.M. Kemble *Codex Diplomaticus* Vol III 419. See P.H. Sawyer *Anglo Saxon Charters* (1968), 612.

13,18 WASHERN. For Melchet Forest see 13,10 note.

13,20 LAVERSTOCK. The Forest is Clarendon, which also included part of Milford. See 27,27 and 67,79 notes.

15,1 EDINGTON. One hide of this land is required in the Tax Return for Whorwellsdown Hundred, the other 1½ hides being in Heytesbury Hundred.

15,2 ASHTON. Required by the Tax Return for Whorwellsdown Hundred. See NV 347a.

16,1 BULFORD. EPNS 126 identifies Bulkington, but Bulford seems to be required by the Tax Return for Amesbury Hundred. See VCH 124, NV 346a and next note.

16,3 ALLINGTON. EPNS 90 identifies Allington in Chippenham. This Amesbury holding seems required by the Tax Return for Amesbury Hundred, and the entries for Bulford and Allington are in sequence with Boscombe and Choulston (16,2;4) which are in this Hundred. See 23,6 note.

16,6-7 WINTERBOURNE BASSETT, MADDINGTON. In Fees 742 and 749, these holdings are a half of Maddington and the whole of *Abbedeston*. The latter, 'Abbot's Tun', survives as Rabson Farm in Winterbourne Bassett EPNS 309. Maddington is Maidens' (i.e. nuns') Tun, earlier *Maydenewynterburna* EPNS 233. It is not clear which DB Winterbourne is which of these, except that the Church of Amesbury's 4½ hides in 16,7 are probably the 'half' of Maddington, Matthew of Mortagne holding 4 hides as the other 'half' in 63,1.

17,1 (Brixton) DEVERILL. EPNS 165-6; named from the pre-conquest holder.

18,1 UPTON (Lovell). EPNS 156 identifies only Upton Scudamore. But an Upton in Heytesbury Hundred is required by the Tax Return.

19,1 (Kingston) DEVERILL. The Tax Return allows this to be placed in Mere Hundred. The 1066 Edith was possibly the Queen. It is held *in pura elemosina* from the King in Fees 743. EPNS 173.

20,1 CONOCK. EPNS 269 identifies Cowage Farm in Hilmarton. But the Tax Return requires this in Studfold Hundred.

20,2 *NECHENDUNE*. The Tax Return places this in Amesbury Hundred. It is possibly Netton (GR 13 36), although the place-names are different.

20,3 CLYFFE (Pypard). DB *Clive* refers to the long steep northern escarpment of the Marlborough Downs and must represent several settlements. Bushton (2,8), Clevancy (26,16) and possibly Broad Town (28,3) can be separately identified.

20,5 LANGFORD. Later held by the Church at Mortain as *Hangindelangeford* (= Hanging Langford) Fees 742. See 37,8 note.

21,1 (Castle) EATON See 66,1 note.
21,3 POULTON. Required by the Tax Return for Cricklade Hundred. It was a detached part of Wilts. in Gloucester until this century. There is no certain DB site in Gloucester between Poulton and the Wilts. boundary and it was possibly integral in 1086.
23,1 COMPTON. In Enford (EPNS 328) in view of the position of Aubrey's other holdings. Held with Winterslow and Ablington in Fees 746.
23,6 TYTHERINGTON. EPNS only identifies Tytherton (Chippenham Hundred). This entry is flanked by Chitterne and Allington and all the lands of the 1066 holder Harding 23,1-6 seem to be in the same area.
23,7 ALLINGTON. The four hides taken from the Church of Amesbury identify this as Allington in Amesbury. See 16,3 note.

Chapter 24. Edward the Sheriff's heirs are the Earls of Salisbury.
24,2 ALTON (Barnes). Edward's heirs hold Alton Berners RH II 274b.
24,7 and 24,10. SHREWTON. EPNS 236: 'Sheriff's Tun'. Only one of the three entries in this chaper (24,7;10;35) need be Shrewton, the others being unidentified Winterbourne (Till) holdings. The Earl of Salisbury also held *Parva Winterburn,* now Asserton in Berwick St. James, (Fees 709,721) and Maddington (Fees 721).
24,11 ORCHESTON. Orcheston St. Mary, and earlier Orcheston Bovyle. *Henricus de Bovill'* held from the Earl of Salisbury in Fees 721. EPNS 234.
24,14 (North) TIDWORTH. Croc also held South Tidworth in Hants. See 4,1 note.
24,18 (Hill) DEVERILL. Held by the Earls of Salisbury as *Hulledeverel* (Fees 728).
24,20 SOMERFORD. The remaining parts of the mill are accounted for by 67,22-23;25 which are probably the same Somerford.
24,21 BLUNSDON. The Salisbury holding is Hanging (= Broad) Blunsdon in Fees 720. EPNS 30-31.
24,27 POOLE (Keynes). Held by the Earl of Salisbury in Fees 709, 722. See Jones 229, VCH p107 n 31.
24,29 MIDDLETON. EPNS 349 identifies Milton Lilbourne, but the Earl of Salisbury's Middleton in Fees (719) is clearly different from the *Middelton* held by Walter de Lillebon (Fees 714,746). See 48,5 note.
24,31 LANGLEY (Burrell). EPNS 105. Held by Thomas Burel in Fees (720), probably a descendent of the 1086 holder.
24,35 SHREWTON. See 24,7 note.
24,41 WINTERBOURNE (Earls) EPNS 383-4. Named after the Earls of Salisbury.
24,42 LANGFORD. Little Langford, see 7,12 note.

Chapter 25. Many of Arnulf's holdings pass to Patrick de Chaworth.
25,3 CHEVERELL. Probably Little Cheverell, see VCH X 54.
25,7 STANDEN. In Chute, EPNS 341, earlier Standen Chaworth. Fees 716,746.
25,8 CHALFIELD. Later in Bradford Hundred, but seems to be required in the Exon Tax Return for Melksham.
25,11 CLYFFE (Pypard). EPNS does not identify *Sclive* which is a Norman-French form for *Clive.*
25,12 *BICHENEHILDE, BECHENEHILDE.* The identification of Jones (p.198) with Beacon
/ 18 Hill in Hilmarton is noticed in EPNS 268, where the derivation of DB *Bichen-, Bechen-* from OE *bēacon, bēcn* is perhaps too readily supposed: OE *bēcen* 'growing with beeches' is also possible. The DB name is not the same as the later one, although the place may be the same.
25,20 CHEDGLOW. See 67,51 note.
25,22 DEVERILL. The Tax Return for Heytesbury Hundred makes it probable that this Deverill is the same as 67,52 and 68,28. Urso, Aubrey and Edgar who hold Deverill in DB are said to have withheld the tax from one hide together with Richard and Durand.
25,23 UPTON (Scudamore). The same place as 32,17 of which Arnulf wrongfully holds ½ hide. Both entries are required by the Exon Tax Return for Warminister Hundred.
25,24 'WINTERBOURNE'. Patrick de Chaworth hold *Berwyke* in Dole Hundred (Berwick St. James) in RH II 254a, Fees 742, possibly Arnulf's Winterbourne.
25,26 EASTON (Piercy). Later in Chippenham Hundred, but it seems required by the Tax Return for Thorngrove.
25,27 YATTON (Keynell). DB *Etone,* which EPNS (45) identifies with Water Eaton, and accepts only *Getone* (32,14) as Yatton. Ekwall, *Concise Oxford Dictionary of English Placenames,* accepts *Etone* as a precursor of Yatton. The place is probably the *Gatton* held in Fees 716 by Henricus Chaynel from Patrick de Chaworth. See 6,1 note.

Chapter 26. Alfred's holdings are later in the hands of Robert Tregoze.

26,1   ALLINGTON. Required by the Exon Tax Return for Studfold Hundred. Held with All Cannings from Robert Tregoze in Fees 725.
26,7   LYDIARD (Tregoze) See Tax Return for Blackgrove Hundred and Fees 712.
26,11-12 UPTON (Scudamore) and NORTON (Bavant). This Upton and this Norton are held together by Galfrid d'Escudamore from Robert Tregoze (Fees 712,725) and are required in the Exon Tax Return for Warminister Hundred.
26,14 FIFIELD (Bavant). The Fifield in Chalke Hundred is held from John Tregoze in RH II 249a.
26,16 CLEVANCY. EPNS 268, VCH 248. See 20,3 note.
26,18 SOMERFORD. John Maltravers holds from Robert Tregoze in Fees 712. Somerford Maltravers is Great Somerford EPNS 73. See 27,10 note.
26,20 HORNINGSHAM. Held from Robert Tregoze as *Parva Horningesham* Fees 738.
26,22 (West) TYTHERTON. EPNS 91-92, formerly Tytherton Lucas. Adam Lucas held from Robert Tregoze (Fees 713,725). Another part of the mill is 24,32.

Chapter 27. Many of Humphrey's holdings pass to the Dunstanville family.
27,2   COMPTON (Bassett). Held by Fulco Bassett from Walter de Dunstanville, Fees 713. The third of two mills at 10s is complemented by the same amounts at 32,3 and 67,63 which are therefore the same Compton.
27,7   WROUGHTON. Held from the Dunstanvilles as *Uverewereston* (= Over Wroughton) in Fees 726. See 2,7 note.
27,10 SOMERFORD. Great Somerford. John Maltravers holds from the Dunstanvilles in Fees 713,726. See 26,18 note.
27,12 BLUNSDON. Held as *Churibluntesdon* by Walter de Dunstanville in Fees 726. Church Blunsdon is Blunsdon St. Andrew EPNS 30-31.
27,13 GROUNDWELL. EPNS does not identify, but this is probably the *Grundevell* held from Walter de Dunstanville in Fees 726. VCH 269.
27,14 ASHTON (Gifford). EPNS does not identify, but Elias Giffard held *Aston* from the Dunstanvilles in Fees (726). The ½ mill at 6s 3d is completed by the fourth parts at 3s and 3s 1½d at Codford 32,10 and 48,6.
27,15-16 BATHAMPTON. Two tenants of Walter de Dunstanville held at *Bathamewily* in Fees (713,726). But the Dunstanvilles also held Wylye to which one of these entries could refer. See 13,11 note.
27,18 WINTERBOURNE (Bassett). EPNS 309. Given by Alan de Dunstanville to Alan Bassett VCH 274.
27,19 POULTON. Required by the Exon Tax Return for Selkley Hundred. See 21,3 note.
27,20 HAMPTON. See 43,2 note.
27,25 HURDCOTT. Required by the Tax Return for Cadworth Hundred. See 37,16 note.
27,26 'FRUSTFIELD'. EPNS 386 does not identify DB *Fistesferie* with Frustfield, but the Tax Return places it in this Hundred. See 67,35. This important village is lost, surviving only in the Hundred name. The Dunstanvilles held Whelpley in Whiteparish (Fees 713,745). Jones 216.
27,27 MILFORD. The forest is Clarendon. See 13,20 and 67,79 notes.

Chapter 28. Miles' holdings passed to Maud of Wallingford.
28,1   WOOTTON (Bassett). Later in Kingsbridge Hundred, but required in the Tax Return for Blackgrove.
28,3-4 CLYFFE (Pypard). The Wallingford holdings were at *Brodeton* (Broad Town GR 09 77) in Fees 315,727. See VCH IX p28 and 20,3 note.
28,7   DRAYCOT (Foliat). EPNS 69-70 identifies Draycot Cerne, but Sampton Foliot holds from Wallingford in Fees 727.

Chapter 29. Some of Gilbert's holdings are in the hands of the Comitissa de Insula in the time of Edward I.
29,2   BINCKNOLL is not identified by EPNS 296, but a holding of Gilbert is required in the Tax Return for Blackgrove Hundred. Bincknoll was in Blackgrove in RH II 243b, 244a, later in Selkley.
29,7   (Broad) HINTON. In Selkley Hundred, held by the Comitissa de Insula (RH II 269b).
29,8   BECKHAMPTON and 29,9 STANMORE. The Comitissa de Insula holds *Batha'pton* and *Stanmere* in Selkley Hundred RH II 269b. See FA VI 539, Jones 197,232. EPNS identifies DB *Bachentone* with Bathampton (227).
32,2   LITTLETON (Pannell). *Liteltone* is also Littleton Drew. William Audrieu is probably the same as William de Aldeleia of the Exon Tax Return for Rowborough Hundred, who held the adjacent Lavington (60,1).
32,3   COMPTON (Bassett) See 27,2 note.

32,5 'CHARLTON' Lost in Hungerford, EPNS (Berks) 302. Together with Standen (39,1) now in Berks., Charlton was in Kinwardstone Hundred in 1086, incorporating Chilton Foliat (28,2), which was later detached, in that Hundred. It was held by the heirs of the Earl Marshall to whom the lands of William of Eu passed. Fees 711,745.

32,10 CODFORD. The mill is shared with Ashton Gifford to which the nearer Codford is Codford St. Peter. See 27,14 and 37,1 notes.

32,13 SEVINGTON. EPNS 27 identifies Sevenhampton in Highworth Hundred, but a Thorngrove Hundred place is required by the Tax Return. Sevington is later in Chippenham Hundred.

32,14 YATTON (Keynell). EPNS 114.

32,17 UPTON (Scudamore) See 25,23 note.

33,1 SHAW. This Shaw is not given a DB identification by EPNS 307 but is required by the Exon Tax Return for Selkley Hundred. See Jones 215.

34,1 SUTTON (Veny). Little Sutton, held by William's heirs in Fees 728, is in Sutton Veny Parish. EPNS 154, VCH VIII p61. See 38,1 note.

37,1 CODFORD. Probably Codford St. Mary, held (as East Codford) by Oliver de Ingham, a descendant of Waleran (Jones 210). See 27,14 note.

37,7 LANGFORD. Probably Steeple Langford held by Sir Lawrence St. Martin, descendant of Waleran. Jones 221, NV 347a.

37,8 LANGFORD. Probably Hanging Langford, the mill being the other half of that at 20,5.

37,11 GRIMSTEAD. The holding was probably both East and West Grimstead, later held by Waleran's heirs in RH II 242a, Fees 747.

37,15 (West) DEAN. East Dean (GR 27 26) is just in Hants. and was also held by Waleran.

37,16 HURDCOTT. EPNS 384. The position of Waleran's other holdings make it likely that this is the Hurdcott in Winterbourne Earls. See 27,25 note.

38,1 SUTTON (Veny). Required by the Exon Tax Return for Warminister Hundred. The two parts of a mill at 13s 4d are completed by the third part at 6s 8d in 56,4. This is probably the *Magna Sutton* of Fees. See 34,1 note.

39,1 STANDEN. Now in Berks, EPNS (Berks) 304-5, formerly Standen Hussey from Richard Husée who held from the Ferrières family. Required by the Exon Tax Return for Kinwardstone Hundred. Bedwyn to which the wood belonged is adjacent. See 32,5 note.

40,1 SUTTON (Mandeville). Galfridus de Mandeville was a descendant of Richard, Jones 234.

41,7 SURRENDELL. Not identified by EPNS 71, but early forms of the name are similar, and it was held by the Mortimers in the 13th century. Jones 231, VCH 360.

42,5 BRIGMERSTON. EPNS 369, named after the 1066 holder.

42,8 FITTLETON. EPNS 330. 'Fitela's Tun'. The name of the 1066 holder is apparently a coincidence.

42,9 SHAW. In Chute, EPNS 341 hesitantly. Robert holds both Biddesden and Fosbury in the area (42,2-4).

43,1 MOREDON and 43,2 HAMPTON. The Tax Return gives Robert 5 hides lordship in Selkley Hundred and 7 hides in Highworth. DB gives him a holding of 1 hide and 1 virgate in *Moredone* and a lordship of 6 hides in *Hantone*. *Moredone* is probably Moredon, placed by EPNS (33) in Shippen Hundred. *Hantone* is either Hampton in Highworth (EPNS 27) or, like *Hentone* (29,7), is Broad Hinton in Selkley Hundred. This edition follows EPNS, but either solution leaves a Tax Return entry not accounted for. A Robert holds Hannington (Highworth Hundred) from Glastonbury (7,2) but the lordship is not given.

44,1 FISHERTON (de la Mere). A detached part of Warminster Hundred in later times, and included there by the Exon Tax Return. See 12,6 note.

45,3 EASTON (Grey). Required by the Exon Tax Return for Dunlow Hundred.

46,1 'FRUSTFIELD'. See 27,26 note.

48,1-2 ELSTON. EPNS 235, earlier *Wintreburn' Elye Giffard* from a descendant of the DB holder. Elias Giffard also held part of Maddington and Shrewton (Fees 721,742).

48,3 ORCHESTON. Also 48,7. One of these holdings was probably in Dole Hundred, and one in Heytesbury (Exon Tax Return). The 48,7 Orcheston falls between Heytesbury places in DB., and there is an Orcheston in Heytesbury Hundred in NV 347a.

48,4 STANTON (St Quintin). Later in Chippenham Hundred, it seems required by the Tax Return for Startley.

48,5 MIDDLETON. EPNS 349 identifies Milton Lilbourne, but the Tax Return requires a place in Warminster Hundred. *Middeldun* was given by Elye Giffard to the Abbey of Fontenay in Fees 743. See RH II 276b, and 24,29 note.

48,6   CODFORD. Probably Codford St. Peter. See 27,14 and 32,10 notes.

48,7   ORCHESTON. See 48,3 note.

48,8   (Hill) DEVERILL. The Giffard holding is *Hulledeverel* in Fees 728.

48,9   KELLAWAYS. Formerly Tytherton Kellaways (EPNS 99) held by Elias de Kayleway from Elias Giffard, Fees 746, FA V 208. Required by the Tax Return for Chippenham Hundred.

49,1a   COLESHILL. EPNS (Berks) 356.

49,2   EASTON. The Tax Return enables the *Estone* of 25,6 and of 45,3 to be identified. This Easton could be either, or the Easton in Kinwardstone Hundred (EPNS 345).

50,1   SHALBOURNE. Half the village was in Berks in 1086 (DB Berks. 1,27). It was transferred to Wiltshire in 1895.

56,4   SUTTON (Veny). See 38,1 note.

59,1   LAVINGTON. In RH II 232a Johannes Marescallus, perhaps a descendant of Robert, holds Lavington Episcopi (= West Lavington EPNS 240).

59,2   GORE. It was in Dole Hundred in the Tax Return. See RH II 254a and NV 347b.

60,1   LAVINGTON. Perhaps Market Lavington. Lavington is held by Roger Gernon from William Blund (possibly a descendant of Robert) in Fees 736. Roger's holding is *Stepel Lavintone* in RH II 236a. See FA V 238, EPNS 240, VCH X p87.

61,1   COWESFIELD. DB *Cuvlestone* which EPNS 140 identifies as Coulston, although from the Tax Return it appears to be in Frustfield Hundred. It must be the same place as *Cuvlesfeld* held in Fees (11,586) by Wilfred Sturmid, probably a descendant of the DB holder. The place is probably part of Cowesfield which is DB *Colesfeld*. *Cuvlestone* and *Colesfeld* have the same derivation, 'Cufel's land', 'Cufel's *tun*' see EPNS 389, and 67,10.

63,1   MADDINGTON. This Winterbourne passed to the Le Moyne family who held it as Maddington (Fees 742, 1178) See VCH 425 and p73, and 16,6 note.

65,1   WINTERBOURNE (River Bourne). The entry refers to half a mill at 3s 9d and is complemented by Winterbournes at 67,36 and 67,95 where parts of a mill each pay 22½d. All three are required by the Tax Return for Alderbury Hundred. They are possibly Winterbourne Gunner, since Saeric held Winterbourne and Laverstock 67,95-96, which latter is adjacent to Winterbourne Gunner.

66,1   (Castle) EATON. EPNS 23-24 identifies Water Eaton. The next mention of the name in EPNS is 1281, and it is safer to regard *Etone* as Castle Eaton (as *Ettone* 21,1) or possibly as Yatton Keynell (6,1. 25,27 notes.) The holding in 21,1 is said to be half of Castle Eaton, so another entry in DB would be expected.

66,2   MANNINGFORD. The remainder of the mill is two parts at 12s 6d in 67,43. These two holdings are probably Manningford Bruce, VCH X p114.

66,3-4   HILPERTON. Probably in Melksham Hundred in 1086 (Tax Return), later in Whorwellsdown.

66,5   GILLINGHAM. In Dorset in 1086. Its presence in Wilts. DB is unexplained.

66,6   EARLSCOURT. It seems required in the Tax Return for Thornhill, although later in Ramsbury Hundred.

67,5 and 67,16   (Monkton) FARLEIGH. EPNS also identifies the Farley in Alderbury Hundred.

67,17   WHADDON. Required by the Tax Return for Melksham Hundred. It is later in Whorwellsdown.

67,22-25   SOMERFORD. See 24,20 note.

67,28   'BARLEY' Lost in South Wraxall, Jones 198, VCH 464. See the Exon Tax Return for Bradford Hundred.

67,35   ALDERSTONE. EPNS 388. The farm in Whiteparish is probably named after the DB holder.

67,36   WINTERBOURNE. See 65,1 note.

67,39   'WINTERBOURNE'. On the river Till, required by the Tax Return for Dole Hundred. It could be one of the several sites later distinguished. See Introduction to Places Notes.

67,43   MANNINGFORD. See 66,2 note.

67,44   STANTON (Fitzwarren). Seems to be required by the Exon Tax Return for Highworth Hundred.

67,47   HILPERTON. See 66,3 note.

67,51   CHEDGLOW. EPNS 57. Jones 206 suggests Chicklade in Dunworth Hundred (GR 9034).

67,52   DEVERILL. See 25,22 note.

67,63   COMPTON (Bassett). See 27,2 note.

67,66   TYTHERLEY. Just over the border in Hampshire, it is included in Wiltshire in RH II 237a.

67,77   LONGFORD. EPNS 221. This *Langeford* is required in the Exon Tax Return for Cawdon Hundred.

67,79 MILFORD. The forest is Clarendon. See 13,20 and 27,27 notes.
67,90 HILPERTON. See 66,3 note.
67,92 LANDFORD. EPNS 386-7.This *Langeford* is required in the Exon Tax Return for Frustfield Hundred.
67,95 WINTERBOURNE. See 65,1 note.
67,99 GROVELY FOREST. In both Cadworth and Branch Hundreds, RH II 233b, 244b.
67,100 BLUNSDON. Edward the Sheriff holds Broad Blunsdon in 24,21 of which this may be a part.
68,21 DRAYCOT (Cerne). Required by the Exon Tax Return for Startley Hundred.
68,27 SMALLBROOK. EPNS 133 identifies Smallbrook in Staverton, but from the Tax Return it appears to be in Warminster Hundred.
68,28 DEVERILL. See 25,22 note.

The Hundreds

DB does not enter Hundred headings in the text of Wilts or the other South-West Counties. The only Hundreds mentioned incidentally are Chedglow and Startley, adjacent to Malmesbury (B5) and (High)Worth containing Lus Hill (24,5). Although the Exon Tax Return gives certain holdings by Hundreds and total numbers of hides for each, it does not usually name places. Many can nonetheless be identified, though with varying probability, and despite the reconstructions of Jones and Darlington, the evidence is insufficient to recover the 1086 Hundreds in their entirety. The later hundreds, as mapped in EPNS in a simplified form, ignoring modern adjustments and amalgamations, are here used in index and map with the exception of Rowborough Regis, a later half of Rowborough, and Malmesbury Hundreds. EPNS includes Shippen *(Scipe)* Hundred which is only evidenced in the Tax Return, and its reconstruction (p30) based on Jones' conjectures differs from the evidence of the Tax Return, from which it would seem to have included Stratton St Margaret, Rodbourne, Lydiard Millicent and Widhill.

Also omitted from the map and index are the geographical detachments shown in EPNS for Dunlow, Thorngrove, Chippenham Melksham, Warminister, Cadworth, Branch, Alderbury and Damerham Hundreds. Only Dinton and Fisherton de la Mere, detached from Warminster, are evidenced in the Tax Return.

The Tax Return points to the general similarity of the DB and later Hundreds, although it indicates important adjustments. Dole Hundred included Gore, later in Rowborough. Staple included Chelworth and Calcutt, later the southern part of Cricklade. Whaddon and Hilperton, later the northern part of Whorwellsdown, were in Melksham, as probably was Chalfield, later in Bradford Hundred. Underditch included ten hides of Salisbury. Thorngrove extended eastwards to included Seavington, Kington Langley and Easton Piercy, later the northern part of Chippenham, which also incorporated Stanton St. Quintin, in Startley Hundred in 1086. Thornhill seems to have included Earlscourt which was later in Ramsbury. In Blackgrove Hundred were Bincknoll and Wootton Bassett, later in Kingsbridge. From the hidages that the Tax Return gives for each Hundred, it is evident that Frustfield Hundred was smaller, and Swanborough, Underditch, Thorngrove and Thornhill Hundreds larger in 1086.

The County Boundary

A number of adjustments, made since the late 19th century, involve places that had been in Wiltshire since DB times. Poulton, Ashley, Long Newnton, Kemble, Poole Keynes, Somerford Keynes and Shorncote were lost to Gloucestershire. Bramshaw, Melchet, Plaitford and Damerham as well as Martin and Whitsbury which are not in DB were transferred to Hampshire. On the eastern border, Charlton and Standen were lost to Berkshire, but Bagshot and a part of Shalbourne mentioned in Berkshire DB were gained. In the West, Yarnfield and Kilmington, long in Somerset, are now in Wilts.

INDEX OF PERSONS

Familiar modern spellings are given when they exist. Unfamiliar names are usually given in an approximate late 11th century form, avoiding variants that were already obsolescent or pedantic. Spellings that mislead the modern eye are avoided where possible. Two, however, cannot be avoided: they are combined in the name of 'Leofgeat', pronounced 'Leffyet' or 'Levyet'. The definite article is omitted before bynames, except where there is reason to suppose that they described the individual. The chapter numbers of listed landholders are printed in italics. Names in brackets are explained in the Notes under at least one of the references given.

Waula, see Wulfric
Wenesi's wife 67,80
Wenesi 51,1. 67,80
White, see Wulfward
Wibert 68,24
Wiflet 49,1
Wigot 28,9;12
William Cornelian 66,4. 68,32
William Delamere 32,4
William Hard 26,22
William Leofric 49, *1a*
William Shield 1,16. 2,4. 68,20
William (Shield) 15,1-2
Earl William 1,3;21
William of Audrieu 32,2-3
William of Beaufour 1,23i
William of Braose 33. 2,1
William of Eu 32. M 8. 8,12. 25,23
William of Falaise 35
William of Mohun 34
William of Picquigny
  son of Ansculf 24,19. 68,22
William (of Picquigny
  son of Ansculf) 68,23
(William of Audley) son-
  in-law of Robert Blunt 60,1
William son of Guy 38
William 2,5;10. 8,6-8. 22,1;5.

24,12. 26,2. 32,13.
50,1;4. 68,4. E 3
Winegot 24,26
Wulfeva Beteslau 68,24
Wulfeva 8,10. 24,7. 26,22
Wulfgar 27,20. 29,6-7. 43,1-2
Wulfgeat Hunter 67,77
Wulfgeat, King Edward's
  Huntsman 1,5
Wulfgeat 26,2;21. 67,79
Wulfmer 24,16. 25,22.
26,21;23. 48,3. 68,8
Wulfnoth's father 67,78
Wulfnoth 67,76;78
Wulfric (Hunter) 67,65;70(?)
Wulfric Waula 67,75
Wulfric's father 67,66-67;72
Wulfric 25,17. 26,16. 27,6.
67,66-69;71-72
Wulfward White 3,1
Wulfward, the King's
  purveyor 67,74
Wulfward 5,5. 25,15. 37,2. 40,1.
63,1. 67,73. 68,20
Wulfwen 24,24;27;41
Wulfwin 27,8
Wulfwy 24,31. 25,19-20
Wymarc, see Robert

Churches and Clergy. **Abbesses of Amesbury** 16. 20,6. St. Mary's, Shaftesbury 12. St. Mary's, Wilton 13. 1,3. St. Mary's, Winchester 14. **Abbeys of Cranborne** 11. Glastonbury 7. Malmesbury 8. St. Peter, Winchester 10. 25,6. **Abbots of Cranborne** 11. Glastonbury 7. M 4. 5,6. 41,8. Jumièges 1,17. Malmesbury 8. M 3. 32,11. St. Peter's, Winchester 10, see Thurstan. **Bishops of Bayeux** 4. M 2. 13,21. Coutances 5. 7,10. Lisieux 6. Salisbury 3. Winchester 2, see Geoffrey, Herman, Osbern Osmund and Walkelin. **Canons of Lisieux** 19. **Churches of Alderbury** 19,2-3. Amesbury 16. 23,7. Malmesbury 8. 30,2. 41,4. Netheravon 56,3. St. Mary, Bec 17. St. Mary, Cranborne 11. St. Mary, Glastonbury 7.(St. Mary), Glastonbury 24,42. 41,8. St. Mary, Romsey 15. St. Mary, Shaftesbury 12. St. Mary, Wilton 13. St. Mary, Winchester 14. 50,5. St. Peter, Westminster 9. St. Stephen, Fontenay 48,5. Salisbury 32,2. **Saint Mary's, Grestain** 20,1. Mary's, Montebourg 56,4. Mary's, Wilton 48,12. 58,2. Stephen's, Caen 1,11. Wandrilles's 1,9;23g. Mont St. Michel 1,15. **Monks, see Alfsi.** **Priests of Aldbourne Church** 1,10. Ramsbury 3,3, see Alfsi, Alfward, Alwin, Brictward, Edgar, Gerald, Leofric, Osbern, Ralph, Reinbald, Rumold, Spirtes and Vitalis.

Secular Titles and Occupational Names. Bowman (*arbalistarius*) ...Warin. Bursar (*dispensator*) ...Robert. Carpenter (*carpentarius*) ...Stephen. Chamberlain (*camerarius*) ...Aubrey, Humphrey, Odin, Thurstan. Cook (*coqus*) ...Ansger, Humphrey. Count (*comes*) ...Gilbert, of Mortain. Countess (*comitissa*) ...Gytha. Doctor (*medicus*) ...Nigel, Theobald. Earl (*comes*) ...Aubrey, Godwin, Harold, Hugh, Roger, Tosti, William. King's Foresters (*forestarii*) ... 67,99. Goldsmith (*aurifaber*) ...Grimbald. Hunter (*venator*) ...Aelfric, Godric, Waleran, Wulfgeat, Wulfric. Keeper of the granaries (*granetarius*) ...Gundwin. King Edward's Huntsman (*venator*) ...Wulfgeat. King's purveyor (*prebendarius*) ...Wulfward. Marshall (*marescal*) ...Geoffrey, Robert. Queen (*regina*) ...Edith, Matilda. Sheriff (*vicecomes*) ...Aiulf, Edric, Edward, Godric. Steward (*dapifer*) ...Ednoth. Usher (*hostiarius*) ...John.

INDEX OF PLACES

The name of each place is followed by (i) the number of its Hundred (numbered west to east working southwards) and its location on the map in this volume; (ii) its National Grid reference; (iii) chapter and section references in DB. Bracketed figures denote mention in sections dealing with a different place. Unless otherwise stated, the identifications of EPNS and the spellings of the Ordnance Survey are followed for places in England; of OEB for places abroad. Inverted commas mark lost places with known modern spelling; unidentifiable places are given in DB spelling, in italics. Difficulties are discussed in the Places notes above. The National Grid reference system is explained on all Ordnance Survey maps and in the Automobile Association Handbooks: the figures reading from left to right are given before those reading from bottom to top. Grid references beginning with 7,8 or 9 are in 100km grid square ST, those beginning with 0, 1, 2 or 3 are in SU. Places with bracketed Grid References do not appear on 1 inch or 1:50,000 maps. Places marked B are now in Berks, D in Dorset, G in Gloucester and H in Hampshire. The Wilts Hundreds with the numbers used in the index are listed after the index, immediately before the map. Because there is insufficient evidence to reconstruct the 1086 Hundreds, the modern Hundreds as given in EPNS are followed ignoring later detachments (see end of Places notes).

	Map	Grid	Text		Map	Grid	Text
Ablington	29-6	15 46	23,4	Boyton	27-13	95 39	24,25
Addestone	28-6	06 43	10,4	Bradenstoke	12-2	00 79	24,19. 68,23;31
Aldbourne	14-5	26 75	1,10	Bradfield	7-5	89 82	41,3
Alderbury	35-13	18 26	19,2-3. 37, 14. 68,33	Bradford on Avon	16-7	82 61	12,4
Alderstone	39-2	24 24	67,35	Maiden Bradley	30-1	80 38	31,1
Alderton	6-5	83 82	41,9. 49,3	Bramshaw (H)	39-7	27 15	67,55;78
Allington	21-1	06 63	26,1	Bremhill	11-15	97 73	8,12
Allington	29-17	20 39	16,3. 23,7	Brigmerston	29-9	16 45	42,5
Alton	29-7	15 46	68,18	Brinkworth	7-4	01 84	8,4. 28,8
Alton Barnes	22-3	10 62	24,2	Britford	37-1	16 28	1,6. 67,58; 70;91
Alton Priors	22-4	11 62	2,4	Brokenborough	1-9	91 89	8,6
Alvestone	16	- -	12,4	Bromham	13-6	96 65	1,14
Amesbury	29-15	15 41	1,3. 24,16; (17)	Broughton Gifford	16-4	87 63	27,1. 67,97
Ansty	31-8	95 26	37,2. 67,37	Budbury	16-5	(81 62)	67,64
Ashley (G)	1-3	93 94	30,5	Bulford	29-12	16 43	16,1
Ashton Gifford	27-11	(95 40)	27,14	Burbage	24-12	22 62	1,23b. 27,4. 68,4;11
Ashton Keynes	2-4	04 94	11,1	Burcombe	32-10	07 30	13,16. 22,4
Ashton	19-6	90 56	15,2	Bushton	12-4	06 78	2,8
Avebury	14-11	10 69	1,23d	Buttermere	24-14	34 61	25,10. 37,3. 68,17.
Badbury	9-3	19 80	7,6	Cadenham	11-6	98 77	22,5
Bagshot	24-5	31 65	E2	Calcutt	2-9	11 93	67,1
Barford	38-3	18 22	37,9	Calne	13-1	99 71	1,1. (3,2. 25,5. 58,1)
Barford St. Martin	32-5	05 31	47,2. 67,81. 68,19	Calstone Wellington	13-4	02 68	25,5. 53,1 58,1
'Barley'	16-6	(82 62)	67,28	All Cannings	21-2	07 61	14,2
Bathampton	33-5	01 38	27,15-16	Bishops Cannings	18-1	03 64	3,2
Baverstock	32-2	02 32	13,17	*Celdewelle*	- -	- -	36,1
Baycliff	27-12	81 39	24,26	Chalfield	16-3	85 63	25,8-9
Bechenehilde	- -	- -	25,18	Chalke	36-2	04 25	13,9
Beckhampton	14-15	08 68	29,8	Charlton	1-10	96 88	8,9
Bedwyn	24-6	27 64	1,2; 23j. (39,1)	'Charlton'	24-2	(32 67)	32,5
Beechingstoke	22-7	08 59	12,1	Charnage	30-11	83 31	3,5
Bemerton	33-11	12 30	55,2. 67,34	Chedglow	1-6	94 93	25,20-21. 26,19. 28,10. 67,51
Beversbrook	12-13	00 73	32,4. 56,5	Chelworth	2-7	08 92	68,30
Bichenehilde	- -	- -	25,12	Chelworth	1-4	96 94	8,7
Biddesden	29-1	29 51	42,4	*Chenebuild*	- -	- -	25,19
Biddestone	11-13	86 73	27,21				
Bincknoll	14-1	10 79	29,2-4				
Bishopstrow	26-6	89 43	24,28				
Blunsdon	4-1	15 90	24,21. 27, 12. 67,100				
Boscombe	29-19	20 38	16,2. 32,7				
Bowcombe (H)	- -	- -	(1,3)				

	Map	Grid	Text		Map	Grid	Text
Cheverell	20-3	98 54	(1,3) 25,3	Kingston Deverill	30-5	84 37	19,1
Chilmark	31-2	96 32	13,5	Monkton Deverill	30-3	85 37	7,3 or 16
Chilton Foliat	24-1	32 70	28,2	Dinton	32-3	01 31	12,6
Chippenham	11-14	91 73	1,5. 45,2. 62,1	Ditchampton	32-7	09 31	4,4. 13,15
Chirton	21-7	07 57	30,1	Ditteridge	11-22	81 69	32,11
Chisbury	24-3	27 66	29,1	Donhead	31-9	91 24	12,3
Chisenbury	23-1	14 52	56,2	Downton	38-4	18 21	2,1
Chisledon	9-4	·18 79	10,5	Draycot Cerne	7-12	92 78	68,21
Chitterne	27-2	99 43	23,5. 24,22-24 25,15-17. 32,8	Draycot Fitzpayne	22-5	14 62	5,1
Cholderton	29-14	22 42	16,4	Draycot Foliat	9-5	18 77	28,7
Choulston	29-3	(15 49)	(1,19)	Durnford	29-18	13 38	13,3. 32,1
Chute Forest	24-24	31 51	41,5	Durrington	29-11	15 44	23,2
Clatford	14-18	15 68	26,16	Earlscourt	15-1	21 85	66,6
Clevancy	12-11	05 75		Easton Grey	6-1	88 87	45,3
Clyffe Pypard	12-8	07 76	20,3-4. 25, 11. 26,17. 27,9. 28,3-4. 29,5. 39,2. 50,3. 67,75. 68,23-24;26	Easton Piercy	11-3	89 77	25,26.
				Easton	- -	- -	49,2
Codford	27-14	97 39	32,10. 37,1. 48,6	Castle Eaton	5-1	14 95	21,1. 66,1
Colerne	11-19	82 71	27,17	Ebbesborne Wake	36-3	99 24	42,10
Coleshill (B)	5-4	23 93	49,1a	Edington	19-8	92 53	15,1. 68,1
Collingbourne Ducis	24-22	24 53	1,19	Elcombe	8-6	13 80	23,8
Collingbourne Kingston	24-20	23 55	10,2	Elston	28-3	06 44	48,1-2
Castle Combe	10-3	84 77	27,23	Enford	23-3	13 51	2,10
Compton	23-2	13 52	23,1	Etchilhampton	21-3	04 60	24,3. 25,4. 67,49
Compton Bassett	13-2	03 71	27,2. 32,3. 67,63	Eysey	2-6	11 94	18,2
Compton Chamberlayne	32-9	02 30	1,8	Monkton Farleigh	16-1	80 65	67,5;16
Conock	21-6	06 57	20,1	Fifield Bavant	36-1	01 25	26,14;23
Coombe Bissett	37-3	10 26	1,13	Figheldean	29-5	15 47	67,61
Corsham	11-20	86 70	1,11	Fisherton Anger	35-8	(13 29)	22,6
Corsley	26-2	82 46	67,33	Fisherton de la Mere	33-3	00 38	44,1
Corston	7-3	92 83	8,6	Fittleton	23-4	14 49	42,8
Corton	27-9	93 40	50,4	Fonthill Bishop	31-1	93 32	2,2
Coulston	19-7	95 54	67,2	Fonthill Gifford	31-3	92 31	47,1
Cowesfield	39-3	25 23	61,1. 67,10	Fosbury	24-19	31 58	42,2-3
Cricklade	2-8	10 93	B4.(1,10.3,3. 7,6. 8,13). 9,1. (10,5. 12,5. 26,7. 27,9. 66,6. 67,1. 68,24)	Fovant	32-13	00 28	13,19
				Foxley	7-1	89 85	45,1
				'Frustfield'	39-1	(25 24)	27,26. 46,1. 67,71;93
Crofton	24-10	26 62	26,4	Fyfield	14-17	14 68	2,3
Crudwell	1-7	95 92	8,11	Garsdon	1-12	96 87	8,10
Cumberwell	16-2	82 63	27,5	Gategram	- -	- -	67,84
Damerham (H)	40-1	10 15	7,1. 11,2	Gillingham (D)	30-13	80 26	66,5
Dauntsey	7-7	97 82	8,2	Gore	20-6	01 50	59,2
West Dean	35-12	25 27	37,15	Grafton	24-16	25 60	32,6. 68,5; 8-9
Deptford	33-4	01 38	24,36	Grimstead	35-11	22 27	37,11. 67, 42;59
Brixton Deverill	27-15	86 38	17,1	Grittleton	10-1	86 80	7,10
Hill Deverill	27-7	86 40	24,18. 48,8	Groundwell	4-2	15 89	27,13
Longbridge Deverill	27-6	86 40	7,3 or 16	Grovely Wood	32-1	05 34	67,99
				Gussage (D)	36-6	98 11	23,10
Deverill	27	- -	25,22. 67, 52. 68,28	Ham	24-9	33 63	2,5
				Hampton	5-5	18 92	27,20. 43,2
				Hannington	5-3	17 93	7,2
				Hardenhuish	11-11	91 74	25,25

	Map	Grid	Text		Map	Grid	Text
Harding	24-11	29 62	68,6	Maddington	28-4	06 44	16,7. 63,1
Hartham	11-17	86 72	22,3. 24, 37. 27,22. 67,46;53;87	Christian Malford	7-13	96 78	7,4 (5)
Hazelbury	11-23	83 68	1,23f. 28, 13. 56,6. 67,41	Malmesbury	1-11	93 87	M. B4-5. 5,4. (7,11. 8,3. 24,20;38. 26, 19. 27,10;23. 28,1. 41,1;9. 45,1. 49,1). 67,40.
Heddington	13-5	99 66	24,4				
Heytesbury	27-3	92 42	1,23e				
Highway	12-12	04 74	8,1. 41,4				
Highworth	5-6	20 92	1,23a. (24,5)	Manningford	22-9	14 58	10,1. 66,2. 67,43.
Hilmarton	12-9	01 75	25,14. 32, 9. 67,19	Manton	14-19	17 68	28,12
				Marden	22-10	08 57	51,1
Hilperton	19-3	87 59	66,3-4, 67, 47;90	Marlborough	14-12	18 69	B4. 1,23 i.
				Marten	24-17	28 60	67,83. 68, 10;13
Broad Hinton	14-4	10 76	29,7.				
Homington	37-4	12 26	57,1	Melchet Forest(H)	39-4	27 22	(13,10;18)
Horningsham	27-5	81 41	19,4. 26,20	Melksham	17-2	90 63	1,12. 67,89
Huish	22-1	14 63	68,3	Mere	30-8	81 32	67,45;68;76
Hullavington	7-10	89 82	41,1	Middleton	26-5	(90 44)	24,29. 48,5
Hurdcott	32-4	04 31	27,25	Mildenhall	14-13	20 69	7,7
Hurdcott	35-4	17 33	37,16	Milford	35-9	15 29	27,27. 67, 79
Idmiston	35-1	19 37	7,14				
Imber	27-1	96 48	41,6	Milston	29-10	16 45	21,2. 42,6
Keevil	19-5	92 58	25,1	Moredon	4-3	13 87	26,9. 29,6. 43,1
Kellaways, see Tytherton							
Kemble (G)	1-1	98 97	8,7	Nechendune	-	-	20,2
Kennett	14-20	11 67	26,21. 37, 5. 50,5.	Netheravon	23-5	14 48	1,18. 56,3. 68,2
Kilmington	30-4	77 36	E4-5	Nettleton	10-2	81 78	7,9
Kington St. Michael	11-4	90 77	41,8	Long Newnton (G)	1-8	90 92	8,8
Knighton	29-8	12 45	67,60	North Newnton	22-12	12 57	13,2
Knook	27-4	93 41	67,14;86	South Newton	33-10	08 34	13,10-11
East Knoyle	30-12	88 30	1,20	Newton Toney	29-16	21 40	26,5
West Knoyle	30-9	85 32	13,7	Norton	7-2	88 84	8,5
Lackham	11-21	92 70	32,12	Norton Bavant	26-7	90 43	26,12
Lacock	11-24	91 68	24,33. 26,15	Oaksey	1-5	99 93	67,6
Landford	39-5	26 20	67,92	Odstock	37-5	14 26	67,9
Langford	33-8	03 36	7,12-13. 13, 13. 20,5. 24,42. 37, 7-8	Ogbourne	14-9	18 72	1,22. 28,11. 67,62;85
				Orcheston	28-2	05 45	24,11-12. 48,3;7
Kington Langley	11-5	92 77	7,11	East Overton	14-23	(13 66)	2,11
Langley Burrell	11-9	93 75	24,31	West Overton	14-16	13 68	13,8
Latton	2-5	09 95	18,2	Pertwood	30-6	88 35	5,5
Laverstock	35-7	15 30	13,20. 67,96	Pewsey	24-15	16 60	1,23c. 10,3. 25,6. 67,50
Lavington	20-5	01 54	59,1. 60,1				
Liddington	9-2	20 81	12,5	Plaitford (H)	39-6	27,19	67,56
Littlecott	12-6	03 77	28,5	Pomeroy	16-11	81 56	66,8
Littleton Drew	6-6	83 80	5,6. 7,5	Poole Keynes (G)	1-2	00 95	24,27
Littleton Pannell	20-4	99 54	32,2	Porton	35-2	19 36	24,40. 67, 72
Lockeridge	14-21	14 67	30,6	Potterne	20-2	99 58	3,1. 25,2. 67,11
Longford	37-6	17 26	67,77				
Luckington	6-4	83 83	30,7. 41,10	Poulshot	17-3	96 59	(1,11)
Ludgershall	29-2	26 50	24,15	Poulton	14-10	(20 70)	27,19
Lus Hill	5-2	16 93	24,5. 27,6	Poulton (G)	2-1	10 00	21,3
Lydiard Millicent	3-2	09 86	1,21	Purton	3-1	09 87	8,13
				Quintone	-	-	(1,3)
Lydiard Tregoze	8-1	10 84	26,7	Ramsbury	15-2	27 71	3,3

	Map	Grid	Text		Map	Grid	Text
Winterbourne Earls	35-3	17 34	24,41	Wolf Hall	24-13	24 61	68,12
				Woodborough	22-8	11 59	42,1
Winterbourne (R. Till)	28	- -	67,39	Woodhill	12-7	06 76	4,2
				Wootton Bassett	12-1	06 82	28,1
see Addestone, Elston, Maddington, Shrewton							
Winterbourne Monkton	14-7	10 72	7,8	Wootton Rivers	24-7	19 63	1,15
Winterbourne Stoke	28-7	07 40	1,17. 24,8-9	North Wraxall	11-8	81 75	24,38
				Wroughton	8-7	14 80	2,7. 27,7. 67,38
Winterslow	35-6	22 32	20,6. 23,3. 67,66;73	Wylye	33-7	00 37	13,11
Wishford	33-9	07 35	13,12. 37, 10. 68,32	Yarnfield	30-2	78 38	E3
				Yatesbury	13-3	06 71	54,1
Witcomb	12-10	02 75	25,13	Yatton Keynell	11-7	86 76	6,1. 25,27. 32,14
Witherington	38-1	18 24	67,54				
'Wittenham'	16-9	(80 58)	5,2	Zeals	30-10	78 31	64,1. 67,32

Places not named
1,23h. 13,21. 16,5. 25,28. 26,19. 65,2. 66,7. 67,21. 67,57. 67,88. 67,98.
In Grovely Wood 67,99.

Places not in Wiltshire
References are to entries in the Indices of Persons and Places.

Elsewhere in Britain

BERKSHIRE ... Charlton. Coleshill. Standen. DORSET ... Cranbourne, see Churches.
Gillingham. Gussage St. Michael. Shaftesbury, see Churches. GLOUCESTERSHIRE ... Ashley.
Berkeley, see Roger. Gloucester, see Durand. Kemble. Poole Keynes. Somerford Keynes.
Long Newnton. Poulton. Shorncote. HAMPSHIRE ... Boscombe, see Alstan. Bowcombe
(Isle of Wight), see 1,3. Bramshaw. Damerham. Melchet Forest. Plaitford. Romsey, see
Churches. Tytherley. Winchester, see Churches and Odo. MIDDLESEX ... Westminster,
see Churches. MONTGOMERY ... Montgomery, see Earl Roger, note. SHROPSHIRE ...
Beslow, see 68,24 note. SOMERSET ... Bath, see B 4. Glastonbury, see Churches.
STAFFORDSHIRE ... Audley, see William.

Outside Britain

Audrieu ... William. Aumale ... Robert. Avranches ... Hugh, note. Bayeux ... Bishop.
Beaufour ... William. Bec ... Church. Braose ... William. Breteuil ... Gilbert. Brionne ...
Gilbert, note. Caen ... St. Stephen's. Coucy ... Aubrey, note. Courseulles ... Roger.
Coutances ... Bishop. Douai ... Walscin. Dreux ... Amalric, Herman. Eu ... William.
Falaise ... William. Ferrers ... Henry. Fontenay ...Church. Grestain ... Church.
Hauville ... Ralph. Hesdin ... Arnulf. Jumièges ...Abbot. Lacy ... Roger. Lisieux ...
Bishop, Canons. L'Isle ... Humphrey. Mohun ... William. Montebourg ... Church.
Mont St. Michel ... Church. Mortagne ... Matthew. Mortain ... Count. Mortimer ... Ralph.
Picquigny ... William. Rivers ... Walter. 'Spain' (Epaignes) ... Alfred, note.

Maps and Map Keys

WILTSHIRE HUNDREDS

The figures used for Wiltshire Hundreds in index and map are:

1	Chedglow	21	Studfold
2	Cricklade	22	Swanborough
3	Staple	23	Elstub
4	Shippen (Scipe)	24	Kinwardstone
5	Highworth	25	Westbury
6	Dunlow	26	Warminster
7	Startley	27	Heytesbury
8	Blackgrove	28	Dole
9	Thornhill	29	Amesbury
10	Thorngrove	30	Mere
11	Chippenham	31	Dunworth
12	Kingsbridge	32	Cadworth
13	Calne	33	Branch
14	Selkley	34	Underditch
15	Ramsbury	35	Alderbury
16	Bradford	36	Stanford (Chalke)
17	Melksham	37	Cawdon
18	Cannings	38	Downton
19	Whorwellsdown	39	Frustfield
20	Rowborough	40	Damerham

The County Boundary is marked on the maps by thick lines, continuous for 1086, dotted for the modern boundary; the Hundred boundaries by thin lines, dotted where uncertain.

National Grid 10-kilometre squares are shown on the map border.

Each four-figure square covers one square kilometre, or 247 acres, approximately 2 hides, at 120 acres to the hide.

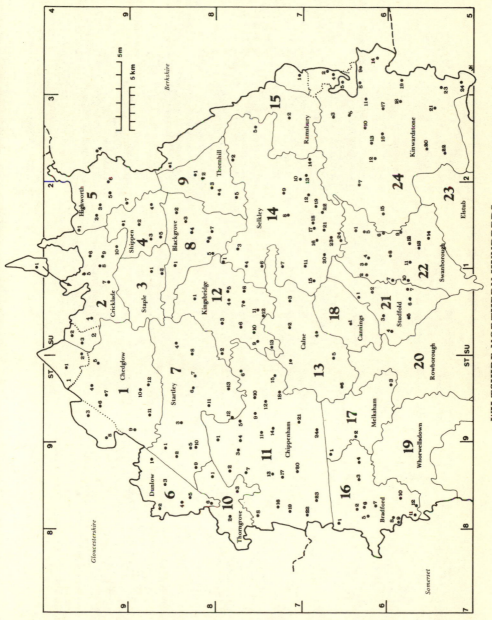

WILTSHIRE NORTHERN HUNDREDS

WILTSHIRE SOUTHERN HUNDREDS

Whorwellsdown 19
1 Whaddon
2 Staverton
3 Hilperton
4 Trowbridge
5 Keevil
6 Ashton
7 Coulston
8 Edington

Rowborough 20
1 Rowde
2 Potterne
3 Cheverell
4 Littleton Pannell
5 Lavington
6 Gore

Elstub 23
1 Chisenbury
2 Compton
3 Enford
4 Fittleton
5 Netheravon

Westbury 25
1 Westbury

Warminster 26
1 Upton Scudamore
2 Corsley
3 Warminster
4 Smallbrook
5 Middleton
6 Bishopstrow
7 Norton Bavant
8 Sutton Veny

Heytesbury 27
1 Imber
2 Chitterne
3 Heytesbury
4 Knook

5 Horningsham
6 Longbridge Deverill
7 Hill Deverill
8 Tytherington
9 Corton
10 Upton Lovell
11 Ashton Gifford
12 Baycliff
13 Boyton
14 Codford
15 Brixton Deverill
16 Whitecliff

Dole 28
1 Tilshead
2 Orcheston
3 Elston
4 Maddington
5 Shrewton
6 Addestone
7 Winterbourne Stoke

Amesbury 29
1 Biddesden
2 Ludgershall
3 Choulston
4 North Tidworth
5 Figheldean
6 Ablington
7 Alton
8 Knighton
9 Brigmerston
10 Milston
11 Durrington
12 Bulford
13 Ratfyn
14 Cholderton
15 Amesbury
16 Newton Toney
17 Allington
18 Durnford
19 Boscombe

Mere 30
1 Maiden Bradley
2 Yarnfield
3 Monkton Deverill
4 Kilmington
5 Kingston Deverill
6 Pertwood
7 Stourton
8 Mere
9 West Knoyle
10 Zeals
11 Charnage
12 East Knoyle
13 Gillingham

Dunworth 31
1 Fonthill Bishop
2 Chilmark
3 Fonthill Gifford
4 Teffont Evias
5 Tisbury
6 Swallowcliffe
7 Wardour
8 Ansty
9 Donhead

Cadworth 32
1 Grovely Wood
2 Baverstock
3 Dinton
4 Hurdcott
5 Barford St. Martin
6 Ugford
7 Ditchampton
8 Wilton
9 Compton Chamberlayne
10 Burcombe
11 Washern
12 Sutton Mandeville
13 Fovant

Branch 33
1 Sherrington
2 Stockton
3 Fisherton de la Mere
4 Deptford
5 Bathampton
6 Stapleford
7 Wylye
8 Langford
9 Wishford
10 South Newton
11 Bemerton

Underditch 34
1 Wilsford

Alderbury 35
1 Idmiston
2 Porton
3 Winterbourne Earls
4 Hurdcott
5 Salisbury
6 Winterslow
7 Laverstock
8 Fisherton Anger
9 Milford
10 Tytherley
11 Grimstead
12 West Dean
13 Alderbury
14 Whaddon

Stanford (Chalke) 36
1 Fifield Bavant
2 Chalke
3 Ebbesborne Wake
4 Trow
5 Tollard Royal
6 Gussage

Cawdon 37
1 Britford
2 Stratford Tony
3 Coombe Bissett
4 Homington
5 Odstock
6 Longford

Downton 38
1 Witherington
2 Standlynch
3 Barford
4 Downton

Frustfield 39
1 'Frustfield'
2 Alderstone
3 Cowesfield
4 Melchet Forest
5 Landford
6 Plaitford
7 Bramshaw

Damerham 40
1 Damerham

Not mapped

Alvestone
Bechenehilde
Bichenehilde
Celdevelle
Chenebuild
Gategram
Nechendune
Quintone
Retmore

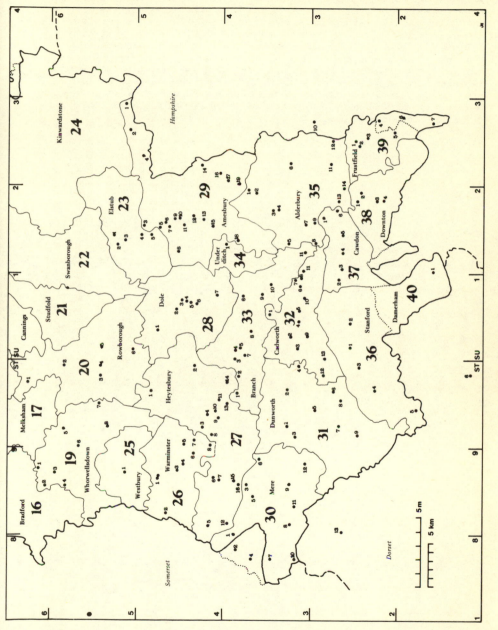

WILTSHIRE SOUTHERN HUNDREDS

SYSTEMS OF REFERENCE TO DOMESDAY BOOK

The manuscript is divided into numbered chapters, and the chapters into sections, usually marked by large initials and red ink. Farley, however, did not number the sections. References have therefore been inexact, by folio numbers, which cannot be closer than an entire page or column. Moreover, half a dozen different ways of referring to the same column have been devised. In 1816 Ellis used three separate systems in his indices; (i) on pages i-cvii; 435-518; 537-570; (ii) on pages 1-144; (iii) on pages 145-433 and 519-535. Other systems have since come into use, notably that used by Vinogradoff, here followed. This edition numbers the sections, the normal practicable form of close reference; but since all discussion of Domesday for three hundred years has been obliged to refer to page or column, a comparative table will help to locate references given. The five columns below give Vinogradoff's notation, Ellis' three systems, and that employed by Welldon Finn and others. Maitland, Stenton, Darby and others have usually followed Ellis (i).

Vinogradoff	Ellis (i)	Ellis (ii)	Ellis (iii)	Finn
152 a	152	152 a	152	152ai
152 b	152	152 a	152.2	152a2
152 c	152 b	152 b	152 b	152bi
152 d	152 b	152 b	152 b2	152b2

In Wiltshire, the relation between the Vinogradoff column notation, here followed, and the chapters and sections is

64 c	M 1	-	Landholders and B1-5	68 a	13,6	-	13,16	72 a	33,1	-	37,10
d	1,1	-	1,5	b	13,17	-	15,2	b	37,11	-	41,6
65 a	1,6	-	1,12	c	16,1	-	19,4	c	41,7	-	45,3
b	1,12	-	1,21	d	20,1	-	22,4	d	46,1	-	49,1a
c	1,22	-	2,4	69 a	22,4	-	24p	73 a	49,1	-	56,1. 51,1
d	2,5	-	2,12	b	24,1	-	24,16	b	56,2	-	66,1
66 a	3,1	-	3,5	c	24,17	-	24,30	c	66,2	-	67,14
b	4,1	-	6,2	d	24,31	-	25,2	d	67,15	-	67,42
c	7,1	-	7,10	70 a	25,2	-	25,18	74 a	67,43	-	67,68
d	7,10	-	8,2	b	25,18	-	26,7	b	67,69	-	67,100
67 a	8,3	-	8,9	c	26,8	-	26,23	c	68,1	-	68,22
b	8,9	-	10,2	d	27,1	-	27,14	d	68,23	-	68,33
c	10,3	-	12,4	71 a	27,15	-	27,27				
d	12,4	-	13,5	b	28,1	-	29,5				
				c	29,5	-	32,2				
				d	32,3	-	32,17				

TECHNICAL TERMS

Many words meaning measurements have to be transliterated. But translation may not dodge other problems by the use of obsolete or made-up words which do not exist in modern English. The translations here used are given in italics. They cannot be exact; they aim at the nearest modern equivalent.

BORDARIUS. Cultivator of inferior status, usually with a little land. *smallholder*

CARUCA. A plough, with the oxen who pulled it, usually reckoned as 8. *plough*

CARUCATA. Normally the equivalent of a *hide,* in former Danish areas. *carucate*

COSCET, COSCEZ. A cultivator who lived in a cottage (see M3 note). *Cottager*

COTARIUS. Inhabitant of a *cote,* cottage, often without land. *cottager*

DOMINICUS. Belonging to a lord or lordship. *the lord's* or *lordship* (adj.)

DOMINIUM. The mastery or dominium of a lord *(dominus);* including ploughs, land, men, villages, etc., reserved for the lord's use; often concentrated in a *home farm* or *demesne,* a 'Manor Farm' or 'Lordship Farm'. *lordship*

FEUDUM. Continental variant of *feuum,* not used in England before 1066; either a landholder's holding, or land held by special grant. *Holding*

FIRMA. Old English *feorm,* provisions due to the King or lord; a fixed sum paid in place of these and of other miscellaneous dues. *revenue*

GABLUM. Old English *gafol,* tribute or tax to the King or a lord. *tribute*

GELDUM. The principal royal tax, originally levied during the Danish wars, normally at an equal number of pence on each *hide* of land. *tax*

HIDA. A unit of land measurement, reckoned at 120 acres. *hide*

HONOR. (B5) equivalent to *feudum,* Holding. *Honour*

HUNDRED. A district within a shire, whose assembly of notables and village representatives usually met about once a month. *Hundred*

LEUGA. A measure of length, usually about a mile and a half. *league*

PRAEPOSITUS, PRAEFECTUS. Old English *gerefa,* a royal officer. *reeve*

QUARENTINA. A quarter of a virgate or league (see 1,1 note). *furlong*

r.,rq. Marginal abbreviations for *require,* 'enquire', occurring when the scribe has omitted some information.

TAINUS, TEGNUS. Person holding land from the King by special grant; formerly used of the King's ministers and military companions. *thane*

T. R. E. *tempore regis Edwardi,* in King Edward's time. *before 1066*

VILLA. Translating Old English *tun,* town. The later distinction between a small *village* and a large *town* was not yet in use in 1066. *village* or *town*

VILLANUS. Member of a *villa,* usually with more land than a *bordarius.* *villager*

VIRGATA. A quarter of a hide, reckoned at 30 acres. *virgate*